# A History of International Thought

International thought is the product of major political changes over the last few centuries, especially the development of the modern state and the industrialisation of the world economy. While the question of how to deal with strangers from other communities has been a constant throughout human history, it is only in recent centuries that the question of 'foreign relations' (and especially imperialism and war) have become a matter of urgency for all sectors of society throughout the world. This book provides the first comprehensive overview of the evolution of Western international thought, and charts how this evolved into the predominantly Anglophone field of International Relations. Along the way several myths of the origins of International Relations are explored and exposed: the myth of the peace of Westphalia, the myths of Versailles and the nature of the League of Nations, the realist–idealist 'Great Debate' myth, and the myth of appeasement. Major approaches to the study of international affairs are discussed within their context and on their own terms, rather than being shoe-horned into anachronistic 'paradigms'. Written in a clear and accessible style, Ashworth's analysis reveals how historical myths have been used as gatekeeping devices, and how a critical re-evaluation of the history of international thought can affect how we see international affairs today.

**Lucian M. Ashworth** is Professor and Head of the Department of Political Science at the Memorial University of Newfoundland, Canada.

# A History of International Thought

From the origins of the modern state
to academic international relations

**Lucian M. Ashworth**

To Valerie

Thanks for being such
a great colleague
here at MUN.
We will miss you!

Luke

Routledge
Taylor & Francis Group

LONDON AND NEW YORK

First published 2014
by Routledge
2 Park Square, Milton Park, Abingdon, Oxon OX14 4RN

and by Routledge
711 Third Avenue, New York, NY 10017

*Routledge is an imprint of the Taylor & Francis Group, an informa business*

*British Library Cataloguing in Publication Data*
A catalogue record for this book is available from the British Library

*Library of Congress Cataloging in Publication Data*
Ashworth, Lucian M., 1964–
A history of international thought : from the origins of the modern state
to academic international relations / Lucian Ashworth.
pages cm.
Summary: "A History of International Thought in International
Relations"-- Provided by publisher.
Includes bibliographical references and index.
1. International relations--History. I. Title.
JZ1242.A8 2013
327--dc23
2013031221

ISBN: 978-1-408-28292-2 (pbk)
ISBN: 978-0-415-73538-4 (hbk)

Typeset in Times New Roman
by Saxon Graphics Ltd, Derby

Printed and bound in the United States of America by Publishers Graphics,
LLC on sustainably sourced paper.

# Contents

**PART III**
**Conclusion: international relations in living memory and
lessons for the future**                                                        **249**

# Preface

Studying the past is like investigating the aftermath of an explosion. The pieces that can be put together to make a coherent story are spread in a seemingly random pattern. While some materials have evaporated entirely, or at best been left scorched and incomplete, others are present in their entirety, but are ripped up and spread around the site. You usually arrive on the scene after others have already tried to make sense of the scene, leaving behind attempts to reconstruct what had been present. These are the stories constructed by those who have already tried to reconstruct, in whole or in part, what had happened. Some have done their job well, while others have made leaps of logic that you now realise are wrong. Others still have made ill-informed assumptions about what had been there, and have failed to properly investigate the material. Even while piecing together what you find, you realise that the task in front of you keeps revealing an increasingly complex picture. You piece together what you can, draw your conclusions, but also realise that you don't quite have all the information you need (and probably never will), and that perhaps someone someday will find something in the debris that you missed.

This book is an attempt to reconstruct a narrative out of the pieces that make up the story of the history of international thought. It is a story that has benefited from the hard work of people that have already sifted through parts of the rubble, but it is also a story that has not received the attention it deserves from scholars of International Relations (IR). It is also a story that I have wanted to write for a long time ever since I realised that the tales we were told about the origins of IR and international thought did not fit the evidence. My first revelation came during my PhD thesis in the early 1990s, when I realised that the story of the realist–idealist first 'great debate' was inaccurate. This led in 1995 to a chapter in my PhD thesis that argued that the realist–idealist debate had never taken place (later presented at the Canadian Political Science Association conference in Montreal in 1995, and published in my book in 1999). I was not the only one on this trail, however. Peter Wilson had discovered the same anomaly, and his excellent 1998 criticism of the idea of a realist–idealist debate is justly regarded as a classic in the historiography of international thought. Peter had been in the year ahead of me during my undergraduate years at Keele University. It was another Keele graduate in the same year as me, David Long, who worked with me during my postdoctoral year at Carleton on a reassessment of David Mitrany. Looking at Mitrany had been a suggestion of my PhD supervisor at Dalhousie, Robert Boardman (Bob had been Mitrany's research assistant). Yet, the seed that led to the writing of this book was probably planted much earlier than this. In my final year as an undergraduate at Keele in the 1984–5 academic year I had signed up for Hidemi Suganami's 'Causes of War' course. We had had to choose three electives, and this course had been my third choice. Despite this, it was to become my favourite course during my entire undergraduate degree (and there was some stiff competition here from Mark Hoffman's excellent Strategic Studies, from the lectures in my second year International Cooperation course delivered by John Vincent, and my first- and second-year tutorials with Alan James and Lorna Lloyd). Hidemi not only introduced me to the work of J.A. Hobson (the first time I realised that secondary sources often got their analysis badly wrong), but also to historiography.

This work has been in the back of my mind since at least the late 1990s, but until now I did not feel that I had enough knowledge to write it. There have been two reasons that have pushed me to break cover and write a history of international thought. First, is the lack of an accessible text on the history of international thought (although Torbjørn Knutsen's quite different 1992 *A History of International Relations Theory* is an exception here); and second is the general lack of knowledge on the history of international thought within International Relations (IR) circles. Obviously the two are related. This is not to say that there have not been plenty of people writing on disciplinary history, many of whom I have acknowledged below, but rather that this scholarship has not managed to make it into the textbooks that train our next generation of scholars, and consequently the vast mass of the profession remains ignorant of the history of their field. The struggle to get people to unlearn the tired old myths that still get trotted out as cognitive shortcuts (to use Kim Hutchings' phrase) goes on. As I write IR textbooks are still being printed that talk about the 'Treaty' of Westphalia, the Westphalian system, the failure of the League, the realist–idealist 'Great Debate', and how appeasement proved a group of people called realists right. If these myths were just harmless distractions – stories we told students to keep them amused – there would be no harm. If only it were that simple. Unfortunately historical myths are rarely anodyne. They serve a purpose, whether intended or not. Historical myths are used as arguments in theoretical discourse. The myth of League failure, for example, is often invoked as an argument against international organisations. Thus, a deeper historical study can have a critical role in discussions of theory. Equally, without a deeper understanding of its intellectual history IR is likely to cling to another myth: the myth of spurious persistence that assumes that ideas have a life of their own outside of the context of writers using them. This can also give our field a little humility. Our ideas and theories do not exist in some unhistorical realm waiting to be discovered, they are the products of, as well as participants in, human history. We need to understand international thought and the field of IR as embedded in a wider historical experience. This also means we need to expose the silences in the myths as well. A glaring example is the way that the industrial revolution is often forgotten in introductory IR textbooks, despite the central role it played in the development of international thought.

The community of scholars interested in the history of international though in general, and the disciplinary history of IR in particular, has grown significantly in the last two decades, and many members of this community have helped me through the intervening years with my understanding of specific parts of this story. At the risk of causing offence through forgetting an intellectual debt, I would like specifically to thank Duncan Bell, Ian Bruff, Randall Germain, Ian Hall, John Hobson, Gaynor Johnson, Torbjørn Knutsen, Tony Lang, Halvard Leira, Lorna Lloyd, David Long, Sean Molloy, Craig Murphy, Nick Rengger, Brian Schmidt, Tim Shaw, Stuart Shields, Hidemi Suganami, Casper Sylvest, Andrew Williams, Peter Wilson and Owen Worth. I would also like to assure Ben Rosamond, Laura Shepherd and Chris Agius that, whatever font this book eventually appears in, it was originally keyed in Times New Roman.

# 1 Introduction

To discover from the history of thought that there are in fact no such timeless concepts, but only the various different concepts which have gone with various different societies, is to discover a general truth not merely about the past but about ourselves as well.[1]

Man has no nature, just history.[2]

*This chapter explores the nature of international thought and international relations, stressing the problems we have in defining what the international is. In providing an introduction to the study of international thought it will explore a number of issues that are important to understanding the study of the international:*

1 *The role of history and historical accounts as gatekeeping devices. The stories we tell about the origins of things are not neutral, but are highly politically charged narratives that can be used to promote some ways of thinking, while marginalising others.*
2 *Texts from the past change their meanings over time, and as the concerns of the readers of the text change. In order to understand a particular text from the past it is important to try and read it on its own terms, rather than just imposing our own concerns and prejudices on it. This is not as easy as it sounds.*
3 *There are two under-analysed assumptions in IR that directly affect the way that we interpret the history of international thought. These are: (a) The way that certain historical myths continue to be repeated in IR, despite the fact that they have been refuted in scholarly publications. The worst of these is the myth of the realist–idealist debate. Forcing all ideas into realist and idealist straitjackets stops us from being able to see the richness and diversity of international thought. (b) That what we know as international thought is, almost entirely, a western interpretation of the world.*

*This book divides international thought into three phases. The first, explored in Part I, involves the creation of an inter-state system as a by-product of the formation of the modern western state from the sixteenth century onwards. The second, examined in Part II, follows the development of a self-conscious analysis of the international during and after the industrialisation of society. The third, the development of IR as a university subject after 1945, is summarised in Chapter 8. This book concentrates on the first two phases.*

In their send-up of English history, originally published in 1931, Sellar and Yeatman declared that history is what you could remember. Theirs was the only 'memorable' history because it was made up of the partially remembered stories of English history overheard in 'golf-clubs, gun-rooms, green-rooms, etc'.[3] What Sellar and Yeatman were satirising was not history *per se*, but rather the way that people construct definite narratives out of half-digested historical 'facts'. Throughout *1066 and All That* the text is broken up by declarations that a certain person or event is a good or bad thing. The whole story is tied to what is the defining feature of whether something is memorable or not: whether it relates to Britain being 'top nation'. Thus, the American War of Independence results in America having no more history, because America was now no longer 'memorable'. While Sellar and Yeatman were satirising a specifically British Whig history[4] that when they wrote was already under attack from a new generation of historians, what is uncomfortable about their approach is that we are all guilty of these kinds of distortions and over-simplifications (a Whig history is one that is written not to understand the past, but to give support to current positions in the present). Historical narratives, tottering on a flimsy base of knowledge, are frequently used to justify certain positions, policies or preferences. Often the shrillness of our claims on an issue is directly proportional to our lack of knowledge of the historical case at its base. Most recently, and since history teaching in schools around the world have come under the control of national curricula, these narratives have been used to justify the existence of specific sovereign states. Yet, these narratives are not exclusive to state-based nationalisms, and can be found among all human collectivities. Even academic fields of study are not immune to this process.

International Relations (IR) has its own set of standard Whig histories. These revolve around the idea of the first great debate and the dichotomy of realism and idealism. The construction of a conflict between realist and idealist approaches peppers many textbooks, and allows lecturers of introductory IR courses to present a simple history of IR that sees it as a long struggle between idealist and realist paradigms. This great debate is often located in the inter-war period, but it is also sometimes placed in the post-1945 period. The fact that there is no agreement on when this 'Great Debate' took place should send warning signals through teachers of introductory courses. Like all good myths the realist–idealist debate is based upon a kernel of historical evidence. Brian Schmidt has located a realist–idealist debate among US foreign policy studies in the late 1940s, while 'realist' and 'idealist' were terms that were traded (often with different and conflicting meanings) between the wars. There is even evidence of a debate resembling the realist–idealist debate before the First World War.[5] On balance, though, the realist–idealist 'Great Debate' over-simplifies the past by ignoring the rich diversity of pre-1950s IR, and imposing anachronistic conditions on to the past. A similar process operates in International Political Economy (IPE), where the myth of a complete separation between the study of politics and economics prior to the 1970s has written out both liberal and socialist political economy approaches to the international that were active prior to 1950.[6]

This book is an attempt to bring some historical rigour to these stories that we tell about the international. I do not presume to be telling the whole and complete story, though. Like Bertrand Russell, I believe that the more we know the less certain we are about the truth. All histories are interpretations and present a particular biased angle, which can be due to factors such as the cultural baggage of the author or the evidence available. There is, however, a major difference between narratives based on flimsy and misleading evidence, and histories (however biased or misleading they still are) that endeavour to understand and uncover as much of the past as humanly possible. Well informed histories, however subject to their own biases, at least provide us with an attempt to recreate the past, and offer a firm foundation for scholarly debate. The central goal of this book is to provide as much understanding of the history and origins of international thought as possible within the confines of a single work. In order to do this I try as far as possible to understand these ideas within the context of their own times. This is more of a struggle than it may at first appear because the past at one level is irredeemably lost to us. Our evidence for the past is always fragmentary and limited to certain forms of evidence that tend to survive better than others. Thus, while we know much about late Republican Rome from the archaeological record and the surviving writings of the period, we are limited by the loss of other forms of evidence, such as the perspectives of the slaves or the mindsets of the citizens themselves that were the context in which the surviving evidence existed and made sense. Added to this there are our own views and contexts. Our own views on slavery, so different from the Roman, mean that we either tend to judge their society by our own standards (as the film *Spartacus* did), or we unconsciously ignore the unpalatable aspects that interfere with our interpretation of an idealised past (as the equally classic film *Cleopatra* did).

That said, there are also very good reasons for studying the past in general, and the history of ideas in particular. First, whether we like it or not, political arguments based on historical precedent or narratives are a central feature of our society. Positions are justified by reference to historical narratives, and thus the spread and acceptance of historical narratives form an effective gate keeping device, where they are used not to understand the past, but to prevent ideas that do not fit the story from being accepted. Second, the predominant tendency in IR theory to read past theorists only in terms of present day concerns and categories limits our understanding of the richness of texts, as well as the tendency of these texts to be interpreted differently by different generations. Related to this is our failure to understand two aspects of a text: its relation to the possible intent of the author, and the way that the attitudes of a particular audience in space and time reinterpret a text. Texts, in short, are not static and unproblematic sources. Third, the placing of a text within its historical context helps reveal the complexities of human existence, and guards us against simplistic formulae for human action that merely extrapolate the particular concerns and prejudices of groups in space or time. In terms of the history of international thought, this imperative to study ideas within a broader historical context has sharpened with the development of international political theory (IPT). The development of a more philosophically nuanced IR theory via IPT means that IR now needs to undergo the same revolution in thought that political theory went through with the debates about the nature of the history of ideas in the late 1960s and early 1970s. In short, we must match our deepening philosophical understanding with an equally deep understanding of how historical context affects the way that we read philosophical insights. The next section confronts this issue.

## What this book is ... and what it is not

Over the last few years there has been a growing body of literature in IR called international political theory (IPT). IPT has been defined as 'that aspect of the discourse of International Relations which addresses explicitly issues concerning norms, interpretation, and the ontological foundations of the discipline'.[7] In other words, it is an understanding of the underlying theoretical foundations of IR and international thought. Applying analysis taken from political theory, IPT has added to our understanding of the history of IR through a deeper analysis of the international thought of past theorists and philosophers within a broader context of the analysis of questions of justice, war, power and sovereignty. While IPT often analyses past thinkers, the primary focus is not to understand those thinkers in terms of their context and place within the history of ideas (although it is not precluded from doing so), but rather to understand those authors in terms of the broader perennial questions that they are involved with asking. Thus, an analysis of A.T. Mahan would be less about the contexts and debates in which his ideas evolved, and more to do with how he can help us answer questions about sovereignty, colonialism and war.

To a certain extent this development of IPT has brought IR into line with the development of political theory. This alignment, however, opens up a question about the relationship between theory and historical context. From the late 1960s onwards political theorists have faced and debated the question of the role of historical context in the interpretation of political theory and past theorists. The first salvoes in this debate were fired by Quentin Skinner in 1969 and have since been organised into what became known as the Cambridge School of political theory.[8] While I do not want to go into the details of this debate here, I do want to stress the point that the Cambridge School helped open up political theory to the history of ideas, and especially to criticisms of the construction of 'traditions' in political thought that owed more to an ahistorical 'spurious persistence'[9] based upon flawed understandings of the context of political thinking. This is not to say that the Cambridge School is not without its critics, indeed Skinner's original 1969 article was the subject of a robust response in 1974 by Parekh and Berki. Even then, Parekh and Berki did not cast doubt on Skinner's argument on the importance of historical context, rather they took issue with how Skinner had employed and (in their view) overstated it. For Parekh and Berki there were different degrees of importance for context depending on the nature of the thinker and the form of his or her work. There were attempts by past thinkers to address what are seen as perennial problems of human existence, and so sometimes we can read them in the same way as we would read a more recent writer.[10] Yet, in the final analysis Parekh and Berki replace Skinner's more bullish support for the understanding of the intentions and context of a thinker with an acceptance of the inability to escape the present, and an acceptance that historical and contextual understanding is always shifting and is never stable. The bottom line that emerges from this exchange is the complexities of the relationship between a text, its writer and their historical context. Any attempt to understand political theory requires us to understand how it interacts with both its historical context and with the audience in the present.

The success of IPT in IR has, therefore, brought with it an imperative to engage with the historical context and linkages of international thought. Greater awareness of the role of political theory in international thought requires us to consider the importance of methods of thought associated with the history of ideas too. This is where the history of international thought comes in. Its importance lies placing international theory within its historical context, and thereby acting as a support for the study of IPT. This is not the end of the matter, though. The history of international thought also acts as a critique (and even a criticism) of current narratives and practices that use historical narratives as a means of bolstering or demolishing certain current theoretical arguments in IR. For example, it is not uncommon – both in IR and in popular debates on foreign policy – to hear the claim that some idea will not work, and the reason for this can be demonstrated 'by the failure of the League of Nations' and of the ideas associated with it. This feeds into a common sense narrative that many are familiar with. But did the League, qua the League, fail? Were the ideas of those who supported the League sunk with the League, and who exactly supported the League, and in what way? The current tendency is to use the League story as a criticism of all approaches that talk about institutional change in IR, and as a support for ideas of power politics based on a particular reading of human nature; and it can be a devastating put-down. The question is, though, is it good history? While an actual analysis of the League is beyond the scope of this study, we will in Chapters 6 and 7 explore many of the thinkers who wrote on the League and League issues. The picture that emerges is instead a very complex one, with many supporters of the League idea coming from what is now regarded as a realist position, while many of those written off now as idealists were critical of some or all aspects of the League. A proper evaluation of how ideas, over time, interact with the world of policy requires a more complex understanding of what those ideas were, and how they evolved as part of a wider historical process. In short, in order to do good theory we also need to do good history.

Thus, this book is not a work of international history, nor is it an account of IR theories, it is also not necessarily a work of IPT, although to a certain degree it contributes to all three. It inhabits the space between these three recognised and well-developed fields. What it will do is confront two little-analysed assumptions that have silently dominated much IR theory. These are:

1   The 'text-hindered' nature of IR's approach to history, or rather how we only interpret past international thought through the categories of 'realist' and 'idealist' that we find in our first year IR textbooks.
2   The view that IR theory is primarily an objective and universally relevant attempt to understand global politics, rather than (in John M. Hobson's view) a parochial celebration and defence of western ideals.[11]

We will deal with both of these in turn, showing how they have shaped the arguments and assumptions of this book.

In a 1997 book on Roman villas John Thomas Smith refers to the phrase 'text-hindered archaeology', which is in common use in archaeological circles.[12] This phrase referred to the tendency to interpret archaeological evidence through the lens of historical texts (especially contemporary or near contemporary texts). Such a reading distorted the interpretation of the archaeological record since it assumed that texts could be taken at face value, rather than read as partial, partisan or just plain inaccurate artefacts. Thus, for example, interpretations of third and fourth century AD Gothic society using the available archaeological evidence has been held back by too close an attachment to the Gothic history of Jordanes, written two centuries later, by a partisan Eastern Roman, and in a different political climate.[13] The analysis of the history of international thought has suffered from its own form of text-hindered fantasy, although it is not historical texts that are the main source of the problem, but rather the interpretation offered by textbooks, and their taking of certain interpretations as the definitive account. With very few exceptions IR textbooks have assumed that the history of IR is marked by a clash between two dominant paradigms: realism and a less well defined second one called idealism, utopianism or liberalism. Much of this interpretation seems to be borrowed (and distorted) from Carr's 1939 *Twenty Years' Crisis* (Carr is to IR, perhaps, what Jordanes is to Gothic history), or from 1950s debates over US foreign policy. Over the last decade IR textbooks have kept this 'realist'–'idealist' split, but have added other 'paradigms' as these approaches have gained some form of acceptance as distinct schools of thought, although with little attempt to say why they can be called paradigms.[14] This often takes the form of grids, in which the paradigms are defined in terms of their assumptions about the study of the international. The most common pairs in this comparison are selfish human nature (realism) vs altruistic or good human nature (idealism); state-centrism (realism) vs states and others (idealism); anarchic international system (realism) vs communal international system (idealism); and national interest (realism) vs internationalism (idealism).[15] The problem here is that so many attempts to properly explore the writings of past international thinkers are shoe-horned into this realist–idealist schema, and this hinders a proper historically nuanced reading of past international thought. Certainly, the lumping of a group of disparate writers into the category 'idealist' has rendered current IR oblivious to the differences between advocates of collective security and the stricter pacifists, or to the raging debate in 1930s IR over the role of capitalism as a cause of war. In this sense, much of IR's perceptions of its own history have been text-hindered – whether that text be more recent textbook over-simplifications, or a too ready acceptance of the objectivity of E.H. Carr. One goal of this book is to release the study of international thought from the realist–idealist straitjacket. Much as archaeologists struggle to allow their finds to structure the story that they tell, so we must try to allow our 'finds' (in this case texts and archival material understood within their historical context) to structure the story we tell. This is, at one level, an impossible task because it is never possible (even for the best historian) to wholly escape our own temporal and spatial context. However, the more we are able to limit the intrusions of these fantasies of the present then the more we are able to fully appreciate the meaning of past thought, and its place within the multiple ironies and contradictions that is the historical record. History, according to the historian Lynn White, 'is a bag of tricks which the dead have played upon historians', and it is the illusion that the written record is 'a reasonably accurate facsimile of past human activity' that is the most remarkable of these tricks.[16] We historians of IR must be aware of these tricks.

Thus, while this book is, to a large extent, a study of texts, I hope to avoid some of the complaints made by archaeologists by stressing two things. First, the importance of context in the development of international thought; and second, seeing texts and ideas not as competing truths and scientific interpretations, but as the equivalent of archaeological artefacts in their own right. Rather than seek to, for example, analyse and critique Norman Angell's *Great Illusion* as a work of social scientific interpretation alone, the goal is to understand what Angell was saying and how his text relates to contemporaries. This leads me to the second of the under-analysed assumptions in IR: that 'international theory does not so much explain international politics in an objective, positivist and universalist manner but seeks, rather, to parochially celebrate and defend or promote the West'.[17] This issue is already the subject of John M. Hobson's 2012 book on Eurocentrism and IR. Here, rather than repeating Hobson's eloquent argument, I would like to take his conclusion in a different direction. Hobson's intent is to point out this Eurocentrism in order to challenge it, and I certainly support this goal. My role here is a different one: to understand the development, richness, complexities, silences, contradictions and form of this fundamentally Eurocentric (and, certainly since the 1890s, Anglocentric) project we call international thought as a thing in itself. As a result, this study is also an unabashedly

Eurocentric one, in the sense that it is studying a product of European (or western) civilisation. This is not to say that the non-western world has nothing to offer. On the contrary there is no doubt in my mind that it does. Rather, just as a study of the Roman Empire will make no reference to the equally important civilisation of China, so a study of the Eurocentric and latterly Anglocentric, tradition of international thought will limit itself geographically and culturally. Thus, what I am studying in this book is not the slow unfolding of a globally-minded scientific project, but rather the development of a collection of western views and interpretations that have tried to make sense of the international, and the west's place in a wider global politics, within a fundamentally Eurocentric world-view. This is a world-view that, like all world-views, may have much to offer humanity as a whole, but is also by its very nature myopic and limited in how much it can be transferred into a truly global vision. In this sense western international thought is little different from its parent body of western political thought.

Thus, at the end of the day this book is a sort of dig into the archaeological record of international thought. The intent is to give some kind of temporal and cultural context to the ideas that have been used to explore the international within western political thinking. Here, though, we do run into an initial problem of nomenclature. What is it that we mean by 'international'? It is to this question that the next section turns.

## What is 'the international'?

Perhaps the first place to start is to untangle what we mean by 'the international'. Like most successful intellectual fields IR benefits from an unspoken vagueness about its subject matter. I call this a benefit because it has given the field a flexibility that has allowed it to meander and change with the times and with intellectual fashions. This is not unique to IR, but rather seems to be the norm. The ideal field of intellectual endeavour seems to combine both a core definition of what it is about with the ability to take in (or even move to) new forms of study as opportunities arrive. To use a planetary analogy here, it seems that to retain a stable orbit any intellectual field needs to combine conservative centripetal forces intent on reigning in the field to within set parameters with centrifugal forces working to move the field away in any and all directions. Alongside this tension there is another that runs to the heart of the definition of the field. Is IR primarily a recent, predominantly American, university-based field reflecting the concerns of later twentieth century global politics, or is it the latest manifestation of much older ideas about human relations? My simple answer to this is a very unhelpful yes to both. While seemingly contradictory, both are true, and our emphasis on one or the other largely depends on our definition of IR, and following on from this the question of what date we see as the founding of IR. The 'when' of IR is, in this sense, not an idle question, but one that cuts to the heart of how IR is defined. If we interpret IR, with Stanley Hoffman, as an American social science of the Cold War, then the field is founded in the 1940s or 1950s, and can be defined as the (US) university-based sub-field of political science that first coalesced around a predominantly American-school realism intent on answering the questions of world order in a bipolar world, but has now branched out to include other approaches (see Chapter 8). If we look to the end of the First World War (a position more popular in Britain, and especially in Aberystwyth where the first Chair in international politics was founded in 1919), then IR is defined more broadly as a field that includes policy-makers and journalists, and the question of the causes of war is focused on as a major founding question (see Chapters 6 and 7). If the foundation is sought in the late nineteenth century then the focus shifts to questions of industrialisation and colonialism, and their effects on the broader states system. Here the attention of IR shifts to a political economy approach over a much longer period of time, where war and the system of states becomes the product of wider modern and modernising forces of material development, class conflict and imperialist ideologies (see Chapters 4 and 5). For others the early modern era of the sixteenth and seventeenth centuries become the key period where territorial state competition becomes the norm, and a supposed clear division between domestic and inter-state politics opens up. Here sovereignty and analyses of the society of states tend to dominate (see Chapters 2 and 3). Finally, there are those who see the fundamentals of IR rooted in forces that transcend time, and as a result IR becomes a field that has always been there, its principles rising to the surface throughout history when perspicacious thinkers in times of crisis cut through the façades of ideological justifications to reveal the permanence of interests and power. Here mention is made of the power-political elements to be found in the works of Thucydides, Kautilya, Machiavelli and David Hume.

Where we trace the origins of IR from is a reflection of what we see IR as being primarily about. The idea of IR as timeless often underscores a belief that the basic premises of IR are rooted in laws of history that have their origins in the nature of humans or of human societies. While more historically nuanced approaches are critical of this view of the origins of the field, and often interpret it as the product of a naive and ill-informed view of the richness and variety of human historical experience, there is a grain of value here for any analysis of the history of international thought. While the devil of IR may lurk in the detail of time-specific conditions, what ties all of IR together – while simultaneously distancing it from much domestic politics – is the issue of the relations between human societies and groups that do not necessarily recognise a higher authority acting as a clear and unequivocal mediator for relations between them. This is a wider question that has at least affected human relations since we first settled down and claimed ownership of territory for farming or grazing, and even if the way that those relations are manifest are managed and organised through time-specific ideas, structures and forms of production. Even the nomads of the Eurasian steppes needed ways in which to regulate grazing rights with strangers outside of their own social group. These relations are qualitatively different to those that occur within the group, and the ultimate sanction of war is never too far away, even if more often than not they are solved peacefully.

Here it is perhaps useful to turn to James Der Derian's analysis of the origins of diplomacy as a means of teasing out this deeper taproot of IR.[18] Der Derian argues that the origins of diplomacy need to be seen in the need to mediate between the estrangement of societies (that is, to deal with the problem of foreignness and alienation we feel towards other societies). Diplomacy, in this sense, represents a temporary solution (a salve, if you will) applied to the problem of estrangement in the absence of a more structured solution. Der Derian also contrasts diplomacy with what he calls anti-diplomacy: the condition where mediation becomes impossible because of religious or ideological differences that cannot conceive of any compromise of principles. What Der Derian has explored in his discussion of diplomacy is a perennial human problem in a world split up into societies that lack clear structures within which to regulate their discourse: how do we achieve a *modus vivendi* (a way of getting along) with other human societies? Underlying this also remains the anti-diplomacy option, which interprets the problem of mediating estrangement as begging the question, and instead turns to the idea of constant warfare against the outsider. Here we also encounter the important distinction between 'politics' and 'relations'. In its essence the idea of politics – deriving from the Greek 'polis', and referring to the basic constitutional and social unit for the classical Greeks – refers to the forms used by a society to organise and manage itself. Often this group was seen as being (in both biological and metaphorical terms) an extended family, hence our continued use of 'domestic' to describe politics within a modern state. Thus, members of a polis were 'born' of it, and thus formed a single *nationem* or 'nation' – derived from the Latin *natus*, meaning to be born. For many cultures in many periods it has been necessary to contrast the normal 'politics' of the nation – the *re publica* ('public matters') to the Romans, from which we take our word 'republic' – from the 'relations' between nations. The former involves the 'normal' intercourse of a people, while the latter is a mediation of estrangement.

There is a danger here of seeing international relations as a fundamentally amoral interaction when compared to the ethics of domestic politics. This is where Der Derian's concept of anti-diplomacy can help. International relations may be necessarily a morally lower order set of interactions from those of domestic politics because it lacks the ethical and extended familial bonds of the nation, yet it too requires rules and agreed ethical norms in order to function. In this sense international relations are different from the war of all against all that would theoretically occur between societies that wished and worked for the total destruction of their neighbouring nations. International relations imply a set of conventions that make relations between nations manageable and predictable. Thus international relations have always been something more than the mere absence of the norms of domestic politics, and have included a just as complex system of norms that are made even more complex by the lack of a clear political hierarchy to enforce and implement them. On top of this, the distinction between the politics of the nation and international relations has never been, in practice, a sharp one. For the classical Greeks there was always the danger that the polis would descend into civil war (*stasis*) in which the politics of a polis would come to resemble the relations between *poleis*. The Greek word for a state where no constitution was agreed – *anarchia* – was adopted by the classicist Lowes Dickinson for his description of the international when he adopted the phrase 'international anarchy' to describe the world of states.[19] On the other hand, there was always the possibility that the relations between nations would in turn lead to a more formal and political structure. Thus Plato saw in the relations between Greek *poleis* the beginning of a sense of family similar to the polis, while notions of Christendom (of a common community of Christians) and the Dar-ul-Islam (community of Muslims) in the Middle Ages presupposed relations between co-religionists that were closer than just mere relations. Sometimes even the rules of diplomatic discourse could take on the air of a sense of closer family ties. The convention of addressing fellow rulers in ancient near eastern diplomatic correspondence as 'brother', or the nineteenth century notion of the European family of nations both demonstrate how there was no necessarily sharp dividing line between the politics of the nation and international relations.

Yet, for all these broader historical precedents, the nature of international relations are historically dependent, and rarely do institutions, norms or the units of analysis survive for more than a few centuries of human history. Even Morgenthau recognised this when he stated that, while the concept of interests was eternal, how interests were manifest was specific to a given period in time.[20] Thus the idea of the national interests of states would only survive as long as the institution of the state survived, to be replaced by the interests of whatever organisation replaced the state. Even the idea of the state – at best five hundred years old, but in its current form perhaps much younger than that – has changed rapidly with the development of industrialised economies reliant on a complex grid of global finance, production, labour, trade and (perhaps most importantly) cheap concentrated energy in the form of fossil fuels.[21] At the same time the ideological context has changed significantly over the period of recorded history, influencing what people feel that they can and cannot do. Modern people generally react with disgust to what the Roman's considered to be just treatment of a defeated enemy, where massacre, plunder and enslavement were seen as normal practice. At the same time, it is worth bearing in mind that a Roman might equally treat with horror the ability of twentieth century civilisation to exterminate an unprecedented 200 million people in the name of so many higher ideals. Roman brutality, by contrast, was small scale and targeted. Ideas matter because we do use them as yardsticks for our own behaviour, and it is the interactions of so many societies with different cultural norms that often make international relations such a dangerous, interesting and crucial set of problems.

The claim that historical difference is irrelevant to IR often centres on the idea, first expressed by David Hume in his essay 'Of the Balance of Power', that the concept of the balance of power cuts across cultures and time. There are two problems with this formulation. First, it assumes that the balance of power meant the same thing in all ages. There is strong evidence that this is not even true for the modern era. Originally expressed in the Renaissance as a metallurgical metaphor implying a mix of elements, the idea of the balance being a pair of scales seems to date from 1612–13, when this analogy was used by Trajano Boccalini in his three-volume *Ragguagli di Parnaso*: a forceful denunciation of Spanish power that relied on a balance of power argument using the analogy of scales that was to become the common way of interpreting it in the centuries to come.[22] Even later ideas of the balance of power do not necessarily describe the same phenomena. Ralph Pettman, in his 1991 textbook distinguishes between three different meanings of the balance of power in history and IR: it can be a mere description of a situation, a prediction of how states will behave, or a proscription for policy in a specific case.[23] Contrary to Hume, who believed that the idea of the balance of power was so basic that it must have been known to the ancients, there is no evidence that ancient authors did consciously recognise or even apply, it. The evidence is always implied, and can only be made to fit when we ignore the equally common examples of bandwagoning and hegemonic domination that occurred in pre-modern relations.[24] There is also no evidence, for example, that the idea of the balance of power existed in the Hellenistic and Roman Mediterranean, while the argument that the balance of power was known in classical Greece rests solely on a particular reading of one passage of Thucydides. In fact, there is no direct evidence that Thucydides used or even understood an idea of a balance of power between *poleis* in general, let alone between Athens and Sparta. Instead, it is inferred from his comment at the end of Bk I ch. 2. That the 'growth of the power of Athens, and the alarm (fear) which this inspired in Lacedaemon, made war inevitable'. Yet, the bottom line is that this is an unsubstantiated inference that lacks further corroborative evidence. It could just as easily be that Thucydides is accusing the Spartans of showing a fear (*phobos*) that the Spartan's own self-image claimed they had overcome. Hence, Thucydides' statement is open to interpretation. Thus, much of the notion that IR consists of an ahistorical set of values rooted in naturally determined 'laws of history' owes more to a Whiggish history of the international that reads modern norms anachronistically into the chance comments of pre-modern authors. Indeed, it is a product of the assumption that ideas have a separate existence from the historical contexts that they inhabit – that they are, in Skinner's words, 'a growing organism'.[25] In other words, ideas are personified as self-contained notions that have their own existence and history, rather than being the products of particular and time-bound, political conflicts and developments.

Thus, while we can talk about a central idea of continuity in the form of the relations of estranged societies and groups, what constitutes international thought is shaped by specific conditions through time. This even applies to the idea of the study of IR itself, which is also a time-bound concept. While we can draw out examples of international thought from the past, it is really not until the late nineteenth century that we can talk about distinct works of international thought. On top of this, it is really not until the early twentieth century that we can discern a body of writers that see themselves as self-consciously part of an IR scholarly community. On top of this, it is really not until the middle twentieth century that this body of scholars becomes associated with a field primarily located within the university. Thus, when looking at the development of western-dominated international thought we may be looking at three interlocking periods:

1   A first phase from the Renaissance onwards, where there are no specific international writers, but in which the nature of the international is explored as part of the study of politics and statecraft.
2   A period of less than a hundred years between about 1880 and 1950 when the international begins to be studied in its own right, but where there is no specific intellectual home for IR.
3   A third phase, that has its roots in the inter-war world, but does not really gather a full head of steam until after 1950, when IR becomes a university-based field that is eventually captured (but not without some resistance) by Political Science.

It is during this last phase that IR becomes a predominantly (but not exclusively) American social science.

## The history of international thought, its phases and form

This book mainly covers the first two phases, and the transition to the third phase. The three chapters in Part I cover this first phase, where the development of the territorial states in Europe saw the development of a distinct body of knowledge on statesmanship that included thoughts on the nature and form of the international. This began with the development of a new statecraft based on a reading of the Roman historian Tacitus (see Chapter 2). This section includes an assessment of the role of the Peace of Westphalia (in Chapter 3). The place of the Westphalian peace in the development of the state system has come under attack in recent years, although it is still common to see the state system described as the 'Westphalian system'. Chapter 3 also explores the various Enlightenment attempts to understand the international, and argues that, by and large, there was much continuity between pre-Enlightenment and Enlightenment international thinking, but that the work of Rousseau and Kant marked an attempt to make a distinct break with the international practice of the past. Part I ends with a discussion of the role of industrialisation and imperialism in the creation of the international system of the nineteenth century (Chapter 4). It is these processes that created the context for the development of specific and self-consciously international scholarship towards the end of the century.

Part II covers the period in which this international scholarship develops in the west, and becomes an important part of the thought of the English-speaking world. From the 1880s, and on through the First World War, there developed a debate over the nature of the competition of states that developed into both an attempt to understand the role of empire and also the nature of the rules that governed competition between the great powers (see Chapter 5). There were three rough strands to this thought: an overtly imperialist group of writers, who saw the competition between states for global mastery as natural; a middle group that explored ways in which states could regularise their competition in order to bring greater security and lessen conflicts, and a group that challenged the role of the nation state. The First World War acted as a catalyst that both encouraged a greater interest in international affairs, while also creating institutions – both globally and domestically – that fostered the study of the international. Between 1919 and 1935 the discussion of the international in the English-speaking world was dominated by the major institutional experiments that were going on both under the auspices of the League of Nations, and within states with the creation of semi- and non-state bodies that were supporting scholarship on international questions (see Chapter 6). Here four loose schools of thought are examined: the liberal geopolitical school that sought to develop an alternative political geography to understand the changes that had occurred since the war; the conservative supporters of the League, who saw the new structures as an important addition to the diplomatic world of states; a liberal socialist group who saw the new arrangements under the League as the beginnings of a new form of international relations; and finally the pacifist and radical socialist opposition to the League and League collective security. Chapter 7 looks at the debates of the late 1930s that led up to the Second World War, and also at the discussions about the shape of the post-war settlement that took place during the war. Involving many of the same writers already introduced in Chapter 6, the discussion here will revolve around the criticisms of Nazi geopolitics, the debates over appeasement, and the wartime discussions over the post-war order.

Part III starts off with a discussion of the development of IR as a university subject in the two and a half decades that followed the ending of the war. Here the role of key meetings and committees on both sides of the Atlantic are discussed (see Chapter 8). The story here revolves around the rise of both American School realism and the English School to dominant positions in the study of IR in the English-speaking world, although important differences remained with the formulation of the functional approach and the split between what was seen as a more classical and historical approach and the more quantitative and positivist analyses of IR (a split that was to be labelled as the second 'Great Debate' in later analyses of the field). This brief sketch of the field will be followed by an analysis of how this can help us understand the nature of the field of IR, specifically the problematic use of paradigms in IR, and how we might rethink our ordering of international theory to better reflect the richness and diversity of international thought.

Throughout this journey I take on a number of myths and half-truths that have dominated IR's view of its own history, frequently drawing on existing works that have presented alternative views of IR's history. As a result, this book also plays an important myth-busting role that is not totally unlike that taken up by the popular television series *Mythbusters*. Among the myths explored will be: the idea of the Peace of Westphalia as the origin of the state system; the pacifism and internationalism of the Enlightenment; the extent to which 1919 represented a break with the past; the existence of an idealist paradigm; the realist–idealist 'Great Debate'; the place of appeasement in international thought; and the effect of the Second World War on international theorising. At the end of the day the best kind of history is one that challenges conventions so that new more nuanced histories can be written. This book, as an exercise in revisionism and rewriting is part of that process. Of course, while I can be confident that the story I tell is a better piece of scholarship than the history I criticise, I can be equally sure that I will be followed by another revisionist wave that will criticise my own inaccuracies and write another history. The story in this book, therefore, is not the last word in a subject, but merely the first step in what will hopefully be a long journey.

## Notes

1 Quentin Skinner, 'Meaning and Understanding in the History of Ideas', *History and Theory*, 1969, 8(1), 53.
2 José Ortega y Gasset quoted in Ernst Cassirer, *An Essay on Man. An Introduction to a Philosophy of Human Culture* (New Haven: Yale University Press, 1944), 172.
3 W.C. Sellar and R.J. Yeatman, *1066 and All That. A memorable history of England* (New York: Dutton, 1931), vii.
4 For the idea of Whig history see Herbert Butterfield, *The Whig Interpretation of History*.
5 On a realist–idealist debate in the US in the late 1940s see: Brian C. Schmidt, 'The American National Interest Great Debate' in Brian C. Schmidt (ed.) *International Relations and the First Great Debate* (London: Routledge, 2012), 94–117. On the different meanings of realism and idealism between the wars, see Lucian M. Ashworth, 'Where are the Idealists in Interwar International Relations?', *Review of International Studies*, 2006, 32, 291–308. On an analysis of the pre-First World War IR see Torbjørn L. Knutsen, 'A Lost Generation? IR Scholarship before World War I', *International Politics*, 2008, 45, 650–674.
6 For an example of this see Benjamin Cohen, *International Political Economy. An Intellectual History* (Princeton: Princeton University Press, 2008), especially pages 1–19.
7 Chris Brown, Terry Nardin and Nicholas Rengger, *International Relations in Political Thought. Texts from the Ancient Greeks to the First World War* (Cambridge: Cambridge University Press, 2002), 1.
8 Quentin Skinner, 'Meaning and Understanding in the History of Ideas', *History and Theory*, 1969, 8(1), 3–53.
9 Skinner, 'Meaning and Understanding', 35.
10 Bhikhu Parekh and R.N. Berki, 'The History of Political Ideas: A Critique of Q. Skinner's Methodology', *Journal of the History of Ideas*, 1973, 34(2), 163–184.
11 John M. Hobson, *The Eurocentric Conception of World Politics. Western International Theory, 1760–2010* (Cambridge: Cambridge University Press, 2012), 1.
12 John Thomas Smith, *Roman Villas: A Study in Social Structure* (London: Routledge, 1997), 6.
13 See the argument in Michael Kilikowsky, *Rome's Gothic Wars* (Cambridge: Cambridge University Press, 2006), 130.
14 John T. Rourke's highly successful textbook, for example, began with a table listing just realism and idealism, but has now added a third 'catch-all' paradigm: constructivism. John T. Rourke, *International Politics on the World Stage*, twelfth edn (Boston: McGraw Hill, 2008), p. 19. Russett, Starr and Kinsella added 'radicals' to their realist and liberal division: Bruce Russett, Harvey Starr and David Kinsella, *World Politics. The Menu for Choice*, third edn (Boston/New York: Bedford/St Martin's, 2000), ch. 2. Some textbooks have been more careful, warning against

seeing paradigms as 'monolithic'. See, for example, Scott Burchill and Andrew Linklater, 'Introduction' in Scott Burchill et al., *Theories of International Relations*, third edn (Houndmills: Palgrave, 2005), 18. One has also tried to give some credence to the existence of idealism by linking it to philosophical idealism: John Baylis and Steve Smith, *The Globalization of World Politics*, third edn (Oxford: Oxford University Press, 2005), 774. Despite this, a depressingly large number of recently published textbooks ignore current scholarship, and continue to trot out the thoroughly discredited idea of a realist–idealist debate. See, for example, Andrew Heywood's *Global Politics* (Basingstoke: Palgrave Macmillan, 2011), p. 4.

15  See, for example, table 2.1 'Assumptions of Realism and Idealism' in Joshua S. Goldstein, *International Relations*, sixth edn (New York: Pearson, 2005), p. 57; and box 4.16 'Prospects for War and Peace. Realists vs Strong Liberals' in Robert Jackson and Georg Sørensen, *Introduction to International Relations*, second edn (Oxford: Oxford University Press, 2003), p. 132.

16  Lynn White, *Medieval Technology and Social Change* (Oxford: Oxford University Press, 1962), v.

17  Hobson, *Eurocentric Conception*, 1.

18  James Der Derian, *On Diplomacy* (Oxford: Blackwell, 1987).

19  Goldsworthy Lowes Dickinson, *The International Anarchy 1904–1914* (London: Century, 1926).

20  Hans J. Morgenthau, 'Another Great Debate. The National Interest of the United States', *The American Political Science Review*, 1952, 46(4): 961–988.

21  For a recent analysis of the effect of coal and oil see Timothy Mitchell, *Carbon Democracy. Political Power in the Age of Oil* (London: Verso, 2011). The differences between the politics of agrarian and industrial societies has been a talking point since the work of Auguste Comte in 1822, and was even recognised by realist systems theory in the 1950s and 1960s: see, for example, George Modelski, 'Agraria and Industria. Two Models of the International System', *World Politics*, 1961, 14(1), 118–143. These changes (especially in their more recent form) are also central to the historical materialism of Robert Cox (see his classic 'Social Forces, States and World Orders: Beyond International Relations Theory', *Millennium*, 1981, 10(2), 126–155).

22  See Satya Brata Datta, *Women and Men in Early Modern Venice: Reassessing History* (Aldershot: Ashgate, 2003), 32.

23  Ralph Pettman, *International Politics. Balance of Power, Balance of Productivity, Balance of Ideologies* (Cheshire: Longman, 1991).

24  See William C. Wohlforth et al., 'Testing Balance-of-Power Theory in World History', *European Journal of International Relations*, 2007, 13(2): 155–185.

25  Skinner, 'Meaning and Understanding', 11.

# Part I

# International relations before the study of International Relations

# 2 The origins of the modern state and the creation of international relations … by mistake

*This chapter explores the causes and effects of the revolution that led to the creation of the modern states, and how this led to an inter-state realm that began to be studied by thinkers during the time.*

*We start by exploring the three traditions of thought that early modern scholars had inherited from the ancient world. The first of these, the philosophical tradition that traced its roots back to Plato and Aristotle, had minimal influence on the development of international thought. The second Roman Republican tradition influenced Machiavelli, and other Italian Renaissance scholars, and is often referred to as Ciceronian humanism (after the Roman writer and statesman Cicero). Ciceronian humanism concentrated on what was seen as the virtues of the Roman Republic: popular participation in politics, a sense of putting the interests of the community ahead of your own interests (civic virtue) and a well-balanced constitution designed to bring the best out in citizens. The third tradition was the one found in the work of ancient historians, especially the writings of Tacitus. This third tradition produced a school of thought that dominated much work in Europe on the nature of statecraft, and is called Tacitist humanism. The Tacitists saw sovereigns as behaving differently from private individuals due to their need to protect their subjects. As a result they were often forced by necessity to do things that would be immoral for a private citizen to do. These ideas are the beginnings of the concept of reason of state.*

*It is this 'Tacitism' that is responsible for laying down many of the early modern notions of inter-state relations.*

*Humanism here is used to describe those writers who attempted to apply classical Greek and Roman writers to the non-religious political and social problems of their age. In this sense both those who applied the Roman Republican tradition (Ciceronians) and the historical tradition of Tacitus (Tacitists) can be described as humanists.*

While we can talk about international relations as on one level the (almost) timeless study of the relations between recognised communities, it is the development of the modern state that gives form to what we would call the international today. In this sense IR as a field is both a product of and a reaction to an ongoing social revolution that occurred over the last four centuries. This revolution has been so successful that few of us alive today, especially in the West, can contemplate a world without states (indeed, they have reached the status of being a natural part of our lives). Yet, a few centuries ago the idea of the sovereign state (let alone the sovereign nation state) was something accepted and experienced by a minority of the Earth's population. While European renaissance writers such as Guicciardini and Machiavelli knew there was a difference in the way that people felt about their fellow citizens and how they treated foreigners, they also wrote about politics as a seamless set of rules that applied as much to individual citizens or subjects of a prince as it did to groups of people. Machiavelli's use of historical lessons freely ranged across all levels of political interaction, and as a result it is fair to say that he did not really have a separate theory of the international. Politics was governed by laws applicable in many circumstances, while the real difference lay between the politics of principalities and the politics of free republics.

That said, there are clear changes going on in the sixteenth and seventeenth centuries that were laying out a separate politics of statecraft and diplomacy. Until quite recently it was common knowledge in IR that there was a major change in the nature of politics after the Middle Ages. This (often uninformed) view would frequently stress the role of the Thirty Years' War and the subsequent peace of Westphalia as a clear break with the past that led to a new international system (the 'Westphalian system'). Recent analyses of past international relations has quite rightly criticised this over-simplification of history. Many have demonstrated the continuity with the past found in the Holy Roman Empire specifically, and European states in general. These studies are right to challenge these simplicities. In particular, the myth of a Westphalian origin (discussed in the next chapter) was due for a serious debunking. There is a danger, however, that in our revisionist fervour we ignore the profound changes that were taking place at this time. No, there is not a sharp and clear break with the past, and no, the modern sovereign state did not just emerge in 1648 and dominate the world for the next three-and-a-half centuries. Yet, there were serious changes to the nature of politics from the late fourteenth century onwards that did create a new pan-European inter-state sphere of political interaction, and it was the development of this new political sphere that would eventually merge into a truly global international system that is the subject of study among IR scholars today. Something happens to politics in these centuries, and where the old simplistic view was right was that there was a marked shift in the nature and exercise of political authority. Where it was wrong was in the extent of that shift, and also in focusing those changes on 1648 and the peace of Westphalia. Much more was going on both before and after.

The development of the modern state led to a qualitatively different approach to politics. What made the state different from what had come before (although there were parallels with earlier empires such as Rome or Persia) were the various forms of centralising control – particularly in relation to taxation; the regularisation of the military; technological developments in fortifications, artillery and shipping; the growth of state diplomacy; the cartographic revolution; changes in class structures as a result of the development of a monied economy; and eventually an idea of sovereignty emerging as a part of absolutism, but increasingly becoming an attribute of the state. What emerged was a state designed to raise revenue primarily for the purpose of spending this revenue on war and war-related activities such as diplomacy, cartography and fortresses. Historians call this the fiscal–military state. While these were profound changes, there was also much continuity with the past, and the forms of the state continued to owe as much to past practices as it did to new innovations. The lack of nationalist sentiment and the continuity of many feudal loyalties meant that there are limits to how similar the early modern fiscal–military state is to the states of the twentieth and early twenty-first centuries. The forms that the state took changed dramatically in the intervening centuries.

The fiscal–military state that emerges in early modern Europe, with its parallel functions of tax gathering and martial preparedness, became increasingly absolutist and centralised from the late seventeenth century, although by the end of the eighteenth ideas of popular sovereignty were challenging these arrangements. Until the nineteenth century these states remained agrarian societies, with power based on land use and ownership. The advent of industrialisation (as we shall see in Chapter 4) wrought major changes to both the state's internal and external manifestations, effectively bringing the fiscal–military state model to an end among the great powers (although elements of these arrangements survived into the twentieth century in many states). The building of the modern state is, consequently, a long process with many twists and turns. It is, therefore, a gross exaggeration to speak of a 'Westphalian' state system in which states are presented as the same kind of unit existing in the same kind of system. The sixteenth and seventeenth century political systems are dead and gone, and our current system has little in common with them. That said, the early modern state did signify a break with much medieval practice, and represents a first step in the development of an international sphere of politics that is worthy of study in its own right. The section after next will explore these major changes that led to the development of the state, and discuss what they tell us about an emerging system of relations between these new states.

Yet, despite the institutional break with the past represented by the state, the writers who explored this new politics still saw themselves as continuing the older classical tradition of writers from the Greco-Roman past. In this they shared the assumptions of Machiavelli and Guicciardini that all political knowledge worth having had already been developed by writers in the ancient world. The goal of the scholar was to uncover and apply this timeless wisdom to the present in order to educate the princes and statesmen of their time. Yet, this classical tradition was not a single body of knowledge. More importantly, there seemed to be three distinct and seemingly contradictory traditions that carried with them two different models of the nature of knowledge in politics. The next section will explore the use of the classical tradition, and how it influenced the writers that were exploring the new politics of the state. This will be followed by a section on the changes that occurred in the form and exercise of power as the early modern state emerged. The final section combines the discussion in both sections by looking at how a new humanism – influenced by specific aspects of the classical tradition – emerged to understand the changes in statecraft wrought by the emergence of the early modern state.

## Philosophy or history? Mixed messages from the classical tradition

For the late medieval and early modern mind the ancient writers were an important source of knowledge. For many the ancient world represented the pinnacle of human achievement, and consequently ancient advice was to be preferred to that of more modern commentators (who were, after all, mere pale reflections of the ancient original). Yet, this veneration of the past was not unthinking, and most would agree that some authors, like the satirist Lucian of Samosata, were suspect because of their negative view of Christianity. Also, because the ancients certainly did not speak with one voice, it was open to interpretation which of them was the more useful or insightful. In addition to this, because these were not necessarily holy texts with a single orthodox view, the ancients were open to different interpretations, applications and even glosses. This was even more so in the case of the ancient historians, where plain narratives could imply (or be used to imply) sophisticated political theories. In some respects the use that modern IR puts Thucydides to is a continuation of this tradition.

While the variety of ancient authors and early modern interpretations makes any classification guilty of oversimplification, it is fair to say that there were three distinct schools of ancient authors that influenced the Renaissance and early modern mind. The first was the classical Greek philosophical school, represented most strongly by the works of Plato and Aristotle. Plato had been central to Christianity and Church doctrine since the days of the Roman Empire, and through Boethius and Augustine Plato's writings became canonical. To a lesser degree this process could also be seen in the Arab world, where Plato influenced a philosophical tradition of which the most famous product was Abu Nasr al-Farabi, *Mabadi' Ara Ahl Al-Madina Al-Fadila* (often translated as the ideal city) written in the tenth century. Aristotle came later to Christian Europe, via Arab scholars who had already studied and integrated Aristotle into their own philosophical output. Plato and Aristotle taught the west about timeless truths and the life of the mind. Aristotle was used to explain nature, to justify human communities based on (Christian) moral principles, and to bolster a conservative political order. The second tradition was based on the Roman Republican tradition, especially the Republican Roman adaptation of Stoicism as represented by the works of Cicero. While the first tradition had found favour with the Church, this second tradition became popular with the fifteenth century apologists for the new breed of Italian city politician. The Ciceronian concern for the core values of Republican politics (civic virtue, immutable/renewed mixed constitutions, and the need for aphorisms to understand the problems of day to day politics) forms the core of the Machiavelli of *The Discourses*, even if the stated source for the ideas in the book was the Roman History of Livy. The third tradition is that of the ancient historians, especially the 'Roman' histories of Tacitus, Livy, Appian and Polybius; the biographies of Plutarch, several texts of Xenophon's; and the two histories of Alexander written by Quintus Curtius Rufus and Arrian. Interestingly the earlier Greek histories of Herodotus and Thucydides had limited influence on the study of statecraft until the seventeenth century. For Herodotus (first translated into Latin in 1450) this may have been the result of the perceived anecdotal nature of his writing, although according to Gibbon Herodotus' account of the Persian wars inspired the English Queen Elizabeth to resist Spain.[1] Thucydides seems absent from the influences on Renaissance studies of statecraft, but gains a new status in the seventeenth century, especially with the new translation of his work by Thomas Hobbes.[2] As narratives these histories were more open to interpretation, but as laboratories of human nature and behaviour they provided a ready source of knowledge for the new class of statesmen that ran the emerging states of early modern Europe. This use of the historians was often mixed with the stoic tradition, although the Republican Roman stoicism of Cicero found less favour than did the later imperial stoicism of Seneca that taught constancy in the face of power, rather than the older traditions of civic virtue in a self-governing republic. Seneca's advice on how to remain constant to your ideals while facing the necessity of being prudent towards powerful authorities seemed to offer better advice to the subjects of the new centralising monarchies of northern Europe.

It was this third tradition that formed the background and intellectual justifications for the state-building of the sixteenth century. The most influential of the historians, Tacitus, actually gave his name to the humanist movement that was to dominate the interpretation of politics in sixteenth century Christian Europe. The surviving sections of Tacitus' histories, whose preservation had received papal support, had been an early subject for the new printing presses, and copies of Tacitus were freely available during the fifteenth and sixteenth centuries.[3] Tacitus' style meant that his text leant itself well to the drawing of historical lessons in a complex and ambivalent political universe, leading Montaigne to marvel at Tacitus' topicality despite the intervening centuries.[4] In addition to Tacitus, the sixteenth century was fascinated by the stories of Alexander and Caesar. Their styles of leadership and statesmanship were studied and emulated through works such as Quintus Curtius Rufus and Appian. This was in sharp contrast to the Ciceronian humanism of Machiavelli. Caesar, for Machiavelli, was the ultimate villain. Not because he was cruel, which for the time he was not, but because he took a functioning virtuous republic and corrupted it into a monarchy. For Machiavelli, the greatest people were those who took a corrupt society and made a functioning and virtuous republic. For the Tacitean humanists a century later it was the mere act of state-building and state-maintaining that had moral worth. The development of Tacitean humanism will be covered in more depth in the last section of this chapter.

What I want to stress here is the importance of this third, historical, tradition to the development of the early modern state, and the relative irrelevance of the first, philosophical, tradition. More specifically, I argue that many of the intellectual justifications of the early modern state were consciously imitated (or at least interpreted) from later antiquity. There was little in Aristotle that spoke to the early modern state builders, but the rich vein of historical commentaries on the empires of Alexander and the Romans provided a wealth of 'best-practice' examples. Thus, what emerges is a political theory based on political practice as found in the great classical historians, rather than based on the philosophical thought exercises of the Platonic or Aristotelian traditions. This pragmatic history-based statecraft merged with the evolving institutions of the Early Modern era – with their roots in the European Middle Ages – to form new ideas about the nature of politics and the responsibilities of both ruler and ruled.

In sum, Aristotle is left behind. His ideas remain a yearning among conservatives. It becomes a living fossil that is picked up by advocates of Senatorial class power in late Republican Rome, but is unable to survive the populist (and military-based) revolution of Caesar. It is picked up again by the Church at the end of the Middle Ages as a shield against the new humanism. Again, it fails to prevent the popularity of a political doctrine associated with the historian Tacitus. Even Machiavelli's attempt to revive the civic virtue of the Roman Senatorial party broke against the imperial policies of Spain and France. The cleverness of Aristotle was no match for the perceived pragmatism of Tacitus.

## The crises of the early modern and the rise of the state

The Europe of the hundred years between 1550 and 1650 faced four profound changes that would leave lasting effects throughout the course of modernity. Even in our own time, at the other end of the process, these changes are still being accommodated and dealt with, although to a certain extent a settlement was worked out with each one of these changes in the middle of the seventeenth century. The first of these was the instability caused by the doctrinal conflicts over religion. This came to a head between 1610 and 1648. While religious conflict is still an important irritant today, it could be argued that the form of religious dispute that developed in the early modern period became the form for ideological conflict in later modernity. In other words, our contemporary ideological and ethnic conflicts are fought with the same intellectual tools as the religious conflicts of the early modern period. Understand the dynamics of one and you understand the other. Secondly, the sixteenth century witnessed the rise of the centralised territorial state, with all of the institutions that came with it. Bureaucracies, direct taxation, professional armies, state-based economic policy all emerge at this time, and all assisted in the development of the war-fighting capabilities of the state.[5] Third, the feudal structure of vertical rights and duties was slowly replaced by a class system. The significance of this change for social relations was that, whereas in a feudal system loyalties and common feeling, via fealty, are expressed as vertical rights and duties between people in different classes, the new class system stressed the horizontal bonds and common interests between people in the same class. These changes in class arrangements can be linked to the rise of commercial relations, and their replacement of the older feudal order.[6] Finally, the sixteenth century witnessed the invention of the home. Medieval houses were the centre of the public life of an extended family, but sixteenth century society separated the public from the private. A new private space opened up in houses where an immediate family could interact away from the world.[7] The political importance of this was the emergence of a new political stereotype, the ruler as loving father. In sum, the sixteenth century witnessed revolutionary changes in four key areas of society: religion, government, class relations and domestic arrangements.

For medieval society religion both held the *res publica Christiana* together, and helped to keep secular authority fragmented. Christianity and the Church maintained a sense of universalism, while acting as an alternative shadow authority to secular power. When religious authority began to fragment in the Renaissance it was not only unity that was threatened. The weakening of the role of the universal Christian ideal allowed secular authorities to extend their power more readily, and without regard for medieval custom. Although the idea of Christian unity remained in the concept of the 'Republic of Letters' (that scholars across Europe shared a common bond). Beginning in fifteenth century Italy, and crossing the Alps towards the end of the century, state authority by the sixteenth century was growing without hindrance from cosmopolitan Christian values. Yet, assisting in the state building process was only one effect (and merely a permissive one at that) of the fragmentation of religious faith. Religious conflict, as a conflict of absolutes that broach no compromise, led to a series of ideological disputes that culminated in the Thirty Years' War between 1618 and 1648. Attempts at compromise between Catholics and Protestants were often met with violence, of which the assassination of the conciliatory French King Henry of Navarre in 1610 was perhaps the most visible, and for many traumatic, example. As religious zeal increased in the late sixteenth century, potential points of conflict were increased by the gradual spread of doctrinal differences to other areas of life. In a process known to German historians as *Konfessionalisierung* (confessionalisation), issues of faith came to prominence in cultural, educational and legal spheres of life.[8] As a result, by 1618 all areas of civil life were open to religious discord.

While religious difference brought conflict and undermined the sense of a common Christian bond between all Christians, the modern state was gradually replacing older feudal forms as the key political institution in Europe. A series of mutually reinforcing developments helped build the large centralised territorial states:

1    The weakening of feudal ties led to the growth of monarchical power.
2    The conflict between the various emerging centres of political power put a premium on military might, and encouraged the development of professional armed forces loyal to the sovereign and the state.

3   As armies became more effective as an instrument of state power they were used to extend the power of states, whether that be the crushing of independent nobles within the state, or absorbing smaller principalities outside.

4   As armies mutated from a collection of feudal levies, to professional mercenaries and finally to professionals hired by the state, states needed to be able to raise significant funds through taxation for the hiring and provision of troops.

5   This situation was further exacerbated by the technological arms race in the early modern period. The need for a blue-water navy and the growing importance of cannon for both siege and field put further strains on the financial resources of the state.[9]

6   The raising of finance and the management of the armed forces played a crucial part in the emergence of bureaucracies in the early modern fiscal–military states.[10]

7   At the same time the need to control territory for taxation and policing purposes led to the development of cartography and state-sponsored geographical societies.[11]

8   The growth of the diplomatic corps changed the form of the relationship between sovereigns, as well as providing sovereigns with much greater levels of information than available to their medieval forebears.[12]

Yet, while all this sounds so very modern, and indeed it represents a break with the medieval past, these fiscal–military states were not militarised societies in the modern sense. The absence of nationalism, and the persistent importance of many feudal ties, meant that there was a limit to the extent that the state was mobilised for war. Rather, it is better to see them as societies 'adequately organised to produce war on demand'. In this they stand in stark contrast to the slower mustering and organisation of European medieval society.[13] This centralisation for war, however, also helped to aggravate religious rivalries, as the new states attempted to impose one religion within their borders in order to decrease the chances of internal dissension, and thereby strengthen the ability of the state to project its power beyond its borders. It was not for nothing that the Treaty of Augsburg in 1555 agreed to the formula *cuius regio eius religio* for the constituent members of the Holy Roman Empire: the religion of the ruler should be the religion of their subjects.

Although state centralisation brought a new kind of conflict between sovereigns, it also created new tensions and conflicts within the state that were often unconnected to the issue of religion (although, frequently the two became linked in one form or another). The new fiscal–military state of the sixteenth century was not only interested in maintaining its security in relation to its neighbours, but also protecting and extending its power within its boundaries. The processes involved in the development of a more aggressive foreign policy go hand-in-hand with the development of a more intrusive security state at home, and a system of state-sponsored violence and control directed at the population that the state was, at least theoretically, meant to protect. Religious splits often helped to create an air of threat and instability that in turn led to the justification and deployment of quite brutal systems of state repression.

Despite the lingering attraction of the myth of the England of 'Good Queen Bess', of which the 1999 film *Elizabeth* was a recent example (although, to be fair to the film, it did not flinch from showing some of the more violent excesses of Elizabeth's supporters), the England of the Virgin Queen was a deeply repressive state. For Curtis C. Breight the importance of the period between 1547 and 1612 in England was that it 'marks a shift in which English domestic policy is wedded to a new global foreign policy run not by monarchs but by a conglomeration of forces recognisable as the "state"'.[14] As a result, domestic policy and control become part of a wider conflict with external threats. This did not mean that the state was without supporters in the wider population, but it did mean that the state apparatus relied on, and made good use of, what D.M. Loades sees as the main strength of the Elizabethan regime: its 'highly efficient intelligence system'.[15] A centralised internal security system, that controlled the activities of the population, was part of a wider conflict with foreign powers. This security system was controlled by a new breed of men, who owed their power to their control of the levers of government. Breight even goes so far as to regard the England of the period as being under a *Regnum Cecilianum* – the rule of the two Cecils and their ally Walsingham, who took it in turns to run the overt and covert elements of the state apparatus under both Elizabeth and her successor James.[16]

One of the most intriguing aspects of the policy of the English state under this regime was the ability to stage conflicts outside of England that could be used both as a means of justifying stricter controls and laws internally, while at the same time providing a pretext for the shipping of conscripted unemployed labour abroad to fight in often hopeless wars. It was not that domestic policy drove foreign policy, nor even that foreign drove domestic, rather that the two were merged into a single political struggle that focused on the political survival of the state. Nor was England unique in this regard. Other emerging states also developed this Janus-faced security apparatus. These developments occurred unevenly though, and concentrations on the developments in England and France often led us to forget that Germany experienced a different form of state-building through the organisation of the Holy Roman Empire. That said, the intellectuals of the age were left to make sense of dramatic changes in the nature of political life, and naturally for the time it was to the classical authors that they turned.

The emergence of the state was also aided by the reordering of class relations. The old feudal order had confined loyalties within a rigid system of client–patron relations in which the monarch or medieval city was only one of many elements. As commercial relations replaced feudal obligations the links between feudal client and patron broke down. The extent of the role of commercial practices in the destruction of feudal ties can be most clearly seen in the steady replacement of feudal tenancy with rent-based tenancy across western Europe.[17] As feudal tenancy died out so did the links of loyalty between 'master and man'. Instead, aristocrats and landlords became distanced from their tenants, and developed a stronger class consciousness with their class peers. This new horizontal class system created state-wide classes, and helped redefine people's loyalties. Feudal loyalties became refocused towards the state.[18] Burgundians began to see themselves as Frenchmen, while tenants of the Dukes of Northumberland were now English. The beginnings of these national sentiments can be seen in the plays of Shakespeare, such as *Henry V*, or in the popular patriotic songs of the day like 'My Lord Willoughby's Return'.[19]

Yet, the collapse of feudalism left a moral void. How were these new states to be justified ideologically? Towards the end of this period, in the middle of the seventeenth century, a ready template for the new politics was found in another new institution: the idea of the home. Domestic life in the early modern period – beginning in France, but quickly adopted and extended to the United Provinces of the Netherlands and England – increasingly became a private sphere that included immediate members of a family and its retainers. Where the medieval house was also a public place of work with no set uses for rooms (furniture was designed to be moved so that a room could serve many functions during the day), rococo France, *Gouden Eeuw* Holland and Stuart England created havens within houses that were private rooms. These rooms had set uses, and were furnished with comfortable and permanent furniture, as well as wall decorations. Eventually the idea of the home spread throughout Europe.[20] In Russia, for example, Catherine the Great created a private 'Hermitage' within her palace complex in St Petersburg where she and her family alone were allowed. Dutch *Gouden Eeuw* painting – such as the touching yet moralising work of Vermeer, or the personal portraits of De Hoogh – reflects this new domestic reality most effectively.

The political structure of the home – with a father figure as the head of the household, and horizontal divisions between adults, children and servants – became the model for the role of the sovereign in the state.[21] This was consistent with the primary intellectual paradigm of the early modern mind: the Great Chain of Being. Early moderns made sense of the world by seeing it as a great complex chain extending from the most simple and inanimate object all the way to God. The chain itself repeated patterns along its way, so that (for example) the animals of the sea were always matched by corresponding land animals (hence the survival of names such as 'sealion' or 'seacow'), while the form of the cosmos was repeated in the structure of humans, animals, plants and rocks.[22] Politically speaking, therefore, the government of the state would be an analogue of other parts of the *Great Chain*, including the heavens above and the family below. Thus, to use the family as a direct model for government was seen as perfectly natural. In fact, the power of this analogy was so great that it was not until Locke's attack on Robert Filmer that we see the beginnings of a consistent opposition to this episteme. The new arrangements of the state, therefore, were interpreted as analogous to the home, with the ruler at home and abroad behaving as a protecting father figure. The duty to protect his family remained a central justification for the statecraft of the era.

Early modern writers were forced to face the consequence of these radical changes. Initially, the humanists of the Renaissance looked to the classical writers of Greece and Rome for explanations of the rise of the state, and the moral citizenship of Cicero became a model of good human behaviour in this new world. The sixteenth century saw the emergence of a school of humanism influenced by the writings of Tacitus. These new humanists rejected the civic virtue that underpinned the political philosophy of Machiavelli, and looked instead for an explanation of state behaviour that was fundamentally amoral. This makes sense if we consider that the new states of the mid-sixteenth century were often too large for a face-to-face system of government based on civic virtue, and also that their feelings of deep vulnerability and insecurity had led to systems of control and repression that could not be justified by reference to the ideas of moral citizenship found in either Cicero or Aristotle. Instead, intellectuals turned to the pages of the Roman imperial historians, especially the works of Tacitus, where they found what seemed like clear parallels with the rulers of their own age. Sovereigns, they believed, were above ordinary morality because of the necessity inherent in *region dell stato* (the Italian original of *raison d'etat*, or reason of state). These sceptical new humanists produced a language that helped justify state behaviour, although most of them dreamed of a return to some form of unity (usually led by their own sovereign). This new language of *raison d'etat*, rather than uniting its users despite their religion, helped justify acts of violence committed in the religious wars. By the seventeenth century a new breed of thinker had emerged. Sick of the carnage around them, they hoped to recreate some sense of order through appeals to natural laws and through a new science that would transcend religious conflict. This last group, however, did not denounce the language of the Tacitist new humanism. Instead they fused *raison d'etat* with ideas of natural law. From this school emerged the norms of state practice that would dominate inter-state affairs up to the Enlightenment of the late eighteenth century, and would also develop many of the norms and practices that are used in the state system today. In the next chapter I will turn my attention to this latter group. The rest of this chapter is dedicated to a discussion of the new Tacitist humanism that emerged as an explanation of the new fiscal–military state of the sixteenth and early seventeenth centuries.

## Humanism and reason of state

Human history is replete with fundamental changes in thinking that result in major social change. Our own western society is still digesting the profound changes in values that emerged in the 1960s, as the continued popularity of television programmes such as *Mad Men* show. A similar change in the sixteenth century has not been given the same recognition today that it deserves. In part this is because it merely involves a change from one Roman author to another. At the beginning of the century Cicero, along with the compatible ideas expressed in Livy, was regarded as the key writer for the humanist tradition. Expressing dissatisfaction with the seemingly out of touch philosophical moralising of theologians influenced by Aristotle, writers like Machiavelli, Sebastian Fox Morcillo and Giovanni Viperani set out to construct a new moral code for the new states of Italy.[23] Although Machiavelli's proposals were of a different order to those of Fox Morcillo and Viperani, all shared Cicero's concern with living a moral life within a moral constitution. Machiavelli, borrowing from Livy's history of Rome, upheld the Republican Roman version of civic virtue, where the citizens of the state behaved with moderation and a sense of pride. Where this was impossible because the state was ill-formed, or under construction, Machiavelli demonstrated in *The Prince* how innovators beyond moral law could construct a state within which civic virtue would eventually be able to flourish.

Ciceronian humanism was centred on Italy, and especially on the Italy of the Renaissance. The early modern period would be dominated not by Ciceronianism, but by its two opponents. Within humanism the Ciceronians would be challenged by the Tacitists; while from outside humanism the advocates of monarchy, influenced by Bodin, would attempt to collapse the distinction between state and family. Where Machiavelli had looked to the Roman Republic, with its dynamic mixed constitution, as the perfect politically ethical community, Bodin argued for the superiority of a centralised monarchy based on family, rather than on a political constitution. For Bodin the family was a natural moral institution, and the father's dominance was tempered both by this naturalness and by fatherly duty and concern for those in his charge (wife and children) who lack the same level of reason. Bodin extrapolates from the family to the state. The sovereignty of the monarch is indivisible, like the sovereignty of the father in a family.[24] Bodin's idea, of extrapolating from family to state, was to be an important ingredient in the re-ordering of early modern thought a generation later.

Yet, the second half of the sixteenth century was not to be dominated by the thoughts of Bodin, but by the revolution in sceptical humanism. The humanism of Machiavelli, while sceptical of the theologians, was still anchored in a Ciceronian morality that advocated civic virtue and moderation in public life. Machiavelli's philosophy rested on the moral base of the good citizen practising public virtue. His intellectual successors in humanism were to become sceptical even of that. The discovery of the works of Tacitus took humanism down another route. The Tacitists were selective readers of Tacitus' history, but it was often the successful ruthlessness of Tiberius in dealing with his opponents that attracted them. There was no moral gloss to Tiberius' actions, which were carried out purely to preserve himself and the Roman polity.[25] Like its forebear, Tacitist humanism began in Italy, and the initial forms of it were first laid out by a contemporary of Machiavelli's, Francesco Guicciardini. Where Machiavelli balked at ultimate cruelty in *The Prince*, Guicciardini, defining interest in an amoral sense, saw violent and cruel acts as the basis of the founding and maintenance of great states 'according to the reason and custom of states'.[26]

Despite its Italian origins, it was the Europeans beyond the Alps who were to develop Tacitism into an effective and popular approach to the political problems of the sixteenth and early seventeenth centuries. In the writings of Montaigne and Lipsius Northern Europeans would find inspiration for a new view of statecraft better suited to their larger societies. From the point of view of international thought the biggest name among the Tacitists of the north is Justus Lipsius.[27] Lipsius combined Tacitus' understanding of ruthless necessary power with the stoic philosophy of Seneca that offered a way of remaining constant to your ideals within a Tacitean universe. Lipsius' two main treatise – *De Constantia* and *Politika* – were translated into all the major European languages. Indeed, *De Constantia* was translated into at least seven languages in over eighty editions, while between 1589 and 1751 *Politika* was translated into at least eight languages in ninety-six editions.[28] The popularity of Lipsius across Europe not only influenced the work of other Tacitists, but also provides a bridge between the earlier humanism of the Italians (both Ciceronian and Tacitist) and the later philosophies of Hobbes and Grotius in the later seventeenth centuries.[29] His influence on the historical plays of Shakespeare, perhaps through the Lipsian works of Bacon and Jonson, has also been noticed.[30] While still strongly wedded to the idea of a pan-European 'republic of letters', Lipsius' work was nevertheless aimed at learning to live with the new realities of the powerful monarchical states that divided Europe up into a patchwork of different centralising jurisdictions. This advice was directed both at the rulers themselves and at their subjects. In his advice for princes he recognised the new realities of power, but tempered this with the need for good counsel (prudence), the importance of the prince as an example of virtue to his subjects, and the importance of discipline for the success of the state (especially military discipline). For subjects of these states Lipsius made free use of his knowledge of Seneca to give advice on how to survive in a dangerous world without necessarily sacrificing virtue. His striving for a stoic Senecan aloofness can in part be seen as a reaction to the passions released by the religious conflicts that haunted him throughout his life.[31] Here, the politically active life championed by Ciceronian humanism disappears to be replaced with a new politics where the subject is no longer a crucial part of the political process, except as a subject of discipline and a consumer of the peace that hopefully prudent monarchical government will bring.

While Tacitist and Ciceronian humanism were at odds about the moral nature of political power, it is important not to forget the strong links between the two, and the debt owed by Tacitism to the earlier humanists. Both were a rejection of what we might see as the esoteric or philosophical school of political theorising, led in the Renaissance by the Aristotelians. Although this may just be a modern conceit brought on by selective reading of the past, political thought seems to be perennially troubled by friction between an esoteric branch, that thinks in terms of atemporal fundamentals outside of the flux of human history, and a secular group, who prize the ironies of history, and see historically conditional (and conditioned) flux as the basis upon which political action is and must be based. Not surprisingly, the roots of this split between the esoteric and historical schools goes back to the ancient texts that formed the basis of Renaissance and early modern learning. Although Plato is perhaps a better paradigm for the esoteric school, it was Aristotle that had become widely known and read in Western Europe from the high Middle Ages onwards. His concepts of timeless principles and a static conservative society meshed with a Church-based learning that saw flux and change in the material (secular) world as a vice, and a further vindication of the superiority of a life directed towards heavenly contemplation (the point that this was a partial reading of Aristotle does not diminish the power of this interpretation). The material political world, and its ethics, should serve a contemplative life, which in turn needed no justification, but was rather an ultimate ideal.[32] By contrast, humanism, in both its key Early Modern forms, prized history.

History was a vast library of human experiences, and especially for the Tacitists it was the form of knowledge most relevant to political life. It is not that they rejected the ideas of virtue found in the philosophies of Plato or Aristotle, but rather that they saw it as a secondary consideration in politics, where issues of right and wrong were often less clear, and often changed as circumstances altered. Political prudence was necessary to learn the particulars of statecraft, and only human experience can teach prudence.[33] Justus Lipsius contrasted an atemporal and divine virtue with prudence. While virtue came from God's laws, prudence was taught by history, and was the knowledge associated with political practice and statecraft. The role of virtue was to temper prudence so that it did not become merely 'subtill (sic) craft, and malice', but was fashioned into prudent statecraft.[34] To ignore history, and to live by atemporal virtue only was to behave like an ancient stoic:

> They seeme not to knowe this age, and the men that live therein, and do give their opinion, as if they lived in the commonwealth of Plato, and not in the dregs of the State of Romulus.[35]

For Lipsius and the Tacitists the old Roman virtue of constancy is modified (under the influence of Seneca's imperial-era stoicism) away from its Republican original form, in which the wise constant man always acts according to specific rules, towards the new Imperial vision of constancy as a prudent outward conformity to authority, but an inward private and philosophical constancy to philosophical ideals.[36] The techniques of this form of constancy can be learnt from the great historians, who recorded the flux of human politics, not from the grand statements of Plato and Aristotle. There is little room here for Socrates' notion of the detached philosopher who always remains true to his own learning. Instead, practical and useful knowledge comes from an understanding of the complexities of human nature as revealed in the unfolding drama of human history. Thus, it was important, the Tacitists thought, to be prudent on the outside, while remaining constant to what we know is right on the inside. We must be privately constant, even while we were publically prudent.

From the 1570s onwards Tacitism caught the mood of European humanists. An Italian circle in Paris spread the ideas to France, and influenced the pamphleteers who justified the St Bartholomew's Day Massacre of French Protestants. In Guy de Pibrac's defence of the actions of the French court the murder of the Protestant leader is justified by necessity.[37] In order to prevent treason the state was justified in breaking a moral law that applied to individuals. Here we see the crucial word that was to justify the actions of many states during the instability of the next seventy years. The action was necessary, and therefore was above moral law. While not advocating immoral actions, Cardinal Richelieu, seven decades after Pibrac, was to warn his sovereign against being too morally scrupulous so as to act against the interest of the state.[38] The two most influential Tacitists of the age, Lipsius and Montaigne, were less direct in their support for necessary evil. Both writers based their thoughts on scepticism about the acquisition of knowledge in general, and moral knowledge in particular.[39] Both were also concerned by the growing instability caused by religious friction and state rivalry. Basing their thought on the idea that self-preservation was a universal and common human goal, they set out to argue that loyalty to the state should not be based, as it was for Machiavelli, on a sense of civic virtue, but on our own sense of self-preservation.[40] This had been taken further by Giovanni Botero, who advised princes never to trust in ties of friendship or kinship, but only in common interests.[41] A strong state that does well and follows its interests protects its citizens from the current instability in inter-state relations.[42] The Tacitists did, however, share the Ciceronian humanists' belief that political knowledge came from human experience expressed through history, rather than from abstract generalisations about human behaviour. Thus, while they were sceptical of generalised claims to knowledge, Tacitists regarded history as a basis upon which to build an understanding of statecraft.[43]

Lipsius and Montaigne extended self-preservation and linked it up to the Tacitist notion of necessity. For Lipsius the structure of political relations and the sequences of events constrained the actions of politicians. Consequently, states were often in a position in which they had no choice but to act in a certain way in order to survive.[44] Without choice there could be no moral imperative. The English Tacitist Stephen Gardiner argued that a prince may be forced to do cruel and evil things, but he is only an evil man if he acts cruelly when compassion is compatible with his interests.[45] Montaigne, betraying the disgust of the hermit for the world, implied that public life requires people to betray, lie and massacre.[46] Thus, the relations between states were governed solely by self-preservation and necessity. It follows from this that pursuing moral choice, when necessity dictates a particular action, is potentially dangerous, both for the actor and for those who rely on them.[47] Perhaps the best statement of this comes in Shakespeare's *Hamlet*. Hamlet's sense of moral choice, in a situation where he should just kill his uncle out of necessity, leads to the deaths of six innocents. By contrast, the amoral Fortenbras, living under the forces of necessity, ends the play as king of Denmark. If Fortenbras had been the main protagonist then the play would (at best) have lasted half an hour: an angry Fortenbras (without Hamlet's misplaced moralising) kills his uncle after being told the truth by his father's ghost.[48] If this was not enough of a break with Machiavelli's civic virtue, Tacitists also looked to the strength of the state in material, especially financial, might, rather than in the Ciceronian virtuous citizenry. This was particularly blatant in Giovanni Botero's work, were the greatness of cities and states is linked to wealth, and in the ability of the state to raise taxes from that wealth.[49]

It would, however, be wrong to assume that the Tacitists were only concerned with self-interest and physical power. Here we must distinguish between their advocacy of *raison d'etat* as the means of state politics, and their stated ends. While self-preservation was seen as the only sure basis of political action and institutions, Montaigne, Lipsius, Botero and Gardiner were also believers in the ultimate good of the unity of Christendom. Botero himself wrote to justify the actions of Habsburg Spain. Through its exercise of *raison d'etat*, Botero hoped that Spain would unite Christendom under the Catholic Church. Similarly, Gardiner's goal was a federated Catholic monarchy under Philip II, which would act as the guarantor of peace in Christendom.[50] Lipsius remained a strong advocate of a cosmopolitan Christian and European republic of letters built around Latin scholarship.[51] Most of the Tacitists associated with Habsburg domains assumed that the law of self-preservation would lead, in time, to a recognition of European unity against the real enemy of the Turk. Here we see the beginning of a two-tier inter-state realm. There are the relations between Christians, which are fundamentally more harmonious in the long run, and relations between Christian and Turk, which are nothing more than a continual state of war. The problem that Tacitism was to face was that the use of their ideas of *raison d'etat* and necessity would not lead to Christian unity, but instead would be used as the excuses for further Christian disunity.

Beyond Lipsius, Montaigne, Botero, Gardiner and the other supporters of Christian unity in the Tacitist camp, lay a second group of Tacitists with a more modest goal for Christendom. Botero, in his historical analysis of Italy, had already mentioned how Lorenzo de Medici had kept peace in Italy by balancing the power of his rivals.[52] If Christian political unity was out of the question (as it was for Tacitists in England and Venice, for example, who questioned Spain's ambitions), it might be possible to argue that the laws of self-preservation would lead to a balanced peace between all the states of Europe. The idea of the balance of power originally had a chemical or anatomical meaning, very different to the modern mechanical definition. Just as the humours of the body needed balance, so the different competing states of Christendom could contribute different attributes to the European body politic that would bring long-term balance and order.[53] Certainly, there was no conception, in the sixteenth century, of a mechanical balance of power responsible for maintaining order between sovereigns. This was all to change in 1612–13 when Trajano Boccalini used the analogy of a pair of scales to explain the balance of power. This idea of a mechanical balance between the interests of states was to be incorporated in the next generation of inter-state theory that emerged after the Thirty Years' War, and came to a head in the eighteenth century. In sum, later Tacitism had played with the idea that self-preservation might lead to an order based on competing state interests.

What the Tacitists were trying to do was part of a project that was wider than political thought, and went to the heart of early modern attempts to find a solid basis for a stable order in all branches of knowledge. As Hirschman has demonstrated, three different interpretations of the royal road to an ordered society emerged. Some advocated repressing destructive passions by force, others suggested pitting better passions against the worst sort, while a third group hoped to use human interests.[54] Lipsius, during his long career, managed to span all three of these, but increasingly it was the idea of interests that formed the basis of Tacitist proscriptions. Even customs and common law were explained by reference to past interests, with jurists like Matthew Hale rejecting the idea of the naturalness of English law, and seeing it instead as a product of the 'exigencies and conveniencies' of earlier generations.[55] Montaigne, ever the sceptic, regarded the laws of conscience 'to be derived from custom rather than nature'.[56] Much as many Cold War realists, such as Henry Kissinger, assumed that their views on power and interest would lead to order between the superpowers of the USA and USSR because it would transcend ideology and lead to a balance of power, so Tacitists assumed that interests would lead to peace through the acceptance of a common language of politics.

Yet, interest, necessity and *raison d'etat* were not enough to create a stable order. Instead of inventing a politics that would transcend religious division, and lead to a stable order, Tacitism put amoral intellectual tools in the hands of religious fanatics and state-builders. By the end of the century even Spanish Tacitists, such as Alamos de Barrientos, were advocating the abandonment of the goal of a universal Christian empire.[57] At the other end of Tacitism, Francis Bacon continued to preach unity, but cast doubt on the politics of *raison d'etat*: 'Concerning the means of procuring unity; men must beware, that in the procuring, or uniting, of religious unity, they do not dissolve and deface the laws of charity, and human society.'[58] Tacitism, with its political theory rooted in a generalised idea of human interests had failed. Yet, surprisingly, much of its ideas were to survive the strife of the Thirty Years' War. *Raison d'etat* was to be welded on to a new conservative ideology that was to be the basis of domestic politics for the next century and a half, and the basis of much inter-state relations, in one form or another, to our own day.

## Notes

1  Edward Gibbon, *An Essay on the Study of Literature* (London: Becket and de Hondt, 1764), 7.
2  Although J.B. Bury sees close parallels between Thucydides and Machiavelli. See his *The Ancient Greek Historians* (London: Macmillan, 1909), 140–143.
3  See the discussion in Rhiannon Ash, *Tacitus* (London: Bristol Classical Press, 2006), 96–9.
4  See the discussion in John Burrow, *A History of Histories* (Harmondsworth: Penguin, 2009), ch. 8, especially 128, 147.
5  These changes are discussed in detail in William H. McNeill, *The Pursuit of Power* (Oxford: Basil Blackwell, 1982); Bruce D. Porter, *War and the Rise of the State: The Military Foundations of Modern Politics* (New York: Free Press, 1994); and Perry Anderson, *The Lineages of the Absolutist State* (London: New Left Books, 1974).
6  These changes are discussed in detail in Samuel Clark, *State and Status. The Rise of the State and Aristocratic Power in Western Europe* (Montreal and Kingston: McGill-Queen's Press, 1995). See also Stephen Toulmin, *Cosmopolis: The Hidden Agenda of Modernity* (Chicago: University of Chicago Press, 1990), 96–8.
7  Witold Rybczynski, *Home: A Short History of an Idea* (New York: Viking, 1986).
8  Ronald G. Ash, *The Thirty Years War. The Holy Roman Empire and Europe, 1618–1648* (Basingstoke: Macmillan, 1997), 17.

9  See the discussion in J.R. Hale, *War and Society in Renaissance Europe, 1450–1620* (Stroud: Sutton, 1998), 46–7.
10  These issues are developed in both MacNeill, *op cit*, and Porter, *op cit*.
11  This idea is developed in Gearóid Ó Tuathail, 'Introduction: Geo-Power', *Critical Geopolitics* (London: Routledge, 1996).
12  Hale, *War and Society*, 45.
13  Hale, *War and Society*, 44.
14  Curtis C. Breight, *Surveillance, Militarism and Drama in the Elizabethan Era* (Houndmills: Macmillan, 1996), 1.
15  D.M. Loades, *Politics and the Nation 1450–1660. Obedience, Resistance and Public Order* (Glasgow: Collins/Fontana, 1974), 283.
16  Breight, *Surveillance*, 22–7.
17  Clark, *State and Status*, 151–3.
18  Toulmin, *op cit*, 97.
19  My Lord Willoughby's Return stresses the Englishness of the brave 'captains three', and stresses that Willoughby's bravery is in the service of England.
20  Rybczynski, *op cit*, especially the first four chapters.
21  For a detailed study of this see R.W.K. Hinton's two-part article 'Husbands, Fathers and Conquerors: 1. Filmer and the Logic of Patriarchalism', *Political Studies*, 1967, 15(3), 291–300; and 'Husbands, Fathers and Conquerors: 2 Patriachalism in Hobbes and Locke', *Political Studies*, 1968, 16(1), 55–67. An excellent examination of patriachalism and the emergence of liberalism can also be found in Jean Bethke Elshtain, *Public Man, Private Woman. Women in Social and Political Thought* (Princeton: Princeton University Press, 1981), ch. 3.
22  Michel, Foucault, *The Order of Things. An Archaeology of the Human Sciences* (London: Tavistock, 1970), ch. 2; E.M.W. Tillyard, *The Elizabethan World Picture. A Study in the Idea of Order in the Age of Shakespeare, Donne and Milton* (New York: Vintage, nd), chs 4–7.
23  Richard Tuck, *Philosophy and Government 1572–1651* (Cambridge: Cambridge University Press, 1993), 12–39.
24  Jean Bodin, *The Six Bookes of a Commonweale* (Cambridge, Mass: Harvard University Press, 1962). A good commentary on Bodin can be found in J.W. Allen, *A History of Political Thought in the Sixteenth Century* (London: Methuen, 1960), Part III, ch. 8.
25  Tuck, *op cit*, 41. It is worth pointing out, however, that the Tacitists used a particularly selective reading of Tacitus to underscore their ideas. Tacitus' defence of the imperial, over the Republic beloved of Cicero, did, however, provide the Tacitists with a template for criticising Ciceronian humanism.
26  Quoted in Tuck, *op cit*, 39. Guicciardini's view of inter-state relations can be gleaned from his *Ricordi*. See Francesco Guicciardini, *Maxims and Reflections of a Renaissance Statesman (Ricordi)* (Gloucester, MA: Peter Smith, 1970).
27  For a full account of the international thought of Lipsius see Halvard Leira, 'Justus Lipsius, Political Humanism and the Disciplining of 17th Century Statecraft', *Review of International Studies*, 2008, 34, 669–92.
28  Leira, 'Justus Lipsius', 685.
29  Leira, 'Justus Lipsius', 689.
30  See Geoffrey Miles. *Shakespeare and the Constant Romans* (Oxford: Clarendon, 1996).
31  See Leira 'Justus Lipsius' for developments of these points.
32  Tuck, 11.
33  See, for example, Giovanni Botero, *The Reason of State* (London: Routledge, 1956), Bk II.3, pp. 36–7.
34  Justus Lipsius, *Six Bookes of Politickes or Civil Doctrine* (London: Richard Field, 1594), Bk 1, 1–9.

35 Lipsius, *Six Bookes of Politickes*, Bk IV, 13.
36 For a discussion of this see Adriana McCrea, *Constant Minds: Political Virtue and the Lipsian Paradigm in England 1584–1650* (Toronto: University of Toronto Press, 1997), 10.
37 Tuck, 41.
38 Cardinal Richelieu, *The Political Testament of Cardinal Richelieu*, edited and translated by Henry Bertram Hill (Madison: University of Wisconsin Press, 1961), 35.
39 Michel de Montaigne, *Essays* (Harmondsworth: Penguin, 1958), Introduction, 10; Justus Lipsius, *Two Books of Constancie* (New Brunswick, NJ: Rutgers University Press, 1939), Part II.
40 Tuck, *op cit*, 51–3.
41 Giovanni Botero, *The Reason of State* (London: Routledge, 1956).
42 See, for example, Walter Raleigh's justification for war in his *A Discourse of the Originall and Fundamentall Cause of Naturall, Customary, Arbtrary, Voluntary and Necessary Warre* (London: Humphrey Moseley, 1650), 1–5. Although published in 1650 this book was written in the sixteenth century.
43 See, for example, Botero, *Reason of State*, 36–7, Bk II.3; and Justus Lipsius, *Six Bookes of Politickes*, 13–4, Bk I.9.
44 Lipsius, *Of Constancie*, 125; and *Of Politickes* Bk IV.
45 Stephen Gardiner, 'A Discourse on the Coming of the English and Normans to Britain, Showing How Princes have Succeeded or Failed Depending Upon Whether They Ruled According to Reason or Appetite [1553–5]', in Peter Samuel Donaldson (ed.), *A Machiavellian Treatise By Stephen Gardiner* (Cambridge: Cambridge University Press, 1975), 138–9, 141.
46 Montaigne, 'Of Profit and Honesty', *Essays*, III.1.
47 Gardiner, *op cit*, 139.
48 Shakespeare's character is very different from the Hamlet of the Saxo Grammaticus story that is the original source for Shakespeare. The fact that Shakespeare so dramatically rewrote the story makes his *Hamlet* a fully contemporary tale of late sixteenth and early seventeenth century politics.
49 Giovanni Botero, *A Treatise Concerning The Causes of the Magnificency and Greatness of Cities*. Lipsius also endorsed this view in *of Politickes*, 82, Bk IV.9.
50 Gardiner, *op cit*, 150.
51 Leira, 'Justus Lipsius', 676.
52 Botero, *Reason of State*, 125.
53 Ralph Pettman, *International Politics. Balance of Power, Balance of Productivity, Balance of Ideologies* (Melbourne: Longman Cheshire, 1991); Michael Sheehan, *Balance of Power: History and Theory* (London: Routledge, 1995), 33.
54 Albert O. Hirschman, *The Passions and the Interests. Political Arguments for Capitalism Before its Triumph* (Princeton: Princeton University Press, 1977), 15–56.
55 Matthew Hale, *The History of the Common Law of England* (Chicago: Chicago University Press, 1971), 34.
56 Montaigne, 'of Custom', in *Essays*, ch. 21.
57 Tuck, *op cit*, 77.
58 Francis Bacon, *The Essays 1601*, http://www.orst.edu/instruct/ph1302/texts/bacon/bacon_eaasays.html.

# 3   Reaction and reform

## Patriarchal order and the Enlightenment response

*This chapter looks at the development of an approach to inter-state relations that replaced Tacitist humanism during the sixteenth century. This patriarchal conservatism adapted Tacitist ideas of the reason of state, but set it into a conservative political philosophy that stressed the importance of both tradition and order. It was patriarchal in the sense that it interpreted sovereign rulers as father figures with a moral duty to protect their subjects. Patriarchal conservatism was the philosophical justification for the power of states from the second half of the seventeenth century, and in the late eighteenth century it would come to be called the* ancien régime. *The Enlightenment of the eighteenth century was a philosophical revolt against patriarchal conservatism.*

*One of the major goals of this chapter is also to explore and debunk the myths about the Peace of Westphalia that is found in so many IR accounts of this period.*

*The second half of this chapter looks at how Enlightenment ideas challenged patriarchal conservatism. I argue that much Enlightenment thought did not actually challenge patriarchal conservative notions of inter-state relations, and that it was not until the theories of Rousseau and Kant that we see the beginnings of an alternative Enlightenment approach to the international.*

The tendency in IR textbooks over the last few decades has been to present the Peace of Westphalia as a watershed. Before it lies a different feudal world, while after it the international system of states begins its three or more centuries of domination. The last chapter has shown the extent to which the origins of the state system – and with it what we know as ideas of the international – is much earlier. This chapter questions the idea of Westphalia as a key watershed in the development of international thought, and focuses on how the development of patriarchal conservative ideas of inter-state politics in the mid-to-late seventeenth and early eighteenth centuries were challenged (with mixed results) by late eighteenth century Enlightenment thought. In this process a clear conception of the difference between domestic (intra-state) and international (inter-state) politics begins to emerge.

Basically, the ideas that emerge during and after the Peace of Westphalia largely continue the earlier sixteenth century view of politics as a fused whole, with no clear differentiation between a domestic and international realm. They do begin the process of splitting these two political realms, however, by conceiving of the world within the state and outside it as different arenas in which the same laws of politics are played out. Interestingly it is during the Enlightenment, when the earlier patriarchal conservatism of the so-called *ancien régime* is criticised, that the idea emerges of separate realms obeying different laws. This idea of separation is accepted (and even championed) by many earlier (mainly British) authors, but challenged and criticised by others, most dramatically by Rousseau and Kant. It has to be said, though, that this separation of realms by Enlightenment scholars was often a device employed in order to discount the international realm, and to encourage the focus of political theorising towards the internal affairs of the state. This is certainly true of David Hume, and to a lesser extent of Adam Smith. Jeremy Bentham's idea of international law is an exception here, as is the concentration on the problems of the international in the later works of Kant. On the whole, though, the international theorising of political philosophers of the Enlightenment remains a weaker branch of knowledge in comparison to the revolution in the development of ideas of domestic government, and it is only after the effects of industrialisation and imperialism at the end of the nineteenth century that we can really talk of the sustained analysis of the international realm. Having said this, both the patriarchal conservatives and the Enlightenment philosophers contributed to the building of an idea of an international sphere. The former brought ideas of conflicts over power in the absence of authority (the origins of what later writers in IR would call the anarchy problématique), while the latter brought an idea of a separate international realm that carried with it a different power-political logic from that of the domestic public sphere. Thus, if we were to answer the question of when the 'Westphalian' system sovereign states emerges, then the answer would have to be sometime after the Enlightenment reaction to the politics of the patriarchal conservatives.

This, of course, begs a very big question about what IR scholars today mean when they talk about a 'Westphalian system'. The bulk of this chapter explores how, first, patriarchal conservative ideas displace the older Tacitist humanism discussed in the last chapter, and then how the Enlightenment in turn attempted to challenge these ideas. Before we do this, though, I would like to address the issue of the Peace of Westphalia, concentrating first on the myth that 1648 represents a founding moment for modern ideas of IR, and following this up with an assessment of the implications and uses of the myth of 1648 on international affairs as it has been practised in the recent past.

## A note on the treaties of Westphalia and the Westphalian myth in IR

Before analysing the changes in international thought from the seventeenth to the eighteenth centuries a quick reference to the treaties of Westphalia is called for. 1648, and the peace reached in that year, are frequently mentioned in IR texts as a watershed that ushered in our world of sovereign states. Why do we associate the development of the modern state system with the treaties that brought the Thirty Years' War to its conclusion, and is this association justified? At face value the texts of the treaties do not seem to support this view. There are no overarching philosophical statements in them, except perhaps with one exception. This has not stopped the peace of Westphalia being regarded, in so many IR texts of the last four decades, as the moment at which the modern states system emerges; so much so that the phrase 'Westphalian system' is routinely employed in IR as the label for the modern system of sovereign states. This use of the adjective Westphalian was given further fuel in the 1990s by the re-emergence of a literature arguing for the failure of the sovereign state, with perhaps the title of Susan Strange's final publication 'The Westfailure System' holding a witty pride of place in this genre.[1] Yet, despite this common-sense belief in the existence of a sovereign states system emerging from the peace of Westphalia, several IR scholars with a deeper knowledge of the period under scrutiny have called into question this relationship between the 1648 treaties and the modern practices of IR. The reaction to the Westphalian system story arguably began with Stephen Krasner's 1995–6 article in *International Security*, but the first sustained criticism came with Andreas Osiander's 2001 article in *International Organization*. This was followed by Benno Teschke's book in 2003, and by a further burying of the myth of 1648 in an article in *Millennium* written by Benjamin de Carvalho, Halvard Leira and John Hobson.[2]

Perhaps the first issue to address is that there was no one treaty of Westphalia, but three – and possibly even four. The year 1648 saw the signing of three treaties within the German territory of Westphalia, two in the City of Münster and one at Osnabrück (although Osiander keeps to a stricter definition, only recognising the two that dealt directly with the Holy Roman Empire, and discounting the Spanish–Dutch treaty. De Carvalho et al. mention the Dutch–Spanish treaty, but also prefer the stricter definition of two. The Dutch Rijksmuseum, perhaps not surprisingly, opts for three).[3] The October treaty of Münster ended hostilities between France, the Emperor and their respective allies. The January treaty of Münster brought the Eighty Years' War between Spain and the Netherlands to an end. While pre-dating the Thirty Years' War, this war had been absorbed into the general conflict in Germany, and the conflict between the Netherlands and Spain had remained one of the most important causes of the instability in Europe, and was not surprisingly a major contributing factor to the outbreak and continuation of the Thirty Years' War. Finally, the treaty of Osnabrück ended the war between Sweden, the Emperor and their allies. War between France and Spain dragged on for another eleven years, finally coming to an end with the treaty of the Pyrenees in 1659. Thus, there is no single Westphalian document, but rather two, three, or even four (depending on whether you include the Franco-Spanish treaty).

The second issue is the question of how much the treaties changed the political alignments of Europe. The straight answer here is that there was little, in terms of power relations, between the main states of Europe that was different in 1648 from 1618. After a long period of weakness France had reasserted itself as a major political power, but this was merely a return to prominence, rather than the emergence of a new constellation in the European political sky. The power of the Spanish and Austrian Habsburgs were not greatly dented, although after 1659 Spanish power would begin a long protracted decline. Sweden was launched on a short career as the dominant power in the Baltic, while the positions of Brandenburg and Bavaria in Germany were strengthened by territorial gains. Finally, the independence of the United Provinces of the Netherlands and the Swiss Confederation were recognised by Spain and the Empire respectfully. Except for the collapse of Bohemian Protestantism, the confessional divisions of Europe appeared equally unchanged. Despite the carnage wrought on Germany, and a few minor revisions of the European political and confessional map, the divisions of 1648 were little different from those of 1618.

One of the claims of the literature in IR is that 1648 saw the final culmination of a conflict between the universal aspirations of the Empire/Habsburgs (with its roots in medieval unity) and the particularistic claims of the largely protestant states (plus France). The latter were victorious, and therefore ushered in our modern era. The problem with this simple antimony is that there is no evidence for it. Indeed, both Osiander and de Carvalho et al. point out that the Empire was actually weaker when the Thirty Years' War broke out.[4] In addition to this, the particular claims of the separate Christian rulers were not necessarily at odds with wider universalist claims that underscored both ideas of Christian unity, and the concept of a cosmopolitan republic of letters based around the use of Latin. Linked to this is the claim that 1648 saw the end of a conflict between empire and sovereignty, with the final victory of the idea of the particularist sovereign state over the claims of universal empire. There are two problems with this. First, although there was a sense of a pecking order among sovereigns, most clearly expressed in the formal seniorities of ambassadors in a posting, there was never any realistic attempt by the Habsburgs to create a universal empire. Certainly, writers associated with the Habsburgs (as mentioned in Chapter 2) often advocated a Habsburg-dominated peaceful union, but this was never turned into an actual bid for Empire. Linked to this, the states that were opposed to the Habsburgs were not recent arrivals on the European stage, but had been around for a long time. Second, the Habsburgs and all other rulers exercised a personal sovereignty, but this did not amount necessarily to the same thing as the idea of a formal sovereignty held by a particular state. Thus, at no time was there a tension between a possible imperial ideal and the notion of the sovereign state. Rather, the development of the sovereign state was a long drawn-out process taking place over the next two centuries.[5]

Even the single overt statement of political principle was a piece of borrowed clothing. The famous *cuius regio eius religio* (the religion of the ruler is the religion of the people), the so-called Augsburg formula, was part of the compromise peace signed in 1555 between the Lutheran and Catholic princes of Germany. The only differences were that by 1648 the Calvinists were also brought into the process, and the religion of the various parts of the Empire were frozen in their confessional affiliations as of 1 January 1624. In all cases this formula, and its subsequent revision in 1648, applied to the lands of the Holy Roman Empire.[6] The applicability of the Augsburg formula outside of the Holy Roman Empire was not necessarily agreed to, although the concept of non-interference in the internal affairs of other states would be invoked in later centuries as a (often contested and frequently transgressed) principle of the state system. Suffice it to say, that the Augsburg formula, as reinterpreted in 1648, did not usher in an unfettered notion of non-interference.

Yet, having said all this, while the treaties associated with the peace where not themselves a major break with the past, the world after 1648 was wildly different to the world of the sixteenth century in one important respect. The intellectual climate had changed dramatically, and the events that had culminated in the peace of 1648–59 were at least partially part of a new way of looking at both politics and relations between political entities such as the emerging states of Europe. It is this intellectual change that is explored in this chapter. Yes, there is an intellectual change in how statecraft is approached in the first half of the seventeenth century, and this change is profound. At the same time, though, that intellectual change itself did not create – fully armed – a state-based international system. Rather, as Osiander rightly points out, the transition to what we know as a state system was a slow one that was also moulded by the diplomatic politics of the eighteenth century, the revolutions of the Enlightenment, and the industrialisation of the nineteenth century.[7] This chapter looks at both the patriarchal conservative intellectual revolution that replaced the humanism discussed in the last chapter, and at the Enlightenment reaction to the world that this patriarchal conservatism bequeathed to the *ancien régime* of the eighteenth century. The incomplete nature of the Enlightenment challenge to patriarchal conservative notions of inter-state politics set many of the parameters of the state system that would interact with industrialisation after the 1850s. The effects of industrialisation on the state system and on the nature of international thought will be the subject of the next chapter.

Before explaining the development of patriarchal conservative approaches to the international it is worth looking at the ideological power and role of the Westphalian myth. While the myth of the creation of a system of sovereign states preserving peace between them has been largely discredited, the myth – or 'Westphalia concept', as Sebastian Schmidt prefers to call it[8] – emerged for two good, but contradictory, reasons. The use of Westphalia as a watershed event dates from at least the nineteenth century, although the lessons that were drawn were many and varied until the 1940s. In fact Westphalia was as likely to be invoked as a support for the changes wrought by the League of Nations as it was for support for state sovereignty.[9] Frederick Schuman, writing in 1933, sees the three treaties of 1648 as being primarily about territory, although he also links it to the toleration of Catholics and Protestants, and sees the peace *as part* of the emergence of the modern state system.[10] The narrowing of the discourse of Westphalia, as Schmidt calls it, started with Leo Gross' 1948 article that sketched the myth of the peace as the start of the modern system of states.[11] Frequent reprintings of Gross' article led to it becoming a key 'best source yet' for those writing on the origins of the modern states system, and Gross' view of Westphalia was taken up again by Quincy Wright in the 1950s, where he argued that 'the Peace of Westphalia … recognised sovereign territorial states as superior to other groupings'.[12] In 1969 Richard Falk took this narrowing further by removing the historical context and talking about Westphalia as a model of authority.[13] After this Westphalia became not an historical turning point, but instead it became a description of our system of sovereign states: the 'Westphalian System'. Out of this myth of the Westphalian system have come two diametrically opposed uses. First, Westphalia became a system that brought peace through sovereignty, and thus was something we changed at our peril. Second, to others it became the name given to an old order that had had its day, and was now being superseded.

First, the Westphalia myth has been, since Gross and Wright, used as an ideological justification for the preservation of the system of states, and has acted as an argument against the development of more interventionist structures of global governance. This notion of stability through sovereignty and non-interference has been a powerful and compelling vision since at least the late nineteenth century (see Chapter 5), and shrill support for these notions find fertile ground at times when it is perceived that the system of states is under threat. For example, during the NATO–Yugoslav war of 1999 Robert Skidelsky, in an open letter to Michael Ignatieff, put the case for the state system when he wrote:

> You also weaken the presumption of non-interference unduly by omitting the most compelling argument in its favour, namely that it offers the only secure basis for good (and peaceful) interstate relations in a world where values differ. This has been the conclusion of three centuries of European stagecraft [sic], first enunciated at the Treaty of Westphalia. Perhaps you rate justice higher than peace. If so, this is a disagreement between us.[14]

This view has become a powerful article of faith among supporters of the status quo in global politics, but it is just that, an article of faith. The first point to bring up is the obvious one that the period since 1648, especially the last hundred years, has not been peaceful. If we are to judge the Westphalian compromise on this argument alone then it clearly broke down in the 1790s, in 1914 and 1939. In addition, if you count the revolutionary and colonial wars, then the system has offered much of the world no peace and stability since the late eighteenth century. This, however, is merely a negative argument, and offers little in the way of understanding. It is worth looking at Skidelsky's statement in more detail.

Very much in the spirit of the myth of 1648, Skidelsky points out that the goal is order *between* states so as to confine differences within borders. It is a recognition that different values exist, and that they are, by their nature, irreconcilable. Thus, these differences must not be allowed to form the basis of conflict, since conflict over values leads to absolute wars for absolute gains. Here also is the basis for the idea that justice and peace are irreconcilables at an international level. Justice is seen as an absolute, which is interpreted differently by different groups with different values. Order is about compromising justice claims. State sovereignty emerges as the means by which justice claims can be mediated, as it restricts what can rightly be brought up as a question of justice between states. For many, like Skidelsky, this means that sovereignty allows a global politics to function on an orderly basis by making the values that divide us (in a world of different and competing values) an issue for internal, and not international, politics. In sum, sovereignty prevents imperialism by protecting the rights of smaller states with different values.

In fact, sovereignty has done little to prevent imperialism if by imperialism we mean the spread of western political norms and the destruction of non-western ways of life. The concept of sovereignty only applies to recognisably western states. All other forms of society are conveniently *terra nullius* (that is, land with no owners that can be claimed by the first sovereign to occupy it).[15] What sovereignty does do is restrict the extent that states can intervene in the internal affairs of other states. Rather than being a shield against imperialism this is a guard against international disorder, which includes imperialism *exercised by one state against another*, but not imperialism by one state against a non-recognised entity. In this sense, western imperialism was at best allowed, and at worst encouraged, by 'Westphalian' notions of sovereignty. The watchword here is order. Key to the Westphalian myth is the idea that states cannot interfere in the domestic affairs of other states, and that as a consequence a major potential cause of inter-state conflict can be removed. To paraphrase, reverse and pervert the maxim of Ferdinand I: 'let order prevail *so that* the world does not perish'. Yet, because this order is premised on the inferiority of justice, force becomes the ultimate means of settling disputes between states. So, the Westphalian myth offers an order based upon organised violence.

Thus we have a political system premised upon the notion that order is the ultimate good above all others, and that it is states who are charged with maintaining this order through a monopoly on the right to protect their own citizens. The maintenance of order becomes 'real', and all other concerns become 'utopian' longings inappropriate to the hard world of international relations. Indeed, attempts to bring in issues of welfare, individual human freedoms, or even domestic political conceptions of justice are often presented as: (a) dangerous meddling with a working system of order; (b) a not too well hidden form of imperialism; or (c) both at the same time. To some the notion that inter-state relations deals exclusively in order was a necessary corollary to the development of a properly ordered rule of law domestically. David Hume, for example, was willing to accept a realm of unfreedom in the relations between states if that meant that the domestic sphere was protected from foreign interventions. Order internationally would keep international disturbances from preventing the development of a proper legal and free society at home. Not for nothing was Hume one of the greatest supporters of the idea of a stable balance of power. Keep the cold winds of inter-state politics at arm's length and the domestic realm can be left free to develop a liberal utopia.[16] This, of course, assumes that the world within a state is a self-contained community. A system based upon a contract between state and citizen, in which the state provides security, is premised on the citizen's acceptance of this role. While this idea has its genesis in the idea of an original contract in Hobbes, it is not until the Enlightenment and after that this relationship develops into a political practice that eventually evolves into the notion of the sovereignty of the citizen and the development of what we know as nationalism. The result is the sovereign nation state, which emerges as both ideal and as practice by the late nineteenth and early twentieth centuries.

Second, and following from the work of Richard Falk, the Westphalia Myth has been equally used as a means to criticise the system of states, and to use that criticism to argue for a different world order based on new organising principles. In the work of John G. Ruggie, Nicholas Onuf and others the construction of the Westphalian System became a foil to their detailed work on the changes in the nature of the international order.[17] Susan Strange, in her examination of three areas (the credit system, environment and social exclusion) in which the current international order was failing, took this genre a step further by re-Christening it the 'Westfailure System'.[18] Indeed, what these studies have in common is that they were not so much interested in what the Peace of Westphalia was, and even less so in how the politics of seventeenth century Europe was constructed, than they were in examining and highlighting how the current system needed to change. In this sense, Westphalia is at one level irrelevant to their work. Strange, for example, has arguably been proven right about the failure of our current state system to deal with the problems of the credit system (she was proved frighteningly right in 2007–8), the environment (if 97 per cent of climate scientists are right) and social exclusion (the costs of which to prosperity and political order are still being assessed). 'Westphalia' as an ideology expressed by people such as Skidelsky (see above) has indeed failed. So is there any harm in referring to a 'Westphalian system'?

The problem here is the myth of permanence and order, which in turn is used to argue for a sudden post-Westphalian revolution. In fact, as we shall see in much of the rest of this book, the three centuries from 1648 to 1948 do not represent a long period of global social stability. Rather global order, and agreed principles upon which that order should be based, have been a rather elusive commodity. This chapter will, for example, highlight the disjuncture between a patriarchal conservative order and the attempts by Enlightenment figures to deal with the inherent contradictions and dislocations of the *ancien régime*. The development of an industrialised economy, and its involvement in the creation of a new era of imperialism further altered global relations, leading to new ways of looking at the world, as will be explored in both Chapters 4 and 5. The disordered nature of the first four decades of the twentieth century hardly points to a successful ordered and peace states system here either. Presenting a long-lived 'Westphalian epoch', which is hopefully due to be replaced by better post-Westphalian order based on something else, ignores the much more glaring instabilities of the global disorder of the last three centuries, and gives us a misleading view of the longevity and effectiveness of global norms. In this sense, as Schmidt has argued, the simplicities of the concept of Westphalia adds little to the detailed work on globalisation that have used it.[19] In the search for an understanding of how change is possible at the global level it is more likely to mislead than to illuminate.

The myth of Westphalia contains within it the assumption that international orders are long periods of relative stability, punctuated by short bursts of chronic instability that led, in turn, to another stable period. What this hides is the extent to which even supposed periods of international constancy have been far from stable. The rules that have meant to mark these periods have often turned out not to be well-accepted rules at all, and basic concepts such as the state or sovereignty have changed dramatically over the intervening years. In short, the myth of Westphalia hides a history of instability and ambiguous rules behind a façade of the idea of stable and permanent rules. As we shall see throughout this book, the history of international thought reflects not a permanent or semi-permanent order of clear-cut rules, but an indistinct sphere of unstable relationships that has constantly changed as other factors have intervened. This is a vision of the world that would have made sense to the Tacitist humanists of an earlier generation, but (like our own myth of the Westphalian system) in the late seventeenth century the intellectual mood was dominated by a search for rules of permanence in a political world that was all too unstable and threatening.

## The 'sorry comforters' and the retreat from history

The great political crisis of the seventeenth century marks a clear break in the development of Early Modern political thought. The Tacitism of the late sixteenth century was both sceptical of truth claims and was a flexible set of political principles that could be applied in a number of ways and to a number of political actors. Prudence in the face of necessity was equally applicable to the ruled as it was to rulers, although Tacitism certainly advocated a particular amoral policy for rulers in the form of reason of state. While ignoring the scepticism, ambiguities and concern for time in Tacitism, the political theorists of the seventeenth century borrowed the notion of reason of state, but justified it by such constants as natural law and an atemporal rationality. Also interesting from our point of view is the way that this notion of reason of state became linked in with notions of state sovereignty and the naturalness of a state-based system of world order. Tacitism, while it had developed a concept of reason of state, continued to view politics as a united field. The conservative theorists of the seventeenth century concentrated so heavily on the role and place of the state that they succeeded, whether they knew it or not, in cutting politics in two. Certainly, the seeds of this had already been laid by Tacitism's justification of a separate public morality through the device of the necessity of preservation, yet it was the seventeenth century conservatives who made this division the basis of their interpretation of politics, and also gave their world-view a veneer of timeless necessity and respectability.

What this also meant was a change in the nature of what could and should be regarded as knowledge. Tacitism had seen the richness of historical ambiguity as a basis for understanding human action. It was the very unsettled and complex nature of the historical record that gave it its value. Since we could not rely on abstract thought, historical narratives gave us some kind of understanding of how human action and politics worked. This reliance on history showed up the complexities of politics, and the need to balance political principles and to respond as the times dictated, rather than on the basis of abstract principles. The importance of historical narrative and complexity led to an understanding and acceptance of the political role of fictional narrative in plays and poetry. Plays, in particular, were a way of expressing this historical complexity, and thus brought a clearer understanding of the problems of political action. Yet, what the tired statesmen of the seventeenth century crisis wanted was not ambiguous narratives, but clear principles of action upon which a stable and static order could be based. Thus, a theory of political action based on historical and dramatic narrative was displaced by a theory based on unchanging principles extracted from abstract rationality and from natural law.

The first half of the seventeenth century saw Europe lurch from crisis to war, and finally to exhaustion, as Tacitism's ideas of *raison d'etat* (reason of state) were combined with religious violence. Although there was a remarkable continuity in the states and other political actors involved in the wars and diplomacy of the seventeenth century, levels of destruction at the local level could be appalling, leading to high loss of life, economic decline and a frequent pessimism about the future.[20] Facing these failures of inter-state politics the scepticism of humanism began to appear a luxury that Europe could ill afford, and increasingly political theorists turned to more dogmatic ideas of order as remedies for the perceived chaos around them. From an International Relations perspective the two names that stand out from this period are Hugo Grotius and Thomas Hobbes. Both thinkers absorbed the ideas of *raison d'etat* of the Tacitists, but both tempered it with an appeal to a universal natural law. The idea of a generalised and knowable set of natural laws would have been anathema to the scepticism of Montaigne and Lipsius. Grotius and Hobbes, along with other later writers such as Leibniz and Pufendorf, developed general rules of human behaviour that were rooted simultaneously in Tacitist definitions of human nature in terms of interest, and in distinctly unhumanist natural laws that had their origins in divine revelation. Natural law enshrined traditional practices that were designed to ameliorate the excesses of conflicts over self-interest. Yet, self-interest still played a prominent part in this patriarchal conservatism. Although state conflict in the theories of Grotius, Pufendorf and Leibniz was to be tempered by laws of conduct (especially in war), the principles of *raison d'etat* remained. This led Kant to dismiss these theorists as no more than 'sorry comforters'.[21]

The dissatisfaction that Grotius and Hobbes felt towards Tacitism's scepticism was being expressed by many of the later Tacitists, especially in England. Walter Raleigh leaned, as far as a Tacitist was able, towards natural law when he stressed that a war had to be just.[22] Despite this, and other shadows of things to come, this emerging patriarchal conservatism was a major break with humanism. Not least because it abandoned the scepticism of the humanists, and based its knowledge on the certainty of generalised rules, rather than on historical example.[23] This, as it turned out, was to be a crucial difference. Patriarchal conservatism was not concerned with using lessons from historical experience as guides for political action. Rather, they wished to abstract general rules that could be applied in all cases. Behind this was a fear of disorder. For order to be maintained it was necessary to have strict definitions on what was or was not permissible under natural law and *raison d'etat*. Questions about the form and origins of states, that had been the basis of humanist questioning of traditions, gave way in the seventeenth century to an abstract theory of sovereignty that assumed the state was a timeless abstraction.[24]

Sixteenth century humanists based their view of politics on a scepticism about the possibility of human knowledge. They doubted moral claims, and so fell back on historical experience and the idea of self-preservation. Seventeenth century patriarchal conservatives had a different agenda: the intellectual defence of a static and ordered society that would guarantee that the wars of religion and of state building would never happen again. While the natural law theories of Grotius, Leibniz and Pufendorf curbed the excesses of *raison d'etat*, this in itself was not enough to build a comprehensive and static system. Tradition was brought in to justify order, and to integrate the institutions of the state into the idea of a static order. Tradition and order – the first being the ideological guarantor of the second – were to be the rallying cries of patriarchal conservatism all the way to its last gasps at the end of the eighteenth century. During the early seventeenth century, therefore, a timeless tradition, based on abstract certainties was constructed.

Patriarchal conservatives faced two comparatively new institutions that had no traditions to support them. The state and the home, by the seventeenth century, had become firmly rooted social institutions. The problem of integrating these institutions into a static political philosophy was solved by reference to the Great Chain of Being, and the collapsing of the distinction between state and the home, in line with the earlier idea expressed by Bodin (see Chapter 2). The new idea of the family expressed in the early modern home was taken as the analogue, on the Great Chain of Being, of the properly ordered conservative state. The sovereign monarch, or republican estates-general, were interpreted as being the father in an extended family, and this link was justified through tradition by reference to the fatherly rule of Adam. Every sovereign was a direct political descendent of the first father.[25] Sovereigns were, therefore, moral forces with a duty to look after and guide their subjects. This concept of duty, which largely supplemented and supplanted the earlier humanist notion of pure self-preservation, became the leitmotif of seventeenth century works on politics, with perhaps the ultimate statement being made by Samuel Pufendorf in the last third of the century.[26]

One of the clearest demonstrations of this patriarchal paradigm in action was what Foucault described as 'The Great Confinement' of the seventeenth century. While madness in the sixteenth century was publicly tolerated as a demonstration of the frailties and vagaries of the human condition (witness the role played by fools and madness in Shakespeare, or even Erasmus' classic *In Praise of Folly*), the order-obsessed world of the seventeenth century felt a duty to protect (an abstract) order from folly, and to treat deviants as threats to the new fatherly role of the sovereign. Foucault dates the Great Confinement from 1656 with the foundation of the Hôpital Général in Paris. After that date all Europe saw the adoption of the confinement of the mad, criminal and bankrupt in corrective houses. Within months of the foundation of the Hôpital in Paris, for example, one in a hundred Parisians had been confined.[27]

Foucault's work has also directed us to another aspect of the patriarchal nature of seventeenth century sovereignty. The break-up of the feudal order, and the development of relations based on commerce and class, left the subject as an individual among other individuals. The state, in order to exercise a centralised control over these individuals needed a new political rationality that would, nevertheless, appear traditional and time-honoured. Here we see the emergence of what Foucault terms pastorship as the means to control individuals.[28] The state, like the father, became analogous to the medieval idea of the good shepherd exercising pastorship over its people. Obedience to the state – like the flock's obedience to the shepherd, and the child's obedience to the father – became a moral duty in itself.[29] This was an important turn away from the humanist notion of loyalty through self-preservation, which was both sceptical about human moral motives and saw the state as a tool for self-preservation and communal interests.

Since the sovereign authority was to be a father figure domestically the analogy was extended to inter-state relations. *Raison d'etat* was given an overt masculine character. The sovereign-father that was a moral force at home became a protector of his subjects abroad. Thus, *raison d'etat*, which had been an open ended concept based on self-preservation in Tacitism, became associated with the idea of warrior-protector. With it came the baggage associated with what I have called elsewhere hypermasculinity, that is the masculinity associated with a warrior ethic. The need to protect one's honour, the moral superiority of the warrior life, and life as a power contest all became central to the practice of inter-state relations. By contrast, theological moralising and normative approaches to inter-state relations became associated with femininity and failed men.[30] The hypermasculine warrior, therefore, used the sceptical instrumental morality of humanist *raison d'etat* for ends that were related to fatherly protection and the preservation of honour. It is probably no coincidence that the foreign service in many modern states were the last to admit significant numbers of women, and were even late in admitting men whose families were in 'trade'. Again, this shift had been evident in earlier attempts to deal with the crisis of Tacitism, for example in the writings of Walter Raleigh.[31]

Thus, the abstract ideology that justified state practice in the seventeenth century had, at its core, an overt patriarchal philosophy that privileged a particular form of masculinity as being natural to government and inter-state relations. The search for abstract laws to justify this masculine order also involved a rejection of history as a basis of knowledge. Humanist thought, whether using Cicero or Tacitus, saw historical example and analogy as the basis of proof. Machiavelli's use of Livy is a classic example of this. The new conservatism of the seventeenth century rejected history as the basis for understanding human behaviour because it was 'inherently and inveterately deceptive'.[32] Where humanists had wallowed in history's ironies, seventeenth century patriarchal conservatism rejected the particularist and varied lessons of historical study. History, as it was used by the humanists, underscored the frailty of human existence and the importance of fortune and the particular. All of these were hostile to the establishment of an order based on concrete and universal principles. The seventeenth century mind looked for universal principles that would justify an atemporal order, and firmly rejected the idea that historical flux could be a basis for knowledge.[33] This anti-historical bent was particularly marked in Hobbes, where the discovery of abstract truth through the life of contemplation was upheld. History, by contrast, was reduced to a second order form of knowledge. It was a register of facts, in Hobbes' vision, rather than a source of practical knowledge.[34]

The search for universals that were exempt from historical flux led to the enshrining of ideas of a common human nature and of common human rationality. For Hobbes the common nature of humans led to the need for a strong, monarchical, order. For Grotius and Pufendorf a common rationality, in tune with a universal natural law, dictated a certain minimum legal order between states. In Grotius' view natural law was so universal that even God, its inventor, obeyed it.[35] *Raison d'etat*, rather than being the fluid and multidimensional basis of Tacitist scepticism about human motives, became rooted in the idea of a single and common selfish human nature, and was constrained by the idea of a divinely rooted common reason that could be used to construct a universal and permanent order between states. *Raison d'etat* was interpreted as a product of a common human nature understood through a common reason. A common and knowable human nature even became the prime cause of war in some writings, and thus could justify the individual's adherence to restraining power structures based on scientific right-thinking.[36] This notion of inter-state politics as a product of laws based in selfish human nature was to reappear in international thought among writers in the late nineteenth century and among realist scholars in the mid-twentieth century. Perhaps, though, it is worth keeping in mind that while writers like Hobbes saw the pugnacity of human nature in the absence of laws as a problem within the state (and hence the need for a leviathan), he was less worried about the state of nature between states. For while 'kings and persons of sovereign authority' are in a constant state of war like that of individuals in the state of nature, it does not do the same damage to human industry 'because they uphold thereby the industry of their subjects, there does not follow from it that misery which accompanies the liberty of particular men'.[37] The worry for Hobbes remains civil strife, and the relations between sovereigns are, for him, of a different order.

Yet, why have patriarchal conservative ideas survived in inter-state relations, while they have almost completely disappeared from domestic politics? Although modernity emerged in the sixteenth and seventeenth centuries, it went through a major renewal process in the eighteenth and early nineteenth centuries as Enlightenment thought replaced the political concentration on tradition and order with the interlocking triad of reason, freedom and progress. Ideas of a static order, based on the family, were rapidly replaced in domestic politics with the idea of a continually progressing and rational constitutional form of government that guaranteed the freedom of citizens. Yet, what is remarkable is that this victory of the Enlightenment in renewing modernity for another two centuries never extended into inter-state relations. The increasingly liberalised states of the nineteenth century West never developed a distinct Enlightenment view of inter-state practice.

Part of the blame for the survival of conservative norms in international affairs has to be placed at the door of the Enlightenment thinkers themselves. Inter-state relations was, to a large degree, written off by many liberal heirs of the Enlightenment as a massive make-work project for the aristocracy, and of little relevance to the day-to-day lives of the productive bourgeois and proletarian classes. Blaming the aristocratic foreign policy establishment for the existence of war became a standard liberal position up to the First World War.[38] As a result, many liberals thought that the worst excesses of international relations, such as war, would just wither and die once states became liberal.[39] Ironically, this left conservative elites, and conservative ideas, in place in foreign offices. It was not really until the last decades of the nineteenth century that liberals began in earnest to counter the conservative ideas associated with international relations practice, as we shall see in Chapter 5. The result would eventually be the development of an academic field of International Relations that often had as its goal the eventual establishment of liberal government and Enlightenment norms at a global level. The ideas of international organisations, of global federalism, of functional integration and transnational pluralism represented direct, but belated, attempts by many liberal heirs of the Enlightenment, especially in the English-speaking world, to reincorporate inter-state practice into the mainstream of modernity.[40]

In sum, humanism, in its Tacitist form, gave way in the seventeenth century to a patriarchal conservative political philosophy that endowed the state with a moral worth legitimised by a constructed tradition. When patriarchal conservatism was challenged in domestic politics by the Enlightenment, inter-state relations continued to be ordered by a rump patriarchal conservative set of assumptions that were left free-floating. The result was a great detour, in which a separate interstate politics continued to be dominated by a form of modernity that had lost its link to a domestic order.

## The crisis of the *ancien régime*

From an intellectual point of view by the middle of the eighteenth century patriarchal conservatism was moribund. The apparent permanence, pomp and stability of the age of absolutism hid the ideological bankruptcy of the governing ideology. The seventeenth century obsession with order and tradition had broken down, or more correctly had found itself only partially realised. The key problem had been that, in the final analysis, tradition had not been up to the task. The patriarchal conservative ideal, as demonstrated by Filmer, Grotius and Pufendorf had seen timeless traditions as the guarantor of order. Traditional fatherly rule and/or an equally timeless natural law, justified an equally timeless order. Yet, tradition is a capricious ally, and more often than not patriarchal conservatives used abstractions such as the state of nature or the original politics of the Garden of Eden to create a conservative-friendly tradition. Yet, precedents from medieval institutions, such as parliaments and city autonomy, coupled with more radical interpretations of scripture, allowed reformers to use tradition to endanger order. In the Great Civil War of the 1640s–50s in England, Scotland and Ireland, for example, tradition was used to undermine conservative order. This led many apologists of the Royalist cause, such as Thomas Hobbes and Francis Quarles, to drop tradition in favour of an order based on practical expediency rather than right of tradition.[41] When faced with a crisis of incompatibility between tradition and order, patriarchal conservatism dropped tradition in favour of order, but in so doing it undermined the moral reason for that order.

Thus, by the middle of the eighteenth century European governments often appeared to educated men to be based on nothing but the brutal exercise of power, divorced from any moral justification. Apologists for the status quo aped the justifications of tradition and legitimacy, but these arguments seemed increasingly hollow when the very rulers themselves broke rules of legitimacy when it suited their ends. The partitions of Poland, Frederick the Great's seizing of Silesia, or the frequent closing of parliaments throughout Europe undermined the moral legitimacy of patriarchal conservatism. Enlightenment thought offered new means of legitimising rule through reform and new thinking. Not surprisingly, therefore, the ideas were often as attractive to monarchs and elites as they were to anti-establishment radicals.

While the richness of Enlightenment political thought makes an honest summary difficult, there are clear threads that run through much of the intellectual debates. First there was a rejection of the static order associated with patriarchal conservatism. The static or cyclical view of politics that had been a mark of seventeenth century political thought was replaced with a notion of secular progress, and the idea that human history could be seen as a slow rise to better systems of government. Second, Enlightenment thinkers rejected the family analogy, and substituted the hypermasculinity of the father-warrior with a new interpretation of rational masculinity.[42] Men were reinterpreted as living separate lives in a public and a private sphere, while women lived solely in the private. Where patriarchal conservatives saw the private as a model for the public, Enlightenment scholars reinterpreted the private as a non-political sphere that was fully autonomous from the public.[43] The home, along with all things regarded as feminine, became alienated from political life. Third, the Enlightenment once again began to play up the importance of citizen participation and civic duty.

Yet, listing the discontinuities does a great injustice to the continuity between patriarchal conservatism and the Enlightenment. First, the Enlightenment did not return to the earlier humanist epistemology. The Enlightenment, like patriarchal conservatism, was interested in general rules, and therefore rejected the particularistic and sceptical assumptions of Tacitist humanism, although in Edward Gibbon Tacitus still found at least one champion.[44] By and large the Enlightenment took the Hobbesian view of a common human rationality, and reinterpreted it as a foundational tool that justified political reordering and reform. Second, although setting out to reinterpret (and even on occasions to limit) the state, the idea of the pastorship of the state remained a strong theme, especially in Rousseau, Adam Smith and Kant. Third, state sovereignty remained unchallenged as a central political concept. Instead the issue of who possessed the right of sovereignty within the state became the issue. Finally, and related to the first point, the Enlightenment limited its rediscovery of history to grand narratives that justified its project of progressive reform. The idea of the irony and uncertainty of history, which was so key to sixteenth century political thought, remained in the background. For some, such as David Hume, agency-driven history belonged to relations between states (but not to relations within a society), while to Gibbon, Smith and Kant individual agency in history was, in the long run, driven by structural causes. For Giambattista Vico, writing at the beginning of the Enlightenment, agency was associated with the heroic age, but the modern age, as an age of reason, was not about 'great men', but about the creativity of civilisation as a whole.[45] To be fair, though, it was less true of Gibbon, who frequently revelled in history's ironies in a way not dissimilar to his hero Tacitus. Gibbon, alone among those writers interested in the relations between states, tried to synthesise the older Tacitist humanism with the new philosophical traditions that regarded history with suspicion as merely an antiquarian collection of anecdotes.[46] Gibbon here is the exception that proves the rule, and even here he is a hybrid of old and new, not a full attempt to return to the old humanist traditions. Indeed, the Renaissance humanist emulation of the classical tradition was seen by Gibbon as a 'timidly imitative' false dawn that compared unfavourably with the civilisation of the eighteenth century.[47]

The concentration on reforming the state, and a belief in history as a slow progression to better systems of government that would reform inter-state politics in its wake, contributed to an intellectual blindness to the problems of politics beyond the state. Indeed, before Immanuel Kant Enlightenment discussions of the problems of inter-state politics, and especially the relations between domestic and international relations, remain at best afterthoughts within more detailed analyses of intra-state politics. Discussions of the problems of inter-state politics are usually buried in works on fundamentally intra-state issues, or in discussions of historical progress. Having said this, however, views on inter-state politics do exist, and there were attempts to integrate the two spheres of politics together. Although there are obvious differences between individual authors, a certain pattern to their prescriptions does emerge. This pattern should not be surprising since many of these writers were in regular contact with each other. The major exception is Immanuel Kant. Not only did Kant write tracts dedicated to inter-state politics, he also recognised, possibly through his familiarity with Rousseau's work, that Enlightenment treatments of the international sphere were not wholly satisfying. As a result of this distinction, the rest of this section will be devoted to adumbrating the works of the non-Kantians (writers that I have categorised, with apologies to Kant, as the 'New Sorry Comforters'). The next section will look in more detail at how Kant attempted to develop a more radical Enlightenment alternative.

## The New Sorry Comforters

The rediscovery of history, albeit in a form that stressed progress rather than irony and uncertaintly, led to the use of historical analogy and progression as a basis for understanding the development of the relations between states. Rome, its decline and replacement became one of the prime means by which to draw analogies and cautionary tales in the present for Enlightenment political theorists. Enlightenment scholars, ever aware of the dangers of anachronism, stressed not only the lessons but also the differences that had, in their view, led to a more optimistic and durable outlook for civilisation in the eighteenth century.

Not surprisingly, the historian Edward Gibbon was in the forefront of the movement for using classical analogies. His monumental *Decline and Fall of the Roman Empire* mixed tales of human agency with a reverence for the long-term effects of structural conditions. Thus, while the late Empire might on occasion throw up a Julian, who embodied for Gibbon the virtues of old Rome, the structures of the new degenerate society would win in the long run.[48] The failures of Rome were, to Gibbon, the mirror opposite to the reasons behind the success of eighteenth century Europe. Rome stood alone as a united civilisation against the barbarians outside its borders (*pace* Persia, whom Gibbon did not have too much time for), and so had no one to emulate, and no competing civilised peoples to compare itself to. Eighteenth century Europe, on the other hand, was 'divided into twelve powerful, though unequal kingdoms, three respectable commonwealths, and a variety of smaller though independent states'.[49] As a result the potential pool of political talent was increased, and competition between these states forced them to continually adapt and innovate in a way that Rome had not needed to. 'In peace, the progress of knowledge and industry is accelerated by the emulation of so many active rivals: In war the European forces are exercised by temperate and indecisive contests.' Hence European civilisation remained robust through balance and competition, and thus was always a match for the barbarians that surrounded it.[50]

Decline, for Gibbon, was primarily due to uncontrolled passions and 'immoderate greatness'.[51] Decline would set in when these two had nothing to prevent their appearance. The lack of a sense of threat led to libertine behaviour, and to a sense of natural superiority. In a unitary civilisation like Rome there was no check on these developments. In eighteenth century Europe, however, each state felt a need to compete with its rivals within the same civilisation, and even if a state did decline due to hubris and libertinism, other nations were there to take its place. Thus the balance of power maintained the vitality of Europe through competition in industry, structure, arts and morals.[52]

So far Gibbon's account seems to share a family resemblance with Polybius' history of the rise of Rome. Polybius had argued that, through combining all three of the stages of the rise and decline of government, Republican Rome had stepped outside of the cycle of history and reached a state of static permanent being where decline would not happen. Gibbon, on the other hand, felt that the balance of power between states in eighteenth century Europe had transferred European civilisation from the cyclical pattern of rise and decline, in which Imperial Rome had become entrapped, into a new form of history in which progress was possible. To demonstrate this Gibbon argued that the development of the technical arts, and their adaptation by rival European states, now made military success a matter more of superior technology than of military virtue. Since the main strength of barbarians is their superior 'rude valour', technological developments tipped the military balance in favour of civilisation. What this meant was that in order to compete with civilisation barbarians would need to gain technological equivalence, but this was only possible through the adoption of a civilised way of life.[53] Thus, progress was assured as long as Europe remained a continent of competing interests locked into a conflictual balance. Interestingly an argument bearing a family resemblance to Gibbon's can be found a century later in the works of A.T. Mahan, who shared many of Gibbon's views on technological advancement and the importance of the European balance of power for the maintenance of Europe's global power (see Chapter 5).

Not surprisingly, Gibbon was a close acquaintance of Adam Smith. Both men's belief in the superiority of a system based on balance and competition is, therefore, not merely the product of the zeitgeist, although the importance of their place in time and space should not be ignored. Maintaining a balance of power in Europe was British government policy in the eighteenth century, and this British policy was to find its strongest supporter in David Hume, who will be discussed below. Smith, like Gibbon, drew analogies from the fall of Rome, and like Gibbon saw a powerful connection between the security structures of a civilisation, and the development of the technical arts and the economy. Perhaps, though, a major difference between both men lies in their views on wealth. Gibbon showed nothing but disgust for the corruption brought on by wealth in the later Empire, while he praised the simple self-denial of both the philosopher- and soldier-emperors. Smith, on the other hand, saw in wealth a source of strength, and in poverty nothing but weakness. Economic development, therefore, formed the main means by which a state could flourish. This development was both dependent on the right political relations, and a cause of political greatness for a state.

Adam Smith's view of history rested on the idea of the primacy of security concerns, and the importance of a certain amount of political instability in the development of higher stages of economic development.[54] Like Gibbon he drew lessons from the fall of Rome, but unlike Gibbon he saw in the progression of the Middle Ages the slow development of a more advanced political economy. Smith believed that societies went through four stages of economic development: hunting, pasturage, farming and commerce. Each one was stronger and richer than its predecessor. The collapse of the Roman world, due to the superiority of the valour of the pastorally-based militias of the barbarians,[55] led to a general decline, Smith claimed, in the opulence of Europe.[56] This decline was, however, merely temporary. The pastoral conquerors soon turned to agriculture as a source of power-through-wealth that was superior to that of herding.[57] Their development of large independent estates allowed them to use the agricultural surplus to keep retainers for the purpose of security and conquest. With time this developed into the feudal system, in which larger kingdoms united a number of independent barons under one ruler. Kings, in turn, fearing the power of their barons, gave privileges to their towns in order to build up alternative power bases and potential allies against the troublesome barons. Thus, without intending it, medieval monarchs allowed the development of commerce, and in time the commercial might of the towns would replace the landed power of the barons.[58]

The central themes here are: (a) the extent to which power is a product of wealth, and how competition of power inadvertently assists the development of higher forms of wealth creation; (b) how the end of power-as-wealth is the development of security for a society; and (c) that the developments that led to more advanced and powerful economic systems are, in the words of Adam Ferguson, the product of human action, but not of human design. There is, therefore, an evolutionary development of human society, based on competition, which leads to progress towards stronger and more sophisticated societies. When Smith turns his attention away from the distant past to his present, however, his argument focuses on what for him was the basic unit of human society in its commercial stage, namely the state.

It is important not to forget that Smith's *magnum opus* (with apologies to partisans of *The Theory of Moral Sentiments*) was called *The Wealth of Nations*. His concern was not the aggregate wealth of humanity, but the wealth (and therefore power) of the new state of Great Britain in relation to its competitors around the world. Smith was clear in his belief that concerns of security came before those of wealth maximisation.[59] He also proposed the paradox that having rich neighbours was a blessing to a state in peace time, since it would encourage commerce and power-through-wealth, but was a curse during wartime, as those very same neighbours were competitors who would use their wealth to raise and maintain hostile armies and navies.[60] This, however, does not remain a paradox for long. At the end of the day Smith comes down on the side of security: 'The first duty of the sovereign, that of protecting the society from the violence and invasion of other independent societies, can be performed only by means of a military force.'[61] Wealth, for Smith, remains primarily a means to the end of security.

Thus, Smith sees two processes going on simultaneously, with one providing unintended consequences for the other. While businessmen pursue only profit they inadvertently boost the power of the state. The state has an interest in promoting business, but it also has a higher duty to preserve the state, of which the businessmen are part. As a result the state must put security ahead of opulence, although opulence is the source of the power behind security. It is because of this relationship between economic development and the security of the state that the balance of power between competing states encourages economic development. States, in short, require a wealthy economy in order to boost there security in relation to other states.

In the final analysis, rather than offering a solution to the problem of human government on a global scale, Smith's political economy never extends beyond ideas centred on the improvement of the state. In part this can be put down to his view, expressed earlier in *The Theory of Moral Sentiments*, that inter-state relations will never be naturally harmonious because philanthropy always develops in concentric circles from the individual. A person feels the strongest ties to their family, strong ties to their neighbours, moderate ties to their compatriots, but little or no ties to people beyond that.[62] Smith's concern, therefore, ends at what, in his philosophy, was the largest possible unit in which human sympathy and interest could operate: the state. Inter-state relations remained, as it had with Gibbon, a site of conflict, although Smith's approach lacked the idea of a natural balance between states that we find in Gibbon. In sum, the balance of power becomes the only possible outcome for global politics because cosmopolitan sentiments are not possible.

This idea of the international as a realm of unreformable strangeness, in contrast to the wonders of domestic intra-state development occurs again in the work of Smith's countryman David Hume. In his analysis of inter-state relations, cursory and tangential though it is, Hume begins from the point at which the Tacitist humanists left off. The main issue for Hume is human interests. Our nature is to be guided by our interests, but our major flaw in this regard is that we prefer our immediate interests to our long-term interests, even though following our long-term goals would serve us better. This, for Hume, is the justification for the existence of the state. The state exists as an institution that can guarantee the protection of our long-term interests, while in a state-free society all would follow merely their more immediate goals.[63] Through this argument Hume manages to simultaneously combine Tacitist arguments for the state and Enlightenment ideas of an ultimate harmony of interests. The ideas of conflict that are basic to Tacitist conceptions of self-preservation and interest are reinterpreted as the short-term (and competing) interests of humanity, while the longer-term interests that are linked to communal living and harmony can only be pursued by the development of government. Since, for Hume, human nature is therefore dangerous to society, the power of the state is justified in order to protect us from ourselves.

Once state power is justified Hume put himself into a quandary. Having demonstrated how the development of national societies was necessary for individuals in order to end the war of all against all, he is left with the problem that these independent states form the same kind of anarchic society as people without government. The situation, as Hume fully realises, is worse, for whereas individuals need their fellows, and are therefore compelled through self-interest into a governed community, states have no such need for companionship.[64] What states do need, however, is certain regulations to make their relations with each other manageable, or what in the eighteenth century was referred to as the law of nations. For Hume the law of nations was a weak set of regulations that included a basic set of agreements regarding the 'sacredness of persons' prohibitions on 'poisoned arms', 'quarter in war' and any other regulation that might be 'calculated for the *advantage* of states and kingdoms in their intercourse with each other'.[65]

Hume's argument is not out of the woods yet. Just as he had said earlier that individuals seek short-term interest in the absence of government, so states without a common government should seek mere short-term gain at the expense of their long-term interests. The weak 'law of nations' is not a guarantor of a society of states. Yet, as we have already seen, Hume sees states as qualitatively different from individuals, and Hume does not need a government of nations in order to advance the long-term interests of his individuals. In fact, for Hume's politics to work he merely requires that inter-state politics does not adversely affect the lives of individuals. Again, the possibility of cosmopolitanism is denied. Like Gibbon and Smith, Hume fell back on the balance of power, although his balance of power is different from Smith's and Gibbon's in one important respect. Competition between states for Gibbon and Smith, although more so for the former than the latter, provides necessary competition for the development of society, for Hume the balance of power is a means by which states maintain their liberty so that they may continue to serve the long-term interests of their citizens. Balance for Hume is also something that occurs naturally: 'the maxim of preserving the balance of power is founded so much on common sense and obvious reasoning that it is impossible it could not altogether have escaped antiquity'.[66]

Despite the popularity of Hume's writing on the balance of power among realist International Relations specialists, his development of it is quite obviously an afterthought, which he felt that he must deal with in order to explain how his vision of domestic society can remain untroubled and free. His disdain for inter-state relations is made clear in another of his essays, in which he contrasts the ordered and reasoned domestic politics with the capricious inter-state relations, which is driven by the unreasoned whim of statesmen.[67] Inter-state politics, in this sense, is beyond reason, and therefore its wilder excesses are kept in check by the balance of power between states. Short-term Tacitist style interest, which produces a static and zero-sum society, remains the only form of interest behind the construction of Hume's international politics.

Gibbon, Smith and Hume had resorted to a mechanistic view of inter-state relations to both account for its existence and to explain why radical change of inter-state politics was not required. Others, however, had taken a more legalistic line. Earlier in the century Christian Wolf and Emerich de Vattel had discussed the rights and duties of nations, while Montesquieu makes fleeting references to the law of nations. Montesquieu's account, however, is short, and primarily based on an extrapolation of individual rights to the state. Just as an individual has a right of self-defence, he argued, so a state may defend itself: 'the right of war, therefore, is derived from necessity and strict justice'.[68] What interests Montesquieu more is not how inter-state relations are managed, or even how order is possible between states, but under what conditions is a state more durable. Montesquieu, like Polybius, sees durability as a product of a state's constitution, and his favourite is a confederal republic, which combines the size of a monarchy with the internal strength of a republic.[69] Montesquieu's federalism, although of a tighter form than Kant's league of peace, remained fundamentally a means for creating a more efficient state in the competition between states. Thus, for all his discussion of law Montesquieu remains closer in spirit to Hume, Smith and Gibbon than he does with Bentham or Kant.

Perhaps the most thorough attempt to solve the inter-state problem via legal means came not from the author of *The Spirit of the Laws*, but from a man who was influenced by him. Jeremy Bentham, having applied his conception of utility to domestic law, turned his hand to applying the same solution to the international. In his *A Plan for Universal and Perpetual Peace* Bentham suggested an international legal code to prevent war. Unlike his earlier compatriots Bentham had little sympathy with the dog-eat-dog simplicities of the balance of power. Through a mutual reduction of forces, the emancipation of colonies, the establishment of an international court, and the convening of a European congress made up of representatives of all states Bentham hoped that war would become a thing of the past.[70] Perhaps because much of Bentham's vision became reality in the twentieth century – we have emancipated colonies, established an International Court, and convened the United Nations – it is possible to see that his vision of a war-free world was optimistic. Bentham's strength, however, lay in both his realisation that the inter-state sphere needed reforming, and in the obvious ultimate establishment (despite their weaknesses) of his proposed institutions. His goal of disarmament has never been achieved. Indeed, the last two centuries have seen a sharp rise in the size and cost of military arsenals.

Yet, in the final analysis, all of these international afterthoughts, from the works of philosophers more at home with re-ordering domestic politics, fail to satisfy. The three advocates of the balance of power commit the same mistake of assuming that a balance of power is innately stable. First, it is a system based on the use of violence, and therefore encourages the militarisation of the state, and second it is a rationally flawed system. Because military power is impossible to accurately calculate the prudent state would not seek balance, but rather a preponderance of power over its enemies.[71] Finally, the balance of power is, at base, the abandonment of international politics to the rules of Tacitist-style interest, conflict and expediency. Under a balance of power laws of state behaviour are decided by relative military strength, and not by considerations of moral behaviour. In sum, it assumes that the moral codes for domestic politics are fundamentally different from those that should govern inter-state behaviour. As a result there is no coherent theory of human political life, only analyses of relative spheres of human relations.

Interestingly, the problems with Enlightenment approaches to inter-state politics had already been explored by Rousseau, although Rousseau had no particular answer to the problem. As Michael C. Williams has pointed out, Rousseau's criticism of the Abbé de St Pierre's *Project for Perpetual Peace* was simultaneously an attack on the naivety of the advocates of a law-based international federation of states, and on the partisans of the current balance of power system.[72] Rousseau had sympathised with the Abbé's aspirations, but believed that it was naïve to believe that the state elites of Europe would voluntarily give up power. Rousseau is as clear in his criticism of these elites, however, whom he declares rule the world by domination and not by right.[73] The current system of the balance of power, for Rousseau, is flawed because it does not allow for freedom and justice. Basically, where there are two spheres with different levels of justice, the less just will ultimately drive out the more just, and come to dominate both spheres. As a result an unjust international system based on the balance of power will ultimately corrupt the system of justice found inside a state.[74] Worse still, a system which relies on the exercise of brute force, he argued, cannot sustain itself, and states that rely on conquest for their survival will ultimately meet a contest in which they perish. In order to prevent the cycle of violent overthrow and replacement it is necessary to transform the rule of force into a rule of law.[75] He freely condemns the system of international politics that is associated with the balance of power because it undermines the development of properly governed republican government,[76] but his only clear suggestions for rectifying the system centre on developing freedom and justice within the state, which in turn is undermined by the requirements of state competition at the international level. Rousseau's temerity comes from his pessimism about cosmopolitanism, both because of the resistance of state elites to these reforms (mentioned above in the context of St Pierre's plans), but also because of the perceived spatial limits of human loyalty. For Rousseau support for cosmopolitan loyalty will be undermined by the fundamentally local (and even sub-national) nature of human political and social loyalties.[77] Rousseau's logic (that the current balance of power system leads to conflict and subverts justice at the domestic level, yet suggestions for cosmopolitan reform fail due to the resistance of elites and to the spatial limits to our loyalty) was taken up by Immanuel Kant. Kant's goal, however, was to find a way to transcend Rousseau's paradox, and consequently to reform global politics.

## Immanuel Kant and the attempt to step beyond Sorry Comfort

Kant's analysis of inter-state relations comes in a number of later works, of which the two major ones are *To Perpetual Peace: A Philosophical Sketch* (1795) and the last two chapters of *The Doctrine of Right* (1797). Other parts of his analysis also appear in his shorter political works including his *Idea for a Universal History from a Cosmopolitan Point of View* (1784). Throughout the development of his approach Kant remains faithful to the boundaries put on the project by Rousseau. On the one hand the project must be achievable, and on the other it must replace the spirit of domination and might with freedom and law. In addition, his approach to the problem is underpinned by two positions that immediately distance him from the utilitarian solutions of Gibbon, Smith and Hume. First, Kant bases his view of politics on a conception of right derived from reason. Thus, in the final analysis there can be only one form of political right for Kant, and the idea of two separate political spheres with two different concepts of rightful action is inconsistent with this position. More specifically, Kant argued that no matter how just a particular political sphere was, the existence of a sphere where force supplanted right would subvert justice in all spheres of life. Law based on reason must be universal to be effective and strong.[78] Second, he regarded human material interests, whether short or longer term, as fundamentally disharmonious. What united people was not their material interests, but rather their common reason. The problem for Kant was, therefore, how to construct a rationally based cosmopolitan order when there were so many non-rational forces working against it. Kant's argument can be divided into three categories, each of which is crucial to the development of his answer to this problem. First there is the 'is' of the problem, or the question of where we stand at present. The second is the 'ought', which establishes what our imperatives are. The third is the 'how', or the establishment of the means of moving from the 'is' to the 'ought'. As Georg Cavallar has argued, to fully understand Kant's approach to international relations it is necessary to realise the distinction between his *a priori* principles, based solely on practical reason, and the means Kant suggests for reaching those principles, which take into account the social and political contexts.[79]

It is as well to remind ourselves from the start that Kant had a low opinion of humanity. Ultimately, for Kant, the cause of war lies in human nature. As Kant outlined in his *Foundations of the Metaphysics of Morals*, humans are simultaneously under the laws of nature and the laws of reason. The former determine that we should fight for our survival against others, the latter allow us the freedom to construct our own laws, and to find means to live together based on right. Civil society for Kant, therefore, was established in order to protect individuals from attack by their neighbours. The state is able to provide a basis by which conflicts can be decided by general laws based on reason, but this is not the case for the relations between states, where no such basis exists.[80] Interestingly, and despite his obvious preference for reason over the laws of nature, Kant regarded reason in man as too weak to achieve the goal of a just society. Rather, it is the very laws of nature that drive humans to cooperate. The natural urges to fight and dominate led to the establishment of societies both as protection and as vehicles for human competition and domination, but these very societies allow for the establishment of laws based on human reason.[81] Reason, therefore, enters later after nature has established the conditions for the development of rational right.

This, of course, does not solve the problem of lawlessness, but simply bifurcates human politics into a potentially free and legal domestic order, and an international politics based on the threat of force. As far as Kant is concerned relations between states, because they are based on the threat of war, represent a condition of perpetual war. Even periods where there are no hostilities are used to prepare for further violence. Since the system is based exclusively on the use of force it cannot be regarded as peace.[82] Similarly, the existence of a system based on solving disagreements by force is by definition one in which there is no law. Law, for Kant, is a product of reason. It is a set of generalised rules, based on rational and consistent argument, which allows people to be treated as ends in themselves, and not as means to other people's ends.[83] In a system based on coercion people are used as means to other people's ends.

This leads to Kant's condemnation of inter-state politics, and his discussion of what ought to exist. From Kant's point of view 'reason, from its throne of supreme moral legislating authority, absolutely condemns war as a legal recourse and makes a state of peace a direct duty'.[84] The long-term goal for Kant is nothing short of the freeing of humanity from the determination of nature, and the introduction of a permanently peaceful order based on reason. This can be achieved by a league of nations, in which independent states accept a social contract that allows their relations to be governed by legal rules, and exclude the possibility of war. This does not mean that these states form a federal constitution, but rather that they enter into this arrangement as free and independent states.[85] Combined with this 'law of nations' is a second 'cosmopolitan law', which should safeguard the right to travel, trade and interact between states.[86] Thus Kant is not trying to merge the two spheres together, but rather hopes to develop a weaker form of legal society at the international level.

In order to avoid the accusation that he has fallen into the same naïve trap as the Abbé de Saint Pierre Kant spends more time on demonstrating how his project is possible than he does in laying out how it would look in practice. Kant envisions two developments leading to a peaceful league of nations. The first is the growth of what he calls 'republican government'. That is government in which there are divisions of powers between the branches of government, and the legal system is based on generalised rules. Republican governments appear because of humanity's 'asocial sociability'. Everyone wants a system in which there are general rules to control their enemies, but in which they are free to opt out. Since this is not possible people naturally seek, as a second best option, a republican system in which all are subject to general rules.[87] In such states the people who will actually suffer from war through enlistment or higher taxes have a say in government, and so there is a strong opposition to waging foreign wars. Republican governments are likely to enter into alliance with each other for these reasons, and as their numbers grow their league of peace will grow too.[88] In addition to this, as commerce grows human selfishness will be redirected towards the peaceful pursuit of commerce, which will reinforce both the league of peace and cosmopolitan right.[89] At the same time, the shear exhaustion brought about by warfare will lead people to seek a perpetually peaceful system of legal order.

In all three cases, the establishment of republican regimes, the rise of selfishness through commerce and exhaustion through war, it is the hand of nature that leads us towards what reason could already have told us:

> The friction among men, the inevitable antagonism, which is a mark of even the largest societies and political bodies, is used by Nature as a means to

establish a condition of quiet and security … Finally, after devastations, revolutions, and even complete exhaustion, she brings them to that which reason could have told them at the beginning and with far less sad experience, to wit, to step from the lawless condition of savages into a league of nations.[90]

There are obvious weaknesses to Kant's argument that I do not want to go in to in detail here. Suffice it to say that his interpretations of reason and his views on human nature have not gone unchallenged. In the conclusion I would like, instead, to concentrate on Kant's state-centrism, which I believe eventually undermines the radical intent of his argument. Kant, though, must be praised for his realisation of the dire problems in separating domestic from inter-state politics. Hume. Gibbon, Smith and Montesquieu all assumed that the existence of two separate spheres of politics – one in which the good life is practised, and one that must be managed so that it serves or, at worst, does not damage, the domestic good life – was an acceptable arrangement. Kant was adamant that leaving the inter-state as a sphere of injustice would undermine justice in the domestic sphere. The constant fear of war would lead to more oppressive taxation and conscription at home, not to mention the need for repression to hone the state down to a war-fighting machine ('What right has a state *against its own subjects* to use them for war against other states?'[91]). War, and the constant threat of war, makes the state a consumer of human resources and wealth, when its true goal should be the establishment of a just order. Thus, the anarchy of inter-state relations becomes the basis for the subversion of Kant's ideal domestic society, what he called the *rechstaat* (literally a state of law, or state based on law. For Kant it meant a constitutional state).

Yet, in the final analysis, Kant is unwilling to go the last step and propose a cosmopolitan answer. Indeed, Kant attempted to find a moral basis for the state, and in so doing his proposal for perpetual peace rested on the assumption that the state was not the major problem, but instead was a cornerstone for the solution of the problem of unregulated inter-state politics. The 'how', was allowed to subvert the 'ought'.

## Enlightenment international thought as business as usual?

The politics of the sixteenth and seventeenth centuries had been marked by the development of the state, and of a system of political thought that attempted to understand the form, actions and consequences of this revolution. The development of patriarchal conservatism in the seventeenth century had been a response to the confessionalisation of state power. Patriarchal conservatism had attempted to tame the excesses of both state politics and religious conflict by fusing *raison d'etat* to a static conception of tradition that included natural law. Although the conservative political universe had been divided into levels – the home, intra-state politics, relations between Christian states, and inter-faith relations – each of these levels were on the Great Chain of Being, and were consequently analogous and driven by the same rules of natural law. The

Enlightenment's conception of politics had also divided up the political world, although the private sphere lost its status as a political realm. By continuing to concentrate on the state as the primary political institution, Enlightenment political theorists entrenched the division of the political into a domestic and an international.

In the thought of Gibbon, Smith, Hume and Montesquieu the inter-state sphere of politics is accepted as having fundamentally different rules of behaviour to the domestic, and indeed it is the domestic sphere that remains the only means through which the good life is realised. The problem with this approach, apart from the over-optimism about the workings of a balance of power, is that it undermines the idea that there can be one science of politics. If there can be different spheres of politics with different rules of behaviour, then how can there be one best way to live based on timeless precepts of reason and human nature? The advocates of the balance of power are also displaying a remarkable faith in the unintended outcomes of international conflicts. The assumption that international conflict is good for societies engaged in the balance of power is based on nothing more than faith. Indeed, Kant's criticism of the effects of militarisation is a timely response to this false optimism.

Perhaps the greatest criticism of the balance of power advocates is not that they did something that they should not have done, but rather that they reneged on their responsibility to do something. While remaining advocates of reform domestically, the likes of Hume and Smith were happy to accept patriarchal conservative notions of inter-state politics as the proper way to conduct inter-state politics. What this represented was a capitulation of the right to have anything to say on international relations. The failure to make international relations a priority for political reform allowed it to remain in the hands of conservative foreign policy elites following conservative notions of *raison d'etat* that were ultimately based on Tacitist notions of competitive interest. Indeed, up to our own day, while domestic politics has become primarily concerned with questions of justice, freedom and representation, international politics often groans under the old Tacitist doctrines of state preservation and necessity; mixed with the patriarchal conservative dicta of order, state sovereignty and supposedly timeless general rules of interaction. In sum, international relations remained a backward conservative sphere, in which Enlightenment political thought hardly made any inroads.

While Bentham's judicial solution to the problems of international relations was a recognition that the inter-state sphere needed reforming, his suggestions still kept the state as the main protagonist in political life. I shall mention below why I regard this as a problem. The same criticisms that Rousseau levelled at Saint Pierre, however, can be turned on Bentham. His proposals for a stronger rule of law rest on the will of state elites to uphold the new rules. Bentham, of course, hoped that liberal states ruled by citizen representatives would have an innate desire to obey international law. Kant had assumed the same for his republican regimes. In both of these cases it was assumed that war between states was a product of aristocratic or monarchical government. Even at the end of the eighteenth century there was ample evidence that this was not necessarily the case. The new United States, for example, far from being less belligerent, fought a number of wars in the first few decades of its existence, one of them against its former ally France. There would have to be more evidence than this to support a liberal thesis that 'good' governments were also more peaceful.[92]

In all, it is Kant's attempt to construct a system of perpetual peace that appears as the most comprehensive and the most directly concerned with finding a solution to the problem of the bifurcation of political thought into separate domestic and international approaches. Kant understood that having an inter-state realm of continual conflict would have dire consequences for domestic politics, both in material and moral terms. Yet, at the end of the day Kant stopped short of advocating a solution that would have reconciled the two political spheres. Instead he constructed a plan that was more in keeping with the patriarchal conservative model of analogous spheres. As a result Kant finally has to rely on the same conceit that Bentham did. Somehow his states are going to have to want to support the system. Neither Kant nor Bentham fully appreciated how representative government, by increasing the sense of belonging to a state, would help develop nationalist sympathies among citizens.

The problem remains the existence of the state. The modern state owes its existence and development to its ability as a war-fighting machine. Indeed, the very structures of the state were established for those purposes. Enlightenment scholars attempted to reform the state into a *rechtstaat*, while maintaining its war-fighting character, form and system of loyalties. The state was to be the guardian of human freedoms, but we are still left with the question of who guards these guardians at a global level? Finding a moral legitimacy for domestic politics does not, by default, establish a moral legitimacy for global politics. Indeed, the primacy of the state as the ultimate focus of political morality in people's lives actually encourages citizens to regard 'outside' global influences as a threat to the 'proper' moral order. Concentrating political power and loyalty in the state, as both patriarchal conservatism and the Enlightenment did, actually undermined cosmopolitanism. Again, this brings us to the contradiction that ultimately dogs Enlightenment political thought: that it propagated universal ideas of right and freedom, but proposed to implement these goals through the particularistic institution of the conservative-inspired state.[93] The warnings about new wine and old bottles come to mind.

Thus, from the point of view of inter-state relations the Enlightenment does not represent a sharp break with conservative practices. Rather, what we see is either a tinkering with conservative notions to make them more palatable, or projects for reform that are flawed from their inception. As a result conservative ideas have continued to flourish in the analysis of international relations, and it was not until the early twentieth century that liberals were able to make a concerted effort at reforming the international sphere. The basis of this continued adherence to a conservative logic at the global level has been the proposition used by Smith, Rousseau and Kant that cosmopolitan loyalty is impossible because our political loyalties form concentric circles, in which loyalty to the state is the most we can hope for. This assumption that loyalties have to be spatial, rather than temporal, familial, cultural or ideological, locks Enlightenment thought into the conservative logic that the state is the vehicle for the achievement of its citizen's interests. This proposition also commits another cardinal error, which was only corrected by liberals in the twentieth century. It assumes that cosmopolitanism requires a single (and impossible) all-encompassing loyalty to all humanity by the peoples of the Earth. This argument can be superseded by redefining cosmopolitan loyalty away from this spatial and totalising logic. Rather, cosmopolitanism can thrive in an environment that encourages individuals to develop multiple loyalties that are not necessarily spatial or, for that matter, fully global. While these individuals' loyalties will be limited, on an aggregate they will form a global web of loyalties that are interlinked and necessarily cosmopolitan. In other words, while individuals cannot be fully cosmopolitan, a group that possesses inter-locking loyalties can be. In sum, the key to freeing Enlightenment thought from its conservative prison, and the answer to the paradox that stumped Rousseau and Kant, is a redefinition of political loyalty. This answer was to be explored more fully by new liberals and socialists in the early twentieth century (see Chapters 6 and 7).

Of course, there is a possible answer to why, despite the seeming illogic of inter-state statecraft, eighteenth century philosophy was less than concerned to reach a fully rational answer to the problem of the international. The wise men of the Enlightenment were living in an agrarian society that, despite its often grave social problems, had yet to undergo an industrialisation that would transform the state's relationship to other states. Industrialisation turned trade from a money-earning luxury into an economic necessity, made control of overseas raw materials and markets a central part of statecraft, made war more destructive and launched a scramble for empire. While the educated eighteenth century gentleman would bemoan the inconsistencies of statecraft, he could also assure himself that to a large extent his prosperity and way of life did not depend on the vagaries of foreign relations. By the end of the nineteenth century that gentleman's grandchild could not rely on that being the case anymore. In the next chapter, the final one in this section on the emergence of the international as a subject of serious study, we explore the last phase in the creation of the modern international system that is the subject of the field of IR: the effects of industrialisation, and the emergence of a truly global system dominated by the predominantly European colonial empires.

## Notes

1  Susan Strange, 'The Westfailure System' *Review of International Studies* (1999) 25(3), 345–354.
2  Stephen D. Krasner, 'Compromising Westphalia', *International Security* (1995/6), 20(3), 115–151; Andreas Osiander, 'International Relations and the Westphalian Myth', *International Organization*, 2001, 55(2), 251–287; Benno Teschke, *The Myth of 1648* (London: Verso, 2003); Benjamin de Carvalho, Halvard Leira and John Hobson, 'The Big Bangs of IR: The Myths That Your Teachers Still Tell You about 1648 and 1919', *Millennium*, 2011, 39(3), 735–758.

3 Osiander, 'Westphalian Myth', 266; de Carvalho et al., 'Big Bangs of IR', 738–9n; for the Rijksmuseum's take, see: http://www.rijksmuseum.nl/aria/aria_assets/SKA405? lang=en&context_space=aria_encyclopedia&context_id=00048377 (accessed on 2 February 2012). Interestingly, the picture of the ratification of the treaty of Münster by Gerard ter Borch (which hangs in the Rijksmuseum) that is often used in IR textbooks to illustrate the October treaty between France and the Emperor is actually the May ratification of the treaty between the Dutch and the Spanish. Such is the confusion about the Peace of Westphalia in IR textbooks that even this matter is usually the subject of confusion. See, for example, Jenny Edkins and Maja Zehfuss, *Global Politics* (London: Routledge, 2009), 201.

4 Osiander, 'Westphalian Myth', 253–4; de Carvalho et al., 'Big Bangs of IR', 741.

5 See the discussion in Osiander, 'Westphalian Myth'.

6 Osiander, 'Westphalian Myth', 272.

7 See Osiander, 'Westphalian Myth', 281 ff.

8 Sebastian Schmidt, 'To Order the Minds of Scholars: the Discourse of the Peace of Westphalia in International Relations Literature', *International Studies Quarterly*, 2011, 55, 602.

9 Schmidt, 'To Order the Minds of Scholars', 604–9.

10 Frederick L. Schuman, *International Politics. An Introduction to the Western State System* (New York: McGraw-Hill, 1933), 75–6.

11 For a discussion of Gross' argument see Osiander, 'Westphalian Myth', 264–5; Schmidt, 'To Order the Minds of Scholars', 610–11; Leo Gross, 'The Peace of Westphalia 1648–1948', *American Journal of International Law*, 1948, 42(1), 20–41.

12 For a discussion of Wright's role see Schmidt, 'To Order the Minds of Scholars', 611. The quote from Wright comes from Quincy Wright, *The Study of International Relations* (New York: Appleton-Century-Crofts, 1955), 137.

13 See Schmidt, 'To Order the Minds of Scholars', 613.

14 Reprinted in Michael Ignatieff, *Virtual War* (London: Picador, 2000). The original letter was written on 6 May 1999.

15 A point summed up by *Star Trek*'s James T. Kirk during an encounter with a society run by a computer. Doctor MacCoy tries to stop Kirk destroying the computer, warning him that the prime directive forbade interference in the development of an alien society. Kirk quipped back that this was not a real society because it was static. The clear message is that if you do not fit our view of a proper society you are not a society.

16 David Hume 'Of the Rise and Progress of the Arts and Sciences' and 'Essay on the Balance of Power' in *Essays Moral and Political*.

17 See Schmidt, 'To Order the Minds of Scholars', 613 ff.

18 Strange 'The Westfailure System'.

19 Schmidt, 'To Order the Minds of Scholars', 619.

20 See M.S. Anderson, *War and Society in Europe of the Old Regime 1618–1789* (Stroud: Sutton, 1998), 66 ff.

21 Immanuel Kant, *Perpetual Peace* (Indianapolis: Bobbs-Merrill, 1978).

22 Walter Raleigh, *Aphorisms of State, Grounded on Authority and Experience, and Illustrated with the Choicest Examples and Historical Observations* (London: Thomas Johnson, 1661), 57–9. Originally written in the sixteenth century.

23 Toulmin, *op cit*, 30–5. For Hobbes' part in this intellectual shift see Quentin Skinner, *Reason and Rhetoric in the Philosophy of Hobbes* (Cambridge: Cambridge University Press, 1996), 260–1.

24 Jens Bartelson, *A Genealogy of Sovereignty* (Cambridge: Cambridge University Press, 1995).

25 See the discussion in Hinton, *op cit*. For a detailed contemporary account of these relationships see Robert Filmer, 'Observations Upon Aristotle's Politiques (1652)', in David Wooton (ed.), *Divine Right and Democracy. An Anthology of Political Writing in Stuart England* (Harmondsworth: Penguin, 1986), 110–12; and Robert

Filmer, *Patriarchia: or the Natural Power of Kings* (London: Walter Davis, 1680), 12–24.

26  See, for example, Samuel Pufendorf, *On the Duty of Man and Citizen* (Cambridge: Cambridge University Press, 1991), especially part II.

27  Michel Foucault, *Madness and Civilisation* (London: Routledge, 2001), ch. 1–2.

28  Michel Foucault, 'Politics and Reason', in *Politics, Philosophy, Culture. Interviews and Writings 1977–1984* (London: Routledge, 1988).

29  Foucault, 'Politics and Reason', 69. For a contemporary example of these relationships see Leibniz, 'On Natural Law', in *Leibniz. Political Writings* (Cambridge: Cambridge University Press, 1988), 77–9.

30  Lucian M. Ashworth and Larry A. Swatuk, 'Masculinity and the Fear of Emasculation', in Marysia Zalewski and Jane Parpart (eds), *The Man Question in International Relations* (Boulder Co.: Westview, 1997).

31  *Op cit*, 58.

32  Paul Hazard, *The European Mind 1680–1715* (Harmondsworth: Pelican, 1964), 47.

33  Toulmin, *op cit*, 32–5, 83.

34  Hobbes is clear on this point, for example, in his dedicatory letter to the Earl of Devonshire at the beginning of his *de Cive*: Thomas Hobbes, *De Cive. The English Version* (Oxford: Clarendon Press, 1983), 24–5. For a detailed discussion of Hobbes' view of history and knowledge see Quentin Skinner, *Reason and Rhetoric in the Philosophy of Hobbes* (Cambridge: Cambridge University Press, 1996), 260–1, 263–4, 291.

35  'Est autem jus naturale adeo immutabile, ut ne a Deo quidem mutari queat'. Hugo Grotius, *De Jure Belli et Pacis Libri Tres* (Cambridge and London: John W. Parker, 1853), Bk I.10.5.

36  This is part of the central argument of Hobbes' *Leviathan*. It can also be found in many popular tracts of the time. For example: 'R.W.' *The Anatomy of Warre* (London: John Dalham, nd), 2.

37  Thomas Hobbes, *Leviathan*, part one (Hammondsworth: Penguin, 1981), chapter xiii.

38  See, for example, John Bright's speech in Birmingham on 29 October 1858, in John Bright, *Selected Speeches of the Right Honourable John Bright MP on Public Questions* (London: J. M. Dent, 1907), 204; Letter from Richard Cobden to Mr Richard, 29 September 1852, reprinted in J.A. Hobson, *Richard Cobden. The International Man* (Toronto: Dent, 1918), 90; Herbert Spencer, 'Militancy and Industrialism' in *On Social Evolution* (Chicago: University of Chicago Press, 1972), 149–66; and for an overview of Spencer's position see Ernest Baker, *Political Thought in England 1848 to 1914* (London: Thornton Butterworth, 1928), 93–4.

39  See the discussion below, and also in Chapters 4 and 5.

40  This argument is developed more fully in my book *Creating International Studies. Angell, Mitrany and the Liberal Tradition* (Aldershot: Ashgate, 1999), chs 1–3.

41  For Francis Quarles' position see his *Observations Concerning Princes and States, upon Peace and Warre* (London 1642), especially the first three observations.

42  For a discussion of the development of these competing forms of rationality, and their influence on the theory of international relations, see Ashworth and Swatuk, 'Masculinity and the Fear of Emasculation'.

43  For a summary of this process see Jean Bethke Elshtain, *Public Man Private Woman. Women in Social and Political Thought*, second edn (Princeton: Princeton University Press, 1993), ch. 3.

44  Edward Gibbon, *An Essay on the Study of Literature* (London: Becket and de Hondt, 1764), 107–9. See also the discussion in John Burrow, *A History of Histories* (Harmondsworth: Penguin, 2009), ch. 21.

45  David Hume, 'Of the Rise and Progress of the Arts and Sciences (1742)', (http://www.utm.edu/research/hume/wri/essays/rise.htm); Giambattista Vico, *The New Science of Giambattista Vico* (Ithaca: Cornell University Press, 1968), book IV. For discussions of the views of Gibbon, Smith and Kant see below.

46  For a discussion of this see Burrow, *History of Histories*, 353 ff.

47  Burrow, *History of Histories*, 363.

48  See Edward Gibbon, *Decline and Fall of the Roman Empire*, chs XXII–XXIV.

49  *Decline and Fall*, ch. XXXIX.

50  *Decline and Fall*, ch. XXXIX.

51  *Decline and Fall*, ch. XXXIX.

52  For a discussion of Gibbon's approach to inter-state relations see Jeremy Black, 'Empire and Enlightenment in Gibbon's Treatment of International Relations', *The International History Review*, 1995, 17, 441–660.

53  *Decline and Fall*, ch. XXXIX.

54  *An Inquiry into the Nature and Causes of the Wealth of Nations*, Bk III, ch. 1.

55  *Wealth of Nations*, Bk V, ch. 1, part 1.

56  *Wealth of Nations*, Bk III, ch. II.

57  Smith, of course, was wrong to class the Germanic invaders as pastoralists. Actually the Germani were also farmers (although the nomadic Sarmatians, Alans and Huns were in all likelihood pastoralists). See Peter Heather, *Empires and Barbarians. Migration, Development and the Birth of Europe* (London: Pan, 2010), especially 2–4. Gibbon seems to have shared this view about the pastoral nature of the Germani (see Burrow, *History of Histories*, 360.)

58  *Wealth of Nations*, Bk III, ch. III.

59  *Wealth of Nations*, Bk IV, ch. II.

60  *Wealth of Nations*, Bk IV, ch. III.

61  *Wealth of Nations*, Bk V, ch. I.

62  *Theory of Moral Sentiments*, Bk VI, ch. II.

63  *A Treatise of Human Nature*, Bk III, part II section vii.

64  *A Treatise of Human Nature*, Bk III, part 2, section xi; republished later as *An Enquiry Concerning the Principles of Morals.*

65  *A Treatise of Human Nature*, Bk III, part 2, section xi.

66  'Essay on the Balance of Power', in *Essays Moral, Political and Literary.* The problem for Hume here is that – despite copious writings by ancient authors in public matters, statesmanship and war – there is no evidence that either the Ancient Greeks or Romans thought in terms of the balance of power. Rather, as discussed in Chapter 2, it looks like the idea of a balance of power, analogous to a pair of scales, dates from the Italian Renaissance.

67  'Of the Rise and Progress of the Arts and Sciences', in *Essays.*

68  *The Spirit of the Laws*, Bk 10, section 2.

69  *The Spirit of the Laws*, Bk 9, sections 1–3.

70  See Jeremy Bentham, 'An International Code' in *Basic Texts in International Relations,* ed. Evan Luard (Basingstoke: Macmillan, 1992), pp. 415–17; *An Introduction to the Principles of Morals and Legislation*, ch. XVII; 'Rid Yourself of Ultramaria', in Jeremy Bentham, *Colonies, Commerce and Constitutional Law* (Oxford: Oxford University Press, 1995).

71  This is, interestingly enough, Hans J. Morgenthau's argument in his *Politics Among Nations.* Despite Morgenthau's belief that only the balance of power could deliver an easy peace, he pessimistically added that the balance of power was inherently unstable because states seeking their own security would strive for preponderance. Hans J. Morgenthau, *Politics Among Nations. The Struggle for Power and Peace*, sixth edn (New York: Alfred A. Knopf, 1985).

72  Michael C. Williams, 'Rousseau, Realism and Realpolitik', *Millennium*, 1989, 18, 185–203.

73  A classic example of Rousseau's attack on these elites, and the philosophical supporters of reason of state, can be found in his 'The State of War' quoted above.

74  Perhaps a good modern example of the process Rousseau is talking about is McCarthyism in 1950s America. The unjust security concerns of the Cold War undermined notions of justice in the American domestic sphere.

75  See, for example, his discussion of this in *The Social Contract*, Bk I, ch. 3 and Bk II, ch. 9.

76  See, for example, the argument he develops in 'A Discourse on Political Economy' in *The Social Contract and Other Later Political Writings*, especially pp. 7, 28–9.

77  For a fuller discussion of this conflict in Rousseau's thought see Georg Cavallar's work.

78  See Immanuel Kant, 'Public Right', in *The Metaphysics of Morals* (Cambridge: University of Cambridge Press, 1991), section 1, 43: 'So if the principle of outer freedom limited by law is lacking in any of these three possible forms of rightful condition, the framework of all the others is unavoidably undermined and must finally collapse.'

79  See the Introduction in Georg Cavallar's *Kant and the Theory and Practice of International Right* (Cardiff: University of Wales Press, 1999).

80  For a fuller discussion of this see Kant, 'Public Right', section 1.

81  'Idea for a Universal History from a Cosmopolitan Point of View' in Immanuel Kant, *On History* (Indianapolis: Bobbs-Merrill, 1963), Fourth Thesis; *Perpetual Peace* (Indianapolis: Bobbs-Merrill, 1978), first supplement.

82  'Public Right', section II, 54.

83  See the discussion of the categorical imperative in *Foundations of the Metaphysics of Morals*.

84  *Perpetual Peace*, p. 18.

85  'Public Right', section II, 54, 61; *Perpetual Peace*, 354–7.

86  'Public Right' section III; *Perpetual Peace*, 357–60.

87  See *Perpetual Peace*, 366, 'Idea for a Universal History', fourth and fifth theses.

88  *Perpetual Peace*, 349–53.

89  *Perpetual Peace*, 368.

90  'Idea for a Universal History', seventh thesis.

91  'Public Right', section II, 55.

92  The argument that liberal states are more peaceful (at least with each other) has been advanced by a number of theorists, although the most comprehensive was Michael Doyle's 'Kant, Liberal Legacies and Foreign Affairs', *Philosophy and Public Affairs*, 1983, 12, 205–54, 323–53. Doyle, however, under-estimates the novelty of the period he is dealing with, and does not appreciate how his analysis of only constitutionally secure liberal states weights his findings.

93  See Ashworth, 'Bringing the Nation Back In?', in Lucian M. Ashworth and David Long (eds) *New Perspectives in International Functionalism* (Houndsmill: Macmillan, 1999), 69–71.

# 4 A new global political economy?

*This chapter explores the importance of the processes of industrialisation in the creation of a truly global political economic system. Several social theorists that explored this new industrialising world are discussed, each of which had a particular take on how the new realities were changing the political sphere. These are: Cobden and Bright, and their concept of free trade; Friedrich List and the effects of industrialisation on cosmopolitanism and nationalism; and Pierre-Joseph Proudhon and the role of war in justice, and how the changing nature of society has changed the role of war. Throughout the discussions of the these three I also bring in the social theory of Karl Marx. Although Marx did not directly write on the international, his ideas about political economy, as well as his engagement with the work of Cobden and List, would be influential in later years.*

*Throughout this chapter I stress the importance of industrialisation in changing the nature of the international.*

On 1 May 1851 Queen Victoria opened the Great Exhibition in London. The opening was attended by senior figures in Britain, and the ambassadors from many of the countries exhibiting their wares under the Crystal Palace. The opening ceremony could even boast a Chinese representative who, although not an official diplomat of the Manchu court, was the captain of the first Chinese merchant vessel to reach European waters. The Great Exhibition helped to usher in much of what we regard as marks of the modern industrial world. Unlike previous commercial exhibitions in France, which had served as the model for the Great Exhibition, entries were welcome from around the world. Indeed, half of the space in the Crystal Palace was dedicated to lands outside the British Empire, of which the American and French sections were the most impressive. This global reach was deliberate, since the ethos of the Great Exhibition was to unite the world in peaceful commercial competition in order to supplant violent military confrontation. So, pervading it was a notion associated with Auguste Comte that a naturally peaceful scientific and industrial society had supplanted a war-prone theological and military one.[1] As *The Times* put it on the day of the opening of the Great Exhibition: the world had not come together to celebrate war and violence, 'but to exhibit the fruits of that industry, of that skill, of that earth which God has given all of us for our common use, and mutual obligation'.[2] For the first time it was decided that cheap 'shilling' days would be instituted in order to allow ordinary people to attend the Exhibition. The original idea was to help the education and elucidation of all sections of the population, although it had two unintended consequences. One was the mingling of the classes at a common venue, and the other was the encouragement this gave to the development of mass tourism. People saved up in special travel clubs in order to attend one of the shilling days, while enterprising proto-travel agents, such as Thomas Cook, organised package trips to the Exhibition. Foreign tourism also developed from this, with especially a large number of visitors coming over from France to see the exhibits. Thus, the Great Exhibition was both a celebration of a (British dominated and liberal) global economy, but also it was part of the new national consciousness that was coming to dominate the political identities of people in the industrialising states of Western Europe. The Great Exhibition was also responsible for promoting the development of the department store, the shopping mall, agricultural mechanisation, the envelope, rubber rainwear, the inflatable life raft, and the Schweppes food empire.[3]

Yet, it is the notion that an increasingly shrinking, industrial and interdependent world required a new liberal outlook, a new political order and a new imperial ethos that is most relevant to our story. When IR textbooks treat international history at all, the key dates are often 1648, perhaps the French revolution, 1919 and 1945, yet the processes that fundamentally altered the politico-economic structures of global society – industrialisation and the creation of an interdependent economy – arguably had more profound effects on both the nature of international affairs and the way that it was thought about than any of these other events. Indeed, it is no coincidence that industrialisation preceded the development of the idea of a self-conscious and autonomous study of international relations. The field of IR is also as much a product of industrialisation. After all, it was during the mid-nineteenth century that we can for the first time talk about a truly global international system. In her classic analysis of the effects of technology on the development of the medieval world Lynn White criticised the tendency of many historians to concentrate on texts, rather than technological changes, as a means of understanding history.[4] Written records of any time understandably play up specific events that happened in specific years. The more glacial 'langue durée' changes are more difficult to spot, while the sudden event has an immediacy and impact that can rarely be ignored. It is, therefore, not surprising that when textbook writers in IR construct an introductory history of the field they concentrate on what one set of writers have called the 'big bangs' of IR: especially 1648 and 1919.[5] I have been equally guilty of this tendency by my concentration on 1851 in the first paragraph of this chapter. Yet, by introducing 1 May 1851 as the start of the modern world I do so not because the world was so very different on 30 April, but because the Great Exhibition is a handy device that sums up so much of what changed during the nineteenth century, especially in Europe and North America, but also in the rest of the World that found itself confronted by the new power realities unleashed by coal and steam. Suffice it to say, though, that so many of the introductory textbooks in IR skim over the period from 1815 to 1914, leaving it as a period marked by an uncommonly long 'peace'. This does a major disservice to our understanding of the development of IR. In fact the early and mid-nineteenth century is skimmed over in most treatments. Yet, the industrialisation and globalisation that started in this period were the developments that created the world that the emerging study of IR was developed to deal with. The changes may have been slow, but they were sustained and profound.

This globalisation had a third leg to it: the international system also became global because of the spread of European imperial aspirations. Of course, these three legs – trade, industry and imperialism – reinforced each other. The hunt for markets and for raw materials provided a push for colonial territories, while the new mass produced goods and industrial technologies made inter-continental empires easier to gain and maintain. The European armies were not superior in numbers or bravery, and often their non-western foes were also equipped with artillery, firearms and other effective tools of war. Western armies and navies, however, could rely on cheap mass produced weapons and other military supplies, efficient sea transportation, the emerging system of railways, telegraph communications, and modern systems of supply. While it is certainly the case that non-western societies were not the push-over that popular mythology, such as the hit BBC series *Blackadder Goes Forth,* has made them (societies as diverse as Persia, Siam, Abyssinia and China managed to successfully avoid being conquered, while other groups won significant victories against imperial powers even though they later succumbed), it is still the case that western imperial expansion did profoundly change the shape of the world. Not least of these changes was the creation of a single global economy.[6]

Behind this link between industrialisation, globalisation and imperialism stands a single product that revolutionised humanity's relationship with wealth production: coal.[7] The abundance of cheap coal (and, increasingly in the early twentieth century, petroleum) led to an unprecedented social revolution. Coal made steam power cheap, and in turn steam-driven trains and ships were able to transport coal cheaply and efficiently. Coal's highly concentrated levels of energy cut society's reliance on extensive tracts of land for energy production – whether in the form of woodlands or food for labourers and animals – and allowed the concentration of populations in industrial cities far from the sources of the raw materials that their industries used. Coal and steel production led to railways and steam-driven shipping that delivered the raw materials and food required by these new industrial conurbations, and also shipped out cheaply the finished goods. This new industrial reality also fundamentally altered the relationship between the west and the rest of the world. Industrialisation made industrial states increasingly dependent on imported raw materials and foodstuffs for the growing work forces. 'The commodities Europe needed as industrial raw materials could not be obtained simply through relations of trade', and as a result it required control of overseas territories outside of Europe. 'These colonial arrangements' secured the supply of agricultural goods 'in quantities that allowed the development of intensive, coal-based mass production in the towns and cities of Europe.'[8] Thus, industrialisation gave Europeans both the necessity and the means to conquer and control the extra-European world. When late nineteenth century commentators such as Friedrich Ratzel (see Chapter 5) said that a world power needed colonial territories in many different areas of the world they were doing more than justifying imperialism, they were also reacting to what was perceived as an industrial necessity.

Thus, industrialisation fundamentally altered global relations. From an international relations point of view there were clear differences between the IR of (to use George Modelski's phrases) Agraria and Industria.[9] Great powers were now truly global powers reliant on economic links beyond their borders. The technology of war changed dramatically, but so also did the nature of the social classes that fought it. Coal, steel and railways now became the sinews of war, necessary for the duels of vast and increasingly destructive war machines. At the same time the political forces unleashed by industrialisation had made general support for the war necessary. This, coupled with the new late nineteenth century industrial war-machines' need for mass conscription ushered in the age of the idea of total war and mass nationalist sentiments that stretched beyond the traditional state elites of agrarian societies. The new studies of international affairs that we will explore in the next chapter were products of this new industrial, imperial and nationalistic world with its war machines that were more capable of inflicting collateral damage on the society around them than they were on each other. The works that we will explore in this chapter, however, are those that were thrown up by the transition towards an industrial society, and therefore share with the writers already discussed in the previous two chapters a lack of a self-conscious international flavour. Their international thought is still a by-product of their wider politico-economic concerns. It is really not until the end of the nineteenth century that the international is recognised as a problem in and of itself. That said, there is still a recognisable view of the international that emerges from these writers, and is, in turn, influential on the development of a more self-consciously international approach to political problems.

Interestingly, and fitting with the neglect of industrial matters often found among so many of the academic commentators of the time, the four main thinkers whose international thought I explore in this chapter were not primarily political thinkers, but were also practitioners in one form or another. Two of their number were liberal politicians, one a financier and entrepreneur, and the last an anarchist pamphleteer who also served as a political representative. Richard Cobden and John Bright explored how the problems of war and inter-state conflict could be dealt with through the development of free trade and other forms of transnational contact. Friedrich List analysed the role of the state in industrial and industrialising societies, and argued that the processes of industrial development would see competing states give way to a congress of western industrial states. Pierre-Joseph Proudhon's approach would interpret the state as parasitic on economic development, and would carry out an in-depth study of the pros and cons of war. Interestingly, it was in France, rather than in Britain, that much of the questions about the role of industry and war were discussed. Furthermore, with a few exceptions few of these commentators on industrialisation and war have been translated into English. Proudhon's two volume *La guerre et la paix* has no English version, nor do the many books written by the prolific journalist and internationalist socialist Constantin Pecqueur. As a result, the accounts of the development of ideas about the international among Anglophones are already hamstrung by the lack of access to many of the mid-nineteenth century works that discussed these problems. Not surprisingly, many of these works were influences on the one French scholar that did break into the Anglo world of IR in the post-1945 world: Raymond Aron. Partially at least, Aron was a continuation of this French discourse on war and the modern world.

There is a glaring omission in this chapter. Arguably the most well-known social theorist of the mid-nineteenth century was Karl Marx. On so many counts he stands head and shoulders above his contemporaries when it comes to influence on future generations. Marxist ideas have also played an important role in the development of international thought. However 'Marx and Engels did not address themselves directly to formulating a fully developed theory of international relations...' and while there are discussions of world markets, imperialism, free trade and (in the works of Engels) war, any international thought 'is only intimated in their work'.[10] Perhaps the major exception here is Marx's later interest in how capitalism was creating a two-tier world divided into imperial powers and colonised peoples. Marx's notion of capitalism as the first mode of production to create a world market fits in to the argument of this chapter. Marx recognised how steam and machinery had revolutionised production and trade, leading to the first global market and a truly global class system.[11] 'The bourgeoisie' Marx and Engels wrote, 'has through its exploitation of the world market given a cosmopolitan character to production and consumption in every country.'[12] By the 1870s Marx had also come to believe that his view of the transition of society towards capitalism only applied to Western Europe, and that the development of the non-Western world was, by the nature of its involvement in capitalism, very different. The link between capitalism and imperialism mattered.[13] We cannot fully understand the growth of the realisation of the importance of the international during the later nineteenth century without an appreciation of the growing cosmopolitan nature of the politico-economic system that Marx charted in his work. While I do not directly address Marx's philosophy here, he and his collaborator Engels lurk in the background. Their critical analysis of the work of Cobden, List and Proudhon have a bearing on an understanding of the international thought of all three writers, and as such I have brought Marx in, where appropriate, below. Marx's analysis of the new political economy of capitalism is, therefore, the string that binds these beads together.

## Free trade as international thought: the work of Richard Cobden and John Bright

The starting point for an appreciation of the ideas of Richard Cobden is the development of a society dependent on industry and commerce for the bulk of its wealth. While war causes damage in any society that is afflicted with it, there is a resilience to war in agrarian societies that allows them to recover quickly. In his classic study of the nature of Ancient Greek hoplite warfare Victor Davis Hanson pointed out 'the sheer difficulty of destroying trees, vines and acres of grain' – something he had experienced personally during an attempt to clear a small farm in the San Joaquin Valley in California.[14] Sharp declines in the prosperity of an agrarian society could come about after violence and war, but only if the post-war period involved dramatic political, social and institutional changes that prevented a return to the *status quo ante-bellum.* The later Roman Empire, for example, fell victim to many civil wars and invasions in the third and fourth centuries, yet the agrarian economy recovered in all these cases. The invasions and wars of the fifth century, on the other hand, reduced the economy of much of the former Western Empire to pre-historic levels. The significant difference here was the collapse of central imperial authority that had allowed a complex trading and manufacturing economy to flourish.[15] Thus, war might cause the events that brought about economic decline, but war itself was rarely a cause in and of itself. The new emerging commerce and industry dependent societies of the nineteenth century, by comparison, were more sensitive to the direct effects of warfare on prosperity – or, perhaps more importantly in a study focused on ideas, nineteenth century society was perceived as being more sensitive to the direct effects of war. The work of Cobden and Bright fit into a genre of political writing (often called the Manchester School) that influenced much liberal thought in the nineteenth century, especially in Britain. Manchester School liberalism supported free trade, but opposed war and imperialism. While the people who came to be identified as the Manchester School never called themselves by that name (the term was generally used by their conservative and socialist opponents, both at home and abroad, after 1848), the two main advocates of this liberalism, Cobden and Bright, formed an influential political partnership.

Basic to the writings and political agitation of Cobden and Bright was the idea that trade and commerce had now become essential to the prosperity of all classes in all countries. As a result, war now threatened to impoverish all of humanity because nations depend on trade for survival, and war cuts trade links.[16] In addition to this, war is a serious drain on the exchequer, leading to over-taxation and national debt.[17] Cobden and Bright were not alone in this argument about the wastefulness and costliness of war, and their ideas mirrored those in the writings of James Mill in Britain and Paul Leroy Beaulieu in France.[18] They also built on the earlier arguments of writers, such as Jeremy Bentham, who had argued that war only made sense in earlier pre-commercial societies.[19] What was original in the work of Cobden and Bright, however, was the way that they developed the idea of free trade. In their thought free trade was not merely a negative removal of trade barriers, but a way of organising the world without government action. Free trade was a vehicle for the promotion of both peace and commerce at home and abroad. At home free trade reduced the cost of living of ordinary workers, and thus diminished what for Bright was the main cause of labour agitation and rioting.[20] This was an issue of topical concern in the mid-nineteenth century given the series of violent (and often organised) labour unrests and violent confrontations that had occurred in Britain since 1815 and the end of the Napoleonic wars. Abroad, as Cobden argued, free trade was a competitive, but peaceful, common purpose that would unite nations in a friendly rivalry over who could produce the best and cheapest goods. When Cobden posed the question 'what is free trade?' to a gathering in London in 1843, the answer he gave was that it meant 'breaking down the barriers that separate nations'.[21] This, of course, was also part of the ethos of the 1851 Great Exhibition discussed at the beginning of this chapter, and it should not surprise us that Cobden was one of the Commissioners of the Great Exhibition.

This definition of free trade revealed an important part of the international thought of Cobden and Bright: that peace would come not from government action or military strength and intervention, but through a weakening of government, and interactions between the various peoples of the world. As Cobden famously put it: 'As little intercourse as possible betwixt the *governments*, as much connexion as possible between the *nations* of the world!'[22] It would be free trade – bringing peoples together in prosperity and healthy competition in the industrial arts – that would bring peace to the world. Governments, through their diplomacy, were incapable of the task. Free trade, without the hindrance of government was 'the means – and I believe the only human means – of effecting universal and permanent peace'.[23] Free trade could also not be imposed by powerful governments, but had to be enthusiastically embraced by the nations of the Earth. For this reason Cobden opposed wars that aimed at imposing either free trade or general liberal values. This was counter-productive, as it merely had the effect of making those forced into free trade resentful.[24] On this issue Cobden and Bright were at odds with their sometime Party leader, and frequent ally, William Gladstone. While Gladstone also opposed the balance of power and foreign adventures, he supported the idea of military intervention in the service of higher ideals against foreign despotisms.[25] Cobden and Bright's position made them simultaneously opposed to both the balance of power and to the extension of international organisations to international affairs. Peace would come by economic and commercial interactions alone, without the assistance of government.

Underlying this analysis of the differences between government and free trade lay a view of a conflict between classes. For Cobden and Bright there was a sharp conflict between the landed aristocracy on the one hand, and the largely urbanised industrialists and their workers, on the other. Industrialists and workers, since they both relied on industry and the trade in manufactures for their livelihood, had a common interest in minimal government interference and free trade. The landed aristocracy, as the former power-brokers of an earlier agrarian age, had a different set of interests and values that put them at odds with free trade. Both Cobden and Bright had been involved in the movement to repeal the 'corn laws' – tariffs on the importation of grains that protected British landed producers, but also kept the prices of bread high for industrial workers and other city dwellers. Even at the time, the conflict over the corn laws was seen as a class war between landed and commercial interests. This aristocratic opposition to free trade was seen by Cobden and Bright as a feature of aristocratic government, and that protectionism was thus the product of an older agrarian and aristocratic society that no longer had any place in the new commercial and industrial world of the nineteenth century. This use of the state to maximise aristocratic profits through protectionism was not the only way in which the state was used by a landed elite in the service of its own class interests. Aristocrats also profited, through military and colonial posts, from both war and imperialism. Bright even borrowed James Mill's phrase and claimed that the British government was nothing more than 'a gigantic system of out-door relief for the aristocracy'.[26] The problem was not the aristocratic class alone, argued Cobden, but also aristocratic values that tended to infect all classes in society.[27] This made aristocratic values a far greater threat than just the existence of the landed class. For Cobden the only way to fully remove these aristocratic vices of protectionism, war and imperialism was through education of the general public.[28]

While Cobden, Bright and the wider Manchester School tended to see the conflict in society as being between a landed aristocracy, on the one hand, and industrialists and their workers, on the other, there were those who criticised them for failing to see that industrial workers did not necessarily share the industrialist's zeal for free trade. While there were many voices in Britain critical of the idea that factory owners and workers shared interests, particularly in the Chartist movement, perhaps the most eloquent critic of Cobden and Bright's enthusiasm for free trade was Karl Marx. Unlike List (see below) Marx was no supporter of protectionism, and did support free trade, but for reasons very different from the Manchester School. For Marx free trade would break up the old nationalities and intensify the conflict between the proletariat and the bourgeoisie, and thus would hasten the social revolution.[29] Marx, though, pointed out that the cost to workers of the corn laws was far smaller than the reductions in wages imposed (through one means or other) by the factory owners themselves and the factory regulations. Free trade was advantageous to the worker, but in the end would make little difference to the livelihood of the proletariat. The big gainers were those who controlled capital, since free trade left it complete freedom of action.[30] In addition to this Cobden's hope that free trade would end war was wishful thinking. It would end the feudal method of warfare, only to replace it with commercial war. Although Marx does not elaborate on this point, he seems to mean that class war would continue.[31]

Although Cobden and Bright were not without their critics of both the right and the left, the power of their ideas in Britain, continental Europe and the United States cannot be doubted. Their view of the replacement of an aristocratic, statist and war-prone order by a commercial, free trade and pacific order was to be one of the dominant liberal strands of thinking about the international until the early years of the twentieth century. Their view that contact and free trade, rather than government and international organisations, was the means towards prosperity and peace remained a compelling idea until the First World War called this *laissez faire* order into question. Certainly, their ideas were influential on Norman Angell's pre-war *Great Illusion*, and even when their antipathy towards international organisation had been severely questioned following the First World War, J.A. Hobson could still write a critical eulogy to Cobden.[32] Their major contribution to international thought was their recognition that the new industrial and commercial society made peace an imperative because of the growing importance of trade and commerce to modern societies. For them the future lay in less government involvement in the relations between nations, but increased interactions between peoples via free trade. Eloquent critics of the 'aristocratic' balance of power, they were so convinced of the superiority of free trade as a means towards a more prosperous and peaceful future that for them it only required education for them to win the argument. Yet, there were other voices who had looked at the lessons of industrial society and come to radically different conclusions. It was not just the aristocrats who saw benefits to protectionist policies, and in the form of a German writer, entrepreneur and railway enthusiast called Friedrich List the Manchester School would find one of its sternest critics.

## The political economy of an industrialising world: Friedrich List

In discussions of different economic policies it is not uncommon to find writers comparing the theories of Adam Smith and Friedrich List. Smith is presented as the personification of a cosmopolitan economics that advocates free trade, while List is presented as the champion of more national and regulatory protectionist policies. In the last chapter I showed how Smith's international theory was very different from this caricature of him as the cosmopolitan free trader. Equally, though, the view of List as the theorist of protectionism is at best only partially true. Rather, the work of List presents one of the early attempts to explore the effects of industrialisation on society. Yet, List's analysis was not only about national policy. His analysis of the political economy of industrialisation also developed into an understanding of both the nature of the relations between nations, and the place of western imperialism in the development of the new industrialising societies of the nineteenth century. Thus, his work blends together an understanding of the intersection of all three of the key elements of the emerging international order: industrialisation, the sovereign nation state and the spread of western imperial control into the non-western world. List regarded the presence of all three as marking a major discontinuity between his own age and that of the world of the previous century. List was, in this sense, trying to make sense of a new world that had different rules from the one that had preceded it.

Arguably, List's most important addition to the arguments about political economy in the nineteenth century was his view of the stages of economic growth. Although the number and names of those stages changed in his work, the basic premise remained the same: that societies went through phases dominated by a largely subsistence agriculture, by an agricultural system that sees growing commerce and eventual industrialisation, and finally reaches full maturity as an industrial society.[33] List's fame rests on the way that he interpreted these stages, and how from this analysis he argued that, while free trade was beneficial for an agricultural society (as well as between mature industrialised economies), limited and strategic policies of protection were needed to nurture industrialisation. Free trade benefited agricultural societies because it allows it to sell its surplus product, while acquiring industrial goods cheaply. This helps foster commerce, cities and ideas associated with a more advanced civilisation. Between advanced industrial states free trade is also beneficial, as the exchange is to mutual benefit. For industrialising societies, though, free trade will prevent the development of a native industry, and will only benefit the industries of more advanced industrial societies that already have the full advantages of industry. To List it was no wonder that Britain fostered free trade, since it was Britain that disproportionately gained from it. For the industrialising nation protectionism would result in some losses of wealth due to the constriction of access to cheaper goods, but this was a reasonable price to pay for future gains in both prosperity and social development.[34] Thus, List was not an advocate of blanket protectionism. Rather he saw different policies being appropriate for different phases of development. What differentiated him from mercantilists was that mercantilism was based on the idea of competition between states over wealth, whereas List believed that there was mutual benefit to be had in exchange between nations, but that the processes of industrialisation, and the reality of the nation state in that process, made targeted protection necessary for economic development and the wider growth of civilisation.[35]

List's political economy was written as a response to what he termed the 'cosmopolitical' or 'popular' school of political economy that he interpreted as being associated with such writers as Adam Smith and Say. His criticism of this tradition (although, of course, he actually misrepresents Smith here) was based around what he saw as three key failures:

1   Their 'boundless cosmopolitanism'.
2   Their extreme materialism.
3   Their 'disorganising' particularism and individualism.[36]

Turning to the first of these, List reasoned that the argument of the free traders of the cosmopolitan school was rooted in a fundamental leap of faith: full free trade presupposed that the nation state did not exist, and that we already lived in a 'world republic'. While List thought that a universal confederation and a regime of global perpetual peace was 'commended by both common sense and religion', he was equally at pains to point out that we need to structure policy around the reality of the existence of nations and national states. Yet, nation states were not just a reality, but also a product of the particular level of economic development found during industrialisation.[37] As a result, they could not just be wished away. It is important to add, though, that List's definition of a nation seems to refer to larger states only. The Netherlands, still an important colonial power, is described by List as 'the mere fragment of a nation',[38] and the references to his homeland are to Germany, rather than to specific states within the then German Confederation. Germany was yet to be unified when List wrote his major works. Thus, for List the nation and nation state is one of the larger great powers, and not the myriad of smaller powers that can never be more than fragments of a potentially greater whole.[39]

This leads to List's second criticism: that the cosmopolitical school, by relying too heavily on materialist arguments, had missed the importance of other non-material factors in the development of an industrial society. For List there were other less tangible factors at play that led to development, and in turn industrialisation had positive knock-on effects on the course of civilisation. At one level, the industrial division of labour that had been so admired by Smith in his example of the pin-making industry, made necessary a level of coordination between these different parts of the production process. At the national level only the state was capable of providing this level of unity. At the same time, the ground for industrialisation and economic development required a move from the physical force associated with agrarian societies, towards the mental and moral force that dominates industrial society. In order to accomplish this there was a need for the state to promote education in both skills and morals applicable to the new realities. In short, in addition to the physical producers society needed mental producers that created the moral conditions that favoured material producers.[40] There was also a feedback loop here. For List the development of an industrial society also unleashed non-material forces that enhanced and promoted civilisation, education in the natural sciences and a more liberal world. In List's words: 'Industry is the mother and father of science, literature, the arts, enlightenment, power and independence.'[41] Industrialisation, thus, is not merely the means towards greater wealth, it is also the basis upon which civilisation develops to a new higher level.

This, in turn, leads to the third criticism, that the cosmopolitical school adopts an individualism that makes it blind to the social factors in labour, especially the important role played by stability and national unity in industrial development. Private industry, rather than developing and flourishing on its own, is dependent on the united efforts of others in areas such as education, infrastructure social stability and law enforcement. 'The unity of the nation forms the fundamental condition of lasting national prosperity.' It was only where the interests of the individual had been subordinated to the will of the nation that 'the nations have been brought to harmonious development of their productive powers'. Or, to put it another way, the state does what individuals are unable to do, and it is for these reasons that the state is justified in regulating and restricting commerce in order that longer-term goals are not sacrificed for short-term individual gains.[42]

Of course, List can be accused of misrepresenting his opponents. Adam Smith, as we have seen, was no stranger to questions of the role of the state, and he certainly also advocated both a role for the state in the provision of security, education and infrastructure, and also saw the individual choices of manufacturers and producers being at odds with society's longer-term interests.[43] Yet, that said, List was criticising a particular mind-set during his time, which was not above using Smith's ideas to say things Smith would not have said. From this criticism of the cosmopolitical school List laid out an approach to the state and industrialisation that was compatible with both the development of new nationalist ideologies and with the growth of the industrialised and imperialist state during the middle of the century. For, underlying List's pronouncements about commercial policy and the nature of civilisation was a view of the state as both a member of a wider society of states, and as a representative of the steady western imperial conquest of the globe.

Like all of the thinkers we have dealt with so far, List's international thought is a product of his much more developed domestic political thought. That said, his approach to the international was not merely an afterthought, but represented an important support for his wider ideas about the nature of political economy, as befits a world traveller who understood that there were major continental and global ramifications to industrialisation. It also fit into his wider stages of development schema. Although he advocated a stronger emphasis on the nation state, he accepted the idea that a 'universal confederation' and perpetual peace were long-term goals for humanity, while the dominance of the nation state was a stage through which civilisation must pass.[44] In the short term industrial and industrialising nations were in competition, and he does at least once make a favourable reference to the balance of power.[45] At this stage List's analysis of the state is concerned with the link between the wealth and the power of the state.[46] That said, internationally List was a supporter of a concert or a permanent congress between the nations of the world. The world that he saw when he wrote was dominated by one industrial power, Britain, which used free trade to slow the development of its continental rivals. The goal of a more protectionist policy was to allow the rise of these continental powers (alongside the United States) to a position of equality with Britain. Not only would this be in the interest of the other powers – bringing them out from under Britain's domination – but it would also be good for Britain in the long term, since fully developed societies in partnership with Britain would be far better trading partners than they are now.[47] Out of this could come a system of commercial treaties between equals that would bring nations closer together, while increasing their material prosperity.[48] At this stage national interest would give way to a higher rational and cosmopolitan interest:

> The highest ultimate aim of rational politics is … the uniting of all nations under a common law of right, an object which is only to be attained through the greatest possible equalisation of the most important nations of the earth in civilisation, prosperity, industry and power, by the conversion of the antipathies and conflicts that now exist between them into sympathy and harmony.[49]

List based his faith on the development of this sympathy and harmony on his view of the effects of different social systems, and on their natural progress through stages. Agrarian societies were based on brute force, but industrial societies opened up the domination of moral and mental force. Thus the spread of industrialisation would have the effect of minimising physical force, and replacing it with more rational, scientific and peaceful forms of force and social interaction. Thus, in a development not wholly dissimilar to the social dynamics found in Marx, List envisioned the full implementation of national industrial policies being the ultimate transcendence of the competition between nation states. For this reason List was able to present himself as both a cosmopolitan and a nationalist. The latter would finally lead to the former, bringing us to another stage of human development.

Yet, despite these superficial similarities with Marx, Marx himself savaged List as a representative of a particular kind of German bourgeois writer on industrial matters. For Marx, List's protection of national industries amounted to the protection of national capital, and that protectionist policies actually worked against handicraft industries. Making national capital stronger and foreign capital weaker did not help the cause of the worker, and at best preserved the social order as it was. In sum, List was, in Marx's view, ignorant of the importance of class divisions in national economies and the wider class relationship found in industrial societies.[50] That said, List's ideas found fertile ground among many socialists on the European continent, especially back in France, where the first draft of his *magnum opus* had been written.

List's views on the nature of the international under industrial society were shared by other continental European writers of the time, most notably Constantin Pecqueur. Pecqueur, an influential French socialist economist and internationalist, was writing during List's period of residence in France. Three of Pecqueur's best known books were published in 1842, the year after List's *National System*, while his *Intérêt du commerce et de l'industrie* came out the year before List submitted his *Natural System* to the Paris-based Academy of Moral and Political Sciences competition in 1837. Like List, Pecqueur argued that inventions and industrial developments had the effect of bringing forth intellectual changes.[51] One of these was the possibility of the creation of a congress or confederation of states that would lead to world peace and the establishment of customs unions. Before this was possible, however, Pecqueur believed that all nations would have to reach the same level of development, and that some protectionism might be needed to create this condition.[52] Both List and Pecqueur were Paris-based journalists in the late 1830s and early 1840s (List between 1837 and 1843), and while Pecqueur was arguably the better known before 1841, List's reputation rapidly grew after that. It is not beyond the bounds of possibility that they either influenced each other, or were both influenced by the intellectual climate in Paris that included ideas on industrial society and its relationship to social order that had emerged from the writings of Saint-Simon and Charles Fourier. This commonality between List and the French socialist writers of the time is often overlooked in discussions of the influences on List.[53]

Parallel to this competition and harmonisation of interests between the western powers lays another set of international interactions for List: the relations between the western nations on the one hand, and the non-western world on the other. List's view of the non-western world was of a world that was living in an earlier stage of development. Indeed, it was in the interests of all that barbarous nations should be civilised by western ones, and Britain had done a great service to humanity (List believed) by bringing the tropics and their 'barbarous races' into cultivation.[54] The reasons for western colonial control were not altruistic. The development of industry for List led to a lucrative world trade in which the industrialised state provided the industrial goods needed by a backward agrarian society for its development. At the same time only an industrialised state had the power to establish colonies and link them in a complex system of imperial trade.[55] So far List's argument seems to follow a 'white man's burden' argument, in which the non-western 'barbarous' world is brought to social development through the actions of westerners following their own economic self-interest. Yet, there is a limit to how far List is willing to go down this road. Climate, he says, also plays a role in economic development, and it is in 'the temperate zone' where soil and climate are 'most conducive to bodily and mental exertion' that manufacturing industry is always most likely to be found.[56] Alongside climate, though, the issue of racial difference also crops up. In his discussion of Asia, for example, List sees no hope for industrial development without the introduction of Christianity, European moral laws, government and also European immigration to the region. Such was the 'dissolution' of the Asian nationalities that they would not be able to accomplish industrial change on their own.[57] The only let-up that List sees in the march of European colonialism is in the effects wrought by the emancipation of the Spanish and Portuguese empires. This now presented the possibility that trade with the tropics might be able to occur without direct western control and colonisation.[58]

At the end of the day, though, List's congress of peaceful industrial powers is restricted to western, and largely European, powers. This same bifurcated international realm (a system of competing equals with common interests among western powers running parallel to a system of western imperial control over the non-western) would be a common feature in much of early IR, and was to be particularly blatant in the international theory of Alfred Thayer Mahan.[59] Indeed, List's idea that the development of maritime trade would lead first to blue water navies and then naturally to colonial acquisition was an earlier version of a similar argument that was fleshed out in the later part of the century by both Mahan and Friedrich Ratzel. List's ideas of political economy, therefore, also provided the basis for the development of geopolitics and geopolitical understandings of international affairs. This geo-political and geo-strategic element to List can be found most clearly in his discussions of how the railways would make Germany strategically important, thus altering the balance of power in Europe.[60] Here he seems to also have some affinities with Mackinder's 1904 pivot of history idea, which is discussed in the next chapter. Thus, despite his avowed longer-term cosmopolitanism, there is an extent to which List is (at least partially) an early proponent of a nationalist, and at times racial, geopolitics.

# War and society in an industrial age:
# Pierre-Joseph Proudhon

List's statist political economy stands in sharp contrast to the anarchist political economy of List's French contemporary Pierre-Joseph Proudhon. Although best known in the English-speaking world for his work on cooperatives and property rights, Proudhon was one of the few writers in the middle nineteenth century to directly consider the problem of international affairs, and his yet untranslated masterpiece on war and peace was a great influence on French-language debates on the role of war. Proudhon is little known in IR circles. The major exception to this is Alex Prichard's 2007 analysis of Proudhon's international theory.[61] To a certain extent Proudhon's absence from IR should not surprise us. Much of Proudhon's work, and especially the writings directly relevant to international affairs, have not been translated into English, and since IR is fundamentally an Anglophone discipline this goes much of the way to explaining Proudhon's absence in the IR canon. However, Proudhon is not totally absent from IR. The French IR theorist, Raymond Aron, was influenced by Proudhon, and E.H. Carr, who is recognised as both an IR theorist and as a historian, was deeply critical of Proudhon, while Proudhon was at least known to Hans J. Morgenthau. Arguably, though, Proudhon's biggest influence on IR came through David Mitrany. Mitrany made good use of Proudhon's political economy and concept of federation in the construction of his own international theory, and while direct quotations to Proudhon are few and far between in Mitrany's published work, his debt to Proudhon is clear and unequivocal. Before going on to look in more detail at Proudhon's arguments in *La guerre et la paix* I want to highlight those ideas of Proudhon's that Mitrany took and used. This boils down to two of Proudhon's ideas, both of which figure prominently in Mitrany's later work. These are his concept of the 'economic organism' and his view of the value of ownership and tenancy.

In 1851 Proudhon affirmed that it 'is industrial organisation that we will put in place of government'.[62] The development of economic organisation is seen as the movement that will undermine the need for exclusive territorial governments, and make possible the end of foreign relations between peoples.[63] Central to Proudhon's analysis of the state (and contrary to List's argument) was the view of the state as parasitic on economic activity, and therefore as draining on the productive members of society as well as on capitalists. Rather, Proudhon argued, political organisation should flow from democratically organised economic organisations such as industrial collectives, which form an organic web of federations.[64] On the face of it this appears to have more to do with domestic politics than international. Yet Proudhon's concept of federation is based on an appreciation of the importance of the international, rather than the Mazzinian assumption that the international will follow where the national leads. Rather, as Prichard has demonstrated, Proudhon was well aware of the importance of an international order in preserving the peace of Europe and the world, as his defence of the 1815 peace of Vienna against an attack by Louis Napoleon demonstrates.[65]   Proudhon   recognised   an   international   problem   (the destructiveness and arbitrariness of war) that could be solved by a political organisation based upon organic social and economic relations. Proudhon, living before the onset of mass globalisation at the end of the nineteenth century sees his economic organisations as rooted in the local, rather than being part of a globalised web of interactions.

In *Marx Against the Peasant* Mitrany singled out Proudhon as one of the few socialists who understood the link between the peasantry and ownership of the land.[66] Proudhon's support for private land ownership consisted of two parts. The first was his acceptance of the emotional attachment that labourers in general, and peasants in particular, had for the individual ownership of their possessions and land: 'the more ground the principles of democracy have gained, the more I have seen the working classes, both in the city and the country, interpret these principles favourably to individual ownership'.[67] Land ownership had value to the peasants in a way that was fundamentally different to the ownership of the land by landlords because the peasant related to the land directly through their labour. In addition to this emotive and non-rational reason for retaining private land ownership, Proudhon also had a progressivist and rational reason for favouring private land ownership: full collectivisation of the land would leave peasant farmers in a position little different from that under landlordism. Under landlordism the peasant cannot change their status, but is tied to the land through necessity and the need to pay high rents to a distant owner. Under collectivisation the authorities give 'a longer lease and a lower rent', but 'my condition is incapable of change; here I am fixed for life and for the life of my children, attached to the soil', because the peasant is unable to accumulate wealth through farming, and unable to use it to provide annuities in old age.[68] What prevents the ownership of land becoming little different from capitalist ownership is the emotional bond. Mitrany was to develop this idea further through his own analysis of the peasant social revolution, but he was well aware that the core of this idea had been laid down by Proudhon a century before.[69] Ideas of peasant land tenure formed the basis of a political economic system that was neither capitalist nor collectivist in its structure. This was the basis of Proudhon's concept of Mutualism, for which private possession could function as a revolutionary force in conflict with the 'absolute right of the State'.[70]

Thus Proudhon's political theory lays out two principles for the future development of human society. First, the development of economic organisation places the state at odds with the unfolding evolution of human society, and makes possible the spontaneous federation of humanity from the bottom up. Second, the idea of private ownership set within a communitarian social structure forms the basis of a political economy that is in opposition to both capitalism and collectivism, while being more in line with the desires of working people, both rural and urban, for sovereignty over their lives. Both of these principles were to underpin the mid-twentieth century international theory of Mitrany, and fed directly into his functional approach to international organisation.

Yet, it was another work by Proudhon that would have a more direct and sustained influence on Francophone analyses of international affairs. *La Guerre et la Paix*, published in two volumes in 1861, was to influence French thought on war throughout the nineteenth century, and was still being quoted by Raymond Aron in the mid-twentieth century.[71] Proudhon's analysis of war took a very different view from the Anglophone anarchists of the early twentieth century, and this might partially explain why *La Guerre et la Paix* has not found a translator. Whereas the American anarchist Randolph Bourne could write in 1918 that 'war is the health of the state',[72] for Proudhon war served an important revolutionary role due to its place in the development of human society. While for later writers like Bourne (a position later taken up by people like Norman Angell) might was the opposite of right, for Proudhon force was an aspect of justice: the law of force. It was on the right of force that all social structures were ultimately based, and revolutionary change was always made possible by the use of force against the current social structure of society.[73] Proudhon makes his case for the justice of war by reference to the spirituality of conflict, and the role of war in creating culture.[74] What this boiled down to was that for Proudhon force allowed new orders to emerge, and thus was a guard against the atrophying of society.[75]

Because of his rather blunt and brutal support for the idea of war, Proudhon was denounced by many later writers as an apologist for war. Quincy Wright lumped Proudhon with other 'radical champions of the oppressed masses and … reactionary entrepreneurs' who opposed limits to violence. While E.H. Carr saw Proudhon's work as (to use Alex Prichard's words) 'a "panegyric" to war and the deranged ranting of a French "chauvinist"'.[76] Yet, the argument contained in volume I of *La Guerre et la Paix* was only part of Proudhon's take on war. Although Proudhon 'paid tribute to the warrior spirit', the second part of his argument 'acknowledged that heroism must now give way to industry … we walk into an era of perpetual peace'.[77] Like List, Proudhon sees modern industrial society as qualitatively different to earlier agrarian societies. The new technologies of war (artillery, rifling, the revolver and other innovations) had turned modern war into a horrific slaughter, and the revolutionary quality of war was now superseded by the technological and capital needs of war. As a result, war no longer had a moral quality because it was no longer a means towards the end of justice. So, having made the case for war, Proudhon then argues that industrialisation has now made this case redundant.[78] Thus, in the end, Proudhon also shares the view that nineteenth century economic development has altered the basic nature of human society.

## Conclusion: understanding the new society and its international consequences

All of the writers discussed in this chapter are attempting to understand the profound changes linked to the development of a commercial and industrial society. All are concerned with how these rapid changes are altering the relations between states and the role of war in those relations. Cobden and Bright are the most pacifist, although both List and Proudhon see a lessening of the role of war in the future. The main difference here, though, is that List can accept war as part of the balance of power during the current stage of development, while Proudhon sees violence as a means of changing the status quo, and therefore potentially a force for justice and change. Cobden and Bright, on the other hand, see war between commercial societies as counter-productive and ultimately pointless. All see different roles for the state in this new world. List sees an increasingly interventionist state using trade policy as a means to promote national industry. Cobden, Bright and Proudhon are all critical, although in the end Cobden and Bright accept a 'nightwatchman' state that does not interfere with economic policy as a necessity, while Proudhon ultimately rejects the state as just another form of oppression. All see the future of the international system in different ways. For Cobden and Bright it will be a world of limited states in a world dominated by global free trade, for List, a confederation of industrial nations, and for Proudhon a non-state federation of industrial organisations. At the end of the day, though, these insights and views are all products of a common realisation among all four that the world is rapidly changing, and that the old certainties of an agrarian and aristocratic-dominated society now no longer apply. Like Marx, they all recognise a different epoch means having to deal with different rules and different phenomena in order to understand the twists and turns of human civilisation. Searching the vast pool of experience in the works of the ancients is no longer an option. There is a need for a new science of political economy.

It is true to say that the study of the international in all four authors is still merely an extension of their domestic political theory, and also that in many respects these writers are still trying to understand the new forces being unleashed by industrialisation. This is a concern they all share with Marx, although obviously they all take a different approach from both Marx and from each other. Of the four, only Proudhon shares Marx's view that the working class is now a new emerging force in western society (although Proudhon's inclusion of peasants differentiates him from Marx), and only List half-heartedly deals with the 'external proletariat' of the non-western world. Yet, at the same time there are clear views on the international in all four that would influence discussions of the international over the next century. Certainly, Cobden and Bright were a central part of future discussions among liberals and socialists over the necessary conditions for a liberal global order, and the ghost of their ideas still hang over current debates on free trade, globalisation and the relationship between commercial freedom and the state. List's view on the place of a national political economy in a wider European-dominated world of states influenced the development of geopolitics, as well as those critical of the idea of a free trade order. List demonstrated the links between the advocacy of free trade and global economic power. Proudhon's ideas informed David Mitrany's mid-twentieth century attempt to find a middle way between Cobden's laissez-faire free trade and List's statist national political economy. In addition to this Proudhon helped inform the study of war, particularly within France. There were two levels to this. The first was the idea that force was necessary to oppose the status quo. It was in an attempt to find a way around this conundrum that force was necessary to change that early twentieth century international experts (especially E.H. Carr and Charles Manning) attempted to develop ideas of peaceful change. This was also a concern of Leonard Woolf, who saw legal answers to international questions as fundamentally conservative. In the second Proudhon had emphasised the social utility of war, and particularly its link to justice. His arguments were to find their way into the discussion of IR in the 1950s and 1960s via the works of Raymond Aron. Proudhon's praise of war, it must be said, harkens back to an agrarian past. It is certainly harder for people, living the other side of the bloody first half of the twentieth century to sympathise with Proudhon's approach. This points to another reason for the sudden growth of interest in the international in the years that followed: the wars of this new industrial civilisation were redder, more destructive and increasingly less glamorous than before. While this is part of Proudhon's argument, it still makes the first half of his study of war difficult to swallow today.

By the late nineteenth century, with industrialisation, globalisation and imperialism in full swing authors began to turn to the international as an important and unique sphere of human interaction. Their concerns about the relations between states, and especially war and imperialism, drew on the ideas and experiences of the emergence of the state since the sixteenth century, and many consciously drew on the works of these early modern and Enlightenment authors. That said, though, it was the dramatic changes to western society, and by extension western society's relationships with the non-western world, that made the need to understand relations between humans at an international level an imperative. Trade had become a necessity, not a luxury, war was increasingly about economic management and technological innovation, and imperial control was gradually more about markets and raw materials, not glory and agricultural colonies. We now pass from the precursors to international thought that have been the subject of these three chapters to the last century and a half in which a recognisable study of international relations and global politics emerges. This study of international relations – IR – is predominantly a western phenomenon, and increasingly it is also the concern of an English-speaking world that dominates the rest of the globe. Two Anglophone world powers dominate this period: first Britain and then the United States. Both produce a flurry of scholars who attempt to understand the world around them, but also often set out to justify the actions of their societies on the world stage.

## Notes

1 Auguste Comte, *System of Positive Policy* (London: Longmans Green, 1877).
2 Editorial in *The Times*, Thursday 1 May 1851.
3 For a full discussion of the effects of the Great Exhibition see Michael Leapman, *The World for a Shilling* (London: Headline, 2002).
4 Lynn White Jr, *Medieval Technology and Social Change* (Oxford: Oxford University Press, 1962), v.
5 Benjamin de Carvalho, Halvard Leira and John Hobson, 'The Big Bangs of IR: The Myths That Your Teachers Still Tell You about 1648 and 1919', *Millennium*, 2011, 39(3), 735–58.

6  See the discussion in John Darwin, *After Tamerlaine. The Rise and Fall of Global Empires, 1400–2000* (Harmondsworth: Penguin, 2007), especially ch. 5.

7  For an analysis of the role of coal see Timothy Mitchell, *Carbon Democracy. Political Power in the Age of Oil* (London: Verso, 2011), ch. 1.

8  Mitchell, *Carbon Democracy*, 16–17.

9  George Modelski, 'Agraria and Industria. Two Models of the International System', *World Politics*, 1961, 14(1), 118–143.

10  David Boucher, *Political Theories of International Relations. From Thucydides to the Present* (Oxford: Oxford University Press, 1998), 362.

11  Karl Marx and Friedrich Engels, 'Manifesto of the Communist Party', in *Marx/ Engels Selected Works*, Volume 1 (Moscow: Progress Press, 1969), 16–17.

12  'Communist Manifesto', 16.

13  For a discussion of Marx's changing views on imperialism and the development of the non-Western world see Kevin B. Anderson, *Marx at the Margins* (Chicago: University of Chicago Press, 2010), especially the summary on 241–2.

14  Victor Davis Hanson, *The Western Way of War. Infantry Battle in Classical Greece* (Oxford: Oxford University Press, 1990), 3–6.

15  For an account of the economic decline of the Western Empire in the fifth century see Bryan Ward-Perkins, *The Fall of Rome and the End of Civilization* (Oxford: Oxford University Press, 2006), especially Part Two.

16  See John Bright, 'Speech in Edinburgh, 13 October 1853', in *Selected Speechs of the Right Honourable John Bright MP on Public Questions* (London: J.M. Dent, 1907), 229.

17  Richard Cobden, 'Speech at Wrexham, 14 November 1850', in *Speeches on Questions of Public Policy by Richard Cobden MP* (London: Macmillan, 1903), 510.

18  James Mill quoted in Michael Howard, *War and the Liberal Conscience* (New Brunswick, NJ: Rutgers Univerity Press, 1978), 37; Paul Leroy Beaulieu, *Contemporary Wars (1853–1866). Statistical Researches Respecting the Loss of Men and Money Involved in Them* (London: Peace Society, 1869).

19  Jeremy Bentham, 'Principles of International Law [1789–90]', in *The Works of Jeremy Bentham* (New York: Russell and Russell, 1962), 557.

20  John Bright 'Speech in Edinburgh, 13 October 1853', in *Selected Speeches*, 230–1.

21  Cobden, 'Speech in London, 28 September 1843', in *Speeches*, 40.

22  Richard Cobden, quoted in Donald Read, *Cobden and Bright. A Victorian Political Partnership* (London: Edward Arnold, 1967), 110. Emphasis in the original.

23  Cobden's letter to Henry Ashworth, 12 April 1842, reprinted in John Morley, *The Life of Richard Cobden*, Volume I (London: Macmillan, 1908), 248. See also Read, *Cobden and Bright*, 113.

24  Cobden, 'Speech at Wrexham, 14 November 1850' in *Speeches*, 518. See also: Cobden, 'Speech in the House of Commons, 26 February 1857' in *Speeches*, 518.

25  See, for example, W.E. Gladstone, *The Turco-Servian War. Bulgarian Horrors and the Question of the East* (New York: Lovell Adam and Wesson, 1876), 31.

26  John Bright, 'Speech at Birmingham, 29 October 1858', in *Selected Speeches*, 204.

27  Letter from Richard Cobden to Mr Richard, 29 September 1852, reprinted in J.A. Hobson, *Richard Cobden. The International Man* (Toronto: Dent, 1918), 90.

28  Read, *Cobden and Bright*, 115–16.

29  Karl Marx, 'On the Question of Free Trade' in *Marx/Engels Collected Works*, Volume 6 (London: Lawrence and Wishart, 1976), 465.

30  Marx, 'Question of Free Trade', 450–65.

31  Karl Marx, 'Capital Punishment – Mr Cobden's Pamphlet – Regulations of the Bank of England', *New York Daily Tribune*, February 17–18 1853.

32  Norman Angell, *The Great Illusion. A Study of the Relation of Military Power in Nations to their Economic and Social Advantage.* (Toronto: McClelland and Goodchild, 1911); Hobson, *Richard Cobden*.

33  Friedrich List, *The Natural System of Political Economy 1837* (London: Frank Cass, 1983), chs 9–11; Friedrich List, *The National System of Political Economy* (New York: Augustus Kelly, 1966), 177–8. The former work, written as an entry in a competition for the Paris-based Academy of Moral and Political Sciences in 1837, remained unpublished until 1929. The latter work is the one published in 1841, and upon which List's reputation was built. The argument of the former was developed, for a different audience, in the latter.

34  List, *Natural System*, 75 ff, 123, ch. 6; List, *National System*, xxviii, 130 ff, 144, 177–8.

35  List, *Natural System*, 189.

36  List, *National System*, 174.

37  List, *Natural System*, 29–30, 190; List, *National System*, xxvi, xxix, 123, ch. XI.

38  List, *National System*, 408.

39  For a discussion of List's view on 'territorial deficiencies' see W.O. Henderson, *Friedrich List: Economist and Visionary 1789–1846* (London: Frank Cass, 1983), 179–80.

40  List, *National System*, 149–51, 159.

41  List, *Natural System*, 66.

42  List, *National System*, 163, 167–8.

43  For this side of Smith see Andrew Wyatt-Walter, 'Adam Smith and the Liberal Tradition in International Relations', *Review of International Studies*, 1996, 22(1), 5–28.

44  List, *National System*, 123; List, *Natural System*, 190.

45  List, *National System*, 412.

46  For an analysis of List that concentrates on this link between wealth and power see Edward Mead Earle, 'Adam Smith, Alexander Hamilton, Friedrich List: The Economic Foundations of Military Power', in Edward Mead Earle, *Makers of Modern Strategy. Military Thought from Machiavelli to Hitler* (New York: Atheneum, 1967), especially 142.

47  See List, *National System*, ch. XXXV; List, *Natural System*, 50–1.

48  List, *Natural System*, 126.

49  List, *National System*, 410.

50  Karl Marx, 'The Protectionists, the Free Traders and the Working Class [1848]' in *Marx/Engels Collected Works*, Volume 6 (London: Lawrence and Wishart, 1976), 279.

51  Constantin Pecqueur, *Economie sociale. Des Intérêts du Commerce, de l'Industrie et de l'Agriculture, et de la Civilisation en général, sous l'Influence des Applications de la Vapeur. Machines Fixes, Chemins de Fer, Bateaux à Vapeur* (Paris: Desessart, 1839).

52  A summary of Pecqueur's international thought can be found in Jacques Fontanel, Liliane Bensahel, Steven Coissard and Yann Echinard, 'French Utopian Economists of the Nineteenth Century', *Defence and Peace Economics*, 2008, 19(5), 339–350. His major works on this subject were *De la Paix, de son Principe et de sa Réalisation* (Paris: Capelle, 1842); and *Des Armées dan Leurs Rapports avec l'Industrie, la Morale et la Liberté* (Paris: Capelle, 1842).

53  Karl Marx certainly saw List as borrowing phrases from (French) socialism in order to support a specific German bourgeois position. See Karl Marx, 'Draft of an Article on Friedrich List's book: *Das Nationale System der Politischen Oekonomie*' in Karl Marx and Friedrich Engels, *Marx/Engels Collective Works Volume 4* (Moscow: Progress Press, 1975), 265 ff.

54  List, *Natural System*, 125, 366.

55  List, *Natural System*, 69–70.

56  List, *National System*, 161–2.

57  List, *National System*, 419.

58  List, *National System*, 416.
59  For a wider analysis of this underlying Eurocentrism see John M. Hobson, *The Eurocentric Conception of World Politics. Western International Theory, 1760–2010* (Cambridge: Cambridge University Press, 2012). List is mentioned by Hobson as a rare example of a Eurocentric institutionalism that brought in climate as an explanation for the failure of non-western societies to take up superior western institutions (see page 5).
60  Earle, 'Smith, Hamilton, List', 148–9.
61  Alex Prichard, 'Justice, Order and Anarchy: The International Political Theory of Pierre-Joseph Proudhon (1809–1865)', *Millennium: Journal of International Studies*, 2007, 35 (3), 623–45.
62  Pierre-Joseph Proudhon, *General Idea of the Revolution in the Nineteenth Century* (London: Pluto, 1989), 245.
63  Proudhon, *General Idea*, 280–2.
64  See the argument in Pierre-Joseph Proudhon, *The Principle of Federation and the Need to Reconstitute the Party of Revolution* (Toronto: University of Toronto Press, 1979).
65  Prichard, 'Justice, Order and Anarchy', 639.
66  David Mitrany, *Marx Against the Peasant. A Study in Social Dogmatism* (London: Wiedenfeld and Nicolson, 1951).
67  Proudhon, *General Idea of the Revolution*, 210.
68  Proudhon, *General Idea of the Revolution*, 213.
69  David Mitrany, *The Land and the Peasant in Rumania* (Yale: Yale University Press, 1930), xxvi–xxvii.
70  H. de Lubac, *Un-Marxian Socialist: A Study of Proudhon* (London: Sheed and Ward, 1948), 177.
71  See Raymond Aron, *Peace and War. A Theory of International Relations* (New York: Doubleday, 1966), 3–5 for Aron's discussion of Proudhon's conception of the use of force.
72  Randolph Bourne, *The State* (Tucson: Sharp, 1998), 9.
73  Pierre-Joseph Proudhon, *La Guerre et la Paix: Recherches sur le Principe et la Constitution Du Droit Des Gens* (Paris: E. Dentu, 1861), especially the summaries in the prologue and chapter XI of volume I.
74  Proudhon, *La Guerre et la Paix*, especially chapters I and II of volume I.
75  Prichard, 'Justice, Order and Anarchy', 634.
76  Quincy Wright, *A Study of War*, volume II (Chicago: Chicago University Press, 1942) 1215; E.H. Carr, 'Proudhon: The Robinson Crusoe of Socialism' in E.H. Carr, *Studies in Revolution* (London: Macmillan, 1950), 38–55; Prichard, 'Justice, Order and Anarchy', 626.
77  Proudhon, *La Guerre et la Paix*, Preface of volume I.
78  For the best summation of this argument in Proudhon see Prichard, 'Justice, Order and Anarchy', 636–7.

# Part II

# The emergence of the discipline of International Relations and the great crisis of humanity

# 5 The geopolitics of empire and the international anarchy, 1880–1918

*While it is common to trace the origins of International Relations (IR) back to 1919, after the First World War IR was in fact heavily influenced by the developments in international thought in the late nineteenth and early twentieth centuries. This is not to say that the First World War did not have an effect on the development of IR. Quite the contrary, the war years were responsible for popularising many pre-war ideas, while many of these ideas were adapted to fit the studies of the new realities of IR, including the League of Nations.*

*There were two major themes in the study of the international between the 1880s and 1918. These were:*

1 *That the system of states is a reality that is here to stay, and that our policy needs to recognise this if it is to succeed. Approaches in this theme included a geopolitical analysis that often saw the state as analogous to a living organism in conflict with other organisms; and a historical and legal view that saw the problems of the international being one of imperial control and growth.*
2 *That the growing interdependence of states was making the old realities of a state-based diplomacy obsolete. This trend tended to stress war between states as a growing problem, and the solution being a reform of the international system of states.*

*These two trends, stressing the dynamics of imperialism and the problem of war in a transnational world, formed the basis out of which the twentieth century study of IR would emerge.*

*In addition to these trends, we can also see three methods being used to understand the international at this time. These were:*

1 *An idea of states competing in an evolutionary struggle (although the way that evolution was used is closer to the work of Lamarck than it is of Darwin).*

2    *A Hegelian view of the state as embodying the 'spirit' of its people, and therefore being a natural entity.*
3    *A view of science as offering options, rather than one best way, and government machinery, whether domestic and international, as merely convenient machines to be used or discarded as necessary.*

*These broad themes and methods give us a convenient way to classify the thought of the time, but we have to be aware that writers often changed their approaches during this time, and it was not uncommon to find writers move from one to the other. Thus Paul Reinsch wrote works that fit within both of the themes mentioned above.*

Where we choose to place the origins of IR reflects both our view of the field, as well as simultaneously disciplining the field by imposing borders upon it. Chapters 6 and 8 will deal, in part and in passing, with the question of the 1919 and 1945 origins of IR. There is, though, yet another series of dates that we could choose, and it is one that has found favour with some historians of international thought. To a large extent what we now know as the study of IR has its origins in the late nineteenth century, and in the decade before the First World War.[1] Many of the categories and ideas that were to play themselves out in debates after 1919 were products of the late Victorian and Edwardian worlds that predated the First World War. This is not to suggest that the two world wars were not major influences on the shape and direction that international thought took, but rather that the intellectual tools and concepts that were taken up in debates over the shape of international organisations and the post-war orders were ones that had been forged in earlier debates over the nature of the state and political power. The intellectual and popular debates that emerged to explain the emerging national state, the new imperialism of the great powers and the rapid changes wrought by industrialisation and economic interdependence produced modes of thought and cognitive short-cuts that framed the international debate long after the world that had formed them had faded from view. As a result, the political thought that emerged from the 1880s onwards is a vital part of the story of international thought in the century that was to follow.

There are two broad themes that emerge here. The first one is a product of the question of the nature of the state, and the extent to which the state has an imperial imperative that is analogous to the biological organism's imperative to grow. Included in this were early attempts to construct a state-centric vision of international politics, and analyses of the role of imperialism. There were two distinct branches to this first theme: one relied heavily on a geopolitical framework that saw the conflict of states in terms of an organic analogy, while the other took a more historic and international law point of view that stressed the long-term trends that had gone into creating the system of state competition and global empires. The second theme was the series of arguments around the idea that the development of a transnational economy had made the political realities of the old diplomatic order obsolete. In many respects these two themes contradicted each other – one focused on the nature of the state, the other on the forces that were transcending state power – but they also interacted and created a series of different approaches to the international. Current IR scholars might be tempted to see in this a manifestation of the realist–idealist myth, but this would be a mistake. Notions of state centrism did not necessarily imply a modern realist conception of power and interests, while politico-economic arguments about the superseding of the state were often contained within arguments about the nature of world order that would be more familiar to contemporary realists. What provided a much cleaner contrast between these two themes was the question of whether the study of the international was fundamentally a question of imperial policy and colonial management, or whether by contrast international thought should be directed to the broader question of the nature and reform of the international system itself. Between these two also hangs the question of whether the origins of IR should be found in the imperialistic policies and justifications of the major powers before the First World War, or whether IR has a more benign origin located in the study of the problem of war.[2] The answer from this chapter is that both are right. The seeds of modern twentieth century IR can be found both in analyses of the problems of empire, and in concerns about the international anarchy and the destabilising effects of war. The first theme will be explored in more depth in two sections below (one dedicated to geopolitics and one to more historical, legal and philosophical ideas of the state), the second theme will be covered in the penultimate section.

Before looking at these themes, however, it is useful to place them within the broader context of the scientific trends of the late nineteenth century, with particular reference to the expansion in the study of political phenomena using the tools forged in the physical and life sciences. The emergence of various studies of the international in the last decades of the nineteenth century was part of a wider emergence of the social sciences, and cannot be divorced from the attempts to bring scientific rigor to the study of human populations. The debates over the role of science in the study of people also brought in discussions of the use of Hegelian concepts and understandings of the state. Indeed, much of what passed for analyses of the international in Britain before and during the First World War was dominated by an argument about whether the state could be seen as a quasi-spiritual being along lines suggested by Hegel in the early nineteenth century. In which case, the arguments for greater global government would run counter to a natural statist order (see the section on the state and the international below). Much of this also fed off interpretations of evolution and natural selection. Thus, much of the early political geography assumed that states, as quasi-organisms, were locked into a conflict that was seen as resembling Darwin's survival of the fittest. This could take on a distinctly deterministic streak where the evolution of states in competition was presented as an inescapable logic. Although, as Stephen Toulmin has argued, the use of evolution in the social sciences was actually at variance with the ideas of natural selection found in

Darwin. In Darwin's view a species does not possess a specific essence, but rather has a distribution of properties that vary from individual to individual, the mean of which shifts as the species adapts to its environment. As a result, there is no specific unidirectional goal for evolution in which all successful members of a species take on the same characteristics; but rather species are made up of individuals with a range of characteristics, and the spread of these characteristics change as the environment does. Much early social science was, in fact, influenced by an older evolutionary view (associated with the work of Lemark and Herder, and introduced to modern sociology via Herbert Spencer) where evolution is interpreted as the march of a cosmic progress where a set of characteristics are always the most successful, and therefore must be followed deterministically. All other characteristics are therefore seen as substandard, idealistic and dangerous to follow. This is a far cry from Darwin's populations with their multiple characteristics that react to an environment without any clear direction or end point.[3]

In addition to these two themes discussed above, there were also three different theoretical methods being employed by writers at this time. The first is a Lemarkian, and decidedly un-Darwinian, interpretation of evolution that attempts to create a science of the international by understanding what are the characteristics of a successful state or society that will lead it in a clear evolutionary path of success. The second is a Hegelian view of the state that interprets societies as having a spirit or natural essence that both underpins state behaviour and also makes any attempt to move beyond the system of states at the international level problematic. The third represented a rejection of both of these first two positions. It saw science as about opening up possibilities, rather than leading to a one best way, and it saw government (including international government) as merely a piece of machinery, rather than linked to any idea of spirit. To a certain extent these three strands are covered, in turn, in each of the next three sections below. Having said this, though, there are overlaps that make the picture more complex. Individual authors often changed their opinions, a good example of which is Halford Mackinder, whose analysis in 1904 looks decidedly environmentally determinist, but whose work after the war stands as a partial rejection of this position. Also, depending on the audience and the subject matter of the work authors had a tendency to stress a different methodology. Thus, Paul Reinsch's attitude to the state changes significantly between his discussion in his 1900 and 1911 books (see below), although underlying the methodological shift is a change of subject matter rather than a change of heart. We impose simplistic certainties on the theory and methods of past scholars at our peril, and when we do we deny the richness, ironies and variety of their thought.

## A geography of society

It is ironic, yet at the same time understandable, that during a period when industrialisation had remade society so that the certainties of the past no longer seemed relevant that so many in the western world looked to science to discover underlying truths. These truths, it was hoped, would allow us to understand our world in order to better control our lives. One of the most prolific attempts to create a science of state relations emerges in the late nineteenth century out of the new field of political geography. Unlike much social science of the time this international political geography emerged not out of law and history, but rather had its roots in biology and physical geography. That said, it was an approach that found favour with many historians and historically-trained social scientists.

The founding figure of international political geography is Friedrich Ratzel. His writings were influential in intellectual developments in Germany, the United States and Britain, although Ratzel's impact declined dramatically in the last two after the First World War. Ratzel, like so many of the early political geographers, came from zoology via physical geography. His attempts to understand how life interacted with the environment moved on from questions of human interaction with the physical environment, to an analysis of the success and failure of different social systems, and finally to studies of the struggle and interaction between states. Ratzel's writings went down two, not always compatible, channels. As a scientist interested in the interaction of peoples and states with the physical environment, he focused on how different societies were best adapted to different environments (the *Herrenvolk* in a particular region), how successful societies spread with or without the help of the state (*lebensraum*), and finally how changes in technology changed these relationships.[4] In his study of state interaction he slipped in to an analysis of states as organic entities struggling for control of space. Yet, he was enough of a good scientist to know that when describing human societies this could never be anything more than an analogy. The state was not a living being in its own right. A state was composed of individuals that were held together by 'moral and spiritual forces'. Consequently, a state was merely an 'aggregate organism' that behaved differently from proper living organisms.[5] Here Ratzel criticised the tendency to see the science of political geography in maps and cartography. Rather, he argued, social connections were mental processes, and thus could only be 'spiritually conceived and grasped'.[6] Thus, while states struggled over space like organisms, they also had the potential to transcend this struggle, or to accomplish it by incorporation or immigration rather than conquest. This explains Ratzel's interest in the United States and in the global spread of the Chinese outside of a state structure.

Ratzel's work as a scientist ran parallel with his pamphleteering and political campaigning. Influenced by US Admiral A.T. Mahan, he was one of the 'fleet professors' who pushed for the acquisition of a blue-water navy for Germany as a basis of Germany's bid for world power.[7] A supporter of an expanded German overseas empire, Ratzel saw control of possessions in all parts of the world (especially in strategic parts), as the mark of a proper world power.[8] In his agitation for a navy and world empire Ratzel hoped that Germany would copy and emulate the success of the British Empire. This notion of Germany's potential as a world power fed back to concepts that Ratzel had developed as part of his studies in political geography. Raw physical factors alone did not make for a successful world power. The population at large needed a 'space-perception' that took in the geographical realities of the world in order to make expansion possible. At the same time declining space perceptions were linked to the decline of the state.[9] Thus, while the physical world was creating the rules for human interaction, without the perception of those geographical rules a nation would be unable to grow. In many ways Ratzel's ideas were a product of the rapidly industrialising world around him (and also perhaps the equally dramatic great depression of the 1870s and 1880s that had destabilised this new industrial civilisation, and seen Britain lose its industrial lead to the United States and Germany). His world is not one of balance, but of frenetic motion and activity only limited by the rules of space.[10]

When Ratzel talked about German world power he used an organic view of the state – albeit as an analogy rather than as a statement of fact. This concept of the state as an organism following laws of necessity was taken up by one of Ratzel's followers, the Swedish political scientist Rudolf Kjellén. While acknowledging that Ratzel had thought that in its higher forms the state could no longer be seen as like a natural organism, but rather took on a more spiritual-moral form,[11] Kjellén nonetheless accepted the organic analogy for the state with alacrity. In Kjellén's geopolitics the state acts as an individual. 'The state stands in front of us as an organically emerged phenomenon … like a single human being. In one word: the state presents itself as a biological manifestation or life form.'[12] Kjellén's ideas about the organic nature of the state are taken further by the next generation of geopolitics experts in Germany, especially by Karl Haushofer. It is Haushofer and his collaborators who become the foil for Anglo-American international political geography as it developed its own alternative view of international affairs in later decades. This organic analogy fed into an environmentally determinist approach that assumed political actors (acting like organisms) needed to react to the dictates of their environment in order to prosper and avoid extinction. Thus we see the Lemarkian unilinear view of evolution, mentioned above, in full spate here. Ironically, given later developments, it was also the more deterministic elements of Ratzel's thought that were to influence and nurture the early years of this alternative Anglo-American tradition of political geography.

The ideas of Ratzel were brought to the United States by his American student Ellen Churchill Semple. In her 1911 magnum opus Semple claimed to be introducing Ratzel's political geography to an American audience, but in fact her interpretation glossed over Ratzel's distinctions between environmental determinism and agency to produce an approach to political geography that was fundamentally and explicitly environmentally determinist: 'History tends to repeat itself largely owing to this steady, unchanging geographic element.'[13] Semple's stress on the determinist element in Ratzel was part of a wider and earlier trend in American identity construction. Indeed, the idea of nation as organism is found in the early nineteenth century proponents of manifest destiny, while the American imperialism of the 1890s onwards looked to nature for its justifications.[14] In 1893 the historian Friedrich Jackson Turner had used a change in policy at the US Census Bureau to construct an environmentally determinist argument to explain the development of American identity.[15] Although Americans had come from different parts of the world, Turner argued, it was their common experience of the frontier and pioneer life that for Turner had forged a common identity out of disparate peoples. Thus, it was the physical environment of the United States that had unified a people and created an identity. In an interesting irony, it was primarily the experience of working on a physical frontier that had *determined* the specific American ideas of freedom: 'the frontier is the line of most rapid and effective Americanisation. The wilderness masters the colonist … The fact is that here is a new product that is American.'[16] As the frontier moves it leaves behind it – just like 'successive terminal moraines resulting from successive glaciations' – a distinctly American society. For Turner the end of the frontier line meant that successive waves of American immigrants would no longer be formed in the frontier environment. Underlying Turner's analysis was a powerful and common American environmental determinism that readily accepted a determinist reading of Ratzel. It also suggested for many, including Turner himself, that the United States needed to take a more activist foreign policy.[17] The new frontier needed to be found abroad in imperial expansion.

Thus Semple's environmentally determinist reading of Ratzel fits neatly with an earlier indigenous US determinism ironically rooted in an attempt to explain pioneer ideas of freedom and self-reliance.[18] Semple's influence on the development of American political geography was profound, and there are direct links to Ellsworth Huntington and his study of the effects of climate on political and social evolution,[19] Isaiah Bowman (who offered a course at Yale on 'anthropogeography' with Ellsworth Huntington) and Derwent Whittlesey (who was a student of Semple's). Both Bowman and Whittlesey will be discussed in more detail in later chapters. American political geography began its life as an environmentally determinist discipline that regarded human politics as a direct result of physical forces. Yet, as I will discuss in Chapter 6, its defining feature after 1919 would be its rejection of this determinism.

Ratzel's geography was not the only external influence on American political geography prior to 1914. Parallel to the developments in the United States, Britain was also developing a German-influenced political geography of its own centred around the pioneering writings of Halford Mackinder. Mackinder is best known for his idea of the geographical pivot of history, which was the subject of his 1904 article and Royal Geographical Society presentation.[20] Basically the geographical pivot of history, or pivot area (later renamed the heartland in 1919), was Mackinder's name for the area of the Eurasian landmass (the 'World Island') inaccessible to sea power. Mackinder's summary of the spatial history of Eurasia followed Ratzel's (and Semple's) argument that technological developments had had the effect of making larger political units both possible and more dominant. The historical trend was from smaller peripheral to larger continental states. Technological developments from the age of discovery had benefited both sea and land powers. Maritime technology had allowed the states of Western Europe to circumnavigate the physical barriers that had penned them in, and turned the ocean from an obstacle to a highway. At the same time those at the eastern margins – Russia – had succeeded in conquering the pivot area of central Asia.[21]

> While the maritime peoples of Western Europe have covered the ocean with their fleets, settled the outer continents, and in varying degree made tributary the oceanic margins of Asia, Russia has organised the Cossacks, and, emerging from her northern forests, has policed the steppe by setting her own nomads to meet the tartar nomads.[22]

Recent technological developments now seemed set to tip the balance in favour of the land power controlling the pivot area. Mackinder singled out the railways, which had opened up the possibility of developing the interior of Eurasia without the need of ocean-going traffic, and air power that threatened coastal sea power was added to this list in his 1919 book. The implication was that the short period of the supremacy of sea power since the age of discovery was an aberration, and that, for many reasons, it was usually land power that was the dominant of the two.[23]

According to Mackinder sea power was always weaker than land power because land power had two effective strategies for overcoming its sea-borne foes. A land power could either conquer all the bases of a sea power, thus creating an internal sea under its control (e.g.: Macedonia, Rome); or it could conquer a greater resource base than possessed by the sea power, and then use this base to build a fleet to confront the sea power (Dorian Greeks, Sparta). Or, as Mackinder put it in 1905: 'half a continent may ultimately outbuild and outman an island'.[24] Britain's dominant role as a sea power was based on the happy accident that the 'Latin peninsula' (Iberia, France and Italy) had historically remained divided, and consequently there was never a land power strong enough to build a fleet to threaten Britain. This had all changed with the technological developments, such as the railway, that now made the pivot area of the World Island conquerable. It was now possible for a land power to dominate a vast area of natural resources that were beyond the reach of sea power, and to use these resources to overcome the relatively resource weak sea powers of the outer crescent. In Mackinder's words the voyagers of the age of discovery four centuries ago had changed our outlook of the sea by making of it one big ocean. 'A similar revolution is in progress in the present generation in the rapid realisation of the unity of the Continent owing to modern methods of communication by land and air.'[25] The great power that was in the best position to create a resource-rich land empire on the World Island was Germany – although Russia and a possible Russo-German alliance is singled out in the original 1904 article – and the Islanders of the Rimland had been slow to realise this.

Although Mackinder was to dramatically revise his ideas on international political geography after the First World War – adopting a less environmentally determinist approach that was deeply critical of the approaches discussed in this section (see Chapter 6) – his pre-war international theory was one in which space limited human action, and consequently determined historical development.

Central to his view of history, however, was the determining nature of technological development. What was missing from Mackinder's analysis was an issue raised by Leo Amery in the discussion after Mackinder had presented his 'Geographical Pivot of History' paper to the Royal Geographical Society in 1904. Amery pointed out that industrial development also had an important effect on the balance of power that could conceivably counteract the spatial advantages of a Eurasian land power.[26] Industrial wealth – concentrated as it was in smaller geographical areas, and especially among the 'Rimland' powers of Britain, the United States and France – played little or no part in Mackinder's geopolitical analysis. Yet, it was the ability to control and marshal industrial production that would play such a pivotal role in both world wars, and would tip the balance in favour of the sea-based western Allies in both cases.

Outside of academic circles ideas of biological and geographic conflict melded with social Darwinist ideas of the evolution of societies to produce other related philosophies of the naturalness of conflict between states. In the United States three of the leading advocates of this approach were Alfred Thayer Mahan, Homer Lea and Brooks Adams. Both Mahan and Lea came to the discussion of international affairs with military experience – Mahan as an admiral in the United States Navy and Lea as a military advisor to the Chinese Nationalists under Sun Yat Sen. Adams, on the other hand, was a patrician historian from the influential East Coast Adams family.

Mahan's approach to international affairs mixed geo-strategic thinking with concerns of both power relations and racial and cultural conflict. His analysis of the balance of power and military balance, shorn of their racial influences, continued to be admired and quoted in realist circles within post-1950 American IR, especially in strategic studies.[27] Mahan's attacks on international arbitration (a popular idea in the decade leading up to 1914) and his dislike of Norman Angell's *The Great Illusion* (the latter often seen, unfairly, as an archetypal 'idealist' text in post-1950 IR) made use of arguments that were not dissimilar to those used by Cold War strategists. Yet, Mahan's argument has always been more than just an analysis of power relations. Central to his writings was also the survival of what he saw as European civilisation: a category that included the lands of European colonisation such as the United States.

Mahan's starting point, however, was the geo-strategic importance of sea-power – perhaps not surprising given that Mahan was an admiral in the US Navy. Like many classical realists of the Cold War American school such as Morgenthau, an unchanging human nature remained central to Mahan's interpretation. Although he did not necessarily attempt to define human nature, as Morgenthau would, Mahan saw it manifest in the unchanging nature of strategy. While the tactics of war were often radically changed by innovations in technology or institutions, the basic logics of strategic thinking remained the same throughout history, resting on the bedrock of human nature.[28] Sea power, for Mahan, remained the essential way a society could build a global empire. The sea, which had always been a 'great highway' or 'wide common' for civilisations throughout history, offered the best means by which an industrial nation could build a profitable empire through the discovery and conquest of rich lands around the world. Efficient industry led to the need to exchange, which found an outlet in shipping, and that naturally led to the establishment of colonies. The shipping and colonial trade routes, in turn, needed a strong navy to protect it.[29] Thus colonialism is linked to the needs of an expanding industry at home. Mahan divided the conditions affecting the sea power of a nation into six factors – three being physical (spatial) and three related to the nature of the society in question. The three physical conditions were the geographic position of the nation, the physical nature of the territory and the extent of the territory. The three that related to the nature of the people were the number in the population, the character of the people and the character of the government.[30] Of these factors, which are all in their way important, Mahan stresses both the three physical factors and the natural character of the people. Thus, in the final analysis Mahan produces a theory of state interaction that is not uncommon in the late nineteenth century, where geographic location and the racial characteristics of a nation (both 'natural' to Mahan) are central for understanding the success of a sea-born society's imperial ambitions. From this Mahan developed a conception of the nature of international relations that was based on what he saw as unchanging principles of strategy, which were themselves rooted in natural conditions.

While Mahan saw the competition of nations as a result of natural forces, this competition had two elements to it. The first was the competition between European civilisation (in which Mahan included the United States) and the non-European world. Mahan often saw this non-European world as barbaric, and therefore the promotion of the interests of European civilisation usually took on a moral quality for him. There was a natural tendency, he argued, for civilised society to expand, and the line of least resistance was to expand into those territories under-utilised by 'incompetent' and 'inferior' races. Force, therefore, played a role in spreading efficient European organisation to lands where the inhabitants (for example, Turks and Chinese) lacked these abilities.[31] Yet the non-European world was not without its own strength. While European civilisation owed its power to its armaments ('velocity') combined with its superior self-assertion ('spirit'), the non-Europeans predominated in population ('mass'). Armaments were, therefore, needed to preserve civilisation by balancing the superior numbers of the non-European.[32] Behind all of this discussion of the western world's relations with the non-western is what John M. Hobson has called a 'racist siege mentality'. A view of the west as an oasis in a desert of racial barbarians, and the consequent need for solidarity among the western powers.[33]

The second element of competition was that within European civilisation itself. It was this natural balance of power that allowed the great European nations to hone and develop their national self-assertion and their armaments so that they were able to triumph over the non-European. Mahan likened the European balance of power to both a constitution – where the balance of powers assures the general welfare of all – and to competing business organisations – where the pursuit of self-interest leads to the general benefit of all.[34] The balance, that often saw fighting in Europe, led ultimately in the direction of competition over the colonisation of the non-European world, while at the same time preserved the smaller states through the balance between great powers.[35] One of Mahan's main criticisms of the idea of arbitration and the extension of law into the regulation of international relations was that it removed European civilisation's ability to protect itself from the non-European by allowing its armaments to atrophy. In short, the disarmament of European states in the interests of peace and law would lead to the collapse of European civilisation.[36] Thus, there was a natural corrective element to the balance of power that preserved European civilisation both from within and without.

It is this idea of naturalness that pervades Mahan's writing on international relations. It is the natural forces of physical geography and race that propel a people to imperial sea-borne greatness, while armaments and the balance of power are seen as the means for reaching a peaceful equilibrium by natural means, rather than by the 'artificial' means of law and arbitration.[37] The use of force and the exercise of power by states are not just natural, they are also the means by which states stand up for moral right. For Mahan the state is naturally a moral entity, with an obligation to do right, even if it is contrary to some formal law imposed on states.[38] This idea of the natural moral obligation of states even translates into the idea that state governments are not naturally bellicose, but that in an era of popular government it is the people that tend to push states into war with other states. The road to peace, therefore, lay in the education of the public, rather than the introduction of means to control the independence of states.[39] This moral aspect of state behaviour, Mahan believed, should be allowed to assert itself, and not to become constrained by legal principles that were so general as to be irrelevant to the particular cases of right and wrong that may emerge in diplomacy. The mistake of advocates of arbitration and law, Mahan argued, was that they failed to realise that these moral disputes between states were not about self-interest, but rather conflicts of honour and vital interests not amenable to law.[40] Thus states in Mahan's view become quasi-organic moral entities with their own (aggregate) personalities.[41] This led Mahan to oppose the peace through law idea that he had witnessed at the two Hague conferences of 1899 and 1907 as ultimately immoral, since these constraints on states would prevent states from behaving ethically. Mahan had one final reason for opposing legal constraints: that ultimately law requires physical force to work, and that consequently compulsory arbitration would require an international army to enforce it.[42] This issue of the need for some enforcing agency for the peaceful resolution of conflict between states was to become a central concern of many supporters of the League of Nations in the inter-war period.

Mahan's view of international relations was a direct emanation of his views on the naturalness of certain topographic and racial categories, and led to a view of a set of natural strategic concepts, of which the role of the balance of power and armaments as natural elements of international affairs were central. War, while an evil, was a necessary evil that even had the sanction of God behind it.[43] This led him to an optimistic assessment of the workings of what he regarded as a natural international order made up of independent states. This optimism was in stark contrast to the pessimism of his contemporary and fellow American Brooks Adams. In two books straddling the turn of the century Adams proposed an understanding of history that combined ideas of race with those of a determining environment, which at the same time suggested that human history was not necessarily open to change by conscious action because it was immutable laws of nature that operate on the human mind.[44] While we could not shape our environment, we could still possibly influence history by understanding how these influences worked, and then adapting to these forces.[45] In his 1896 work Adams laid out how human societies were influenced first by fear and then by greed. Fear produced a centralised authority through religious, military and artistic figures. The excess energy accumulated by a centralising race was stored as wealth. With the rise of wealth a new figure emerged, the usurer, who triumphed due to his superiority in economic matters. This growth of greed rapidly dissipated the energy of a race, leading to its decline.[46] Only an influx of 'barbarian blood' could reinvigorate a race in decline through usury.[47] By 1902, Adams had, while not abandoning the racial element, come to stress the role of geographic conditions, which he argued 'have exercised a great, possibly a preponderating, influence over man's destiny'.[48] While geographic conditions now became the forces that shaped the directions of the flow of history,[49] race still remained an important factor in the level of adaptability in any given society, and the idea of racial exhaustion developed earlier continued to feature.[50]

This combination of a racialised and geographically-influenced long history of the rise and decline of quasi-organic nations also became the central assumptions of the work of a later American writer: the adventurer, and military advisor to Sun Yat Sen, Homer Lea. In two critically acclaimed works Lea outlined the threats to both the United States (from Japan) and Britain (from Germany and Russia).[51] Like Mahan and Adams before him, it is never completely clear what Lea means by race, and while it carries racist overtones on occasion, it also seemed to be a sloppy short-hand for nation. Underlying this interpretation of the nature of international competition in the works of Mahan, Adams and Lea was the assumption that true scientific knowledge meant an understanding of the ahistorical forces that were always directing human society. This stood in stark contrast to the more liberal and left-leaning interpretations of science found in the works of people such as L.T. Hobhouse, Norman Angell, J.A. Hobson and H.N. Brailsford that saw radical change and human agency as central (see below). The works of Mahan, Adams and Lea were to be the bête noire of a later generation of internationalist liberals. Yet, this hunt for the underlying atemporal forces that shaped civilisation also seems to have been a response to the realisation that industrial society was changing at an increasingly rapid rate. In the writings of Ratzel, Mahan and Adams we find concerns about the need to adapt in a society in which the velocity of change was increasing in a bewildering way. While this change would be embraced by people like Angell, who saw it as a sign of fundamental change, for conservatives like Adams it was a threat that required ever increasing skills at adaptability.

Although pre-1914 political geography and its supporters constructed an interpretation of inter-state relations that we can interpret as a distinct international theory, its assumptions meant that it had little interest either in global order or the nature of what would later be called the international anarchy. In the words of Richard Ashley, they had about as much reason to consider the anarchy 'problématique' as a fish has for exploring the nature of water.[52] This was certainly true of Ratzel, Kjellen, Mahan, Adams and Lea, although increasingly not so for Mackinder after 1919. Basically, their view of international affairs was as an arena where the great powers fought out a struggle for survival in which imperial greatness was the mark of success. What is missing here is a concept of the international order as something mutable and open to human action and organisation. In other words an approach that takes the nature of the international system itself, rather than the nature of the imperial contest, as the object of study. Before looking more closely at studies that did turn towards an analysis of the nature of the international order it is worth looking at how those more influenced by history, law and philosophy were interpreting the relationship between states.

## The state and the international

The geopolitical analysis of the state was only one possible interpretation of the nature of the world of states, and not necessarily the only one to place imperial competition as the central issue. Experts in the field of law, history, philosophy and the new field of political science also explored the interaction of states, and made pronouncements on state competition, imperialism and the nature of modern war. Among these were those who supported the institution of the sovereign nation state, as well as those who were critical of the resulting state-based 'international anarchy'.

Paul Reinsch's international thought has been comprehensively explored in Brian Schmidt's *The Political Discourse of Anarchy* (1998), where Schmidt regards Reinsch's *World Politics* (1900) as 'the first work to investigate directly the subject matter implied by the title'.[53] Indeed, although much of the book is dedicated to exploring the immediate concerns of the effects of colonial competition over China, and in turn the question of American foreign policy towards China, it also contained a discussion of the dynamics of international politics as it related to the state of the world at the close of the nineteenth century. *World Politics* was not Reinsch's only foray into international thought, and his *Public International Unions* (1911) dealt with the questions of international cooperation as a solution to the problems he had outlined eleven years earlier. In addition to this, his interest in colonial government, while not strictly speaking international in its outlook, explored an area that Reinsch regarded as an important part of both the cause and the solution of international instability. Based at the University of Wisconsin, where he came into contact with the historian Frederick Jackson Turner, Reinsch's approach to international thought is firmly tied up with the questions of nation-building and the role of the individual in relation to the powerful impersonal forces of industrialisation and irrational passions that appeared at the time to so dominate politics since the late nineteenth century. While *World Politics* lays out the nature and problem of international affairs at the start of the twentieth century, *Public International Unions* seems to offer a solution that was still, crucially, sensitive to the dominant and embedded nature of the system of national states.

For Reinsch in 1900 nationalism seemed to be an unstoppable force that had been gathering steam for the last five centuries. Indeed, the move from a medieval universalist principle to a nationalist one is presented as a historical trend that statesmen opposed at their peril. 'The reputation of a statesman ... depends on his power to understand and aid the historical evolution ... of strong national states.'[54] While nationalism undermined both cosmopolitanism and local particularities, it remained for Reinsch a guarantee of the vitality of civilisation by allowing different competing approaches and cultural forms to co-exist. This prevented the kind of cultural uniformity that Reinsch saw as the cause of the destruction of civilisations like the Romans that had relied on a single imperial state.[55] Thus nationalism – constrained by international law, a weak cosmopolitan sense and the balance of power – allowed civilisation to flourish. There was, however, a problem. The nationalistic principle, while guaranteeing the vitality of civilisation, also held within it the seeds of its own destruction. National differences led to competition and a belief in national superiority that eventually became imperialism. It was this new national imperialism that threatened the very vitality of civilisation by leading to a competition between the great powers that could end in the eventual establishment of a stagnant world empire akin to that of the Romans. Nationalism (the guarantor of a vibrant civilisation) would lead to imperialism, that in turn would lead to world empire (and a stagnant civilisation). For Reinsch the nineteenth century had been the era of nationalism, but the twentieth century would be the era of national imperialism.[56]

There were wider implications in politics as a whole for these changes. Central to Reinsch's world-view was an interpretation of the development of nineteenth century attitudes to politics. An early rationalist optimism had, he argued, given way by 1848 to a pessimism rooted in the view 'that humanity is swayed not so much by reason, as by the blind and passionate forces of the will'. This pessimism, in turn, had given way to a new optimism of force that gloried in the 'violent energy' of the contest between the strongest national wills.[57] This development had seen the strengthening of ideas of national will, and a corresponding decline of individualism as ideas of social solidarity and aristocratic virtues replaced ideas of liberal reform.[58] The balance of power that had helped preserve civilisation is replaced by an impersonal struggle for survival.[59] Yet, Reinsch felt that all was not lost. While we were entering a new stage where passionate forces were pushing humanity along, there was still the hope that we could use our intellect to understand these forces.[60]

What separates Reinsch from so many of the geopolitical interpretations of the world discussed above also allowed him to chart a way out of the dangers of national imperialism. For Reinsch the passionate forces that were at large were not ahistorical, but rather products of quite specific historical developments. This did not mean they could be ignored, but it did mean that knowledge of these forces would yield solutions that could work with historical realities. In 1900 Reinsch was well aware that much of the form of world politics was a product of changes in economic and industrial relations. The modern imperialism he witnessed was for him, despite the emotive appeals to nationalism used to sell colonisation, predominantly commercial, rather than territorial. The strength of commercial interests shaped the form of the new imperialism, and it was the rise of investment at the expense of industrial concerns that was creating the need for some kind of world policing to safeguard the world of high finance.[61] In 1900 Reinsch had mentioned colonialism as a safety-valve that could distract this new commercially based national imperialism away from direct great power confrontation.[62] This view of colonialism partially explains his interest in colonial government.[63] In 1911, however, Reinsch looked in a new direction towards the creation of international institutions that would build a new world unity without imperilling the separate national identities that were so central to modern civilisation.

The subject that Reinsch addressed in 1911 was the development of the Public International Unions (PIUs) in the late nineteenth and early twentieth centuries. These early experiments in international organisation, some of which such as the Universal Postal Union still exist today, were designed to deal with specific functional problems of global governance.[64] It was the development of these organisations that suggested a solution to what Reinsch saw as the problem of competition under national imperialism. Although the 'historical experience of generations has accustomed men to think in terms of national sovereignty' we are now 'building up cooperation in constantly widening circles, so that it transcends national bounds to become universal joint effort'.[65] By dealing with specific issues of international cooperation the PIUs allowed for cooperation between states on vital issues, without challenging the political and ethnic identities of states. This also represented, Reinsch claimed, a reinterpretation of national independence away from self-sufficiency towards international cooperation.[66] This left the age in a strange paradox: a 'striking growth of world-wide enterprise' contrasted with 'an insensate competition in military armament'.[67] Thus, humanity stood at a crossroads, and it was by building the new international cooperation that humanity both built the conditions for the prevention of war while also fulfilling the imperative of the age for action along lines that William James in 1906 had called 'the moral equivalent of war'.[68]

Central to Reinsch's support for a state-based world order, despite his concerns about its tendency to drift to imperialism, was his view that loyalty to the national state and the national idea was important to human development over the last five centuries. It was this idea of the centrality of loyalty to the national community that underscored the international thought of the British philosopher Bernard Bosenquet. Bosenquet represents the high-watermark of a trend within British thought referred to as idealism, and it was this British idealism that would come under powerful attack by the generation of liberal writers that endorsed an internationalist alternative to the state system after 1914. Before exploring

Bosenquet's contribution to international theory in more detail it is worth stopping to deal with the problem of the phrase idealism. Idealist and idealism in contemporary IR is used, rather sloppily, to describe a whole clutch of non-realist approaches to international affairs, especially those who support stronger international organisations (see the discussion in Chapter 1 on this). This usage dates from at least the 1920s, although it does not gain common currency until after 1945. Confusingly, Bosenquet's idealism is of a different order, and is in fact at odds with the current common usage in IR textbooks, even though one textbook has attempted to square the circle by trying to link so-called inter-war IR idealism to Bosenquet's philosophical idealism.[69] The problem here is that idealism is being used in two distinct ways. In current IR textbooks idealism is used as a synonym for utopianism, and refers to theories that reputedly attempt to build future global structures without reference to harsh realities. Bosenquet was a philosophical idealist in the tradition of Plato and Hegel, meaning that he based his philosophy on the view that ideas (and particularly people's views on the nature and extent of their community) shape political institutions. As a consequence of this, as I will show below, Bosenquet was hostile to many of the ideas of global governance that have been called idealist by later textbook writers. Indeed, Bosenquet was almost universally reviled by liberal and socialist supporters of the League of Nations, and his ideas often reach conclusions that today we would consider quite realist.

Generally speaking, Bosenquet's philosophy was not directly concerned with international politics, and his primary focus remained the study of domestic political life. Increasingly, though, he was forced to address the issue of the external relations of the state, leading one commentator on his philosophy to claim that the First World War forced Bosenquet to deal more thoroughly with the international role of the state.[70] Whether or not the relationship was as direct as that, there is little doubt that in the years after 1914 Bosenquet paid significant attention to the question of international relations, although this did not necessarily mean that he made any significant changes to his overall philosophy. Rather, through 1915 to 1920 Bosenquet explicitly applied his philosophical position to the problems of the international in response to criticisms of his work. Throughout this attention to the international, however, Bosenquet was primarily providing a defence of his philosophical approach to the internal structure of the state, and so (unlike Reinsch) his international theory is an unintended by-blow that emerged from the attack on his ideas by advocates of a more formal system of global governance. As a result, it is worth summing up his political philosophy before exploring his international thought.

The definitive statement of Bosenquet's philosophy can be found in his 1899 (and frequently updated) book *The Philosophical Theory of the State*. The primary focus of the book was to give a *philosophical* account of the state, by which he means the development of an understanding of the essence, or ideal nature, of the state. Thus, Bosenquet was less interested in the history of the state or in empirical observations about the working of states (although these were important to him if they helped reveal the state's nature).[71] The state could be understood as a product of both the human mind (ideas) and the environment inasmuch as the state is a result of human actions, and human actions are the product of the human mind reacting to its environment.[72] The role of the mind in creating the state can be found in the concept of the general will, which Bosenquet adapted from Rousseau. Basically, the extent of the successful (and natural) state was co-terminus with the extent of the general will. In other words, a successful state enclosed and contained a single general will. 'General will' in this form is the sense of community and the willingness of a group of people to act together for the common good. When this general will forms a 'communal mind' and is brought to life through the organs of a state it creates a moral community where free men are willing to subordinate their individual wills to the compulsion of the community.[73] A stable and free state can only exist where it encloses this general will. The limit of the extent of the general will is the limit of free and stable government. Where government extends without a general will it becomes 'external and tyrannical'.[74] In short, and to put it into a recent context, a properly functioning moral state where free people freely submit to authority can only exist if there is a sense of patriotism or national identity that unites people in a general will.

This idea of the general will, or spirit of the community, has implications for how Bosenquet saw international politics. At one level at least Bosenquet is a cosmopolitan. Philosophically-speaking humanity is a unified whole, with common 'purposes and possibilities of human life',[75] but we articulate our universalism through particular states. As a result this philosophical unity is expressed differently in different states, and therefore may be expressed in different ways by different societies. Thus, in the absence of a real existing unity, expressed through a general will encompassing all humanity, the state remains the ultimate moral agent, and the only possible institution in which we can live a free and moral life.[76] Because states remain the largest expression of our moral life this means that their actions cannot be judged using the same criteria as that used to judge individuals, since states do not live in a moral community alongside other states. Equally, states represent a moral way of life that the individual should find worth defending. For these two reasons war is a natural and reasonable part of our lives, especially when it is justified as a defence of our way of life as expressed in the state.

It is here that Bosenquet ran afoul of a growing body of liberal thinkers who saw in the state's propensity for war and organised violence a threat to civilisation. For many liberals the First World War demonstrated the inherent failure of the system of states to provide security, and Bosenquet's theory of the state seemed to be the ultimate philosophical justification for the failed system. Among these attacks the most devastating were in a symposium involving C. Delisle Burns, Bertrand Russell and G.D.H. Cole published in 1915–16, and L.T. Hobhouse's *The Metaphysical Theory of the State* published in 1918.[77] The former looked exclusively at the issue of the external relations of the state, while the more comprehensive criticism in the latter included a long section on the international implications of Bosenquet's thought. Before looking at these criticisms in more detail it is worth pointing out that these works were written during the First World War. Bosenquet's critics were all dedicated to the creation of a system that would prevent another world war, and so were hostile to the idea that the state was the highest moral ideal. At another level, the War had also fostered a strong anti-German feeling in British society, and the fact that Bosenquet's idealism had roots in a German philosophical tradition (via Hegel) did Bosenquet no favours. Indeed, Hobhouse's 1918 book specifically contrasted German philosophy (conservative and anti-individual) with British and French philosophies of freedom, while G.D.H. Cole's caustic comment about 'any Prusso-phile philosopher' was aimed at both Bosenquet and other British idealists.[78]

Key to the criticism of Bosenquet's understanding of the state was the perception that he failed to appreciate the extent to which the state was also a product of its external relations. Delisle Burns listed six instances, ranging from diplomatic activity to agreements to regulate common global problems, where other states influence and direct the nature of the state. Here he constructs a view of the state as a product of its embeddedness in a wider world of states, and not just the product of the general will of its population.[79] Cole and Hobhouse took a similar line, arguing that the mistake of the idealist approach was to see the world inside the state as the only one in which human relations took place. Instead, people were involved in any number of ties inside and outside the state and owed loyalties to many other associations beside the state.[80] For Russell the problem lies in the irony that the state emerges out of a desire for security, but the result of this externally is to create insecurity in relations between states. 'Every nation arms in self-defence, but in doing so acquires the means of aggression.'[81]

Bosenquet's defence against these criticisms was to reiterate his argument that the extension of any political authority was only possible if there was a coherent community able to support the institutions. Without such a 'general will' these institutions would merely be imposing a tyranny by force. In other words the sense of community had to precede the establishment of the organs of state government.[82] Indeed, he even cautioned that if a new international 'league of peace' machinery undermined the general will found in the state that this, in turn, would lead to war: 'All who are satisfied with machinery of this kind are practically together in being votaries of force, for take away the general will and nothing but force is left.'[83] His answer was to offer two possible world order solutions that were compatible with his view of the state, and would leave the general will intact. The first was a longer-term goal of the creation of a truly global general will that would then allow for the development of a world state. While not an immediate possibility, Bosenquet was not hostile to the idea of a world-will supporting a world state.[84] The second was a more practical and immediate option for Bosenquet: a peace made up of a world of properly constituted states living side-by-side in amicable relations. Underlying this was his view that war was a disease found in imperfect states, and that properly constituted states that provided a peaceful and just life for their citizens were themselves naturally peaceful and amicable in their relations with other states.[85]

Like Reinsch, Bosenquet preferred this solution for another reason: he worried that a possible world state (and its general will) could not be 'achieved without the sacrifice of the valuable individual qualities of national minds'.[86] Unity would be bought at the expense of diversity.

This league of peaceful properly constituted states did not satisfy Hobhouse. He cast doubt on Bosenquet's optimism about the pacific nature of states, arguing instead that such a world of independent states had no mechanism for preventing some states from following a more aggressive foreign policy.[87] Against Bosenquet's argument that government institutions could only be properly constituted after there was a general will, Hobhouse claimed the opposite: that an organised moral world was what would emerge from the development of the League of Nations machinery.[88] Not only was a moral and peaceful world order a possible result from extending government control, but Bosenquet's ideal of properly constituted states constructed upon a general will was itself a dangerous fiction. Rather, there was no sharp division between the 'real self' of the state and the 'mechanical relations' beyond it. The state itself did not enclose a moral unity at all, and beyond the state 'men are involved in innumerable relations with their fellows, which require organisation ... all sorts of differentiated organisations are required to deal with the different relations of men'.[89] In sum, Bosenquet overplayed the unity of the state, while underplaying the interactions at the international level that required proper governance if they were to be managed properly and not become a cause of war.

Underlying this split between Bosenquet and Hobhouse was a fundamentally different view of the nature of the state, and of the role of the state and state institutions in the modern world. Bosenquet's idea of the ethical state, which owed much to the idea of the *rechtstaat* found in Kant and Hegel, saw the state as enclosing a self-contained moral community, regardless of economic interdependence (which was an irrelevance for Bosenquet[90]). Hobhouse, on the other hand, saw the changes in industry, class relations and the global political economy as fundamental shifts that had altered the role of the state and human government. Governance (or 'government' as it would have been called in the early twentieth century) had to contain and manage the new world of economic interdependence, not Bosenquet's old-fashioned notion of a more limited moral community based on a general will. For Hobhouse, as for many left-liberals of the time, Bosenquet's talk of the general will hid the extent to which industrial relations had undermined this at home through class divisions, while creating new global inter-linkages that, if left without a proper global level of management, would lead to dangerously destabilising modern industrial wars. In short, international liberals argued that industrialisation and interdependence had radically altered the world, and Bosenquet's idealism no longer described the realities that humanity faced at the global level. To a certain extent, despite his early opposition to ideas of the League of Nations, Bosenquet was not oblivious to these trends, even conceding in later editions of *The Philosophical Theory of the State* that the League of Nations, if built on solid foundations of a world-will, was a possibility.[91] Indeed, J.H. Muirhead went so far as to claim that Bosenquet 'lived to become an ardent supporter of the League', although there is no strong evidence of this from his writings.[92]

While there are some similarities with Bosenquet's ideas of international order and later more classical realist ideas in IR that emerged after 1945, Bosenquet's immediate influence on the development of international thought in the English-speaking world was slight. Indeed, his importance lies in his role as a foil for the development of an international tradition that grew out of the writings of thinkers like Hobhouse. In a world of class divisions, global industrial development and dangerously destructive wars Bosenquet's faith in the perfection of the state seemed at best quaint, and at worst dangerous to Hobhouse and other left liberals. Bosenquet's international thought was also fundamentally an afterthought to protect his view on domestic politics from attack by a new breed of more internationalist thinkers who were questioning the role of the state as a means of governing the globe. It is these writers, and not Bosenquet, who would influence the post-1918 debates on international order in the English-speaking world.

## Moving beyond the state?

Despite Reinsch's view in 1900 that the predominant theme in the last half-millennium had been the rise of the national state, a growing group of writers (that, interestingly, came to include Reinsch) in the lead up to the First World War saw the state order as fundamentally flawed. While there were wild differences before 1914 in their prescriptions for world order, the war years saw a significant number of them turn their talents towards the idea of a league of nations. Yet, this unity of purpose hid deep divisions over what this league would mean, and the eventual release of the draft Covenant of the League of Nations in 1919 left many advocates of the League – especially on the left – deeply disappointed and underwhelmed. Underlying much of this tradition in international thought were two, often contradictory, views: an optimistic conception of the possibility of progress; and a pessimistic view of the trajectory of industrial society towards violent conflict and decline unless something was done to avert it. These two different positions informed the writings of many key thinkers on international affairs in the years running up to war in 1914. This position could be summarised in the words of H.G. Wells, writing in 1920, that 'history becomes more and more a race between education and catastrophe'.[93] Indeed, this juxtaposition between a faith in rational progress and a fear that society was sleepwalking into disastrous conflict remained a hallmark of thought in the inter-war period, only that after the experiences of the First World War emphasis became laid more on the march to barbarism and less on the potentials of rational progression.

The idea that civilisation needed to step beyond the nation state found greater acceptance in Britain than it did in the United States. That said, the idea that the state system itself needed to change, even while the nation state remained the key institution of political life, found supporters among American academics.

Reinsch himself, by 1911, was arguing that the rapid interdependence of the social and economic life of the national state meant that there was a compulsion to cooperate. Unfortunately, this growth of a 'world-wide enterprise' was matched by growth in armaments and international competition. It seemed to Reinsch that the mark of his age was energetic action, and that this would either find outlets in conflict and war (cf: Homer Lea and Brooks Adams discussed above), or in some 'international construction'.[94] Reinsch saw hope in the development of the Public International Unions (see above), which he saw as a level of government that would fill the void 'between humanity and the individual'.[95] Yet, for Reinsch the layer of international government would be an addition to the national state. He saw the state as remaining the prominent political organisation for humanity.[96] The state would remain, but the international state system would be changed in order to encourage cooperation.

Reinsch saw the public international unions as a means of changing human mindsets from one of a clash of local interests towards the idea of an international consciousness.[97] This idea of an international mind was the central feature of the ideas of another US academic, Nicholas Murray Butler. In many respects the ideas of Reinsch and Butler were strongly similar, although Reinsch put more emphasis on the important role of the national state than did Butler, and Butler put more emphasis on the role of international public opinion and less on global institutions. Butler began from the proposition that public opinion was a major cause of war in the modern world. Governments, he argued, had ceased to dominate, and instead they were led in their foreign policy by public opinion that frequently got carried away by bravado when sober thought was required.[98] Yet, it was in this strong role of public opinion that Butler saw hope. If public opinion now dominated government then there was the possibility of educating public opinion towards supporting international law and a more international mind-set.[99] Butler called this the international mind:

> that habit of thinking of foreign relations and business, and that habit of dealing with them, which regard the several nations of the civilised world as friendly and cooperating equals in aiding the progress of civilisation in developing commerce and industry, and in spreading enlightenment and culture throughout the world.[100]

Thus, through his view of the dominance of public opinion in the bellicose acts of states, Butler saw hope in the education of public opinion towards a more international mind. Having said this, though, Butler did not see international public opinion as the sole possible guarantor of peace. Rather, the failings of human nature meant that there would also need to be some kind of international police, quite different from armies and navies, to supplement the policing efforts of individual states.[101] He also did not see uninformed public opinion as the sole cause of war, arguing that the causes of conflict were grounded in social and economic activities.[102] Yet, an international public opinion remained the cornerstone of Butler's conception of the way towards a world without war.

This view of the use of international public opinion to bring about peace was to find fertile ground in the inter-war period, especially among those who opposed the collective security arrangements of the League, and looked instead to a system of global order that did not rely on the threat of military force (see Chapter 6). The idea of international public opinion found itself particularly savaged by IR writers after 1950. While Butler's hope for an international mind can be seen as just an exercise in wishful thinking, it is worth pointing out that it was based on the idea that it was uninformed public opinion that had been an immediate cause of war, and also that Butler did not see the international mind as sufficient for the maintenance of peace, hence his turn to ideas of international policing. What we can see in Butler, however, is a possible response to Bosenquet's argument that international government would require a global general will. In many respects, Butler's international mind was a global general will that was meant to respect the differences that writers such as Reinsch and Bosenquet saw as a positive attribute of a world of states.

Many of the themes hammered out by Butler were simultaneously developed in Britain by Norman Angell. An admirer of the United States, who had spent part of his youth as a homesteader and journalist in California, Angell developed the twin themes of the double-edged nature of global economic and industrial development, and the need for a better rational understanding of the futility of war. While I will explore his inter-war thought in more detail in the next chapter, here I will examine the development of his pre-1914 ideas. Although none of Angell's ideas, as expressed in his magnum opus *The Great Illusion* were particularly original, his genius lay in bringing a number of common themes together in a larger argument, and then presenting them in an accessible style that soon made him a household name in Britain and the United States, and turned his book into a global publishing phenomenon translated into 10 languages. It is arguably the greatest bestseller in the history of IR.[103] One of the effects of *The Great Illusion* was to polarise and frame the debates over international order and war for the next thirty years, and such was its popularity that, even when Angell overhauled his ideas in the wake of the First World War and the subsequent development of the League of Nations, Angell found himself returning to the argument of *The Great Illusion* as the book went through new (and cheaper) editions in the 1930s. Elsewhere I have talked about Angell's thought going through two distinct phases (which I have called 'Angell I' and 'Angell II').[104] The argument of *The Great Illusion* was the core of Angell's first phase, when he still thought that rational argument would be enough to convince people of the futility of war. The inter-war Angell would come to see rationality as insufficient.

Central to Angell's pre-1914 work was the tension between an optimistic high-Victorian faith in progress – especially an admiration for the new complexities of a technologically advanced and internationalised economy – and a pessimistic view of our inability to construct new ideas that reflected the realities of this world economy. We were, in short, running a complex interdependent world using ideas better suited for an earlier and simpler age. For Angell the way out of this situation was to study the realities of our political–economic life, and from that to construct new more modern ideas that are better suited to the world we live in now. Underlying this argument was a materialist view of human society in which our rationality led us to greater prosperity and comfort, but this economic development was increasingly threatened by our passions that were driven by ideas founded on a less complex and less globalised political economy.

In contrast to Mahan's notion of a strategic universe, where the rules have not changed because human nature has not changed, Angell suggested that change had produced a very different world, and that this change was actually accelerating at such a rate that it was difficult for our ideas to keep up with the new rules of society.[105] For Angell this change was progressive and unilinear, leading to ever greater interdependence, and to a decline in the utility of force. Here his argument follows the work of Ivan Bloch. Bloch's claims, backed up by a wealth of statistical analysis, that interdependence and military technology now made war a threat to European civilisation had first appeared as an English translation in 1899.[106] His work had been cited by Angell in the 1912 edition of *The Great Illusion*, but there is no evidence that Angell had read Bloch beforehand.[107] While Angell believed that force could capture wealth in the past, two factors now made military might particularly anachronistic. The first was the intangibility of wealth, based as it was now on issues of financial confidence and on links of trade and private commerce that crossed state boundaries. Dreadnoughts were not capable of controlling the myriad of private transactions that now made up the reality of the international economy. The upshot of this was that armed force was not capable of capturing wealth in a way that it was able to in earlier periods of history when wealth was more tangible, and finance and trade less central to the economy. The second was that the brute simplicities of armed force would actually have the opposite effect to the one intended. Such was the complexities of wealth creation in the global economy that a great power war was liable to destroy the fragile connections that made modern prosperity possible, and thus threaten the existence of civilisation itself.[108] At one point Angell likened the international financial system to the sensory nerves of the international economy, easily damaged by war.[109] Angell illustrated these two trends by following an example of what would happen if a German army captured London and the Bank of England. Despite London being the world's financial hub, an invading German Army would only be able to realise a tiny fraction of this wealth via the gold reserves of the Bank of England. At the same time the collapse of the global financial system caused by the sack of London would see German banks and trade suffer disproportionately to the plunder realised. Thus, even a successful German invasion of Britain would bankrupt Germany.[110]

From this analysis Angell came to two contradictory conclusions. On the one hand the natural progression of the economy was towards peace. Each increase in the complexity and interdependence of the international economy meant that peaceful pursuits (however ultimately selfish they were) were favoured over violence. This had been a mark of human development since pre-history. What is more this movement was going on without any conscious control and often despite the will of individual financiers or diplomats.[111] On the other hand, humanity is governed by theories and ideas, more specifically we are ruled by the ideas of a previous age, and it is only with careful and rigorous analysis that we are able to form new ideas that conform with the realities of the world we live in. The upshot of this is that the human race finds itself engaged in policies that actually work against its material interests, even when it firmly believes that it is actually following its interests. Thus, militaristic policies, suited for a simpler age, will be followed under the illusion (the 'Great Illusion' of the title) that they will bring security and wealth to the state. In fact, these policies bring ruin by destroying the very foundations of security and prosperity. The only way to counter these false atavistic theories is to use our reason to understand the real relation of things. By doing this we create new and obvious truths more in keeping with the nature of contemporary society.[112] Thus, we have two currents at work: an evolution of society towards interdependence that favours more peaceful methods of human interaction, and the need to counteract older ideas that, when applied to current conditions, undercut and endanger the growing complexities of our civilisation. The argument in *The Great Illusion* suggested that rational education alone would accomplish the necessary changes in ideas, although increasingly Angell had to accept that reason was not enough, and that political activism was necessary to get his ideas across to a wider audience.[113]

The implications of Angell's ideas for the state system are, at this stage at least, less radical than they appear. While his approach questioned the underlying basis of *realpolitik*, the state as an institution is not questioned. Rather, Angell's whole argument in *The Great Illusion* leaves the state untouched. True, the shift in power wrought by growing interdependence means that there exists a web of inter-locking communities that cross state borders,[114] but Angell assumes that this is not necessarily a threat to the state. Rather, once statesmen realise that the best interests of their citizenry lies in peaceful co-existence they will adjust their policies accordingly. A system of states will survive into the future, as will nationalism,[115] it is just that their interests will lie in a set of relationships that are markedly different from those of the past. This complacency in Angell's thought towards the role of the state would not survive Angell's experience of war after 1914, and in his later works he did see the need to change the structure of what we would call global governance (see Chapter 6), but at this stage Angell was optimistic that change could come about without altering the fundamentals of government.

In the period leading up to the First World War the most sustained attack on Angell was directed at what was regarded as the overly materialist nature of his argument. An example of this was the criticism levelled at *The Great Illusion* by Mahan. For Mahan the issue of the unprofitableness of war was irrelevant, since the object of arms in the modern era was as a means for settling disputes of right between nations, especially in the question of ownership of 'unutilized regions of the world'.[116] In other words, it was the existence of different views of right and wrong that could not be settled by law, which made armaments necessary. Mahan had also picked up on an over-generalisation in Angell's thinking: the claim that the use of force could not be translated into economic advantage. While it is fair to concede that in the case of a possible European great power war it is hard to see how the use of armed force could benefit either party, even supporters of Angell had to admit that in some circumstances military might could be used for economic gain.[117] In Angell's own time the Spanish American war was perhaps a good example of this. Later Angell would be forced to admit that his argument was based on a pre-war notion that private property was inviolate.[118] In the world after 1918 the collapse of this consensus would mean that the use of force did become a means of gaining economic advantage, even if Angell's point about the overall unprofitableness of war still held in terms of great power rivalry. Here, though, was another weakness of the argument of *The Great Illusion*: that it also assumed that the economic interdependence of the half century before 1914 was an irreversible fact.[119] The inter-war years would teach Angell that he had been overly optimistic.

It might be tempting to see the debate between Angell and Mahan as a manifestation of a realist–idealist debate: a conflict where the arch-apologist for *realpolitik* meets his nemesis the advocate of a new order. The problem with this interpretation, though, is that in this case the familiar classical realist argument, found fully articulated in the later writings of Hans J. Morgenthau, that human interests drive politics is being articulated by Angell, while it is Mahan who employs arguments about the nature of a moral right and wrong. Despite his back-peddling in the second half of *The Great Illusion*, Angell's argument is fundamentally one in which an understanding of our material self-interest leads to a correct evaluation of the right policies to follow. Mahan, on the other hand, sees armaments as a means of upholding the superior Christian and European civilisation that he identified with so strongly. Material self-interest takes a back seat to moral considerations. Yet, there are also parallels that we can draw between the two. Angell's materialist philosophy and Mahan's Christian one both led them to uphold the superiority of western civilisation, and to support imperialism as bringing civilisation to the non-western world.[120] For Angell, the west brought liberal values and prosperity, for Mahan, it brought Christianity and security from barbarism. For all their hostility the two remained united on this point at least.

While Angell was well aware of how the world economy had changed since the middle of the nineteenth century, there is little discussion of how industrial society had affected class interests. This is not to say he was blind to it. On several occasions he mentions the importance of the conflict between capital and labour in modern society. Yet, here Angell sees the ubiquity and cross-border nature of class conflict as another reason for the obsolescence of militarised state conflict.[121] What Angell did not do was to see in this class conflict the possibility that different classes might have interests in different kinds of foreign policy. In short, that while society as a whole might not gain from war, perhaps some economic groups did. It was this line of thinking that inspired the work of J.A. Hobson and H.N. Brailsford.

Hobson's work on imperialism represented a different take from Angell on the causes and nature of international conflict. Specifically interested in the case of recent British imperial expansion, Hobson claimed that it was the class structure at home that was leading to conflict abroad. By keeping wages low and profits high, domestic capitalists had created a situation in which the domestic market lacked the means to consume the goods produced by industry at the same time as investment capital accumulated from profits. The result of this situation was that Britain (and by implication other modern states) needed both markets for its goods and opportunities for financial investment. The new imperialism at the end of the nineteenth century, while it was a net drain on the economy, served the interests of a particular rentier class by providing protected markets for goods and capital. Thus, while imperialism did not benefit society as a whole, it did serve the ends of a particular influential class. Hobson's solution was domestic reform that would lead to greater purchasing power by workers at home, and to better democratic control of vested interests.[122]

It was upon the basis of this argument that Brailsford in 1914 constructed his own view of the nature of the international system. For Brailsford Angell's analysis had been correct but one-sided. There were, in fact, two different and interlocking systems at play that created the current realities of international life. These were the balance of power associated with the international anarchy that existed between states, and the capitalist system of managing economic relations. For Brailsford, the balance of power was a concept dependent on the interests and goals of elites. He thoroughly rejected the idea that power is sought for its own ends as naïve, arguing instead that the nature of the balance of power was dependent on the ends that power, at any given time, was put. While power in an earlier aristocratic age had been vested in land (and thus the balance of power in the eighteenth century revolved around land ownership), it was now to be found in the acquisition of capital. As a consequence, the balance of power in 1914 was centred on investment opportunities and market share.[123] The practical result of this shift in the nature of the balance of power was for the replacement of the direct control of land, to a system whereby capitalist interests in the great powers used indirect control on nominally independent states. In formal political terms the smaller and weaker state remained independent, but in informal and economic terms it was now turned into 'a human cattle farm', whose wealth was extracted for the benefit of elites in one or more of the great powers.[124] In this system arms were not used directly in wars over territory, but instead existed as tools of intimidation in an 'armed peace'. Indeed, it was in the interest of the great powers as a whole to keep this confrontation at a level that stopped short of war.

In terms of the immediate future Brailsford's prediction – that the great powers would avoid war in the interests of their capitalist-controlled armed peace – proved wide of the mark. Two world wars showed that capitalist great power confrontation was far less successfully managed than Brailsford had argued. That said, Brailsford's ideas about low-level conflict linked to the exploitation of weaker societies is remarkably similar to what happened to the international system after 1945, where a largely managed bipolar system of confrontation overlaid a system of indirect control by both superpowers. The era of neo-colonialism – where formally independent and sovereign states were in one way or another controlled by either a capitalist west or a soviet east – conforms to Brailsford's international theory. Thus, while he was certainly wrong in 1914, there is an extent to which he had caught something of the essence of the new international system associated with industrialisation and capitalist production that was emerging out of the old nineteenth century European balance of power.

Brailsford's approach represents an early variant of what to later generations of IR scholars would be called critical international political economy (IPE), and there are echoes of List's analysis of the difference between the older agrarian politics and the new politics of industrialisation (see Chapter 4). While as a journalist immediate events did interest Brailsford, like List, his concern was the longer-term effects of major changes in the economic and political relations within society. As a result, although his immediate prediction in 1914 was wrong, this did not necessarily undermine the basis of his argument (although it did demonstrate, perhaps, that Norman Angell had been right that older agrarian ideas that no longer applied to an industrialised world were still powerful). *The War of Steel and Gold* continued to be republished during the war, with additions, and Brailsford, like many other writers on current affairs at the time, turned his attention to the nature of the forthcoming peace. The shock of the First World War led Brailsford to investigate the possibility of the establishment of a league of nations as a means of preventing the outbreak of future wars. The wartime debates on the future nature of this league would, in turn, influence the nature of the study of international affairs during the inter-war years.

## War and the coming peace. Towards a 'league of nations'

The First World War was a catalyst for interest in international affairs. While many of the ideas expressed on the form and future of the international during and immediately after the war were the products of pre-war debates, the war had two major effects. First, it attracted a host of people previously uninterested (or only partially interested) in international relations to the study of the problems of the international. This was no small matter. Not only did it create a critical mass of scholars who were now writing about the international and its problems, it also created in the wider public in many of the major western nations (and not a few of the non-western) a heightened sensitivity for foreign affairs. The threat that some aspect of political life might, at any moment, drag you off to a trench and threaten you with death for four years has a way of concentrating the minds of an electorate. Second, the experience of the war gave the idea of a 'league' designed to minimise conflict between states popular appeal, not just among the wider publics, but significantly among senior politicians in the great powers. This simultaneous increase in interest in the international coupled with the very real possibility of the establishment of a new set of international machinery for the regulation of relations between states is a watershed in the development of international thought. Having said that, though, the ideas that were discussed after 1914 had their origins before the war, even if the war years often helped to give new names and even meanings to these concepts. One such concept, developed by Lowes Dickinson, was the idea of the international anarchy.

To be precise, the phrase 'international anarchy' actually only dates from Dickinson's updated and expanded study of pre-war diplomacy published in 1926. Dickinson's wartime analysis of the causes of the war was actually entitled *The European Anarchy*.[125] That said, Dickinson's use of anarchy (inspired, no doubt, by his classics background) gave a name to a concept that formed the backbone to the pre-war analyses of the international found in Angell and Brailsford. The idea of the international anarchy has been explored in more depth by later writers such as Richard K. Ashley, Helen Milner and Alexander Wendt; and now is often given Ashley's title of the anarchy problématique.[126] Although not named, this anarchy problématique was the unspoken underpinning of the works discussed in the last section: that the lack of rules and regulations at the international level was at least a permissive cause of the problems of war and state conflict. Early statist and geo-strategic writers did not need to have a concept of the international anarchy for the simple reason that they took the structure of the state system as an assumed given, and therefore had no need to worry about it in the same way. Or, as Ashley so eloquently put it: 'Students of national security who are nationalistically inclined ... have no more reason to speak of global anarchy than fish have reason to speak of water.'[127] By giving a name to the problem Dickinson made possible a whole genre of focused analyses of the problems associated with global governance within a state system. Among this genre was his own influential analysis of the problem.

At one level Dickinson's analysis of European history supports much of the geopolitical arguments of Ratzel, Semple, and Kjellén. States exist in a world dominated by conflict:

> For it is as true of an aggregation of States as of an aggregation of individuals that, whatever moral sentiments may prevail, if there is no common law and no common force the best intentions will be defeated by lack of confidence and security ... and there will be, what Hobbes truly asserted to be the essence of such a situation, a chronic state of war, open or veiled ... and the more the States arm to prevent a conflict the more certainly will it be provoked, since to one or another it will always seem a better chance to have it now than to have it on worse conditions later.[128]

'While this anarchy continues' Dickinson goes on to argue, states 'will endeavour to acquire supremacy over the others for motives at once of security and of domination, the others will combine to defeat it, and history will turn upon the two poles of empire and the balance of power.'[129] After this, though, the agreement with the advocates of geopolitics breaks down. For Dickinson this state of anarchy is not a natural order, but rather, one that was established by states, and perpetuated by them. It was the creation of the sovereign state in the fifteenth century that saw the establishment of an international anarchy.[130] Not only is the international anarchy a construction of the state, it is also increasingly unstable and dangerous. Each war is becoming 'more terrible, more destructive, and more ruthless than the last'.[131] At one level, states are responsible for the problem of the international anarchy because they have allowed the situation to develop and perpetuate. At another, though, identifying the cause of war as the anarchy between states meant that Dickinson could argue that no one specific nation was responsible for the war.[132] Since the international anarchy was the creation of a particular time in history, rather than a natural phenomenon, the answer lay in developing a new system to replace it:

> … so will the States of Europe and the world be unable to maintain the peace, even though all of them should wish to maintain it, unless they will construct some kind of machinery for settling their disputes and organising their common purposes, and will back that machinery by force. If they will do that they may construct a real and effective counterpoise to aggression from any Power in the future.[133]

Dickinson was not alone in his view that it was the international anarchy that was the root cause of the First World War (even though he was the first to explicitly use the phrase anarchy). Writing the year before in another influential text Leonard Woolf argued that '… society is so complex that though the majority of men and women do not want to fight, if there are no laws and rules of conduct … they will find themselves at one another's throats before they are aware of or desire it'.[134] The views expressed by Woolf and Dickinson influenced most British and American commentators during the inter-war years.[135] Part of the attraction of the idea of the international anarchy was its hearty rejection of the pre-1914 rationalism that had assumed that if people were to fully appreciate their situations then states and statesmen could be convinced that their interests lay in preserving peace. The international anarchy argument centred around the idea that the current structure of the system of states caused wars by the absence of a machinery to prevent it, and that this lay outside the wishes and desires of people. Norman Angell, who had by his own admission been guilty of a pre-1914 rationalism, adopted the concept of the international anarchy wholeheartedly after 1918, even using it as a title of one of his publications.[136] While the idea of the international anarchy had existed (without its catchy title) before 1914, it was the First World War that made it an important argument in favour of the establishment of a league of nations.

Agitation for the establishment of a league to deal directly with the problem of the international anarchy had begun as early as the first few months of the war. In Britain, what would later be called the Bryce Group was already being organised by Lowes Dickinson in August 1914,[137] while its American equivalent – The League to Enforce Peace – was established less than a year later in June 1915. The Bryce Group merged with other organisations in 1915 to become the League of Nations Society, and its close links with The League to Enforce Peace guaranteed a free flow of proposals on the league across the Atlantic. Much of these proposals were summarised in Leonard Woolf's popular book *International*

*Government*, written under the auspices of the left-of-centre Fabian Research Bureau, where the problem was highlighted as a lack of institutional machinery:

> In its broadest aspect the problem is to develop a whole system of international relationships in which public war shall be as impossible between civilised states as is private war in civilised states: in its narrower aspect the problem which the world has still to solve is the development of a machinery capable of settling international differences and disputes.[138]

Here we have the elements that would dominate discussions in IR over the next few decades:

1   The unfavourable comparison between international and domestic politics, where the former was seen as inferior to the latter.
2   The need for some kind of governmental machinery in order to bring the international in line with the rules found in the domestic, but going along with this a recognition that any international machinery was going to have to be different from domestic machinery due to the differences in scale and to the role played by the sovereign nation state at a global level.

The need for some form of global machinery was driven by two underlying conditions, both of which Woolf explored. First, and underlined by the jingoism experienced during the war, Woolf anticipated Niebuhr in arguing that humanity 'in national or international masses is not yet an orderly or reasonable animal'. Rather, the passionate nature of humans made some kind of international judicial process necessary, as we were not rational enough to reach a peaceful and just world without it.[139] Woolf's addition of a 'yet' left open (as Niebuhr would not) the possibility that, in the future, people might be rational enough to live without a strict judicial process. Second, 'that in every department of life society has become international',[140] and consequently the state was no longer capable of managing or protecting the life of its own society. Both of these points were, for both Woolf and his contemporaries, underscored in blood by the ongoing First World War.

A more radical take on the shaping of a new 'league of nations' was taken by H.N. Brailsford, whose own 1917 contribution to the debate started from the common position that the goal of any league must be to promise humanity security from further wars. Brailsford, however, was much more critical of the institution of the nation state, arguing that the 'traditional refusal of the sovereign state … to allow any interference with its internal questions' was the greatest obstacle to peace since it meant that problems of justice and equity could only be solved by war.[141] A peace based on nothing more than 'existence side by side of nations, which just contrive to avoid bloodshed' would be a weak and unsustainable one. Instead, any secure peace would need to address questions of justice, and by justice Brailsford also included issues of economic equity.[142] The need to deal directly with the problem of state sovereignty led Brailsford to propose that the new representatives at the League should be made up of appointees from national parliaments, rather than the representatives of governments. This would allow the new league to represent all the ideological fissures within humanity as a whole, rather than just specific sovereign national entities.[143] This 'league of peoples' as an alternative to a 'league of cabinets' remained central to Brailsford's arguments for international organisation up to and including his suggestions for the new United Nations two decades later. It was also adopted by the Labour Party as its official position on the formation of the League.[144] Not surprisingly, Brailsford was deeply disappointed with the peace treaties and League of Nations Covenant that emerged from the Paris Peace Conference of 1919. This disappointment fuelled his pessimism about the League, expressed most bitterly in his book *After the Peace*, and although he did become reconciled to some aspects of the League experiment, he continued to regard it as insufficiently free from state and capitalist interests to deal with the wider problems of nationality, economic injustice and imperialism.[145]

Yet, despite the misgivings of many, such as Brailsford, the idea of the league caught the imaginations of not just intellectuals and writers, but also senior politicians. While Woodrow Wilson is justly credited with pushing the idea and making the league a principle goal of the coming peace, it was actually the South African Prime Minister Jan Smuts who composed the first draft of the League Covenant.[146] Smuts' draft so impressed Wilson that it formed the basis of American proposals at Paris. Other major public figures, such as Lord Robert Cecil in Britain and Léon Bourgeois in France were also associated with the campaign for the establishment of the league. While the resulting League of Nations that met in January 1920 was without precedent, it was also not without its critics, especially among those on the left who had expected more from the organisation. This would mean that much of the debates about the League in the decade to come would focus on a clash between more conservative politicians who were largely happy with the League as it was currently constructed, and more liberal or socialist opinion formers who either supported reform of the League Covenant to 'plug the gaps' in its machinery, or dismissed the League as a capitalist and potentially war-mongering club. That said, the League did open up avenues for new groups that had previously had little input into the practices of international politics and diplomacy. Non-western governments and peoples found the League a useful venue for expressing their concerns about western-dominated great power politics, while women for the first time were able to express specific gendered issues through either the regular organs of the League, or through the League-associated organisation The Women's International League for Peace and Freedom. These will be discussed in more detail in the next chapter.

The attention that the League would give to the issue of women was itself a product of the effect that the war had had on the life of women. In both Britain and the United States one of the effects of the war was to demonstrate the importance of international affairs to the life of women, and to put into sharp relief the relationship between the campaign for the right to vote and the role of war in modern society. The campaign for women's right to vote stimulated interest in international affairs among feminists and suffrage campaigners for two reasons. First, as newly enfranchised voters many feminists saw the involvement in public affairs as the next logical step. Second, many also saw a direct link between the right to vote in domestic politics and the campaign for a more peaceful order globally.[147] For some this intrusion of international affairs came as a shock.[148] Yet, like the men who organised in 1914–15 for a league of nations, feminists on both sides of the Atlantic were quick to organise, with Jane Addams and Emily Greene Balch being particularly active in the United States (and both later earning Nobel Peace Prizes for their efforts).[149] Helena Swanwick, in this sense, was ahead of the curve. She was a founder member of the Union of Democratic Control (UDC) in 1914, an organisation dedicated to preserving debate and discussion about war aims and containing many of the major centre-left international activists of the time such as Norman Angell, J.A. Hobson and H.N. Brailsford. As early as 1913 she had been making the link between the nature of a militarised society, that upholds the physical force to destroy, and the denial of women's rights.[150] For Swanwick a pacific society would be the only one to give women their due place as political equals. In 1935 she wrote that her transition to peace work from agitation for suffrage had been a smooth and easy one:

> I regarded peace not as a state you could work for in the abstract, but as the condition which would result from a just and fair conduct of national and international relations. And I felt that in working for the emancipation of women, I was contributing to the cause of peace.[151]

Swanwick's key wartime UDC pamphlet *Women and War* set out the contemporary feminist case against war, and helped set the tone for denunciations of war throughout the inter-war period. Here Swanwick took aim at the myth that soldiers defended their women-folk by going to war. Instead she argued that not only were armies singularly incapable of defending women and children (either from bombers or from the horrors of occupation by the enemy), but that women suffered more from war than men. Left to fend for themselves on the home front women were subject to solitary horrors, while denied the one positive aspect of war: the camaraderie of the fighting man. Swanwick finished by arguing that militarised societies reduced women to the role of brood-mares, and that the only way for women to enjoy equal rights with men was for a reduction of the role of militaristic physical force in society, and its replacement with more peaceful forms of force and cooperation.[152] Swanwick's analysis of the way that, even in peacetime, militarisation undermines women's position in society was an early example of an argument taken up in feminist IR after the Cold War by Cynthia Enloe,[153] and demonstrates how feminist thought has been an integral part of international thought from at least the First World War. In fact, the emergence of feminist approaches to international affairs owes much to the effects of the war.

There was one more important legacy of the war, and one found on both sides of the Atlantic, but was most sharply delineated in Britain. This was a combination of a deep pessimism about the future of western civilisation and a frantic belief that there was very little time in which to accomplish the goals necessary to save the world from another great cataclysm. This mood is well caught in Richard Overy's *The Morbid Age*, which traces the passage of this pessimism through British society in the 1920s and 1930s. While there had been pessimism before 1914 without a doubt, it now became a strong part of the spirit of the age. It was not for nothing that, following the war Norman Angell could declare that the individualistic pre-war world upon which his *Great Illusion* had rested was dead.[154] Peace, for Angell and many of his contemporaries, could only be secured by some kind of global organisation such as the proposed league. This was not a flight of optimistic idealism, but rather a pessimistic recognition of the failure of the old liberal pre-war world to manage itself without institutional help.

## Conclusion

The period from the 1880s to 1914 represents a crucial watershed in the development of international thought. Rapid industrialisation and globalisation of the economy, combined with changes in the social and ideological make-up of the world, led to a series of studies on the nature of the international. For some, such as Mahan, the emphasis remained the continuities of international strategy, shaped by the perennial forces of human nature. For others the new industrialised world dominated by finance capital and the conflict over natural resources meant that the fundamental rules of international affairs had now changed. In among these intellectual arguments we often find a tension between a nineteenth century optimistic faith in progress alongside a pessimistic sense that human reactions to these changes were dominated by older pre-industrial ways of thinking. Often these two ideas could be found wrapped up in the same argument. Differences of emphasis also abound. Some looked to the effects of space and environment, turning to the physical sciences for their inspiration. Others rested their ideas on a view of unchanging human nature, while others saw the fundamentals of human existence in the development of ideas of community and the realm of ideas.

Thus, all the ingredients for a debate over the international were in place before 1914. What was missing was a crisis to spark off serious debate about the nature and future of the international. The First World War was, in that sense a catalyst, rather than a cause. The international thought of the inter-war period did not emerge as a product of the embers of war, and much of what would emerge as inter-war IR had precedents and antecedents in the pre-1914 period. That said, it would be naïve in the extreme to assume that the war would have no effect on the trajectory of international thought. The first point is that the war acted as an effective recruiting sergeant for the study of international affairs. Although many, such as Angell, Butler or Brailsford had been interested in international affairs before the war, after the war they were joined by others who, until that time had written more on domestic political issues. These new converts included Leonard Woolf, Helena Swanwick and Isaiah Bowman. In the work of one convert, the classicist Lowes Dickinson, the emerging analysis of the international status quo found both a superior summary and a new name for the problem: the European (later international) anarchy. While not the first person to develop what Richard K. Ashley called the anarchy problématique, Lowes Dickinson was the man who gave it its name for future IR scholars. The second point is that the war created an interest in international affairs among the general publics of the major western states. This was tinged with a sense of desperation brought on by the carnage of the war years that led many to believe that a full understanding of the international, leading to reform of the structures of global governance, was necessary in order to prevent another conflict. Finally, the third point is that the war helped crystallise organisations and venues around which writers interested in international affairs could congregate and discuss different approaches to the international. The development of the League of Nations, its associated bodies, the Royal Institute of International Affairs, the Council for Foreign Relations, the Women's International League for Peace and Freedom, the Union of Democratic Control and a myriad other smaller organisations and venues represented a sea-change in the structures that existed for the discussion, dissemination and fostering of ideas about the international. Thus, while the ideas might not have been new ones, as a new world dawned in 1919 the attitudes, critical mass of interested parties, and the institutional structures for the study of the international certainly were.

Even the peace conference in Paris itself helped to push interests forward. Many of those involved in the conference (either directly as delegates or indirectly as advisors or authors of briefing notes) went on to careers that involved both the practice and the study of the international. These included Isaiah Bowman, John Maynard Keynes, Harold Nicolson, Robert Cecil, Philip Noel-Baker and David Mitrany. For those outside, such as H.N. Brailsford or E.H. Carr, opposition to the peace treaties remained a major part of their work over the next two decades. De Carvalho et al. may be right about the over-emphasis of IR textbooks on 1919 as a founding date,[155] but it is also true to say that it does mark – if not a fundamental break with the past – at least a quickening of interest in global problems.

## Notes

1 On this see especially Brian Schmidt, *The Political Discourse of Anarchy. A Disciplinary History of International Relations* (Albany NY: SUNY Press, 1998); Torbjørn Knutsen, 'A Lost Generation? IR Scholarship Before World War I', *International Politics*, 2008, 45, 650–674; and Casper Sylvest, 'Continuity and Change in British Liberal Internationalism, *c.*1900–1930', *Review of International Studies*, 2005, 31, 263–83.

2 On the imperialist origins of the study of IR see: John Hobson, *The Eurocentric Conception of World Politics: Western International Theory, 1760–2010* (Cambridge: Cambridge University Press, 2012) as well as David Long and Brian Schmidt (eds), *Imperialism and Internationalism in the Discipline of International Relations* (Albany NY: SUNY University Press, 2005).

3  Stephen Toulmin, *Human Understanding Volume 1* (Oxford: Clarendon, 1972), ch. 5.
4  On Ratzel's concept of *Lebensraum* – Ratzel also used the terms *Landerraüme, Erdraum* and *Die Politischer Raüme* – see Ratzel (1897).
5  Friedrich Ratzel, 'Die Lebensraum', in *Politische Geographie* (Munich/Berlin: Oldenburg, 1897), 11–12; Friedrich Ratzel, *Anthropogeographie* (Stuttgart: J. Engelhorn, 1899), 2.
6  Franco Farinelli, 'Friedrich Ratzel and the Nature of (Political) Geography', *Political Geography*, 2000, 19, 953. The quote, used by Farinelli, is directly from Ratzel.
7  Friedrich Ratzel, 'Flottenfrage und Weltlage', *Münchner Neuste Nachrichtung*, 1898, 51, 1–2.
8  Ratzel, *Politische Geographie*, 357.
9  Quoted in Hans W. Weigert, *Generals and Geographers. The Twilight of Geopolitics* (New York: Books for Libraries Press, 1942), 99–100.
10  Weigert, *Generals and Geographers*, 101–2.
11  Rudolf Kjellén, *Der Staat als Lebensform* (Leipzig: Hirzel, 1917), 21. It was Kjellén who first coined the term geopolitics.
12  Kjellén, *Staat als Lebensform*, 203.
13  Ellen Churchill Semple, *Influences of Geographic Environment on the Basis of Ratzel's System of Anthropo-Geography* (London: Constable, 1911), 2.
14  Richard Hofstadter, *Social Darwinism in American Thought* (New York: George Braziller, 1955), 172.
15  Frederick Jackson Turner, 'The Significance of the American Frontier in American History', in Frederick Jackson Turner, *The Frontier in American History* (Tucson: University of Arizona Press, 1994). This address was originally given in 1893.
16  Turner, 'American Frontier', 3–4.
17  Frederick Jackson Turner, 'Social Forces in American History', in Turner, *The Frontier in American History*, 315. Originally presented in 1910. See also: William Appleman Williams, 'The Frontier Thesis and American Foreign Policy', *The Pacific Historical Review*, 1955, 24, 379–95.
18  Of course, this idea of frontier freedom went along with the idea of expansion into a 'wilderness' that conveniently airbrushed out the native Americans and Mexicans that lived on that land.
19  See Ellsworth Huntington, *Climate & Civilization* (New Haven: Yale University Press, 1915).
20  In 2004 the importance of Mackinder's 1904 article to the development of geography was recognised by a special issue of the *Geographical Journal* dedicated to Mackinder's work.
21  Halford J. Mackinder, 'The Geographical Pivot of History', *The Geographical Journal*, 1904, 23, 432–3.
22  Mackinder, 'Geographical Pivot', 433.
23  'Geographical Pivot', 434; Halford J. Mackinder, *Democratic Ideals and Reality. A Study in the Politics of Reconstruction* (London: Constable, 1919), 66–9, 84, 143.
24  Halford J. Mackinder, 'Man-Power as a Measure of National and Imperial Strength', *National and English Review*, 1905, 45, 136–43.
25  Mackinder, *Democratic Ideals and Reality*, 93.
26  See Leo Amery's comment in Mackinder, 'Geographical Pivot', 441.
27  See, for example, John H. Mauer, 'Mahan on World Politics and Strategy: The Approach of the First World War, 1904–1914', in John B. Hattendorf (ed.), *The Influence of History on Mahan* (Newport, RI: Naval War College Press, 1991), 157–76.
28  Alfred Thayer Mahan, *The Influence of Sea Power Upon History 1660–1783* (Boston: Little, Brown & Co., 1890), 88–9.
29  Mahan, *Influence of Sea Power Upon History*, 25–8; Alfred Thayer Mahan, *The Interests of America in International Conditions* (Boston: Little, Brown & Co., 1918), 87.

30  Mahan, *Influence of Sea Power Upon History*, 28–9.
31  Alfred Thayer Mahan, *The Interest of America in Sea Power. Present and Future* (Boston: Little, Brown & Co., 1898), 165–6; Alfred Thayer Mahan, *Armaments and Arbitration or the Place of Force in the International Relations of States* (New York: Harper, 1912), 113–17.
32  *Armaments and Arbitration*, 9.
33  John M. Hobson, *The Eurocentric Conception of World Politics. Western International Theory 1760–2010* (Cambridge: Cambridge University Press, 2012), 129.
34  *Armaments and Arbitration*, 10, 86–7, 107–9.
35  *Armaments and Arbitration*, 13–14, 145.
36  *Armaments and Arbitration*, 120.
37  *Armaments and Arbitration*, 8.
38  Alfred Thayer Mahan, *Some Neglected Aspects of War* (Boston: Little, Brown & Co., 1907), 38–9, 51.
39  See *Some Neglected Aspects of War*, x, xx, 47; and *Armaments and Arbitration*, 122–3, 126–7.
40  *Some Neglected Aspects of War*, xvii, 38–9; and *Armaments and Arbitration*, 12.
41  *Armaments and Arbitration*, 142.
42  *Some Neglected Aspects of War*, xviii, 33.
43  See, for example: *Some Neglected Aspects of War*, ch. IV.
44  Brooks Adams, *The Law of Civilization and Decay* (New York: Vintage, 1943 [1896]), 4, 295.
45  Brooks Adams, *The New Empire* (New York: Bergman, 1969 [1902]), xvi.
46  *Law of Civilization and Decay*, esp. 6–7, 292–3.
47  *Law of Civilization and Decay*, 7, 293.
48  *New Empire*, Iii.
49  *New Empire*, 44, 113–14, 181–2.
50  For example, *New Empire*, 44.
51  Homer Lea, *The Valour of Ignorance* (New York and London: Harper, 1909) and Homer Lea, *The Day of the Saxon* (New York and London: Harper, 1912).
52  Richard K. Ashley, 'Untying the Sovereign State: A Double Reading of the Anarchy Problematique', *Millennium*, 1988, 17 (2), 240.
53  Schmidt, *Political Discourse of Anarchy*, 70.
54  Paul S. Reinsch, *World Politics at the End of the Nineteenth Century As Influenced by the Oriental Situation* (New York and London: Macmillan, 1900), 3.
55  *World Politics*, 5–6, 24–5.
56  *World Politics*, 14.
57  *World Politics*, 8.
58  *World Politics*, 70–1, 78.
59  *World Politics*, 16.
60  *World Politics*, 79–80.
61  *World Politics*, 40.
62  *World Politics*, 11.
63  Paul S. Reinsch, *Colonial Government an Introduction to the Study of Colonial Institutions* (New York and London: Macmillan, 1902), and Paul S. Reinsch, *Colonial Administration* (New York and London: Macmillan, 1905).
64  For a good summary of the development of these organisations see Craig Murphy, *International Organization and Industrial Change. Global Governance Since 1850* (New York: Oxford University Press, 1994), chs 2–4.
65  Paul S. Reinsch, *Public International Unions. A Study of International Administrative Law* (Boston and London: Ginn, 1911), 1, 2.
66  *Public International Unions*, 3–5.
67  *Public International Unions*, 6.

68 Reinsch, *Public International Unions*, 7; William James, 'The Moral Equivalent of War', in Harrison Ross Steeves and Frank Humphrey Ristine, *Representative Essays in Modern Thought* (New York: American Book Co., 1913), 519–33 (originally delivered as a speech in 1906).

69 John Baylis and Steve Smith, *The Globalization of World Politics*, third edn (Oxford: Oxford University Press, 2005), 774.

70 P. Savigear, 'Philosophical Idealism and International Politics: Bosenquet, Treitschke and War', *British Journal of International Studies*, 1975, 1(1), 48.

71 Bernard Bosenquet, *The Philosophical Theory of the State*, fourth edn (London: Macmillan, 1923), 1–2. The first edition was published in 1899, with further editions appearing in 1910, 1920 and 1923.

72 This is discussed in Stefan Collini, 'Hobhouse, Bosenquet and the State: Philosophical Idealism and Political Argument in England 1880–1918', *Past and Present*, 1976, 72, 93.

73 See Bosenquet, *Philosophical Theory of the State*, chs VI–VII; and Bernard Bosenquet, *Social and International Ideals. Being a Study in Patriotism* (London: Macmillan, 1917), 307.

74 Bernard Bosenquet, 'The Function of the State in Promoting the Unity of Mankind', *Proceedings of the Aristotelian Society*, 1916–17, 17, 29.

75 *Philosophical Theory*, 305.

76 See the discussion in Peter P. Nicholson, 'Philosophical Idealism and International Politics: a Reply to Dr Savigear', *British Journal of International Studies*, 1976, 2 (1), 78–9.

77 C. Delisle Burns, Bertrand Russell and G.D.H. Cole, 'The Nature of the State in View of its External Relations', *Proceedings of the Aristotelian Society*, 1915–16, 16, 290–325; L.T. Hobhouse, *The Metaphysical Theory of the State. A Criticism* (London: George Allen & Unwin, 1918).

78 Burns, Russell, Cole, 'Nature of the State', 312–13.

79 Burns, Russell, Cole, 'Nature of the State', 298–9.

80 Burns, Russell, Cole, 'Nature of the State', 313, 317–18; Hobhouse, *Metaphysical Theory*, 108–9.

81 Burns, Russell, Cole, 'Nature of the State', 303–8. Quote on 304.

82 Bosenquet, 'Function of the State', 306–7.

83 Bosenquet, *Social and International Ideals*, 313.

84 Bosenquet, 'Function of the State', 50; Bosenquet, *Philosophical Theory*, lix.

85 Bosenquet, 'Function of the State', 35, 51; Bosenquet, *Social and International Ideals*, 307, 309.

86 Bosenquet, 'Function of the State', 53.

87 Hobhouse, *Metaphysical Theory*, 106.

88 Hobhouse, *Metaphysical Theory*, 107.

89 Hobhouse, *Metaphysical Theory*, 108.

90 Bosenquet, 'Function of the State', 51.

91 See lix.

92 Quoted in Nicholson, 'Philosophical Idealism and International Politics', 81.

93 H.G. Wells, *Outline of History* (Toronto: Doubleday, 1925), 1100. The quote appears at the end of chapter XL.

94 Reinsch, *Public International Unions*, 5–6

95 Reinsch, *Public International Unions*, 3.

96 Reinsch, *Public International Unions*, 3–4

97 Reinsch, *Public International Unions*, 7.

98 Nicholas Murray Butler, *The International Mind. An Argument for the Judicial Settlement of International Disputes* (New York: Charles Scribner's Sons, 1912), 36, 105.

99 Butler, *The International Mind*, 41.

100 Butler, *The International Mind*, 102.

101  Butler, *The International Mind*, 9–10.
102  Butler, *The International Mind*, 80.
103  For a discussion of the critical success of the book see Martin Caedel, *Living the Great Illusion. Sir Norman Angell 1872–1967* (Oxford: Oxford University Press, 2009), 109 ff.
104  Lucian M. Ashworth, *Creating International Studies. Angell, Mitrany and the Liberal Tradition* (Aldershot: Ashgate, 1999), 48.
105  *The Great Illusion. A Study of the Relation of Military Power in Nations to their Economic and Social Advantage* (Toronto: McClelland and Goodchild, 1911), 179–80.
106  I.S. Bloch, *Is War now Impossible* (Aldershot: Gregg Revivals, 1991 [1899]).
107  Caedel, *Living the Great Illusion*, 111.
108  Angell, *Great Illusion*, 27–8, 54, 46–7; Norman Angell, *Foundations of International Polity* (London: William Heinemann, 1914), 95–8.
109  *Foundations of International Polity*, 89.
110  *Great Illusion*, 48–9.
111  *Great Illusion*, 252–3; *Foundations of International Polity*, 89, 83–4, 88 Norman Angell, *Peace Theories and the Balkan War* (London: Horace Marshall, 1912), 49.
112  *Foundations of International Polity*, 52–5; *Peace Theories*, 114–15; Norman Angell, *War and the Essential Realities* (London: Watts, 1913), 24–5.
113  Caedel, *Living the Great Illusion*, 101–2.
114  Angell, *Great Illusion*, 153.
115  *Foundations of International Polity*, 74, 141; *Peace Theories*, 44.
116  Mahan, *Armaments and Arbitration*, 122–3.
117  See Caedel, *Living the Great Illusion*, 98.
118  Norman Angell, *The Fruits of Victory* (New York: Garland, 1972 [1921]), 61.
119  Caedel, *Living the Great Illusion*, 102.
120  For a fuller discussion of this issue see Hobson, *Eurocentric Conception of World Politics*, chs 4–5.
121  *Great Illusion*, 155, 266; *Foundations of International Polity*, 78.
122  J.A. Hobson, *Imperialism. A Study* (London: Nisbet, 1902).
123  H.N. Brailsford, *The War of Steel and Gold. A Study of the Armed Peace*, ninth edn (London: Bell, 1917), 29–32.
124  Brailsford, *War of Steel and Gold*, 72.
125  G. Lowes Dickinson, *The International Anarchy 1904–1914* (London: Century, 1926); G. Lowes Dickinson, *The European Anarchy* (London: George Allen & Unwin, 1916).
126  Helen Milner, 'The Assumption of Anarchy in International Relations: A Critique', *Review of International Studies*, 1991, 17, no. 1, 67–85; Richard K. Ashley, 'Untying the Sovereign State: A Double Reading of the Anarchy Problematique', *Millennium: Journal of International Studies*, 1988, 17(2), 227–62; Alexander Wendt, 'Anarchy is What States Make of it: the Social Construction of Power Politics', *International Organization*, 1992, 46(2), 391–425.
127  Ashley, 'Untying the Sovereign State', 240.
128  Dickinson, *European Anarchy*, 9–10.
129  Dickinson, *European Anarchy*, 10–11.
130  Dickinson, *European Anarchy*, 9. On Dickinson's notion that his view of the international anarchy was meant to deal with a specific problem, rather than an ahistorical structural issue, see: E.M. Forster, *Goldsworthy Lowes Dickinson* (London: Edward Arnold, 1962), 173. For a detailed examination of Lowes Dickinson's international thought see Barbara Plank, 'Goldsworthy Lowes Dickinson and the Causes of War: A Theoretical and Historical Analysis', London School of Economics, PhD thesis, 2011.
131  Dickinson, *European Anarchy*, 145.

132  G. Lowes Dickinson, *The Autobiography of G. Lowes Dickinson*, edited by Denis Proctor and Noel Annan (London: Duckworth, 1973), 199.

133  Dickinson, *European Anarchy*, 152–3.

134  Leonard Woolf, *International Government* (London: George Allen & Unwin, 1916), 7.

135  Knutsen, 'A Lost Generation?', 668.

136  Norman Angell, 'The International Anarchy', in Leonard Woolf (ed.), *The Intelligent Man's Way to Prevent War* (London: Victor Gollancz, 1933).

137  Dickinson, *Autobiography*, 190.

138  Woolf, *International Government*, 4.

139  Woolf, *International Government*, 124–5.

140  Woolf, *International Government*, 312–13.

141  H.N. Brailsford, *A League of Nations* (London: Headley, 1917), 80.

142  Brailsford, *League of Nations*, 266–7, 287.

143  Brailsford, *League of Nations*, 313.

144  H.N. Brailsford, *Our Settlement with Germany* (Harmondsworth: Penguin, 1944), 137–8. Labour Party, 'Short Statement on War Aims', Advisory Committee on International Questions memo no. 6 25 June 1918, p1, Labour Party Archives, Manchester; Arthur Henderson, *The Peace Terms* (London: Labour Party, 1919), 12.

145  H.N. Brailsford, *After the Peace* (London: Leonard Parsons, 1920).

146  Jan Smuts, *The League of Nations: A Practical Suggestion* (London: Hodder and Stoughton, 1918).

147  See the discussions in B. Haslam, *From Suffrage to Internationalism* (New York: Peter Lang, 1999); J. Vellacott, *Pacifists, Patriots and the Vote* (Houndsmill: Palgrave Macmillan, 2007); and L. Ashworth, 'Feminism, War and the Prospects for Peace. Helena Swanwick (1864–1939) and the Lost Feminists of Inter-War International Relations', *International Feminist Journal of Politics*, 2011, 13(1), 25–43.

148  See Haslam, *From Suffrage to Internationalism* , 40.

149  See the discussion in Harriet Hyman Alonso, 'Nobel Peace Laureates, Jane Addams and Emily Greene Balch: Two Women of the Women's International League for Peace and Freedom', *Journal of Women's History*, 1995, 7(2), 6–26. On the broader shift in the women's movement from suffrage to peace and foreign policy see Vellacott, *Pacifists, Patriots and the Vote*, ch. 9.

150  H.M. Swanwick, *The Future of the Women's Movement* (London: Bell, 1913), 1938.

151  H.M. Swanwick, *I Have Been Young* (London: Victor Gollancz, 1935), 264.

152  H.M. Swanwick, *Women and War* (London: Union of Democratic Control, 1915). See also H.M. Swanwick, 'Towards a Permanent Peace VI: The Case for Women's Participation in National and International Affairs'. *Labour Leader*, 29 April 1915, 5.

153  See Cynthia Enloe, *The Morning After. Sexual Politics at the End of the Cold War* (Berkeley: University of California Press, 1993).

154  Angell, *Fruits of Victory*, 61–70, 300–1.

155  Benjamin de Carvalho, Halvard Leira and John Hobson, 'The Big Bangs of IR: The Myths That Your Teachers Still Tell You about 1648 and 1919', *Millennium*, 2011, 39(3), 735–58.

# 6 The new world

## International government and peaceful change, 1919–1935

*The first step in understanding the IR of the years between 1919 and 1935 is to forget the idea of the realist–idealist debate. It never happened, or at least not between these years, and also not before or during the Second World War. The first decade and a half after the First World War, though, does see many important developments. IR begins to be taught in the universities; the development of the League leads to debates over how it should be used (for example: should it be based on state membership? Should it use primarily legal or psychological tools to maintain peace and security?); and also a growing pessimism about the prospects of human civilisation.*

*There were four main themes in this period:*

1  *The development of a geopolitical or political geography approach to the study of international relations.*
2  *Various conservative and liberal writers who were broadly supportive of the League of Nations as predominantly an organisation of states.*
3  *A cohesive liberal socialist community in Britain that hoped to reform the League in order to build an effective collective security system.*
4  *Radical socialists and strict pacifists, who opposed collective security and were either hostile to the League, or saw it as primarily a longer-term psychological tool for peace.*

In 1986 Michael Joseph Smith likened inter-war international theory to 'a civic meeting punctuated by communal singing of hymns by S.S. Wesley' that had interrupted 'a performance of Wagner's Ring Cycle'.[1] While few writers have shown Smith's flair for imagery when describing inter-war IR, this view (in one form or another) is probably the most common one found in introductory textbooks. An ongoing and venerable realist tradition is suddenly nudged out temporarily by a bunch of moralising idealists. Common it may be, but Smith – and so many of the textbook accounts – give a misleading picture of international thought both before and during the inter-war period. When dealing with the international thought of the inter-war period the historian of international thought is faced by two challenges. The first is the frequent alluding back to the inter-war period within IR scholarship, which means that most (if not all) IR scholars feel that they know what happened. Any analysis of international thought of the period has to deal with existing assumptions about the debates and the paradigms involved. The second is that so much of the common sense understandings of the inter-war period found in IR scholarship are just plain wrong. At least when we approach a period that is less well referred to in IR, such as the late nineteenth century, the historian of international thought has the luxury of writing on an almost blank page. The historian of inter-war international thought has to come well-armed with barrel-loads of white-out. The problem here, to extend the analogy, is that past simplistic explanations keep coming through the correcting fluid, making the goal of constructing a narrative out of the historical record difficult unless it returns to follow the lines of anachronistic interpretations already laid down. In short: it is easier to learn something new than to unlearn a deeply ingrained mistake. Perhaps the best example of this persistent error is the continued belief in the existence of an idealist paradigm in inter-war IR.

On the positive side, mistaken though it may be, the broad IR interest in the inter-war period has at least meant that the period has attracted a wide range of scholars interested in re-examining and overturning IR's myths about its recent past. In fact, so much work has been done that coherent counter-narratives exist which challenge the inaccuracies of the mainstream mythic histories. Indeed, in some quarters these new interpretations are successfully replacing the simplistic myths, although if a survey of recent IR introductory textbooks is anything to go by there is still a great mountain to climb here.

Perhaps a first issue to address is why is the inter-war period so important to IR scholarship? Why was it deemed necessary to construct myths of IR's origins located in this period, and why has the new, more historically nuanced, analyses been deemed necessary in the first place? Part of the explanation lies in the continued fascination of the inter-war period in especially the wider English-speaking world. Sandwiched between two world wars, the period has been a source of cautionary tales about roads not taken, and of the struggles between liberalism, fascism and communism. In IR more specifically, the inter-war period appears to serve two contradictory roles. From the 1950s onwards it was not uncommon to see stories of the failed experiments of inter-war international affairs held up as a cautionary tale that showed the dangers of stepping off the well-worn paths of traditional 'realist' statecraft.[2] In this form the inter-war story became a warning against 'utopianism', and a support for a more conservative and stable statecraft built upon interests and power. Ideas like arbitration, collective security and international public opinion became the chimeras that had led the world to the brink of disaster. Interestingly the myths of the inter-war period served a different role from the 1980s onwards. Taking the earlier idea of a failed utopian (or idealist) age being replaced by a successful realist challenge, non-realist scholars began to embellish this into a story that actually challenged realist interpretations of IR. The central element of this was the idea that there had been a realist–idealist debate in the 1930s, which had been won by realism. Classed as the first great debate, these writers then added two more great debates: a behaviourist-traditionalist debate in the 1960s that ushered in more social scientific studies of IR, and a third ('inter-paradigm') great debate from the 1970s onwards between realism and two newly popular 'paradigms': structuralism (neo-Marxism) and liberalism.[3] In the 1990s a fourth great debate was added, in which the plethora of new paradigms had effectively broken the realist paradigm's stranglehold of the field.[4] Throughout this presentation of the great debates there was a barely concealed subtext: much as realism had successfully seen off a flawed idealism, so (in line with Thomas Kuhn's view of scientific revolutions) the domination of realism was now giving way in turn to new ideas. Conceding realism's victory in a first great debate was a rhetorical device used to argue that realism was now suffering the same fate as idealism, and could be just as easily tossed into the dustbin of outmoded ideas.[5]

What both boosters and knockers of a realist approach to IR shared was a need to present the inter-war period as essentially a struggle between idealists and realists, and thus while they disagreed on so much, common ground could at least be found in writing off non-realist approaches in the past as idealist. For realists it represented the reason why realism triumphed (and should continue to do so), for those critical of realism it was an example of the natural replacement of paradigms over time (and showed realism its future). As a result, textbooks from the 1980s onwards embellished a story of a great debate in which two paradigms struggled for mastery of the new field of IR. The only problem with this comfortable story was that it had little or no basis in the historical record.[6] Much like the Arthurian legends, which have had a similar limiting effect on our understanding of sixth century Britain, the realist–idealist great debate myth has become accepted through frequent retelling rather than through rigorous academic study. As a result, any attempt to understand the history of international thought in the inter-war period has to start by completely ignoring the categories created by the realist–idealist myth. Indeed, that is what much recent scholarship has done.

Yet, like all myths, the realist–idealist debate is based on a kernel of truth. Realism and idealism, along with utopianism, were traded as insults during the first few decades of the twentieth century, even if the terms lacked precise definitions. Two of these terms – realism and utopianism – were then given a more precise meaning by E.H. Carr in 1939.[7] Similarly, idealism and realism as modes of thought were certainly employed in the late 1940s and 1950s by American IR scholars, and here at least the labels did seem to fit a real debate over US foreign policy.[8] Here ideas of realism and idealism were frequently invoked as two necessary sides of proper social scientific thought.[9] These will be covered in more detail in the next two chapters. The purpose of this chapter lies in a different direction: to make sense of the early inter-war debates on international affairs, and to ask whether we can talk about a distinct intellectual field of IR emerging after 1919. We can certainly talk about emerging communities of scholars, and much of the concepts discussed survived to become part of post-1950 IR. Indeed, there is much more continuity between inter-war IR and post-1950 IR than many textbooks are willing to admit. That said, the international thought that emerged in the inter-war years was also in many ways distinct from the IR that we know as a largely US-based sub-discipline of Political Science that emerged after 1950. The past, in this sense, is also a foreign country.

This chapter examines the international thought associated with the period before the threat of fascism became a major international security concern, and therefore covers the period in which the League of Nations was at the height of its influence. The first section assesses the status of international thought immediately after the First World War, laying out how the immediate post-war period set the agenda for the discussions about the form of the international over the next fifteen years. The second section explores the emergence of a particular Anglo-American geopolitics during this period that, building on the lessons of earlier geopolitical approaches, produced a liberal analysis of the nature of the international order that would later have a powerful influence on United States post-1941 planning for the post-war world. The third section looks at various conservative and liberal writers on both sides of the Atlantic that supported the League of Nations in its current form, and only saw a need for minor revisions of the Covenant. This group was partially supported, but also challenged, by liberal socialist writers that will form the subject of the fourth section. These liberal socialists were supportive of the League idea, but also saw the current Covenant as no more than a first step in an on-going project. The final section brings in the radical socialists and pacifists who opposed the collective security of the League. Although this last group often included League supporters, their vision of what the League should be was radically different to all the three previous groups. While charting these four groups and reconstructing the international debates of the inter-war period, this chapter adds further weight to the argument about the uselessness and inaccuracy of the idea of a realist–idealist debate. This theme will also be taken further in the next chapter, where the complexities of international thought in the immediate pre-war and Second World War years will be explored in more depth. First, though, we need to return to the immediate effects of the First World War.

## International thought in the wake of the First World War

A number of scholars have cast doubt on the importance of the First World War in the history of international ideas, pointing to the continuity in thought between the pre-1914 and post-1919 periods.[10] They are not wrong. Not only did pre-1914 ideas survive the Great War, but also so did the pre-war scholars. The 1920s and 1930s were dominated by writings from those who had first articulated their ideas of international order before the war. Norman Angell, Nicholas Murray Butler, H.N. Brailsford, J.A. Hobson and Halford Mackinder all straddled the war, and in one way or another brought with them their pre-war conceptions and arguments, which in turn often dominated the debates on international order.

That said the First World War had two major catalytic effects that go unnoticed when we concentrate on the continuity of concepts and modes of thought. First, the War, directly or indirectly, spurred a number of intellectuals, writers and activists – many of whom had had little to do with studying the global until then – to write about international affairs. These included the geographer Isaiah Bowman, the journalist and suffragette Helena Swanwick, the economist and politician Hugh Dalton and the economist Emily Green Balch. This was part of what Philip Noel-Baker in 1924 called the 'psychological effect of the war', where the shock of 1914–18 forced people to take an interest in the international society of states.[11] Second, by bringing forth the League and calling into question both the political and economic versions of *laissez faire* the war encouraged the discussion of new forms of global governance. This was most clearly seen in the work of Norman Angell, and summed up in his 1921 *Fruits of Victory*, where he declared that the old individualism (on which so much of the argument of his *The Great Illusion* had been built) was dead by its own hand.[12] As a result the new order required a new system of international governmental machinery that had not been envisaged by Angell before 1914.

Underlying all this was a growth in the perceived importance of international affairs in certain quarters that had previously been little concerned with the international. Looking back to 1914 in a 1968 interview, the feminist and suffragette Kathleen Courtney lamented that she and her fellow activists 'knew nothing about foreign affairs, we had no idea of the causes of war'.[13] The shock of the war led many of Courtney's fellow suffragettes to embrace an active interest in international affairs, and to see this as a logical extension of their advocacy of women's rights at home. A similar sea-change occurred in the British Labour Party, where the new 1918 Party constitution for the first time committed the Party to an internationalist agenda. Previous to this the Party had seen foreign affairs as an unimportant distraction from domestic economic and social problems. This change on the left was matched by a similar change in more official circles, with perhaps the establishment of both the British Royal Institute of International Affairs and its American equivalent the Council on Foreign Relations marking a general realisation that international affairs were worthy of both study and also of public debate. Harold Nicolson noticed this change in attitude towards the international after the war, and worried that this new democratisation of foreign policy would lead to an erosion of the effectiveness of diplomacy. His answer was a division of labour, in which democratic accountability would play a larger role in the prescription of foreign policy, but that diplomats needed to be given freedom from direct interference when they were implementing policy.[14] Thus, while we can argue that the First World War did little to change the available ideas found in international thought, its role as a catalyst for the increased popularity – and urgency – of international issues is hard to deny.

Yet, it was not just the First World War that concentrated the minds of many. The process of building the post-war peace also stimulated interest and debate. The conference process that formally ended hostilities proved to be a deeply divisive process, and even today attitudes on the peace conferences of 1919 tend to be polarised and strongly held. I remember about a decade ago a poster exhibition in the Limerick City library on Anne Frank that described the Versailles treaty as 'notorious', and seemed to blame the Treaty for the rise of fascism. The irony that the attitude of the poster to the Treaty was identical to those of the Nazi's who had hounded the Franks was not lost on me at the time. Throughout the early years of the 1920s debate raged across a wide spectrum of opinion about the content of the treaties, and there were frequent calls for the renegotiation of the peace, calls that only really began to ebb after 1924. The debates about the peace and the treaties were fuelled by a series of analyses written by those who had been participants. These mixed with the resentment of groups (especially on the left) who felt excluded, and by the deeply divisive nature of the issues involved, made the process and the treaties controversial among former enemies and allies alike. Looking back at these debates from the hindsight of 1944 Mary Agnes Hamilton, an important figure in British centre-left circles, claimed that the left's opposition to the peace would have occurred whatever the outcome of the negotiations. For Hamilton the Treaty of Versailles in particular had been singled out for abuse it did not deserve.[15] On the other side, several senior figures were deeply critical of the treaties for being too easy on Germany. Marshall Foch, the French general and Allied supreme commander, pushed for harsher terms, and refused to attend the signing ceremony of the Versailles Treaty. Foch was convinced that the Treaty left Germany too strong, and would lead to a second war in the future.[16] These debates and opinions left a deep mark on the public consciousness in many parts of the world, and have in turn led to many commonly held myths about the peace and its treaties. There is, for example, no such thing as the 'war guilt clause'. Article 231 says no such thing. Rather it was a legal device by which the German government accepted responsibility for damage caused to Allied states and nationals, and thus provided the legal basis for asking for reparations from Germany for damage done to civilian property. Equally, German reparations were whittled away at a series of conferences to a value far lower than the figure that had angered Keynes. Apparent Allied capriciousness over national self-determination appears more reasonable when it is understood that self-determination was only one of three criteria used to assess the new borders. Security and economic viability were the other two considerations. Even the Mandate system (often denounced as a fig-leaf for continued imperialism), by recognising that colonial territories were the property of their populations, laid the foundations for the movement for decolonisation after the Second World War.[17]

These arguments about the Treaties and the origins of the League aside, the new international governmental structures set up or renewed at Paris also opened doors to groups that previously had not shown either the interest or the ability to debate and change international affairs. Thus, while the First World War pushed people previously uninterested in international politics towards engagement, the new structures around the League of Nations also exercised a pull factor on many of these groups. Women were among the beneficiaries of this new awareness and new structures of global governance. The League itself proved friendlier to women than the old pre-war diplomacy, with the Covenant guaranteeing that League positions would be open to women and men equally. As a result women's representation to the League was significant by the standards of the day. This was also reflected in the official delegations to the League. In 1929, for example, the British delegation to the League consisted of three men and two women (the women in this case being H.N. Swanwick and Mary Agnes Hamilton). In addition to this the League gave a special status to women through the Liaison Committee of Women's Organisations that regularised cooperation between the formal League structure and organisations such as the Women's International League for Peace and Freedom (WILPF).[18] At the Disarmament Conference of 1932–3 these women's organisations were given an official status akin to the NGO status that has become common at UN conferences today, while in 1937 the League established a Committee of Experts on the Legal Status of Women.[19]

The League also opened up the diplomatic world to those outside of the European and European settler states. While the peace conference had failed to add a clause to the League Covenant on racial equality (something pushed by Japan, but opposed by others including the Prime Ministers of Australia and New Zealand), both the peace conference and the League included a number of powers from outside the Western orbit. One of these, Japan, had already made its mark as a great power before the war, but the other five represented at the Peace Conference – Siam (Thailand), Haiti, Liberia, the Hedjaz and China – were new to the top tables of world diplomacy. In addition to this, British India was represented by two Indians (Ganga Singh, the Maharaja of Bikaner; and Satyendra Prasanno Sinha, Lord Sinha). In all, six non-western states (four from Asia, two from Africa, and one from the Caribbean) joined the League as founder members. Four more joined over the next seventeen years. Along with the Mandate provisions under the Covenant, that formally recognised that the inhabitants of a territory were the owners and ultimate sovereigns, the Peace conference and League had started the process that would break the western monopoly of global politics. Although it still left western domination in place, and had failed to break up the colonial empires via an extension of the mandate system to all colonies as some advocates of decolonisation like Leonard Woolf had hoped, precedents had been set.[20]

The debates about the future shape of the post-war world order after 1919 were fought out in many arenas, including the press, within and between political parties, in popular pamphlets, public meetings and reports. There was also the growth of the teaching of international affairs in universities. The year 1919 saw the foundation of the first professorial chair in international politics at University College of Wales in Aberystwyth (the aptly named 'Woodrow Wilson Chair'). The London School of Economics also started to offer courses in international affairs. In the United States the University of Chicago was among the pioneers in the establishment of courses in international relations, a development that has been dated from the arrival of Quincy Wright in 1931.[21] Chicago also boasts that its MA programme, founded in 1928, is America's oldest graduate programme in international affairs. Yet, Chicago was a relative latecomer, despite its influence. 1924 saw the opening of the Los Angeles University of International Relations, which is now part of the University of Southern California. Claims are also made for Georgetown University's Edmund A. Walsh School of Foreign Service, founded in 1919. Another claimant in the lists to be the oldest centre of learning in IR is the Graduate Institute of International Studies in Geneva, founded in 1927, and linked to the League of Nations located in the same city.

That said, though, peaking above the surface of these debates were four key books all written in the wake of the Paris Peace Conference of 1919. Tellingly, three of the four were written by people who had, or would have, a university affiliation during this period. Two were also written as a result of participant observation in the peace process, while one was written from experience of the frayed edges of the post-war world in southern Russia. The only one that was not produced by either an academic or participant in the events of 1919 was written by one of the top internationally renowned experts on world affairs. These four books were Isaiah Bowman's *New World*, Halford Mackinder's *Democratic Ideals and Reality*, John Maynard Keynes' *The Economic Consequences of the Peace*, and Norman Angell's *The Fruits of Victory*. The first two, as works of geopolitics, will be discussed in the next section, while the other two will appear in later sections. Important though these four books were, they were not the only works of international thought being produced in the English-speaking world and the following four sections will address the four major strands of inter-war thought in the English speaking world at the time. These are:

1   British–American international political geography.
2   The liberal and conservative supporters of the League.
3   The liberal–socialist challenge.
4   The pacifist and radical socialist critics of the League.

## The geopolitics of the new world: Mackinder and Bowman

Arguably, two of the four most influential books on the new post-1919 world came from the pens of two geographers, one in the United States and one from Britain: Isaiah Bowman and Halford Mackinder. Mackinder's pre-1914 ideas have already been discussed in the last chapter. For both Bowman and Mackinder the experiences of the war and the subsequent peace did not necessarily change their ideas, but they did lead to modifications of their thought as well as a greater concentration in their work on the form and structures of what they both saw as the new realities of a League-based international arena built around major changes in people's outlook on the world.

Although Bowman began work on his *The New World* during the 1919 Peace Conference, it was Mackinder's work that came out first. Mackinder had dramatically rejected environmental determinism after the First World War. That said, Mackinder's earlier more determinist views were incorporated into a broader view of the changes that had occurred in international politics. Partial readings of Mackinder, especially in strategic studies, exploit this, and often ignore Mackinder's arguments about the fundamental changes that have made the older strategic realities obsolete, dangerous or both.[22] Part of the reason that Mackinder could be presented as an environmental determinist rests with his view that conformity to environmental limits was one of two choices open to policy-makers. Under conditions of continued conflict between states for global power, Mackinder argued, the physical environment benefited continental land powers based on the 'World Island' of Eurasia/Africa. Mackinder identified a region of Eurasia (in 1904 called the 'pivot area', in 1919 the more catchy 'heartland') that was not accessible to sea power. This region, consisting of the area of at least three great powers and rich in both resources and manpower, could be used as the basis for a programme of world conquest by a single land power.[23] This situation was particularly disadvantageous for the liberal sea powers of Britain, France and the United States, and suggested that the threat of world empire came from either a Russian–German alliance (1904) or Germany (1919).

Yet, it is important to point out that this environmental determinist interpretation of power politics was only one possibility associated with one of two policy-maker ideal types explored in *Democratic Ideals and Reality*. For Mackinder there were two ways of approaching politics (and, by implication, world politics), either as an organiser or an idealist. While Mackinder treated these ideal types separately at the beginning of his book, the force of the argument, and Mackinder's own preferred view, was that it was important to be both an organiser and an idealist. Thus, his view of the relationship between the two centred, like Carr's concept of the relationship between realism and utopianism discussed in the next chapter, on the importance of a mix. The organiser was the expert in a particular field, who combined depth of knowledge with a narrow focus. In terms of running the state the organisers were the strategists who knew how to efficiently organise resources for the growth and development of the state. 'The great organiser is the great realist ... his imagination turns to "ways and means" and not to elusive ends ... The organiser inevitably comes to look upon men as tools.'[24] In terms of state policy organisers are the experts in grand geopolitical strategy. They are the great map-makers, who pour over plans and then make them happen. This deep and narrow knowledge base is both their strength and their weakness. They know how to accomplish specific goals, but are unable to fathom solutions outside of their ken. By contrast the idealist is the consummate dilettante with a broad knowledge, but no specific expertise. Weaker on organising for specific tasks, the idealist is able to think outside of the box and to come up with novel solutions that draw on a variety of fields of expertise. 'Idealists are the salt of the earth; without them to move us, society would soon stagnate and civilisation fade.'[25]

For Mackinder the interplay of these ideal types could be seen in the different international policies of Germany on the one hand and Britain and the United States on the other. German education was strictly technical, and its policy-makers successfully executed narrow strategic plans, but were imprisoned by their inability to see non-military solutions based on broad plans for international organisation. By contrast, the liberal training in Britain and the United States produced policy-makers who understand values and ethical considerations, but are weaker on strategic questions.[26] Precisely twenty years before Carr, Mackinder had already laid out Carr's realist/utopian categories, and like Carr had seen the fusing of them as central to good policymaking.[27] Mackinder saw hope in a cooperation between the strategic genius of the organiser and the progressive ethics of the idealist, but while he admired the technique of the organiser, he was deeply critical of the organiser as ruler. Organiser statesmen were 'unhuman' and used men as tools.[28] Yet, while the democracy of the idealist was preferable to live in, 'democracy is incompatible with the organisation necessary for war against autocracies'.[29]

Herein lay the problem for Mackinder. Following the logic of the organiser is to stick to the competing foreign policies that had led to the First World War. If the world remains wedded to this logic then the physical layout of the world's landmasses put a premium on the control of the Heartland through its conquest by one of the powers bordering the Heartland. Once the Heartland was under the control of a single land power then the world island could be conquered. The conquest of the world island would give this land power the resources to build up a fleet for the conquest of the democracies on the Rimland. Hence Mackinder's advice to the peacemakers in Paris: 'Who rules East Europe commands the Heartland; Who rules the Heartland commands the World Island; Who rules the World Island commands the World.'[30] In 1919 Mackinder saw Germany – whose education system was (in his view) structured to produce a bias toward the organiser ideal type – as the state poised to carry out this world conquest. There was a second alternative. The World could be made safe for democracy by changing the rules of the game – a strategy that involved a mix of idealist and organiser traits. By copper-fastening states into a system of international organisation through the League, geopolitical strategies of conquest could be replaced by a world built around ideas of democratic government that nevertheless also was aware of the importance of geopolitical realities. This would also solve a further problem for Mackinder: that the technologies of war now made hostilities between great powers a catastrophe.

> The League of Nations … represents a much more hopeful effort for the peaceful settlement of international disputes than anything that has been attempted before the Great War. The Court of International Law at The Hague is now a fact. If success does not attend these or similar endeavours the outlook for mankind a generation hence will be very black.[31]

Thus, for Mackinder, the geopolitical realities must be understood and worked with, but they also need to be transcended and overcome in a realistic fashion. This requires us to be both organisers and idealists. A similar interplay between material reality and ideas can be found in Mackinder's American contemporary Isaiah Bowman.

Bowman was one of the most influential intellectuals in twentieth century America, and also one of the group of scholars that developed and popularised IR in the United States. Through his role as the director of the American Geographical Society he became involved in war work from 1917, and it was from this that he became a senior member of 'The Inquiry' – the group that provided information and advice to the US government – and eventually the Chief Territorial Specialist of the American delegation at the Paris peace talks. Paris changed Bowman. Already beginning to doubt the environmental determinism that had dominated so much pre-war discussions of political geography in the United States (see Chapter 5), Bowman's exposure to the less-deterministic geography taught in France[32] and his realisation at the conference that individuals could make a difference led him to a re-evaluation of his view of the effect that the physical environment had on politics.[33] The result of this intellectual conversion was *The New World.* On the back of this book, and his credentials as a senior member of The Inquiry, he became a key expert on IR in the US, helping to found the Council for Foreign Relations in New York. In the Second World War he was to replay his advisor role, leading Neil Smith to call him 'Roosevelt's Geographer'. The core idea of Bowman's IR was his interpretation of the interaction between the physical environment and human agency.

Like most of inter-war IR scholarship, Bowman's ideas do not fit into a neat 'realist–idealist' dichotomy. Rather, Bowman's IR combines an appreciation for the physical 'realities' that create the initial conditions for IR with an understanding of the 'spiritual and mental attitudes' that interpret and condition the effects of the environment. Thus, in common with so many inter-war experts on international affairs he saw the nature of international affairs as a product of a determining physical reality and a human agency rooted in a world of ideas. It is how Bowman interprets these two influences that distinguishes him from other inter-war writers, and especially from his fellow geographer Mackinder.

For Bowman environmental factors created conditions with which human ingenuity has to deal. While the importance of various environmental factors varied through time and space, the key issue as far as the mid-twentieth century was concerned was the uneven spread of the raw materials necessary for modern society. The need to guarantee a full supply of materials to modern urban centres was, for Bowman, a major reason that great powers pursued policies of imperialism that coerced colonised peoples into subservient providers of manual labour and the extraction of minerals for the colonising power.[34] Yet, as this example shows, environmental factors did not have an independent life from human social factors, but were often responses to them as human use of the environment changed. The importance of raw materials, especially the recently vital oil, was itself the result of changes in the structure of human society.[35] While these physical and social concerns were real constraints on human action, they did not define how humanity should react to them. The major factor that defined the form of international relations was found in the realm of ideas. It was the issue of the distribution of raw materials that particularly concerned Bowman in the inter-war years.

The problem that raw material distribution posed for collective security was well known at the time, and formed a key part of many discussions within the International Studies Conference (ISC).[36] Bowman himself was an active member of the ISC, and the book he edited on land settlement was originally a report prepared for the tenth ISC conference.[37] Bowman's position on raw materials and the prospects for international order was reaffirmed by a US memorandum reported to the ISC conference in 1937 entitled 'Raw materials in peace and war':

> Just as disarmament is a hopeless ideal save through the prior or concurrent achievement of collective security against aggression, so raw material conflicts between nations are hopelessly insoluble in a world where each country must depend on its own strength to meet the menace of war.[38]

On the face of it raw material distribution pointed to seemingly unavoidable conflict between great powers for control and market access. Yet, for Bowman, it was within the grasp of humanity to alter the political structures and create a world in which this mal-distribution was not a source of conflict. The raw facts of geographical spread need not dictate how humans confronted the problem. In other words, scientific facts of environment and geography were only part of the story.

As a fully trained physical scientist Bowman understood the limits of the scientific study of human society. This did not mean he dismissed the importance of physical science to an understanding of human affairs, but rather that he saw the non-tangible and spiritual side of human affairs as the essential force creating a society. It was this view of spirit that underpins Bowman's view of a lived tradition that interprets and deals with the physical facts that it finds. As the very structure of Bowman's *New World* was designed to show, the physical constraints were not difficult to uncover, and were not what made a world new. 'The World becomes new the moment a new idea is applied to it and its workings.'[39] Far more difficult was the attempt to understand how attitudes of mind were changing and reacting to these constraints. International Relations for Bowman was about an understanding of these changes of the collective public mind. The opening lines of the fourth edition of *New World* emphasised this point.

> In the eventual history of the period in which we live, it is reasonable to think that the greatest emphasis will be put not upon the World War or the peace treaties which closed it, searching and complex and revolutionary as their terms proved to be, but rather upon the profound change that took place in the spiritual and mental attitudes of the people that compose this new world.[40]

Crucially for Bowman, it was this defining element of spirit that guaranteed that there were different social alternatives to the problems faced by the world.

In the immediate future, Bowman saw economic crises and inequalities as the main problem thrown up by the background human environment. The growing complexity of international economic relations had made current national boundaries unviable.[41] The state's reaction to this had been to retreat into an economic nationalism, which damaged business and economic stability.[42] In an atmosphere dominated by economic nationalism and the maldistribution of raw materials stronger states will be tempted to use military might to obtain adequate access to necessary resources, thus leading the world to war.[43] The answer to this problem for Bowman lay in a change in political attitude toward systems of international control, especially in the area of raw materials.[44] The major sign that these problems could be sorted out at an international level came from the development of the post-1919 'new diplomacy' that had originally emerged in response to the problem of war. Bowman was particularly hopeful about the system of legal arrangements since 1919 that had meant that states now approached problems of global politics in the spirit of friends rather than competitors.[45] While Bowman saw this as an example of a change of spirit, he did not see the legal agreements alone as a cause of peace, nor did he think that the 'old' diplomacy associated with competing states was dead. The legal arrangements that made multilateral diplomacy possible were a product of the new spirit, rather than a cause of a more peaceful order. In this sense Bowman was no simple advocate of formal legal structures. Similarly, he recognised the continued presence and even need for the 'old' diplomacy. The roots of the new multilateral diplomacy were shallow, and the continued habits of conquest were still ingrained in human politics. As a result, war was still an ever-present possibility, and the need for even the most benign and advanced society to prepare for war was clear.[46] Rather, it was the case that the dictates of the old diplomacy were no longer practical in the post-1919 era, and those who trumpeted the simple superiority of military power over all other considerations were victims of a pseudo-scientific approach that failed to grasp that 'the only permanent thing in this world is change'.[47] Thus, Bowman rejected the argument that a static human nature dictated that the prime concern in politics was the relative power between groups (a common concept in pre-1914 geopolitics, for example), and argued instead that the changes in spirit, while still not dominant, were a product of human interests that had adapted to changing global conditions.[48] This put him at odds with the human nature argument found in Morgenthau's classical realism, even though Bowman also saw policy as defined by interests. Bowman's arguments were to inform the development of United States global strategy during and after the Second World War.[49]

Although Mackinder never grasped the importance of the internationalisation of the economy as Bowman had done, his presentation of the idealist policy-maker and the need to merge this with the organiser followed Bowman's logic that the science of (physical) geography was not in and of itself enough to understand the behaviour of states. While this idea of the necessity of fusion contradicts the myth of the realist–idealist debate (where realism and idealism are constructed as separate paradigms pursued by separate people), it does align Mackinder's thinking with the realism of Carr (and to a lesser extent with that of John Herz), where the concepts of idealism and realism are treated as distinct ways of thinking, but are then brought back together in the idea that the best basis of foreign policy is a combination of realist and idealist outlooks. The inclusion of an idealist element to foreign policy meant that grim realist/organiser strategic logics could be transcended, and indeed this offered the best hope for the Anglophone democracies if they wished to make the world secure for their values and ideas.

While Mackinder's book had been published first, it was Bowman's *The New World* that was to be most immediately influential. In this sense the fate of the two books could not have been more different. Bowman's was lionised throughout the 1920s and early 1930s, while Mackinder's made little immediate impact. By the outbreak of the Second World War, however, Bowman's book slipped out of the collective consciousness, while Mackinder's was rediscovered on both sides of the Atlantic, and briefly became a must-read for those interested in post-war reconstruction. Despite the fact that Bowman was active in the Roosevelt Administration's war effort and post-war planning, it was Mackinder who influenced the development of strategic studies, and became popular with a new wave of international thinkers in the United States such as Nicholas Spykman. These influences will be discussed in more detail in the following chapter.

In some respects we should not be too surprised by this variation in fates. Bowman's book, with its stress on a shift in ideas, fit the zeitgeist of the 1920s, where all seemed new. While the 1920s had its fair share of pessimism, especially in British cultural and intellectual life, Bowman's book as a 'verbal atlas' laying out the current state and future of the world offered an unfettered hope where the only limits were our understanding of both the physical realities and the spiritual possibilities of the post-war world. By contrast, Mackinder's book, while also emphasising the interaction between ideals and material realities, was written more as a cautionary tale for those he feared would be carried away by ideals, and thus ignore the constraints imposed by the physical world. By the later 1930s, and certainly by the early 1940s, Bowman's optimism about the new spirit was hard to justify, while Mackinder's sense of dark foreboding fit the mood better. Equally, Bowman's concern with issues of imperialism and free trade seemed less immediately relevant to the conflict with fascism than did Mackinder's notion of the role of the Heartland and the threat posed by Germany through the realities of space. That said, it was Bowman's ideas of decolonisation linked to free trade that would become the basis of the long-term United States strategy through the Cold War, even while it was Mackinder's notion of political space that would influence military strategy against the Soviet Union. As a result, both deserve to be seen as precursors to Western American-led strategy after 1945.

## The reality of the League: conservative and liberal interpretations of a new world

In IR it is not uncommon to see textbooks treat the League of Nations as part of a realist–idealist, or conservative–liberal, split. In this story the League is seen as the creation of idealists and liberals, while it is realists and conservatives who oppose it. As the example of Mackinder above shows, this was not the case. Rather, many conservatives, such as Mackinder, were strong supporters of the League; while at the same time many liberals and leftists, especially those who supported more radical reforms of the international order, opposed it. On further analysis, this should not surprise us. Support for the idea of the League before 1919 had been common among socialist and more left-leaning liberal circles, but it was not these writers who were responsible for the drafting of the Covenant in 1919. Rather, the League Covenant had been the product of rather old-fashioned diplomacy by those statesmen associated with the right of the political spectrum, and much of the motivation for the establishment of the League came from businessmen and free-marketeers.[50] For more conservative statesmen the League would be just an extension of the old diplomacy.[51] True, many of the top leaders in the peace talks were people of the centre and left. The French Prime Minister Clemenceau had been a radical in the past; Britain's Lloyd George was traditionally on the left of the Liberal Party; and while the US President Woodrow Wilson was far more conservative than his reputation, he was certainly liberal in much of his politics. Once we leave the top table, however, the political hue of the League's founders takes on a more conservative colour. The first draft of the Covenant was composed by South Africa's Prime Minister Jan Smuts, an able statesman, but no radical, while within the British part of the British Empire Delegation it was the Conservative Robert Cecil who played a leading role, and would remain one of the strongest supporters of the League during his lifetime. While there was never any consensus about what the League should be, it is certain that in more left wing circles the initial announcement of the Covenant was met with anger and despair. H.N. Brailsford wrote a whole book denouncing the new 'league of cabinets' that to him seemed to be just a continuation of the old diplomacy, while the socialist and feminist H.M. Swanwick, looking back to 1919, referred to the League that emerged from the negotiations in Paris as 'half aborted'.[52] This section explores some of the conservative and right wing liberal writers who supported the League. While a diverse group, whose individual members were not without their criticisms of the League and the peace treaties, they were nevertheless a fair cross-section of centrist and centre-right opinion on the nature of international order and the place of the League in that order.

Among the more conservative advocates of the League were the members of the Round Table movement that had been founded before the war to promote a confederal British Empire and Commonwealth. Three of its leading members – Philip Kerr (later Lord Lothian), Lionel Curtis and Robert Cecil – were influential members of the British Empire delegation. While some writers have cautioned that the Round Table's influence was limited at Paris, individual members of the movement did play lead roles in the negotiations that led to peace.[53] The League that emerged out of the negotiations very much resembled the League that many Round Table members desired. Kerr supported the idea of an international organisation that would be based more on the principle of law than of the balance of power (a concert of nations). Yet, he also wanted this new body to be primarily consultative, and he opposed a League based on solemn covenants and on sanctions because it would infringe national sovereignty.[54] Kerr's vision of the League was not far off the body that emerged: a sovereign-state-based organisation that, while it had sanctions provisions, did not have the machinery to enforce it without the agreement of its members. In later years Kerr (Lord Lothian after 1930) and Curtis would have doubts about the sovereign state, and they would both move to a more federalist view of global politics. This federalism, though, often saw the British Empire and Commonwealth as the template for a new order, and Curtis in particular was influenced by the American Clarence Streit's call for a world order based around a British–American union.[55] In the immediate post-war period, however, both favoured a looser international order based on the sovereign state.

One of the most long-standing and consistent supporters of the League, Robert Lord Cecil, had also been a member of the Round Table.[56] As part of the British Empire delegation to the Paris Peace Conference and founder member of the Royal Institute of International Affairs, Cecil was active at Paris. While much of his work at Paris was in step with the positions of Kerr and Curtis, on one major issue he diverged, and here Cecil moved closer to the position being taken by many on the centre left. Cecil strongly supported the key articles included in the Covenant that formed the basis for a League collective security system based on the threat of sanctions: Articles 10 to 15. For Cecil these articles formed the main goal of the League: 'that, before resorting to war, international disputants should try every means, whether by negotiation, arbitration or mediation, to settle their quarrel'; and that the 'League was brought into existence as an alliance to stop war, open to all civilised states'. While still a state-based institution for Cecil, the League's existence was primarily a means by which to prevent war through diplomatically agreed principles.[57] In this sense it was a more stable form of international alliance that also possessed a set of permanent institutions to support it, rather than being a radically new organisation. Indeed, early in the negotiations at Paris Cecil pushed for a League Council controlled by the great powers, since for him it was as well to recognise that the great powers would dominate.[58] Cecil, as a member of the League of Nations Commission at the Paris Peace Conference, fought particularly hard for Article 16, which required members to cease 'financial, commercial or personal intercourse' with an aggressor, and also contained a bare bones structure for possible military sanctions against an aggressor. He was, however, aware that there was a danger that the League could become merely an instrument for imposing the status quo, and it was for this reason that he had objected to Article 10. Article 10 stated that: 'The Members of the League undertake to respect and preserve as against external aggression the territorial integrity and existing political independence of all Members of the League.' This left no room for 'correcting international justice', and so had to be balanced by Article 19, which allowed the League Assembly to consider peaceful modifications where 'international conditions … might endanger the peace of the world'.[59] Although coming from a conservative

Round Table background, Cecil was to work most closely in the inter-war years with those on the centre-left who advocated a tighter collective security system.[60]

Cecil was a member of the British Conservative Party, and served in several Conservative governments. By contrast, his colleague in the League of Nations Union, Gilbert Murray, was a long-time associate of the British Liberal Party, although Murray's attempts to enter Parliament were never successful. Cecil and Murray worked with each other in the organisations that were to become the League of Nations Union, through which both first advocated and then (once it had been formed) supported the League of Nations. A strong supporter of democracy and liberal freedoms, Murray was also an elitist for whom progress was defined as a top-down process in which a liberal privileged elite extended their privileges to other groups.[61] This patrician reading of democracy meant that Murray, with the single exception of his personal links to his former student the radical journalist H.N. Brailsford, remained largely detached from the centre-left internationalism of the Labour Party. He was not, for example, among the large number of internationalists in the Liberal Party who defected to Labour in the years after 1914. Murray seems to have been influenced somewhat by the Neo-Hegelians, such as Bernard Bosenquet,[62] but as Peter Wilson has argued Murray never developed Bosenquet's concept of the general will that had formed the basis of the neo-Hegelian objection to international organisations (see Chapter 5).[63] Rather, Murray's ideas about the possibilities of international government demonstrate that his sympathies were much closer to those of L.T. Hobhouse and his supporters as described in the last chapter.

Throughout the inter-war period Murray would, through his work at the League of Nations Union, become closely associated with the idea of the League in general, and collective security in particular. In a 1934 cartoon by David Low, for example, Murray is shown driving the 'League of Nations' fire engine while Robert Cecil goes door-to-door collecting subscriptions to League collective security (the 'fire brigade'). Murray's support for the League was founded on his agreement with Lowes Dickinson (see Chapter 5) that the great flaw in nineteenth century western civilisation was the international anarchy: that with no higher authority above them states were allowed to fight out their differences through war, and in complete disregard to questions of justice.[64] This very use of war by states in the international anarchy also exacerbated the problem by firing up national sentiments, and was thus at the root of racial and religious tyrannies.[65] Indeed, even the most democratic countries, where domestic disputes are handled fairly, cannot be relied upon to behave responsibly internationally.[66] Here Murray certainly rejected Bosenquet's view that well-ordered and patriotic states behave responsibly internationally. Murray showed sympathy for the use of both law and military force to rein in aggressors, but was equally well aware that such a 'frontal attack' on the sovereign state was unlikely to succeed. Instead he turned to the idea of international conferences within the League system, as well as the role played by the institutions of the League that were creating a new international ethos. He endorsed Cecil's view that 'the system of conference *plus* a Permanent

Secretariat is the real essence of the League'.[67] Through these aspects of the League Murray hoped that a mix of arbitration and conciliation would prevent the outbreak of war, but that this would need to be backed up by some level of sanctions by the main League powers. Yet, Murray saw the system as flawed. States were required to agree to a near-unanimous position on sanctions if there was to be an effective means of dealing with rogue aggressive states. What was missing for Murray was 'a much more whole-hearted acceptance of the League spirit and League methods on the part of the Great Powers'.[68]

Murray's greatest contribution to the League project lies in his work for the International Committee for Intellectual Cooperation (ICIC), first established in 1922 with Murray as vice-president (he was later to become its president). Despite the years that he put in to the Committee, Murray was initially unhappy with being involved in it, but soon found himself attracted to the work,[69] and he presented a detailed summary of the contributions of the ICIC in an American publication in 1944, in which he presented it as a basis for the future cooperation in the coming United Nations.[70] For Murray the ICIC's goal was to move beyond nationalism towards the very 'League spirit' missing in the institutional structure of the League.[71] To a certain extent Murray saw this spirit as a return to the classical liberal virtues of the nineteenth century,[72] but it was always in opposition to a narrow nationalism and in support of a rational expertise that was above 'national and party jealousies'.[73] While there is a strong elitist core to Murray's view of intellectual cooperation – he very much saw it as a western-led and elite culture that would be spread to both other classes and the non-western world[74] – his view of the importance of intellectual cooperation to international organisations would survive the League to become the inspiration behind organisations such as UNESCO that institutionalised intellectual cooperation.[75] From the point of view of the study of IR, the ICIC played an important role in promoting the International Studies Conference (ISC), the earliest attempt to bring together experts on international affairs in a regular conference.[76] His view of the importance of experts as a community above factional and national infighting was to reappear in modified forms in the second half of the twentieth century in the functional approach of David Mitrany, in neo-functionalism and in the much later work of Peter Haas on epistemic communities.[77]

The idea of the importance of a moral spirit to the success of institutions dedicated to peace can also be found in Murray's American contemporary Nicholas Murray Butler (see Chapter 5 for a discussion of Butler's pre-war views). While Murray had attempted to change the spirit of the age via the ICIC, Butler had been instrumental in the establishment of the influential Carnegie Endowment for International Peace. Butler had been among those who had persuaded Carnegie to make the initial endowment, had then gone on to found the European branch, and finally was president of the Endowment from 1925 to 1945. In 1931 he was awarded the Nobel Peace Prize for this work with the Carnegie Endowment. For Butler (and in contrast to the liberal socialists discussed below) the legal and institutional basis for a peaceful world had already been constructed in the decade after the war. Key for him was the Kellogg–Briand Pact, in which states had (in Butler's view) renounced the Clausewitzian notion that war was an instrument of policy. All that was needed now was for states to be able to keep their word. Here lay the problem for Butler. In order for states to keep their word the ideals of a selfish national sovereignty had to be replaced by respect for a common moral law, but this was always a solution that required an indeterminate long time to bring to fruition.[78] The role of organisations like the Carnegie Endowment was to create that respect for moral law through the development of a new spirit.

The ultimate solution for Butler, which would come after many years of cooperation and conferences, would be a world federation that would emerge much in the same way that American federalism had emerged out of the petty squabbles of the thirteen original states.[79] Butler gave little detail on how this federation would come about, but for him the failed experiments of world conquest and of nation-building, both of which led to war, pointed to a free federation bound by common global interests as the obvious answer. Behind this idea of federation, however, lay a bias in favour of western values that was as marked as those found in Murray. For Butler, though, the central core of the superior western conceptions of liberty and government were the English-speaking peoples of the British Commonwealth and the United States. Ideas that had emerged from England via agreements like Magna Carta had evolved and progressed up to the American Bill of Rights, and while on the defensive in the 1930s, this tradition offered the best solution for the world to the problem of war and injustice.[80] Thus Butler's vision of a better world was one in which the institutions of the League and the Permanent Court were backed up by a moral spirit that was firmly wedded to the liberal traditions of the English-speaking peoples, especially English common law. Even his notions of education and public opinion had its strongly elitist side. Like Murray, it was to the education of elites that Butler turned to first, with the hope that through a top-down process this would reach wider circles as time went on. For Butler the goal of the Carnegie Endowment was 'to change men's minds with regard to war through an educational program taught by a citizenry of knowledgeable people in positions of authority'.[81]

In the end Butler's solutions to the problem of war proved unsatisfying. His concentration on changing public opinion on war and the international machinery to prevent war relied on there being a long period of peace in which to accomplish the task. Even then, his notions of what the moral spirit should be was hopelessly parochial in a world in which global politics was increasingly multicultural and politically diverse. There was, at the end of the day, no firm mechanism in Butler's thought to prevent war. That having been said, the organisation that he helped to develop, the Carnegie Endowment for International Peace, flourished in the inter-war years, providing a forum for the discussion of ideas about global politics that helped inform debates not only in the inter-war period, but also well into the post-1945 period. David Mitrany, for example, first explored ideas about functional government in a Carnegie-supported publication.[82] These ideas would later become his functional approach that would have a major impact on IR from the 1940s until the 1980s.

Among the intellectuals who worked and wrote for the Carnegie Endowment for International Peace was the Economist John Maynard Keynes. Although Keynes was one of the League's supporters, he was also one of the staunchest critics of both the process that led up to the treaties in 1919 and of the treaties themselves. His *Economic Consequences of the Peace* was arguably the most influential book in the English-speaking world on subsequent attitudes to the treaties of 1919. Although Keynes' voice was not the only one criticising the treaties, his articulate attack resting on his own experience as representative of the British Treasury at the Peace Conference would frame popular opinions of the treaties (especially the Treaty of Versailles) to this day. Keynes' criticism of the Peace was matched by his support for the League system, although even here he shared with much of the centre-left the view that there were problems with the League that needed attention. Yet, while many of his pronouncements sound remarkably like those on the left who were lukewarm to the League, Keynes' position was based on an ideological position that was far more classical liberal in origin. Donald Markwell has characterised Keynes as brought up a classical liberal believing that free trade promotes peace, but concluding after 1919 that state action was necessary in order to make an interdependent world work in the interests of peace and prosperity.[83] Thus, Keynes' work on the peace and the League provides a bridge between the liberal and conservative supporters mentioned above and the self-consciously socialist approaches discussed below. Unlike the major figures of the centre-left explored in the next section, Keynes remained committed to making capitalism and the free market work, yet his views on how the League should work to encourage an interdependent capitalist world free from the scourge of war had parallels with many of his contemporaries to the left. Like H.N. Brailsford he contemplated the economic causes of war, but unlike Brailsford he sought to find a way to develop institutions that would make a capitalist and free market system work for populations in a new globalised world. There are, perhaps not surprisingly, parallels here with Isaiah Bowman's role in the creation of a functioning American-led global order based on free trade and international institutions. Keynes, like Bowman, was also to be a participant in the development of the post-war institutions that were set up by the Allies as part of the post-Second World War settlement. Here, though, I would like to concentrate on Keynes' reaction to the peace, and his views on the League system after that.

Keynes' opinion on the Peace took as its start the idea that the success of the political economy of Europe rested on economic interdependence (especially the easy flow of capital and trade) and the security of property and person across the borders of the various states. Making an argument not wholly dissimilar to that of Norman Angell in his earlier work *The Great Illusion*, Keynes shows his debt to his Cobdenite free-trade-as-peace upbringing by painting a picture of a prosperous interdependent society that had taken root after 1870.[84] Yet, from the start this politico-economic system was built upon shifting sands. Right at the start of *Economic Consequences* Keynes states that very few of his readers 'realise with conviction the intensely unusual, unstable, complicated, unreliable, temporary nature of the economic organisation by which Western Europe has lived for the last half century'.[85] Built on low wages for labour and self-restraint by capitalists (Keynes called this a 'double-bluff or deception'), the system had fallen victim to the war, which exposed this double deception.[86] Here Keynes parallels the change in thought of other writers of the time. Norman Angell, a few years later would also write of the fragile nature of the pre-war interdependence, and consequently of the need for international institutions to protect the fragile recreation of interdependence out of the ashes of war.[87] This need for international institutions would occur in later works by Keynes, but in 1919 his concern was more with the effects of the actions of the peacemakers via the peace treaties, and by implication the need to re-establish the conditions that had maintained prosperity.

Central to the argument of *The Economic Consequences of the Peace* was the view that the pre-war prosperity had been a fragile one built on political arrangements that had been damaged or destroyed by the war. Yet, however fragile the basis of this prosperity, the fact was that it had made Europe a single economic unit, and that any damage to this fragile interdependence would lead to economic ruin, which in turn would mean revolution and war.[88] The economic problem of the location of raw materials and labour had been irrelevant in the pre-1914 system of free trade, but with the drawing of new political boundaries this free trade had been destabilised by the corresponding drawing of new economic boundaries that matched these political ones. The result of this was sharp decline in economic activity at a time when Europe needed economic resources for reconstruction.[89] The fault for this lay in the way that the new treaties of peace were being composed. Most famously, Keynes also attacked the reparations regime. Contrary to popular belief, Keynes was not opposed to reparations *per se*, in fact his job at Paris was to help set the nature of reparations that Germany needed to pay as compensation for damage done to civilian property.[90] Rather, it was the scale he objected to, and it was the wider financial implications of impoverishing Germany by excessive demands that would undermine trade and finance in Europe. In effect, the peacemakers were blind to the fact that 'the most serious of the problems which claimed their attention were not political or territorial but financial and economic, and that the perils of the future lay not in frontiers or sovereignties but in food, coal and transport'.[91] The issue of reparations was complicated by the inter-Allied debts, especially those in which the United States was the creditor. Indeed, many claims for reparations from European states were linked to unpaid debts especially to the US, but also Britain. Keynes called for the cancellation of inter-Allied debts as part of the reduction of reparations payments. Indeed, his reasons for calling for the cancellation of war debts were identical to his reasons for opposing excessive reparations demands.[92] Without drastic measures to deal with these economic and financial measures Keynes foresaw 'the rapid depression of the standard of life of the European populations to a point which will mean actual starvation for some'.[93] Yet, this pessimism did not remain long unmodified. By 1921 Keynes saw reasons to be optimistic. Changes in public sentiment and an end to the 'megalomania of war' saw the crumbling of the reparations regime. 'There is little prospect now of the disastrous consequences of its fulfilment.'[94]

Keynes' arguments about the economic and financial dangers of the peace were a product of his involvement in the negotiations that led up to the reparations provisions and side-agreements of the treaties. They also rested, though, on his belief that free trade promotes peace.[95] Here, and up to a point, there were clear similarities between *The Economic Consequences of the Peace* and the pre-war work of writers such as Norman Angell (see Chapter 5). Keynes' work certainly owes a great deal to the 'philosophy' of *The Great Illusion*, but there are also clear differences, as Donald Markwell has made clear.[96] While both Keynes and Angell wrote in support of the pre-war interdependent economy, and both had seen it as fragile in the face of political conflict and nationalist aspirations, Keynes had rejected Angell's claim that post-war financial indemnities (such as that imposed after the Franco-Prussian war) were necessarily futile and counter-productive. Equally well, Keynes did not accept Angell's view that under the pre-war interdependence that states necessarily shared a common interest in each other's economic prosperity. Germany and Britain were in economic conflict with each other, and the question of ownership of territory was not necessarily economically irrelevant. These differences between Keynes and Angell have frequently been glossed over, not least by Angell himself, who based the financial part of the argument of his *Fruits of Victory* on Keynes' earlier text. Indeed, the erroneous view that Keynes opposed reparations in their entirety probably originates from Angell's post-war re-statement of his argument of the indemnity fallacy using references back to Keynes to add support for it.[97] That said, in *Fruits of Victory* Angell converged with Keynes' argument, agreeing that states were now capable of owning and controlling raw materials, and that consequently great powers could now use economic and financial muscle in their foreign policies in a way that they could not before.[98] Angell's recognition that the international order was unstable, and that economic concerns could now be wrapped up in political and national conflicts led him to concede that some form of international organisation was needed to regulate international life.[99] This was a step that Keynes had also taken.

While Keynes' support for the development of international organisations as a necessary step for the safeguarding of economic prosperity (and thereby peace) led him to back the League of Nations, he was not averse to pointing out the structural weaknesses of the League. High among this list of weaknesses was the 'Wilsonian dogma, which exalts and dignifies the divisions of race and nationality above the bonds of trade and culture'. It struck Keynes as a paradox that 'the first experiment in international government should exert its influence in the direction of intensifying nationalism'.[100] Not always supportive of individual aspects or acts of the League, Keynes was appreciative of the League's work in preventing war. He also supported the idea of developing international organisations to manage economic issues, early on advocating that the Bank for International

Settlements be used as an international monetary authority. More famously, Keynes during the Second World War worked to help found the post-war Bretton Woods system.[101] In this sense Keynes, despite his opposition to state planning of the economy, remained close to many of the more centre-left international experts discussed in the next section. Like them he had come to the conclusion that a return to the pre-war interdependence required the management of international relations via some system of international organisation. Unlike the left, though, he also remained wedded to the idea of the importance of free trade and of a free market, even if that free market was preserved by timely interventions by international organisations.

Keynes was not the only disillusioned British participant of the Paris Peace Conference who would go on to write about both the Peace Treaties and the nature of international relations. Harold Nicolson, though, would wait until 1933 to publish his account of the 1919 Peace, and his work that explored the new realities of the League system of diplomacy appeared in book form only in 1939, just as that system was in its last stage of unravelling. Like Keynes, a man he admired, Nicolson regarded the reparations provisions as the main failing of the Treaty of Versailles. He saw reparations as 'immoral and senseless' and 'impossible to execute'.[102] Yet, unlike Keynes it was less the actual provisions of Versailles and the other treaties that incensed him, and more the way that the peace had been conducted. Like Keynes Nicolson was later to argue that the Treaty of Versailles had become a red herring. The territorial clauses were the least alterable, and 'the other more flagrant anomalies' had since 'righted themselves'. Rather 'the fundamental errors of the Treaty of Versailles were errors not of mathematics or geography, but of morals'.[103] The man who came to embody that failure for Nicolson was President Woodrow Wilson. Wilson's 'rigidity and spiritual arrogance' undermined good diplomacy, and led in turn to the immoral peace that Wilson had set out to prevent.[104] Wilson was the worst sufferer of this moral failure, but the problem also ran through the whole conference. The higher purpose that so many of the participants believed in was undermined by imprecision, rigidity of thought and the lack of awareness at how slips of the pen on maps were deciding the fates of millions. 'We came to Paris confident that the new order was about to be established', Nicolson wrote in retrospect, 'we left convinced that the new order had merely fouled the old.'[105] A disillusioned believer in the new world struggling to be borne, 1919 for Nicolson led him to believe that the 'new diplomacy' contained flaws that could only be overcome by an appreciation for what the old diplomacy could offer the new, as I will describe in more detail below.

Nicolson's approach to the international was to a certain extent a combination of an acceptance of the changes that had occurred in the process of international affairs with an attempt to maintain certain views and practices that he still saw as vital to international order, but had been unduly dismissed by the advocates of the new international order. In this sense Nicolson's ideas on the international were a hybrid of conservative notions of a stable state-based order resting in the threat of force and of more liberal ideas of progress towards an internationalist and pacific order. His ability to link these is shown in his attempt to discredit the idea that 'a sudden gulf sunders the concept of diplomacy as it existed before and after the war', and that 1919 had seen the dawn of a very different Wilsonian international order.[106] Instead Nicolson proposed that if we thought historically then the competing ideas of the doctrine of power and the doctrine of peace existed side-by-side, with the former slowly giving way to the later.[107] The implication of this view was that the power doctrine, with its base in nationalism, never fully goes away. Instead its logic needs to be understood as part of what the international order will be, even as the doctrine of peace and its internationalist principles gain in strength. For Nicolson this meant that the balance of power, based on individual state interests remained the best way to maintain peace until such time as 'international society evolved towards more pacific inter-state relations'.[108] Wrapped up in this was a view of national interest as, in its better arrangements, a form of enlightened self-interest where national egoism was tempered by what Adam Watson called a *raison de système*: that part of a nation's interest rested in the success of the international system as a whole.[109] Thus Nicolson's support for the League and collective security flowed from his interpretation of Britain's enlightened egoism. 'Our aim in supporting the League was not, therefore, altruistic; it was a hard and level headed calculation of needs – enlightened perhaps, but still selfish.'[110] Nicolson's reasons for supporting the League and collective security, therefore, were like the other more conservative advocates of the League: a result of conceptions of national interest and concerns of power balance. Yet, like many conservatives of the time, he fused this with an idealistic belief that (within the confines of practical reality) progress is possible. This progress was more likely to occur if we were able to fully understand the nature of diplomacy, and the challenges facing democratic 'new' diplomacy. This change, if it was to work, had to flow from (and therefore not be in opposition to) the world as it currently was. The new diplomacy must emerge as a product of the old.

As a former career diplomat (he had left the diplomatic service in 1929) Nicolson's major contribution was to re-imagine the place of diplomacy in the new post-war world. During the war it had become common to blame the old pre-war diplomacy for the outbreak of war in 1914 (see the discussion at the end of the last chapter), and in the immediate aftermath of the war many writers contrasted this old diplomacy associated with the international anarchy with the new diplomacy associated with the new League system. This contrast between old and new diplomacy formed an important part of Isaiah Bowman's discussion of the international affairs of the post-1919 new world. Nicolson's analysis of diplomacy accepted that changes had occurred to diplomatic practice, but by drawing out an atemporal essence of diplomacy he constructed a view of the new diplomacy that laid out those areas open to democratic control and those that were the domain of the professional diplomat.

Nicolson's defence of diplomacy in a democratic era began from two premises: first that diplomacy is an atemporal form of interaction that can be defined as the management of international relations by negotiation; and second that the new democratic diplomacy was a reflection of current society, and was consequently here to stay.[111] The problem for Nicolson was that, despite its many advantages, the new diplomacy brought with it problems that needed to be addressed if democratic diplomacy was to function as a proper means of guaranteeing international order. Central to the problems of the new diplomacy were the role of public opinion, the involvement of politicians in diplomacy (instead of professional diplomats) and the growth of conference diplomacy as an alternative to 'secret' bilateral diplomacy. The essence of diplomatic success for Nicolson was precision. Precision on goals and policies led to good negotiations and workable agreements between states.[112] The main problem of democratic diplomacy was that in adjusting the emotions of the masses to the thoughts of the rulers imprecision in negotiations became rife.[113] Openness in the negotiations of the new diplomacy increased this tendency, while 'diplomacy by conference' encouraged imprecision by moving the diplomatic discussion away from the precision of documents towards the imprecision of conversation between statesmen.[114] Here Nicolson diverged from Robert Cecil, who regarded the very public nature of diplomacy in the League as a major guarantee against both injustice and misunderstanding.[115] Gilbert Murray, although a strong supporter of the League conferences and conference system, did share Nicolson's worry that democratic accountability left statesmen at the mercy of the basest forms of public opinion during a crisis.[116] Interestingly, Nicolson's analysis was at odds with Frederick Sherwood Dunn's analysis of conference diplomacy written in 1929. Dunn, who would go on to be regarded as one of the founders of the classical realist tradition in post-war American IR, saw conference diplomacy as a spontaneous development emerging from the 'needs of international life' that was distinct from the more traditional judicial concepts of international organisation.[117]

The problem for Nicolson became one of how to keep the new democratic diplomacy while grafting onto it the advantages of precision found in the old oligarchic diplomacy. His answer lay in drawing a distinction between policy and negotiation. Policy should and must be controlled by democratic institutions and open to public opinion. Once policy had been developed then negotiation should necessarily be organised by professional diplomats working in secret.[118] Where policy discussions spread over into diplomatic negotiation then the result usually was to debase the value of agreements and to sow confusion. This was often the case in multilateral conference diplomacy, and while Nicolson did see a role for these big conferences, he did not see them as an adequate substitute for bilateral links.[119] Thus, Nicolson finishes by defending the professionalisation of the diplomatic service, while also welcoming the new era of democratic statesmanship. As Derek Drinkwater points out, Nicolson's international thought evolved into an attempt to balance what is practicable with what is desirable.[120]

What all these liberal and conservative approaches have in common is an attempt to bring forth a new world that builds upon the best of the old. While many of them foresaw a distant future where the nation state had been replaced, nonetheless they all assume that the central elements of the old order would continue to frame the new. All assumed a continuing nation state, and many accepted that some form of the balance of power might continue as the main framer of the system of states. Most would agree with Keynes that a continuation of a capitalist system based on broad free-market principles would also remain the central reality of the new world, and the new structures of the League and its companion organisations were interpreted as means for bringing out the best in the old institutional arrangements. The development of international organisations, therefore, was to be welcomed, but as a way of bringing about an organic change in the order that already existed, rather than as a wholly new order based on vastly different principles. For this reason we can see these writers, as far as their international theory was concerned, as fitting into one of Michael Freeden's definitions of conservatism: the view of change as only good if it builds upon the natural progression of the world as it is.[121] This did not mean there was not much common ground between this set of writers and more radical ones – Nicolson was a great admirer of Angell's later work, while both Cecil and Gilbert Murray worked with many on the left in the League of Nations Union – but it does mean there was a significant difference in approach between these liberal–conservatives and liberal–socialists that was often hidden by their agreement on a vast range of policy issues. It is to these liberal–socialists that we now turn.

## The liberal–socialist challenge: reordering the international

While many on the left had shown suspicion and even hostility to the League in 1920,[122] this was to change dramatically after the mid-1920s. In fact, by the later 1920s many of the most constructive suggestions for League reform and for a League-based world order came from those to the left of the political spectrum. What emerged from this was a policy for League reform that was based on a particular reading of the nature of the international system. In Britain this group can be best described as liberal–socialists, and they formed an integrated 'school' of inter-war IR sharing a common intellectual language and venues for the discussion of their ideas. Although the term liberal–socialist does not roll off the tongue as easily as realism or idealism, I have chosen it for four reasons. First, liberal–socialist was not an unknown phrase at the time, and writers on domestic affairs that had moved from the Liberal Party to Labour after 1918, such as L.T. Hobhouse, often used it to describe themselves. Second, it emphasises their intellectual affinity with earlier liberal writers, while underscoring the more radical take that they had developed on matters related to the capitalist system and the class divisions under capitalism. Third, the views of the group discussed below fit with Michael Freeden's definitions of liberal and socialist ideologies. They subscribe to what Freeden calls the 'Millite core' of the liberal grand project that places liberty as the central political virtue, and then links it to ideas of both individualism and progress.[123] This liberal approach is filled out by key socialist core concepts such as the social embeddedness of humanity, the importance of welfare (through the welfare state), and the ultimate goal of equality.[124] Finally, the liberal epithet demonstrates the distance that existed between their views of international affairs and other socialists. There was clear blue water between them and Stafford Cripps' brand of socialism that denounced the League as an international burglar's union,[125] on the one hand, and Leninist conceptions of foreign affairs on the other. While clearly overtly socialist, the liberal–socialists had arrived at their socialist position via liberal ideas of freedom, equality and the rule of law. They were keen to abolish war, capitalism and the rank unfairness of twentieth century global life, but the route to be taken was via a system of global institutions that would encompass pooled security, decolonisation and democratisation. Far from being utopians – giving more attention to building future worlds than to understanding the mechanics of this one – the liberal–socialist prescriptions were often heavily influenced by what was achievable in the already existing international system.

Perhaps a major reason for the concentration on the analysis of current events at the expense of theory was that these writers came from different intellectual and professional backgrounds that had different theoretical and literary conventions. Among those with a firm academic background Philip Noel-Baker came from law, Hugh Dalton from economics, Alfred Zimmern from classics and David Mitrany from political science. Others had a professional background: J.A. Hobson, Norman Angell and H.N. Brailsford were journalists and Leonard Woolf started in the imperial civil service. While it is clear from their Labour Party Advisory Committee work that they had developed a common language by which to understand the world, they were still at the early stages of synthesising a clear theoretical framework. Even then, as I will discuss below, they were beginning to put down firm theoretical roots notwithstanding the lack of any precedent for a specifically international theory.[126] Despite the lack of a rich vein of international theory, the international was not completely devoid of theory. J.A. Hobson's economics informed many, including crucially H.N. Brailsford (although this was a source of friction with Norman Angell).[127] Perhaps more importantly G. Lowes Dickinson's ideas on the international anarchy influenced all the major liberal socialists, giving them a baseline understanding of the operations of the international system in the absence of proper institutions.[128]

There were four key values that emerge from the debates between liberal–socialist writers that can allow us to define their view of international affairs.

1    The ultimate point of studying International Relations was to abolish it as a separate sphere by introducing the norms of domestic politics into the international. While the state as an institution need not be abolished, the concept of national sovereignty was at the root of many of the problems of international coordination. National sovereignty was behind the unstable international anarchy, and while the principles of the international anarchy might have been applicable to an earlier less interdependent era, they were dangerous in the changed conditions of the modern world.

2    This meant that the main immediate need was for the establishment of the rule of law (although with provisions to prevent this law becoming the tool

of supporters of the *status quo*) and the proper international political institutions to manage that law and give it force.

3    This could be established through international agreements, and that the impetus for these agreements would be international common interests in peace and prosperity. An exclusive nationalism was the major impediment to realising this, as well as vested (often capitalist) interests that profited from the state.

4    The success of these agreements could only be based on very precise and accurate information about the nature of the international system as a whole, as well as knowledge of the myriad of specific disputes and issues that dog international relations.

The main writers in this subculture that accepted these four points were Leonard Woolf, Norman Angell, Philip Noel-Baker and Hugh Dalton. Others, such as David Mitrany, H.N. Brailsford, J.A. Hobson and Alfred Zimmern, buy into most of these core views, but have reservations about certain aspects. For example, Mitrany would be in accord with (1) and (4), but he would have seen (2) as a longer-term goal, and (3) as unobtainable and naïve. Brailsford would have agreed with (1) and (2) up to a point, but would have given a greater prominence to what he saw as the ultimate problem of the failings of capitalism. He would have agreed with (3), with the added protocol that this would be most likely among democratic socialist states, and he would have had little problem with (4). Thus, liberal–socialism in IR clearly had fuzzy boundaries, although it was centred largely in Britain, and its influence on the United States was limited to its transmission through such trans-Atlantic writers as Norman Angell and David Mitrany. In Britain it was mainly associated with the Labour Party, and a large number of its thinkers were members at one time or another of the Labour Party Advisory Committee on International Questions. This Advisory Committee acted as one of the key venues for these writers. In fact, the writing, distribution and discussion of Advisory Committee memos served as one of the major ways that this group kept close intellectual contact. The Advisory Committee also brought these writers into regular contact with another branch of Labour thought on international affairs, the stricter pacifists such as C.R. Buxton, Helena Swanwick and Arthur Ponsonby, who will be discussed in the next section.[129] These strong pacifists were opposed to the second of the liberal–socialist core views, although they shared some (but not all) of the liberal–socialist language. While they often supported the establishment of international institutions like the League, they were opposed to any use of force, even in the name of the League.[130]

The important point about liberal–socialist analyses of international security is that, rather than ignoring the realist view of security as a zero-sum game, they accepted it as one of many possible security realities. A world of competing military powers, acting under the logic of the balance of power was, for liberal–socialists like Angell, Woolf and Noel-Baker, the logical result of a world that failed to build effective international security institutions. The problem with the balance of power was, as Morgenthau would concur in the 1950s, that it was inherently unstable. It was also no longer workable in a modern and interdependent global society. Despite initial misgivings about the League, its Covenant, and the 1919 peace treaties in general, the liberal–socialists saw the League as the only substantial international organisation, and hence the most likely institution upon which some form of collective security to guarantee international peace could be built. The League was, therefore, central to their policy prescriptions at the time, but was not necessarily vital to their overall world-view. If the League proved itself to be no longer up to the job, then many liberal–socialists were prepared to abandon the immediate institutions of the League, while still supporting the idea of League-like institutions. Liberal–socialist interpretations of collective security revolved around two key points. The first was that the League itself in the 1920s was still not ready to take up its role as a fully-fledged pooled security system. There were serious gaps in the Covenant of the League that would have to be filled first. The second point was that a successful pooled security system would have to combine three interlocking elements to work effectively in a world of states. These were an effective and workable system of arbitration between states, a properly functioning system of sanctions to make the arbitration system believable and widespread disarmament to lessen the effectiveness and promise of aggressive war. Arbitration–sanctions–disarmament formed a 'wonderful trinity', each one of the three helping to reinforce the other two. If, however, one of these three proved weak and ineffective, then the viability of the other two would be called into question. In this section I will first look at the reasons why liberal–socialists attacked the League, and then analyse their suggestions for closing the collective security 'gaps' in the League in order to develop a viable arbitration–sanctions–disarmament regime. Finally, I will look at how they reacted to the failure of pooled security after 1931. This analysis will, in turn help to separate what the liberal–socialists saw as time-bound expedient policies, and what they held to be their main theoretical understanding of international security.

The liberal–socialist approach to security developed out of a sustained criticism of the way that the League was currently constructed. With the exception of Brailsford's 1920 attack on the League,[131] little of the flavour of the debate within liberal socialism over the future of the League is captured in print. Rather, the best sources for this come in the exchanges in Labour Party memoranda, speeches and private correspondence between the members of the group. Memoranda remained a safer vehicle for ideas on the League since all the liberal–socialists remained committed to the League idea, but in Britain before 1924 it was difficult to publicly support the League Covenant and maintain your credentials as a left-winger. Here we see the limits of using printed matter alone to understand a group of scholars. As a form of public face print often obscures conflicts or positions that the scholar does not want on public display.[132] The memoranda of the Advisory Committee allowed both free-rein for the criticism of the Covenant, while also providing a space for constructive support for the League and League reform at a time when public endorsement of the 1919 peace was still a political liability on the left. A series of memoranda laid the foundations of what would become the liberal–socialist formulation of the pooled security alternative to the international anarchy.[133] The conversation contained within these memoranda criticised the League for continuing the anarchic system of states, but also recognised that it was highly unlikely that there was a will to dramatically re-negotiate the Covenant. Indeed, any renegotiation would likely reduce, rather than increase, the power of the League.[134] Instead, their attention turned to the creation of a pooled security system out of the existing Covenant in an exercise that became know as 'closing the gaps in the Covenant'. The Covenant remained vague on how states were to deal with aggression.

The development of an effective pooled security based on arbitration, sanctions and disarmament was seen as a necessary alternative to the war-prone international anarchy that had been the main cause of the Great War. By the 1920s there was already a history of successful arbitration on a bilateral basis, and the machinery existed for the settlement of simple judicial disputes in the Permanent Court of International Justice.[135] Support for arbitration as a means of avoiding war were tinged with a concern for the natural conservatism of legal methods, and Leonard Woolf was an early advocate of turning over many non-legal disputes to international conferences instead, since the legal machinery was incapable of dealing with primarily political problems.[136] Realisation of the complexities of international disputes, tempered by the success of bilateral arbitration treaties, led Arnold-Forster and Woolf to draw up a plan for the development of an arbitration and conciliation system under League auspices.[137] It was, however, recognised that no arbitration regime would be fully workable without a system of internationally-agreed sanctions that could prevent states opting out, or resorting to war rather than go through a system of international conciliation. Drawing an analogy from domestic politics, Hugh Dalton argued that all successful legal systems required the threat of coercive action, while David Mitrany insisted that arbitration would lead 'a precarious existence' without some means to enforce it.[138] Discussions of sanctions were tempered by a realisation that, while necessary, there was strong opposition from the publics and governments in many states to the use of military force, and consequently weaker economic sanctions (required under the Covenant anyway) might be all that was available to the League.[139] Yet, a strict sanctions regime under the League and guaranteed by all the major League powers was seen by France and many of the minor powers as a precondition for the establishment of a disarmament regime under League auspices. Disarmament in this context referred to a reduction of arms to a level consistent with League membership (that is, that allowed a state to still participate in the deterring of an aggressor). Liberal–socialists were well aware that armaments and arms races could exacerbate tensions by breeding insecurity.[140] Disarmament agreements could help ease tensions, as well as saving state resources for other purposes.[141] Thus disarmament, by making aggressive war less likely, would reinforce arbitration, while arbitration needed to be guaranteed by sanctions that, in turn, would allow for states to confidently agree to a common disarmament regime.

While this triad of arbitration, sanctions and disarmament remained the goal of liberal–socialist work on the League, there remained widespread concern that there were forces that would not allow this system to be established – or, if established, to work. Mitrany doubted that there was the will among states, while Woolf was concerned that the system would be too wedded to the status quo, and Brailsford was suspicious of a system that did not deal with the wider inequities of capitalism.[142] Yet, this proposed pooled security system bears all the hallmarks of a social democratic answer to the problem of society. Far from ignoring capitalism, it represented part of a classic social democratic tactic codified for the Second International in the Branting Declaration of 1919: the need to establish a stable democratic shell state first in order to create the environment conducive to the development of a mature democratic socialism.[143] In this sense solving the security problem via the League was seen as a necessary step prior to dealing with the social and economic unfairness of capitalism. Consequently, arguments about the question of when the problems of capitalism should be dealt with remained unresolved – with Brailsford at one extreme believing that without an early confrontation then capitalists would do their best to undo the gains made in the security field, and Angell at the other seeing many capitalists as potential allies in the campaign against war.[144]

## Challenges to a League system: pacifists and radical socialists

The system of collective security, as laid out by the liberal socialists, was not universally welcomed by the left. Indeed, key elements were deeply opposed to it either because they saw in collective security a fig leaf for capitalist imperialism, or because they opposed the idea of war in all its forms, including a war fought in the interests of the League. Here we have yet another vision of the League. If conservatives and conservative liberals saw it as an extension of a concert of states and the liberal socialists hoped the League would be a functioning collective security system that would precede any development of socialism, the radical socialists and strict pacifists either interpreted the League as an organisation involved in a longer-term change of attitudes, or rejected the League entirely as an extension of great power politics. Admittedly, those who rejected it were in a minority within this group, and for most strict pacifists the problem was more one of the League being misused – or, more correctly, of the League not playing to its strengths of moral suasion and longer-term psychological change. Among this group were three major figures in the Labour Party, one of the top women journalists in Britain and a future American Nobel Peace Prize laureate.

In her analysis of the converts who joined the British Labour Party during and after the First World War Catherine Cline saw Arthur Ponsonby as the leader of the Party's pacifist wing.[145] A former Diplomat and Liberal Party candidate, Ponsonby became a major figure in the Labour Party in the inter-war years. As Parliamentary Under-Secretary of State for Foreign Affairs in the 1924 first

Labour government he was responsible for the introduction of the Ponsonby Rule that established Parliamentary oversight of international treaties. The introduction of the Ponsonby Rule was part of Ponsonby's desire to make diplomacy and the diplomatic service more democratic. Elevated to the House of Lords in 1930, he was Labour leader in the House of Lords from 1931 until his resignation in protest at the Labour Party's support for sanctions against Italy in 1935. A strict pacifist opposed to all forms of war and League sanctions, Ponsonby differed from many of his political allies by not coming to it predominantly via his religious faith. In a letter written in 1933 to the then Labour leader George Lansbury, a Christian socialist and pacifist, Ponsonby stated that he wished he 'had as much faith and *hope* in Christianity as you have!'[146] Thus, like his colleague H.M. Swanwick, Ponsonby's pacifism lay more in his political than in his religious faith.

Ponsonby's main contributions to the study and conduct of international affairs were in two areas. The first was his work on the democratisation of diplomacy and the making of foreign affairs (the culmination of which was his introduction of the Ponsonby rule); the second was in his criticisms of collective security and the attempts to close the gaps in the Covenant, where he also laid out an alternative role for the League. His call for the democratisation of diplomacy dated from before the First World War, but reached its culmination in his 1915 book *Democracy and Diplomacy*. Here Ponsonby made the connection between the lack of democratic control in diplomacy and the continuation of the international anarchy that had caused the war. The bottom line for Ponsonby was that democratic control would tap in to a growing popular sentiment across many countries that war was too destructive and counter-productive. Ponsonby's suggested reforms stretched from reform of the diplomatic service itself to Parliamentary consent to treaties and the establishment of a Parliamentary foreign affairs committee to oversee the foreign policy of the government.[147] Ponsonby's views on the need to democratise diplomacy were also taken up by another former diplomat working for the Labour Party, George Young, and his and Young's ideas became the basis of a Labour Party pamphlet in 1920.[148] Underlying all this work was the idea that the oligarchic nature of diplomacy was dragging the world into wars that would have been opposed by the majority of citizens. This enthusiasm for democratic 'new' diplomacy would be embraced by Isaiah Bowman, but also tempered by Harold Nicolson's scepticism (see above).

Ponsonby's agitation for democratic control of diplomacy and foreign affairs found a ready and unconditional home in Labour Party circles. His criticisms of collective security were considered more controversial, and eventually distanced him from the Party leadership and the wider body of liberal–socialist writers on international affairs. Like many other Labour leaders and thinkers, he was deeply critical of both the peace treaties and the League Covenant in the early 1920s.[149] His first major concern was the problem of defining the aggressor, something that was required under Article 10 of the League Covenant as part of League collective security. If an aggressor in a dispute could not be identified then it would be hard for the League to organise sanctions. Aggressor for Ponsonby was a subjective term used by both sides to discredit their opponents in a dispute or war, and from a jurists point of view proof of aggression was not legally possible. He did, though, concede that supporters of collective security were using 'aggressor' as a refusal to submit to arbitration.[150] Ponsonby's main criticism of collective security, though, was based on his view that the role of governments in building peace was limited. Governments, he argued, could work to prevent wars from happening, but the only sure-fire way of maintaining peace was to change the attitudes of the vast bulk of the population. Thus, while government action to prevent war was not without its role, in the long run only a psychological change in populations could guarantee enduring peace.[151] Collective security was a weak way to bring about peace because it was only an attempt by governments to mechanically prevent war, and Ponsonby was suspicious about the 'comparative ease with which it has been accepted by so many nations'.[152] Thus Ponsonby took a long-run view of the building of peace based upon psychological changes in the broader population, and was suspicious of the role of governments. This suspicion of governments contrasted with a faith in public opinion. In this sense, Ponsonby was very much at odds with the view of Reinhold Niebuhr in the late 1930s that groups of people actually behaved in an amoral and interest-seeking way (see next chapter).

While Ponsonby was one of the most senior strict pacifists in the Labour Party, he was certainly not its most high profile. That accolade should go to George Lansbury. A cabinet member in the second Labour government of 1929–31, he became leader of the Party after the disastrous defeat of 1931, resigning in 1935 over the Party's support for League sanctions against Italy during the Abyssinian crisis. Unlike Ponsonby, the source for Lansbury's pacifism was his strong Christian belief, and as a result he interpreted the problems of international affairs as products of moral failing. He denounced the Treaty of Versailles for being a 'peace of hate',[153] and saw the faults of modern statesmanship as the product of a 'creed' that saw 'moral evil' as 'politically right'.[154] War for him was wrong whatever the reason for it, and he opposed all forms of the use of force including war fought under League auspices.[155] Instead he promoted (unilateral) disarmament by example as the means to creating a more peaceful world. In a message to the Fulham East constituency during a by-election in 1933 Lansbury declared that his answer to the problem of war would be to 'close every recruiting station, disband the Army and disarm the Air Force. I would abolish the whole dreadful equipment of war and say to the world: "Do your worst."'[156] Although a much-loved figure on the British left, his disarmament by example views were not shared by the majority of the Party (and was even at odds with the views of the Labour candidate in the Fulham East by-election[157]), and Lansbury's resignation, along with Ponsonby's departure as Labour leader in the House of Lords, marked a change in Labour towards full support for collective security, and eventually rearmament and collective defence against Hitler.

A different form of opposition to collective security under the League came from the radical socialist Stafford Cripps. Unlike Lansbury and Ponsonby, Cripps was not against war *per se*, and indeed by 1939 he became a strong supporter of collective defence against fascism, even declaring in the House of Commons during the debate over the Munich Agreement in 1938 that 'You won't forever satisfy rival imperialisms by handing over to them the smaller nations of the world. The time will come when the clash will be at your own door.'[158] Before then, however, Cripps had opposed collective security as an extension internationally of a capitalist system, and at the Labour Party conference of 1935 he even referred to the League as an 'International Burglars' Union'.[159] In the late 1930s Cripps became associated with the Socialist League, an organisation within the Party that, among other things, dismissed the League as a tool of capitalism.[160] While pacifists like Ponsonby and Lansbury could see some good in the League as a force for moral suasion, radical socialists like Cripps saw the whole experiment as nothing more than a tool of capitalism. At the same time, though, Cripps found himself able to support a war against fascism since it was capitalism, and not war, that he saw as the major problem facing humanity.

Perhaps, though, the most articulate left-wing opponent of collective security was Helena Swanwick. Like much of centre-left thinking in Britain, Swanwick's attitude to the new League of Nations and its Covenant was mixed. On the one hand she, and others, had campaigned vigorously for a league of nations from the early years of the war. On the other hand, she was deeply unhappy with the result that emerged in 1919 and came into force in 1920. She disliked the Versailles Treaty with which the Covenant was (for her) so worryingly linked, was troubled by the refusal to allow the defeated Central Powers and Soviet Russia to join the League, and she saw the domination of the League by governments and cabinets rather than peoples as a major weakness of the League. While these attitudes to the League were common even among supporters of collective security (see above), Swanwick parted company with the liberal–socialists in her equally strong opposition to League sanctions, especially military sanctions. Swanwick believed that the possibility of League sanctions and military action would actually undermine the League, and were based on a faulty understanding of current conditions.[161] Beside these 'crippling errors' there were also other initial irritants that, according to Swanwick, undermined the League's credibility even before it was officially convened. These were the link between the Covenant and the Versailles Treaty; restricting League membership to states; and the insistence of French and British statesmen in continuing to act unilaterally in Russia, Hungary and within the reparations commission, which at least undermined the spirit of the Covenant.[162]

Yet, Swanwick never lost hope. There was, she argued, enough of substance in the Covenant that people of good will could make it work. She likened the League to a skeleton, which different groups had already been adding flesh to: 'the first Council has met; the first steps towards a Labour Bureau have been taken; women are organising to put forward the claims of women under Article 7; commissions are being appointed to carry out certain work allotted to them by the Treaty.'[163] Since the alternative to the present League was not a new order, but rather a return to the pre-war international anarchy, the League had to be recognised as the best route towards a more cooperative and peaceful world. 'The Realist in us must admit that the League is in being', she argued in 1920. 'The

Idealist must admit that it is not the League of his loyalty and his devotion and must ask himself how best this can be established.'[164]

Yet, for her the answer did not lie in the 'closing of the gaps' in the Covenant, and the establishment of a collective security system. As she later recalled in her memoirs, she had already made up her mind during the First World War that the League-sponsored wars made necessary by a full collective security system would be counter-productive.[165] Generally, her objections revolved around three arguments. The first, a continuation of her wartime criticism of the use of war (see the discussion in Chapter 5), that a 'League war' had the same effect on the ground as any other kind of war waged for less exalted reasons. Tied up with this was her criticism of the distinction, found in the arguments of Norman Angell among others between the use of military might for conquest and its use in a policing role. Second, she believed that the threat of sanctions weakened the League, because there was no will among states or publics to use these provisions. Third, she criticised what she saw as the highly legalistic approach by the advocates of the closing of the gaps in the Covenant, arguing instead that the road to peace was through changes in psychology.

During the war years Swanwick had set out to show how war affected women and children, and how for whatever noble ideals a war was fought, its effect on society and civilians was the same. Advocates of military sanctions under the League argued that, when used by the League, military force would serve a policing role, which would be substantially different from the way that force was used under the old international anarchy. Swanwick strongly attacked this policing analogy, arguing that it hid the extent that a League war would have much of the same consequences as any war. A League 'police force' would not be operating under the same conditions as a domestic police force, but instead would be using military force against military force. Rather than taking a criminal nation into custody, a League army would be attacking the offending nation's people and infrastructure. War passions would have to be aroused in League states in order to justify the action, and any League army would be armed with the latest weapons for war and devastation. Also, while a policeman is meant to operate within a supportive community that he is required to protect, a League army would be invading a country whose inhabitants would be hostile to it.[166] Swanwick also doubted whether, once a League war was begun, that the states contributing to the conflict could resist using the pretext of the war to pursue their own interests.[167] In addition, the active involvement of League powers in a local conflict would represent a widening and escalation of the conflict analogous to that of the 1914 crisis. Swanwick returned here to her earlier arguments about the dangers of a society based on physical force. The concept of a League war merely returned to the physical force argument, and the use of the threat of war by the League extended and legitimised arguments based on physical force.[168]

Swanwick's most often used argument against League sanctions, however, was the more immediate issue that she did not think there was the will or the capability to use the League for military security. She was willing to concede that the threat of sanctions against smaller powers had brought an end to conflicts in the 1920s, but she argued that there was no will at all to bring effective, and military, sanctions against any great power should it break the provisions of the League Covenant.[169] By simultaneously threatening sanctions, while clearly not having the capability to make good on those threats, the League threatened to discredit itself. 'A League which threatens "I'll whip you" and never does, would be much stronger if it never threatened.'[170] She continued to see the sanctions provisions of the Covenant not as unfinished business in need of legal tightening up, as did the advocates of the closing of the gaps in the Covenant, but rather as compromise provisions that the state representatives at the Paris peace talks put in with the intention of leaving vague because they had no intention of using them in the first place.[171] As a result of this view, she rejected as idealistic the argument that they should be tightened up, and instead suggested that they should be abolished since the sanctions provisions got in the way of the far more important peace work undertaken by the League.[172]

So, if she opposed a 'League with teeth', what did Swanwick – who was after all a supporter of the League – suggest that the League should do? To answer this, we need to understand her final reason for rejecting League sanctions, namely that the idea of 'closing the gaps in the Covenant' was frequently based on misguided legalistic assumptions. What particularly surprised Swanwick about many of her 'sanctionist' colleagues was that they trusted in the agreement of legal formulae worked out in paper treaties. This seemed to her to be an amazing leap of faith. States had been breaking treaties and legal agreements for centuries, and many had been broken since 1919 alone, yet the more legalist supporters of sanctions (e.g. Noel-Baker) assumed that if the treaties and agreements were legally binding and precise that states would not be able to wriggle out of them.[173] Swanwick felt that, however strong the legal language, states would find a way to dodge their obligations.[174]

What Swanwick proposed was an abandonment of the search for a legal formula, and instead the concentration on more psychological matters. Generally, she felt it was not legal obligations, but rather attitudes of mind that would bring about a more peaceful world. War fighting was based on a particular physical force mentality, which had largely disappeared from domestic politics. The same process could happen, she felt, at the international level. In the long term we had to try to understand why people fought wars. This was no easy step: 'Cut-and-dried little sets of laws are easier to understand and simpler to state than the strangely and irrationally mixed motives which cause men to act as queerly as they do.'[175] Furthermore there 'is no short-cut to the promised land of Security' using legality and force as a substitute for confidence building.[176] In the shorter-term the League of Nations could foster a more peaceful international atmosphere through tendering 'its good offices for conciliation and bargaining and compromise; its incomparable Civil Service; its adroitness at saving face'.[177] This would help states to change their psychological attitude to international politics, leading to the replacement of the norms associated with physical force for the norms that underlie a post-physical force society.[178]

Swanwick's feminist and pacifist opposition to collective security found common cause with her American colleague from the Women's International League for Peace and Freedom: Emily Greene Balch. Like Swanwick, Balch thought that women's maternal role gave them a particular view on war that tended towards pacifism. It 'is natural' wrote Balch in 1922, 'that the half of mankind ... which has always had the responsibility for the Children and the suffering of the weak should be especially ready to make sacrifices on behalf of peace'.[179] Although Balch was also willing to concede that women were as likely as men to be 'inflamed by nationalism, intoxicated by the glories of war, embittered by old rancors'.[180] Like Swanwick, Balch was not opposed to the League, and saw the need for a twin track approach towards peace consisting of both the creation of the formal 'machinery of peace' via organisations like the League, and a deeper change of psychology that would lead to a greater respect for peace.[181] Yet, she also agreed with Swanwick that military sanctions under League auspices was not the answer. She also objected to the use of the term 'police force' when describing military action in the defence of collective security. She was particularly dismissive of the claims made by several international experts that an internationalised air force could be used to police aggression.[182] 'I understand by police force' Balch told the Women's International League Congress in Grenoble, 'something absolutely unlike fire, explosives and gas, rained from the air'.[183] Thus, for Balch the key to a more peaceful world lay in changing human psychology and attitudes towards war, and the enfranchisement and political involvement of women was an important step in this development. These similarities between Swanwick and Balch aside, there was one major difference between them that is relevant to the next chapter: while Swanwick's support for changes in mind-set and opposition to collective security led her to support later attempts to appease the fascist powers (especially Nazi Germany), Balch, by contrast, moved in the other direction. Balch endorsed the imposition of economic sanctions against aggressors and became increasingly hostile to American neutrality and isolation, despite her strong pacifist convictions.[184] In the end, a shared intellectual understanding towards peace and the role of the League were not enough to guarantee a shared agreement on the preferred policy in dealing with fascist aggression. While Swanwick would commit suicide in 1939, partially as a result of her gloom over the international situation (although also because of her deteriorating health), Balch would go on to earn the Nobel Peace Prize in 1946 for her long service to peace.

There is a temptation to see the traditions discussed in this section as a dead-end in the history of international thought, and the subsequent development of a university-based academic field of IR. In this story the path leading down to the European part of the war in 1939 becomes a final refutation of the idealism of the strict pacifist, and the knee-jerk anti-capitalism of the radical socialist. Certainly, looking back from the other side of both the Second World War and the subsequent Cold War between communism and capitalism, those who particularly advocated a renunciation of war in the late-1930s can seem naïve. This fits the narrative often found in IR textbooks too: a jejune opposition to war comes up against the realities of fascist power, and the response, 'in good Kuhnian fashion', is the emergence of realism as an alternative paradigm.[185] Perhaps one of the most well-known figures in the pacifist movement in the 1930s was the charismatic activist and organiser of the Peace Pledge Union (PPU) Reverend Hugh Richard Sheppard. Dick Sheppard based his full renunciation of all forms of war on his Christian faith, although he attracted and converted to an absolute pacifist position many non-believers too. It was Sheppard who had helped convince Vera Brittain to renounce her support for collective security, and the PPU attracted support from both Arthur Ponsonby and George Lansbury.[186] Much of this came after the Abyssinian crisis of 1935–6, when collective security became associated with calls for military intervention and even war. Many of those who had formerly supported the League now moved over to a pacifist position that opposed much of the League architecture (it was at this time that E.H. Carr also lost faith in the League). One young man – who had recently written his first article (entitled 'Christian Pacifism') in 1936 joined the PPU, worked for the PPU bookshop – became very close to Sheppard in the last year of Sheppard's life. Sheppard's brand of Christian pacifism was to remain a life-long part of this young man's interpretation of international politics, even leading him to become a conscientious objector during the Second World War. That young man's name was Martin Wight, who in later life was to become one of the key thinkers in post-war British IR (and perhaps the central figure in the 'English School'), and regarded by some as a realist thinker.[187]

## Conclusion

The understanding of IR in the inter-war period has been badly served by the simplistic (and inaccurate) description of it as dominated by a realist–idealist split. Rather, as the discussion above demonstrates, inter-war IR in the English-speaking world prior to the mid-1930s was a far more complex affair. Also, rather than being driven by metaphysical concepts such as realism or idealism, the debates of the time were dominated by more pragmatic and prosaic concerns linked to the immediate problems of international affairs. This pragmatism was at least partially the result of a sense of urgency. The international system had just thrown up a bitter four year war that had killed millions, the sense that the global order was broken and in need of serious fixing dominates these discussions. Even the men of the right, such as Mackinder, looked to the League of Nations as the best hope for a better world. There was also a sense of urgency here, with the League system seen, even by its supporters, as a currently weak and half-formed entity. Writing in 1927 Philip Noel-Baker, a major proponent of the League, wrote that 'there still remains one doubt about the future of the League … Will its institutions be given time to build up their strength before the catastrophe of a new war sweeps them all away?'[188]

In Britain at least, this sense of urgency was given a sharper edge by a general sense of pessimism about the future. A feeling of being part of a civilisation in decline made the search for a new world order appear both more pressing and less likely to succeed. It is no coincidence that it was this British context that eventually produced both Arnold Toynbee's *A Study of History*, with its concerns about how we can evaluate decline in civilisation, and Robert Graves' *I, Claudius*, with its subtext of the ebbing away of Republican Roman traditions. Even the emergence of eugenics occurs as a product of a sense of racial decline, rather than as part of a triumphant belief in the superiority of a particular race. George Orwell's anti-hero in *Keep the Aspidistra Flying* half looks forward to the appearance of the bombers that will obliterate civilisation, while in H.G. Wells' film *Things to Come* (1936) movie-goers were shown how swift and devastating that destruction would be.[189] This pessimism lent an air of desperation to much of the writing of international experts. The status quo was seen as dangerously precarious, and the need for structures of international organisation came to be seen as a necessary safeguard for peace that had to be brought in to being at all costs. This mix of the necessity of change and the requirement to boost organisational alternatives can be read, without the benefit of context, as a woolly-headed support for utopian ideas. Yet, a look at the context, and an analysis of other texts such as the Noel-Baker quote above, reveals that rather than being the product of optimistic naivety, these arguments for international government were the product of a desperate generation fearful of a return to the violence of the Great War. The very reason that writers such as Woolf and Angell supported stricter international organisations was that they did not trust people or states when left to their own devices. Once a threat worse than war emerged, in the shape of fascist aggression, many of those same writers that had so feverishly supported League of Nations collective security – especially Norman Angell, Leonard Woolf and, a little later, Philip Noel-Baker – switched their allegiance to rearmament and support for a close Anglo-French alliance. This will be discussed in more detail in the next chapter.

Returning to the 1920s and early 1930s, while it is true to say that opinion on the nature of the League was divided, it is also true that there was widespread support for the organisation. This support certainly straddled the left-right divide, although at any given time there was often strong resistance from some groups to the perceived direction the League was taking. Strong support for the League and the League idea, however, masked differences over what form the League should take. Since the League was an evolving institution, rather than a finished product, differences emerged most often over the form the League should take in the future. That said, there was much common ground between conservative enthusiasts for the League, such as Robert Cecil, and the pro-League left. The major split, at least in British political opinion, was between the liberal–socialist supporters of collective security and a coalition of stricter socialists and pacifists who opposed collective security and championed the idea of the League as a force of moral suasion rather than of legal sanctions. This split was to take on a new role in the late 1930s, as the next chapter shows.

Behind all this is an important point about the League-based international order of the immediate post-1919 period: that the League was never a complete institution with clear goals. It remained a project (or, more correctly, a series of projects) that were in various stages of construction by the time war came in 1939. As a new and unprecedented organisation, even those who were building and using it were not agreed on how it should work. The world's statesmen, in this sense, were in uncharted waters. Bowman was right to see the new world emerging after 1919 as a mix between the old and the new diplomacy. Thus, we have to see the period between 1919 and 1935 as one in which, while the status quo had been discredited, there was no clear and settled idea of where the world should go. Rather than an intellectual conflict between conservative realists supporting things as they are, and radical idealists out to change everything, what we see are debates between different proponents of change. Interestingly, figures as politically and intellectually diverse as Isaiah Bowman, Gilbert Murray, Nicholas Murray Butler, Helena Swanwick and Emily Greene Balch were stressing the need for a change in 'spirit' or 'psychology' – often alongside institutional changes – as a central part of any future new order. As these different groups argued on the sunny shores of Lake Geneva, forming different alliances of convenience on the way, each knew that they were in a race against the time in which the dark storm-clouds of war would once again menace humanity.

## Notes

1 Michael Joseph Smith, *Realist Thought from Weber to Kissinger* (Baton Rouge and London: Louisiana State University Press, 1986), 54.
2 See, for example, Roland N. Stromberg, 'The Idea of Collective Security', *Journal of the History of Ideas*, April 1956, 17(2), 250–63.
3 See Michael Banks, 'The Inter-Paradigm Debate', in Margot Light and A.J.R. Groom (eds), *International Relations: A Handbook of Current Theory* (Boulder, CO: Lynne Rienner, 1985); and Mark Hoffman, 'Critical Theory and the Inter-Paradigm Debate', *Millennium*, Summer 1987, 16(2), 231–49.
4 Steve Smith, 'Introduction', in T. Dunne, M. Kuki and S. Smith (eds), *International Relations Theories: Discipline and Diversity* (Oxford: Oxford University Press, 2007), 10.
5 For this argument see Joel Quirk and Darshnan Vigneswaran, 'The Construction of an Edifice: the story of a First Great Debate', *Review of International Studies*, 2005, 31, 89–107.
6 For a discussion of the literature on the myth of the realist–idealist 'great debate' see Brian Schmidt (ed.), *International Relations and the First Great Debate* (London: Routledge, 2012).
7 E. H. Carr, *Twenty Years' Crisis* (London: Macmillan, 1939).
8 See Brian Schmidt, 'The American National Interest Great Debate' in Schmidt, *IR and the First Great Debate*, 94–117.
9 See, for example, John Herz, *Political Realism and Political Idealism* (Chicago: University of Chicago Press: 1951).
10 See, for example, Brian C. Schmidt, *The Political Discourse of Anarchy* (Albany: State University of New York, 1998), especially 34 ff. Also: Torbjørn L. Knutsen, 'A Lost Generation? IR Scholarship Before World War I', *International Politics*, 45(6), 650–74. And: Casper Sylvest, *British Liberal Internationalism 1880–1930* (Manchester: Manchester University Press, 2009).
11 Philip Noel-Baker, 'The Growth of International Society', *Economica*, 1924, 12, 262–77.
12 See Norman Angell, *The Fruits of Victory* (New York: Garland 1972 [1921]), especially 61, 293–300.

13  Beryl Haslam, *From Suffrage to Internationalism* (New York: Peter Lang 1999), 40.

14  Harold Nicolson, *Diplomacy: A Basic Guide to the Conduct of Contemporary Foreign Affairs* (New York: Harcourt Brace, 1939).

15  Mary Agnes Hamilton, *Remembering My Good Friends* (London: Jonathan Cape, 1944), 104–6.

16  See the discussion in Margaret MacMillan, *Peacemakers* (London: John Murray, 2002), especially, 177 ff, 469, 486.

17  See MacMillan, *Peacemakers* for a full discussion of all of these issues.

18  WILPF was a non-governmental organisation that spanned the globe, but was particularly strong in Britain and the United States. Its membership included many of the key inter-war feminists including Emily Greene Balch and H.N. Swanwick.

19  For more on the League and women's organisations see Carol Miller, *Lobbying the League: Women's International Organizations and the League of Nations* (Oxford: Oxford University Press, 1992). See also Hilkka Pietilä, *Engendering the Global Agenda* (New York and Geneva: UN NGLS, 2002), 1–8.

20  See Leonard Woolf, *Mandates and Empire* (London: League of Nations Union, 1920), 17–18.

21  Kenneth W. Thompson, *Schools of Thought in International Relations. Interpretors, Issues, and Morality* (Baton Rouge: Lousiana State University, 1996), 14 ff.

22  See, for example, Colin S. Gray, 'In Defence of the Heartland: Sir Halford Mackinder and his Critics a Hundred Years On', *Comparative Strategy*, 2004, 23, 9–25.

23  Halford J. Mackinder, 'The Geographical Pivot of History', *The Geographical Journal*, 1904, 23: 421–37; and Halford J. Mackinder, *Democratic Ideals and Reality. A Study in the Politics of Reconstruction* (London: Constable, 1919), especially chapters 3–5.

24  Mackinder, *Democratic Ideals and Reality*, 18.

25  Mackinder, *Democratic Ideals and Reality*, 9.

26  Mackinder, *Democratic Ideals and Reality*, ch. 2.

27  See E.H. Carr's *Nationalism and After* (London: Macmillan, 1945).

28  Mackinder, *Democratic Ideals and Reality*, 18, 30.

29  Mackinder, *Democratic Ideals and Reality*, 20.

30  Mackinder, *Democratic Ideals and Reality*, 106.

31  Halford J. Mackinder, *The Modern British State. An Introduction to the Study of Civics*, second edn (London: George Philip, 1922), 276.

32  Here, perhaps, the work of the French human geographer Jean Brunhes was important to Bowman's conversion. To Brunhes 'natural facts' were things that humans modify, shape and interpret. Bowman was one of the editors of a 1920 edition of Brunhes' work: Jean Brunhes, *Human Geography. An Attempt at a Positive Classification Principles and Examples* (London: George G. Harrap, 1920).

33  In a 1924 letter Bowman stated that the 'last shreds' of determinism were 'completely removed from the fabric of my own integral life' by the experience of the 1919 Paris Peace Conference. See Neil Smith, 'Bowman's New World and the Council on Foreign Relations', *Geographical Review*, 1986, 76: 438. On the influence of French geographers see Geoffrey J. Martin, *The Life and Thought of Isaiah Bowman* (Hamden CT: Archon, 1980).

34  Isaiah Bowman, *The New World. Problems in Political Geography*, fourth edn (Yonkers-on-Hudson: World Book Company, 1928), 12–14; Isaiah Bowman, *International Relations* (Chicago: American Library Association, 1930), 18–21.

35  Bowman, *New World*, 735–7

36  The ISC was the organisation that brought together experts in international affairs, and was a key focus of intellectual collaboration in the inter-war period. See David Long, 'Who Killed the International Studies Conference?', *Review of International Studies*, 2006, 32, 603–22.

37  Isaiah Bowman (ed.), *Limits of Land Settlement. A Report on Present-Day Possibilities* (New York: Books for Libraries, 1937).

38 Quoted in Pierre Denis 'International Aspects of State Intervention in Economic Life', in Charles Carlyle Colby (ed.) *Geographic Aspects of International Relations* (Chicago: University of Chicago Press, 1938), 81.

39 Isaiah Bowman, 'The Pioneer Fringe', *Foreign Affairs*, 1927, 6, 63.

40 Bowman, *The New World*, 1; see also his *International Relations*, 14–15.

41 Bowman, *The New World*, 735.

42 Bowman, *The New World*, 23.

43 Bowman, *International Relations*, 18.

44 Bowman, *The New World*, 738.

45 Bowman, *The New World*, 7–9; Bowman, *International Relations*, 9–10.

46 Bowman, *International Relations*, 10–13.

47 Bowman, *The New World*, 4; Bowman, *International Relations*, 28.

48 Bowman, *International Relations*, 29–30.

49 Neil Smith, *American Empire. Roosevelt's Geographer and the Prelude to Globalization* (Berkeley, Los Angeles and London: University of California Press, 2003).

50 For a discussion of this 'businessmen's peace movement' see Craig N. Murphy, *International Organization and Industrial Change: Global Governance since 1850* (New York: Oxford University Press, 1994), 157–9.

51 On conservative support for the League see D.S. Birn, *The League of Nations Union 1918-1945* (Oxford: Oxford University Press, 1981), 25.

52 H.N. Brailsford, *After the Peace* (London: Leonard Parsons, 1920); H.M. Swanwick, *I Have Been Young* (London: Victor Gollancz, 1935), 266.

53 See, for example, John E. Kendle, *The Round Table Movement and Imperial Union* (Toronto: University of Toronto Press, 1975), 248 ff.

54 Kendle, *Round Table Movement*, 250–2.

55 See, for example, Marquess of Lothian, (Philip Kerr), *Pacifism is Not Enough (Nor Patriotism Either)* (Oxford: Clarendon, 1935); Lionel Curtis, *Civitas Dei: The Commonwealth of God* (Macmillan: London, 1938). See the discussion in Kendle, *Round Table Movement*, 292 ff.

56 For a full discussion of Cecil's work as a statesman and internationalist thinker see Gaynor Johnson, *Lord Robert Cecil Viscount Cecil of Chelwood: Politician and Internationalist* (Aldershot: Ashgate, 2013).

57 Robert Cecil, *A Great Experiment* (London: Jonathan Cape, 1941), 74, 78.

58 See D.H. Miller, *The Drafting of the Covenant*, volume I (New York: Putnam, 1928), 57–61.

59 Article 19 of the Covenant. Cecil discusses this on pages 76–7 of *A Great Experiment.*

60 For a detailed discussion of Cecil's internationalism see Gaynor Johnson, *Lord Robert Cecil Viscount Cecil of Chelwood: Politician and Internationalist* (Aldershot: Ashgate, 2013).

61 See the discussion in Peter Wilson, 'Gilbert Murray and International Relations: Hellenism, Liberalism, and International Intellectual Cooperation as a Path to Peace', *Review of International Studies* 2011, 37(2), especially 896 and 906.

62 On the influence of the neo-Hegelians on Bosenquet see Jeane Morefield, *Covenants Without Swords. Idealist Liberalism and the Spirit of Empire* (Princeton: Princeton University Press, 2004), ch. 1.

63 Wilson, 'Gilbert Murray and IR', 895.

64 Gilbert Murray, *The Ordeal of this Generation. The War, the League and the Future* (London: George Allen & Unwin, 1929), 57 ff.

65 Gilbert Murray, 'Self-Determination of Nationalities', *Journal of the British Institute of International Affairs*, January 1922, 1(1), 6–13.

66 Murray, *Ordeal of this Generation*, 67–8, 125–8.

67 Murray, *Ordeal of this Generation*, 79.

68 Murray, *Ordeal of this Generation*, 97.

69  See the discussion in Wilson, 'Gilbert Murray and IR', 902.

70  Gilbert Murray, 'Intellectual Cooperation', *Annals of the American Academy of Political and Social Science*, 1944, 235, 1–9.

71  Gilbert Murray, *From the League to the U.N.* (Oxford: Oxford University Press, 1948), 4, 211. For Murray's early antipathy to nationalism see Gilbert Murray, 'National Ideals; Conscious and Unconscious', *International Journal of Ethics*, October, 1900, 11(1), 1–22.

72  Gilbert Murray, *The Problem of Foreign Policy. A Consideration of Present Dangers and the Best Methods for Meeting Them* (Boston: Houghton and Mifflin, 1921), preface. See also Murray, *Ordeal of this Generation*, 196–7, where the emphasis is on intellectual cooperation in order to restore a lost Cosmos.

73  Murray, *Ordeal of this Generation*, 191.

74  See the discussion in Wilson, 'Gilbert Murray and IR', 905–6.

75  See Julie Reeves, *Culture and International Relations: Narratives, Natives and Tourists* (New York: Routledge, 2004), 50.

76  Murray, 'Intellectual Cooperation', 4–5. On the ISC see Michael Riemens, 'International Academic Cooperation on International Relations in the Interwar Period: The International Studies Conference', *Review of International Studies*, 2011, 37, 911–28.

77  On Mitrany and Neo-functionalism see Chapter 8. On epistemic communities see Peter M. Haas, 'Epistemic Communities and International Policy Coordination'. *International Organization*, Winter 1992, 46(1), 1–35.

78  Nicholas Murray Butler, 'The Alternative to War [1934]', in Nicholas Murray Butler, *The Family of Nations. Its Need and its Problems. Essays and Addresses* (New York: Charles Scribner, 1938), 11–15.

79  Nicholas Murray Butler, 'Some Problems of World Federation [1937]', in Butler, *The Family of Nations*, 362.

80  Nicholas Murray Butler, 'Where are the Leaders? [1934]', in Butler, *The Family of Nations*, 23; and Nicholas Murray Butler, 'The Duty of the English-Speaking Peoples [1934]', Butler, *The Family of Nations*, 47–55.

81  Charles F. Hewlett, 'John Dewey and Nicholas Murray Butler: Contrasting Conceptions of Peace Education in the Twenties', *Educational Theory*, December 1987, 37(4), 453, see also 454.

82  David Mitrany, *The Land and the Peasant in Rumania. The War and Agrarian Reform* (London: Humprey Milford and Oxford University Press, 1930); and David Mitrany, *The Effects of the War in South Eastern Europe* (New Haven: Yale University Press, 1936). Other volumes in this series included work by James T. Shotwell (the general editor), G.D.H. Cole and John Maynard Keynes.

83  Donald Markwell, *John Maynard Keynes and International Relations. Economic Paths to War and Peace* (Oxford: Oxford University Press, 2006), 3 ff.

84  John Maynard Keynes, *The Economic Consequences of the Peace* (London: Macmillan, 1920), chapter II.

85  Keynes, *Economic Consequences of the Peace*, 1. Page 3 of the American edition (New York: Harcourt Brace and Howe, 1920).

86  Keynes, *Economic Consequences of the Peace*, 17–19 (19–22 in the American edition).

87  Norman Angell, *The Foundations of International Polity* (London: William Heinemann, 1914), 61–8.

88  Markwell, *John Maynard Keynes and International Relations*, 102 ff.

89  See, for example, his discussion of the situation with coal, iron and labour: Keynes, *Economic Consequences of the Peace*, 91–2 (99–100 in the American edition).

90  See the discussion in Gregor Dallas, *1918. War and Peace* (London: John Murray, 2000), 243 ff. See also Keynes' own calculations on what Germany could pay, and why the indemnity fallacy argument was also, in its turn, wrong in John Maynard Keynes, *A Revision of the Treaty* (London: Macmillan, 1922), ch. 6.

91 Keynes, *Economic Consequences of the Peace*, 134 (146 in the American edition).
92 Markwell, *John Maynard Keynes and International Relations*, 65–6.
93 Keynes, *Economic Consequences of the Peace*, 213 (228 in American edition).
94 John Maynard Keynes, 'The Change of Opinion (1921)', reprinted in his *Essays in Persuasion* (London: Macmillan, 1931), 51. Also published as part of Keynes, *Revision of the Treaty*, 7.
95 Markwell, *John Maynard Keynes and International Relations*, 3.
96 Markwell, *John Maynard Keynes and International Relations*, 107–9.
97 Markwell, *John Maynard Keynes and International Relations*, 108.
98 Angell, *Fruits of Victory*, 68, 87, 297.
99 Angell, *Fruits of Victory*, 301.
100 Keynes, *Revision of the Treaty*, 11.
101 For a more detailed analysis of Keynes' support for international organisations see: Markwell, *John Maynard Keynes and International Relations*, chs 5–6.
102 Nicolson's letters to his wife and father, reprinted in Harold Nicolson, *Peacemaking 1919* (London: Methuen, 1964), 350 and 359. This book was originally published in 1933.
103 Harold Nicolson, 'Modern Diplomacy and British Public Opinion', *International Affairs*, 14(5), 1935, 603.
104 Nicolson, *Peacemaking 1919*, 195 ff.
105 Nicolson, *Peacemaking 1919*, 187.
106 Harold Nicolson, 'The Foreign Service', *Political Quarterly*, 7, 1936, 208.
107 Nicolson, 'Modern Diplomacy', 606–7.
108 Derek Drinkwater, *Sir Harold Nicolson and International Relations. The Practitioner as Theorist* (Oxford: Oxford University Press, 2005), 77.
109 See Adam Watson, *Diplomacy: the Dialogue Between States* (London: Eyre Methuen, 1982), 20, 93. On Nicolson and foreign policy see the discussion in Drinkwater, *Harold Nicolson and International Relations*, 64–70.
110 From an unpublished paper dated 1935. Quoted in Drinkwater, *Harold Nicolson and International Relations*, 77.
111 Nicolson, 'Modern Diplomacy', 599; Nicolson, 'Foreign Service', 220; Harold Nicolson, *Diplomacy* (New York: Harcourt Brace, 1939), 1–2, 4, 30.
112 Nicolson, *Peacemaking 1919*, 207.
113 Nicolson, *Peacemaking 1919*, 190.
114 Nicolson, *Peacemaking 1919*, 208–9.
115 Cecil, *A Great Experiment*, 92–3.
116 Murray, *Ordeal of this Generation*, 59–61.
117 Frederick Sherwood Dunn, *The Practice and Procedure of International Conferences* (New York: AMS Press, 1971 [1921]), 6.
118 Nicolson, 'Modern Diplomacy', 611–12; *Diplomacy*, 42.
119 Nicolson, 'Foreign Service', 220.
120 Drinkwater, *Harold Nicolson and International Relations*, 208.
121 Michael Freeden, *Ideologies and Political Theory. A Conceptual Approach* (Oxford: Oxford University Press, 1998).
122 Robert Cecil noted that in 1920 the Labour members of the House of Commons 'were at that time doubtful' about the League. Cecil, *A Great Experiment*, 101.
123 Freeden, *Ideologies and Political Theory*, 144–5.
124 Freeden, *Ideologies and Political Theory*, 425–6.
125 Labour Party, *Report of the Thirty-fifth Annual Conference* (London: Labour Party, 1935), p. 174. Cripps at one point even likened the League to the Anti-Comintern Pact of fascist powers. See Eric Estorick, *Stafford Cripps: Prophetic Rebel* (New York: John Day, 1941), p. 82.
126 For the lack of international theory see David Mitrany, *The Progress of International Government* (London: Allen & Unwin, 1933), especially p. 33.

127  J.A. Hobson, *The Evolution of Modern Capitalism* (London: Scott, 1894); and *Imperialism: A Study* (London: Nisbet, 1902).

128  G. Lowes Dickinson, *The European Anarchy* (London: George Allen & Unwin, 1916).

129  Confusingly, pacifist in the inter-war years was used as a term to cover both those who opposed all war without exception, and those who saw a role for force as a final sanction in a proper collective security system. On this issue see Louis R. Bisceglia, 'Norman Angell and the Pacifist Muddle', *Bulletin of the Institute of Historical Research*, 1972, 45, 104–19; and Martin Caedel, *Pacifism in Britain 1914–1945* (Oxford: Clarendon, 1980).

130  See, for example: Arthur Ponsonby, *Now is the Time. An Appeal for Peace* (London: Leonard Parsons, 1925); and H.M. Swanwick, *Collective Insecurity* (London: Jonathan Cape, 1937). For a fuller discussion of the interaction between these two see Lucian M. Ashworth, 'Rethinking a Socialist Foreign Policy: The British Labour Party and International Relations 1918 to 1931', *International Labor and Working Class History*, 75, 2009, 30–48.

131  *After the Peace* (London: Leonard Parsons, 1920).

132  A good example of this can be found in David Mitrany's response to the second edn of Georg Schwarzenberger's *Power Politics*. In January 1952 *International Affairs* published Mitrany's non-committal and polite review of the book. After finishing the review in September 1951 Mitrany wrote to A.P. Wadsworth of the *Manchester Guardian* saying that Schwarzenberger 'is a slimy little Germanic worm and I don't know who pays for or buys this kind of book ...' The letter reveals what the review could not. DM to APW 15 September 1951, 338/1/122 *Manchester Guardian* Archive, John Rylands Library, Manchester University, UK.

133  See especially the following Labour Party Advisory Committee on International Questions memoranda: J.A. Hobson, 'Economic War after the War', no. 24, nd; H.N. Brailsford, 'A Parliament of the League of Nations', no. 44, January 1919; Norman Angell, 'Peace Terms', no. 61, May 1919; David Mitrany, 'Memorandum on Labour Policy Concerning Commissions to be Set up Under the Peace Treaty', no. 125, January 1920; C. Delisle Burns, 'Notes on the League', no. 143, 8 June 1920; Anon, 'Revision of the Treaty of Versailles', no. 254a, 1922; Leonard Woolf, 'The League of Nations and Disarmament', no. 251, 1922; and Anon, 'The Need for a League Foreign Policy', no. 287, 9 July 1923. All available in the Labour Party Archives in Labour History Archive and Study Centre, Manchester, UK.

134  'Need for a League Foreign Policy', p. 4.

135  See William Arnold-Foster, 'Commentary on the British Government's Observations to the League, on Arbitration and Security', Advisory Committee on International Questions memo no. 386, February 1928. Labour Party Archives, Labour History Archive and Study Centre, Manchester, UK.

136  Leonard Woolf, *International Government* (London: George Allen & Unwin, 1916), 52–9.

137  William Arnold-Forster and Leonard Woolf, 'Proposed Recommendation to the Executive Regarding a Convention for Pacific Settlement', Advisory Committee on International Questions memo no. 355a, nd. Labour Party Archives, Labour History Archive and Study Centre, Manchester, UK.

138  Hugh Dalton, *Towards the Peace of Nations. A Study in International Politics* (London: Routledge & Kegan Paul, 1928), 211; David Mitrany, *The Problem of International Sanctions* (London: Humphrey Milford and OUP, 1925), 2. See also David Mitrany, 'A Labour Policy on Sanctions', Advisory Committee on International Questions memo no. 366, May 1927. Labour Party Archives, Labour History Archive and Study Centre, Manchester, UK.

139  See, for example, Mitrany, 'Labour Policy on Sanctions', 1–2. The political problems of sanctions led to its disappearance from much Labour Party literature. See James Ramsay MacDonald, *Protocol or Pact? The Alternative to War* (London: Labour

Party, nd [1925]), p. 5; and Labour Party, *Labour and the Nation*, first edn (London: Labour Party, 1928), 41.

140  See, for example, Angell, *The Foundations of International Polity*, 163–93.

141  Philip Noel-Baker, *Disarmament* (London: Hogarth, 1926), 7.

142  Mitrany, 'Labour Policy on Sanctions', 2, 7; H.N. Brailsford, 'Arbitrate or Disarm. A New View of Security', *New Leader*, 12 September 1924, 3–4; Woolf, *International Government*, 52–9.

143  Ashworth, 'Rethinking a Socialist Foreign Policy', 44–5.

144  For a summary of this debate see Henry Brinton (ed.), *Does Capitalism Cause War?* (London: H. & E.R. Brinton, 1935). This book brought together an exchange of letters in the *New Statesman*, and included an introduction written by Lord Cecil.

145  Catherine Ann Cline, *Recruits to Labour. The British Party 1941–1931* (New York: Syracuse University Press, 1963), 93.

146  Letter from Arthur Ponsonby to George Lansbury, 22 October 1933. George Lansbury Papers, British Library of Political and Economic Sciences, London School of Economics and Political Science. Emphasis in the original.

147  Arhtur Ponsonby, *Democracy and Diplomacy. A Plea for Popular Control of Foreign Policy* (London: Methuen, 1915).

148  See the following Labour Advisory Committee on International Questions memos written by George Young: 'Memorandum on the Reform of the Foreign Services' no. 10 July 1918; and 'The Reform of Diplomacy: A Practical Programme', no number, May 1921. Both in the Labour Party Archives, Labour History Archive and Study Centre, Manchester, UK. See also: Labour Party, *Control of Foreign Policy: Labour's Programme* (London: Labour Party, 1920).

149  See, for example, Arthur Ponsonby, *The Covenant of the League of Nations* (London: Union of Democratic Control, 1920).

150  Arthur Ponsonby, *Now is the Time. An Appeal for Peace* (London: Leonard Parsons, 1925), 107–9.

151  Ponsonby, *Now is the Time*, ch. VIII.

152  Ponsonby, *Now is the Time*, 160.

153  Quoted in Henry R. Winkler, *Paths Not Taken. British Labour and International Policy in the 1920s* (Chapel Hill: University of North Carolina Press, 1994), 54.

154  George Lansbury, *My Life* (London: Constable, 1928), 214.

155  George Lansbury, 'To the Electors of Bow and Bromley', electoral flyer for the 1935 General Election, 2–3. Paper no. 361, George Lansbury Papers, British Library of Political and Economic Science, London School of Economics and Political Science, London.

156  Quoted in Thomas Sewell, *Intellectuals and Society* (New York: Basic, 2009), 227.

157  C.T. Stannage, 'The East Fulham By-Election, 25 October 1933', *The Historical Journal*, March 1971, 14(1), 190.

158  Quoted in Adolf Sturmthal, *The Tragedy of European Labour. 1918–1939* (London: Victor Gollancz, 1944), 265.

159  Stafford Cripps, quoted in Labour Party, *Report of the Thirty-fifth Annual Conference* (London: Labour Party, 1935), 174.

160  See the discussion in Lucian M. Ashworth, *International Relations and the Labour Party. Intellectuals and Policy Making from 1918–1945* (London: IBTauris, 2007), 139.

161  Swanwick, *I Have Been Young*, 266.

162  H.M. Swanwick, *The Peace Treaties Explained. No. 1 The Covenant of the League of Nations* (London: Women's International League, 1920), 12.

163  Swanwick, *The Peace Treaties Explained*, 15.

164  Swanwick, *The Peace Treaties Explained*, 16.

165  Swanwick, *I Have Been Young*, 267.

166  H.M. Swanwick, *New Wars for Old* (London: Women's International League, 1934), 23–4; H.M. Swanwick, *Collective Insecurity* (London: Jonathan Cape, 1937), 230–1.

167  Swanwick, *Collective Insecurity* , 89–90.

168  H.M. Swanwick and W. Arnold-Forster, *Sanctions of the League of Nations Covenant* (London: London Council For Prevention of War, 1928), 22–5.

169  Swanwick, *New Wars for Old*, 6–7.

170  Swanwick, *I Have Been Young*, 268.

171  Swanwick, *New Wars for Old*, 16.

172  H.M. Swanwick, *The Roots of Peace* (London: Jonathan Cape, 1938), 139–48; Swanwick, *New Wars for Old*, 9; Swanwick and Arnold Forster, *Sanctions of the League*, 17.

173  Swanwick, *Collective Insecurity*, 19–20.

174  Swanwick and Arnold Forster, *Sanctions of the League*, 20–1.

175  Swanwick, *Collective Insecurity*, 20–1.

176  Swanwick, *New Wars for Old*, 21–2.

177  Swanwick, *New Wars for Old*, 21.

178  Swanwick, *The Roots of Peace*, 78–82.

179  Emily Greene Balch, 'Women's Work for Peace', *The World Tomorrow*, November 1922, 336.

180  Balch, 'Women's Work for Peace', 334.

181  Emily Greene Balch, 'The Habit of Peace', *McCalls Magazine*, February 1919.

182  See especially, Philip Noel-Baker, 'The International Air Police Force', and Hamilton, 'No Peace Apart from International Security', both in Storm Jameson (ed.) *Challenge to Death* (London: Constable, 1934). This idea of a global air force in the service of peace also appears in H.G. Wells' 1933 book *The Shape of Things to Come* (made into a film entitled *Things to Come* in 1936).

183  Emily Greene Balch, 'The Relation of Civil Aviation to Disarmament', Speech to the WIL Congress at Grenoble, 24 April 1932. Emily Greene Balch papers, Wellesley College, Massachusetts, Series III reel 22.

184  See the discussion in Harriet Hyman Alonso, 'Nobel Peace Laureates, Jane Addams and Emily Greene Balch: Two Women of the Women's International League for Peace and Freedom', *Journal of Women's History*, 1995, 7(2), 6–26, especially pages 18–19.

185  See Steve Smith, 'Paradigm Dominance in International Relations: The Development of InternationalRelations as a Social Science', *Millennium: Journal of International Studies*, Summer 1987, 16(2), 192.

186  On Dick Sheppard and the PPU see Richard Overy, *The Morbid Age. Britain and the Crisis of Civilization 1919–1939* (Harmondsworth: Penguin, 2010), 243 ff.

187  On Wight's pacifism and link to Sheppard see: Ian Hall, *The International Thought of Martin Wight* (New York: Palgrave Macmillan, 2006), 29–35. Wight's status as a realist is disputed, but many see him this way. See Sean Molloy, 'The Realist Logic of International Security', *Cooperation and Conflict*, 2003, 38(2), 83–99.

188  Philip Noel-Baker, *The League of Nations at Work* (London: Nisbet, 1927), 131.

189  For a discussion of this pessimism see Richard Overy, *The Morbid Age.*

# 7 Collapse and war

## Continuity and change in IR theory, 1936–1945

*The concept of appeasement is frequently brought up both in IR texts and in common speech as an argument to support specific ways of doing IR or specific foreign policy positions. This chapter begins by confronting the myth of appeasement, and argues that both the nature and the legacy of pre-Second World War appeasement are more complex than most IR textbooks suggest. Here I stress that IR is often too obsessed with structural causes for events, and not enough with agency and the role of historical accidents.*

*This chapter explores five themes that were influential in the years between 1936 and 1945, and argues that, contrary to the realist–idealist 'Great Debate' myth, no single approach to IR emerged out of the war years and the years just prior to the war. Rather, by the time the war ended in 1945 there were many approaches to the study of the international competing for dominance in the English-speaking world. These were:*

1   *Interpretations of the international crisis that built upon the revolution in archaeology over the last few decades. Here particular mention is made of how Arnold Toynbee used archaeological knowledge to construct a longer-term view of the international.*
2   *Anglo-American political geography, which built its views of world order in part on a criticism of what was perceived as the German geopolitical view. Political geography would be influential on United States wartime planning for the post-war order.*
3   *Approaches that saw the problems of international order in the relationship between capitalism and war, and in the decline of the liberal politico-economic order. This includes both the participants in the 'does capitalism cause war' debates, and the work of political economists such as Karl Polanyi.*
4   *A functional alternative to global order, first mentioned by Harold Laski, developed by David Mitrany, and adapted by E. H. Carr.*

5    *Various power political approaches, that emphasised the importance of national interest and also the nature of the society of states. This contained writers who would, in the decades after the war, influence and/or go on to found both classical realism in the United States and the English School in Britain.*

The decade between the Abyssinian crisis and the final defeat of the Axis is a story well known to the collective Western consciousness. Reinforced by a mountain of war films and popular documentaries (not to mention frequent uses of the 1938 Munich Agreement as a cognitive shortcut), the global crisis that led to the relative global stability of the Cold War is a period frequently used and alluded to in popular debates about politics. Yet, surprisingly, knowledge about the theoretical debates surrounding the nature of international order is thin on the ground in IR circles. In fact, when we turn to introductory textbooks this decade's sole role seems to be to use the rise and fall of the Axis powers as an explanation for the fall of idealism and the rise of realism. 1936–45, therefore, becomes the explanation for a major sea-change in IR thinking. It heralds the end of a supposed short-lived idealist IR, and an assumed return to a pre-1914 power politics. In the last chapter I have already shown how the categories of realist and idealist did not exist – at least not as conscious paradigms. In this chapter I aim to show the complexities and multiple ironies of thought just before and during the Second World War. In doing this I demonstrate that while there certainly were innovations and changes, there was actually far more continuity between inter-war and wartime IR than the myth of the realist–idealist debate allows. Indeed, many of those tagged as realist innovators in the 1940s shared a common conception of the nature of IR with many inter-war writers since written off as idealists. Examples of this continuity can be seen in the similar treatment of power politics in the work of Woolf and Schwarzenberger, and the common use of functional ideas in Mitrany and Carr. In both of these cases the *post hoc* categorisation of Woolf and Mitrany as idealists, and Schwarzenberger and Carr as realists hides and obscures common theoretical threads that makes a nonsense of the simple categorisation employed in so many introductory IR textbooks. In short the post-1945 realism that was meant to have been such a break in international thought involved a lot more continuity with pre-1939 thinking than is often given credit.

There are, though, a number of themes that do emerge in the world order debates of the decade. The first is the emergence of an attempt to understand the crises of the world order through a wider understanding of the nature of the histories of civilisations, and the sketching of longer-term patterns that might make sense of the ongoing international crisis. While taking inspiration from the earlier work of Oswald Spengler, particularly *Decline of the West*, this genre also drew from a deeper knowledge of the ancient world of Greece and Rome found especially in Britain. Perhaps its most famous proponent was Arnold J. Toynbee, who was also influential in foreign policy circles through his role as the Director of Studies at the London-based Royal Institute of International Affairs. The second theme is the conflict over the proper interpretation of geo-strategic factors in international affairs, especially the perceived differences between the geopolitics supposed to dominate Nazi ideology, and the political geography found in American and British strands of strategic studies. The third strand is a discussion of the crisis of capitalism and of the decline of the old liberal order that particularly involved key thinkers on the left; while the third was the conflict between predominantly federalist and functionalist alternative views of the nature of the post-war international order. Finally the fourth is the development of the idea of the nature of the power political system of the society of states, and the extent to which it was open to reform. Out of these emerge a number of groups or positions whose interaction shaped the nature of post-war IR as a field of academic study. These groups include a German-based geopolitics, which in turn acted as the foil for the further development of an Anglo-American international political geography that helped form immediate US policy towards the post-war world. There was an early international political economy approach that heralded the birth of a new world out of the crisis of capitalism, which was often closely associated with debates over whether the form of the new world should be federal or functional. Finally, there were power political approaches that were trying to make sense of the crisis of the last few decades through an understanding of power and political interests. This last group would contain thinkers who would later be seen as the classical realists responsible for the founding of a realist approach to world affairs. All of these groups of thinkers were active during this period, although only a few would eventually be accepted as canonical IR thinkers. Some of the reasons for the different fates enjoyed by the various authors will be discussed in more detail in the next chapter.

Before discussing these strands of international thought, though, there is another issue that needs addressing because it has such a strong influence on both textbook accounts of the origins of IR and on the attitudes of the wider public to international affairs. Appeasement and the lessons of the Second World War are commonly used in IR textbooks to explain why IR took the route it did after 1945. This myth is bolstered by the frequent use of the appeasement trope in popular discussions of international affairs. References to appeasement and to Hitler are frequently brought up in public debates as a cognitive shortcut in order to press the argument for intervention or military confrontation. Even among quite sophisticated thinkers on IR's history there is a tendency to assume, without any clear evidence, that somehow appeasement was wrong and that there is a mistake that needs answering for in the statesmanship of Britain and France before 1939 (see the argument below). If the myth of appeasement is wrong, then by extension there may not be anyone at fault in the first place. Similarly, if the myth of appeasement used in textbooks to explain the sea-changes in IR is wrong then we may have to look elsewhere to explain why IR turned out the way that it did. As a result, the first section of this chapter will use recent work by international historians to reassess appeasement and the first year of the war in order to grasp how it affected the development of IR. What emerges from the work of historians is a very different story from the one taught to undergraduates in introductory IR textbooks.

## The problem of appeasement and the myths of May 1940

On the morning of 3 September 1939 a world leader sat immobile and stunned. Against all his predictions war had now broken out, and he had miscalculated. He had very early on realised that he had been diplomatically outmanoeuvred during the negotiations in the previous September that had led up to the Munich agreement of 1938. One aide at the time had accused him of giving in 'thoroughly' to diplomatic threats of war. The policy he had been working on was now in tatters, and over the coming months he was forced to recognise that he would now have to fight a major war. Not only that, but that war would have to be fought without a potential ally that had decided on neutrality after the Munich negotiations. Suddenly he turned to his advisor – who had reassured him that war would be avoided – and with a savage look on his face he snapped 'What now?' Was that Neville Chamberlain? No. Then perhaps it is French Prime Minister Edouard Daladier? Again, no. That despondent and uncertain world leader was Adolf Hitler.[1]

Appeasement plays a central part in the story of the origins of IR, and that drama is played out in the IR textbooks used to teach introductory IR courses. Generally speaking, IR textbooks rely on what Kimberley Hutchings calls cognitive shortcuts when discussing appeasement. In most cases the point of introducing appeasement is to underscore the failure of inter-war approaches to IR, and explain the ascendency of a more clearly power politics approach after the war usually referred to as realism. Thus, appeasement forms an important part of the narrative that highlights and reproduces one of the dominant identities associated with the field of IR. This should not surprise us, given that all human identities are sustained and reproduced by the telling of foundational or defining fables, and that these myths often play fast and loose with historical accuracy. Generally, the majority of textbooks in IR rely on the emotive appeal of the term appeasement, mentioning the policy and then relying on its negative connotations in order to direct the reader to the specific conclusion that there was something fundamentally misguided about inter-war IR. This, in turn, then stands as an explanation for the rise of a power politics approach to IR during the Cold War. Perhaps it should be highlighted here too that the goal in the textbooks is rarely to understand inter-war IR, but rather to use the period as an explanation for the emergence of a particularly realist-dominated IR after 1950. This also explains why the textbooks rarely attempt to engage with texts written in the 1930s and early 1940s, or even with more recent secondary texts on the period. The inter-war era stands as a point of mythic origins, rather than as a period studied in its own right.

The story that emerges from the textbooks is a familiar one to those brought up in Britain, Canada, Australia, New Zealand and the United States, and is one that is equally well reproduced in popular films, television documentaries and literature. In Andrew Heywood's recent 2011 text appeasement is said to have encouraged Hitler to believe that he could invade Poland 'without precipitating war with the UK and eventually the USA'.[2] While Heywood attributes this view of appeasement to unspecified 'others', John T. Rourke is more willing to nail his colours to the mast. For Rourke 'Great Britain and France vacillated timorously' when Adolf Hitler came to power. They gave way to Hitler's demands at Munich in 1938, and British Prime Minister Neville Chamberlain is singled out among 'other leaders' for his mistaken view that 'an appeasement policy toward Germany would satisfy it and maintain peace'.[3] For Jackson and Sørensen the policy of appeasement pursued by Britain and France had 'disastrous consequences for everybody, including the German people' because it allowed a great power to get out of control.[4] For Goldstein and Pevehouse 'the Munich Agreement seemed only to encourage Hitler's further conquests', and thus gave appeasement a negative connotation.[5] Bruce Russett and Harvey Starr top this familiar story off by pointing out that realists were sceptical of appeasement, and that 'the worst of World War II could have been avoided by earlier resistance to Hitler derived from a "realistic" understanding of conflict and power in international politics'.[6] Some are a little more careful. While agreeing that 'Britain and France would have actually enhanced their national security by standing firm in 1938', Roskin and Berry argue that the only difference between successful détente diplomacy and appeasement is whether you succeed or fail. It is difficult to tell in advance what the outcome will be.[7] While not necessarily contradicting the view of appeasement as a failure, Len Scott points out how recent debates on appeasement 'have focused on whether there were realistic alternatives to negotiation, given the lack of military preparedness with which to confront Hitler'.[8] Joseph Nye is careful to point out that as a policy of statecraft 'appeasement is not bad per se', but it was 'the wrong approach to Hitler'.[9] Nye also urges us not to be too hard on Chamberlain, whose intentions were good, even if he is culpable for 'his ignorance and arrogance in failing to appraise the situation properly'. Although this failure was not Chamberlain's alone.[10] Chris Brown is more conciliatory, arguing that the situation in the 1930s was anomalous, and hence judging 'a set of ideas by their capacity to cope with a Hitler or a Stalin seems to set far too high a standard'.[11]

Although these accounts differ they are united by their view that appeasement was a failure. Many see the goal of appeasement as the maintenance of peace, while for some appeasement was also marked by a failure to understand the realities of power relations. Russett and Starr even make the claim that appeasement was contrary to a realist understanding of IR, neatly glossing over E.H. Carr's and George F. Kennan's support for appeasement. For the overwhelming majority of IR textbooks appeasement becomes a cautionary tale in which a misapplied policy of peace leads to a worse war. Not only does this feed in to an explanation for the rise of realism during the Cold War, it also taps in to a popular discourse about standing up to dictators that has been used to support so many interventions since. The Dutch re-colonisation of Indonesia after 1945, the Anglo-French intervention in Suez in 1956, the American involvement in Vietnam in the 1960s and early 1970s, and the American-led invasion of Iraq in 2003 have all been, at one time or another, justified in editorials, cartoons or speeches via the use of the appeasement cognitive shortcut.

Even the more scholarly and nuanced analyses of the history of the discipline are not immune to the lure of using appeasement to make claims about the implications to IR theory of appeasement. While they may avoid the more obvious simplicities and confusions found in textbook accounts, they are still likely to use appeasement as part of their criticism of certain thinkers. I have certainly done this in the past. In my 1999, 2002 and 2007 analysis of the myth of the realist–idealist debate I present appeasement as a failed policy, and then showed how appeasement was a conservative policy that was actually opposed by writers such as Norman Angell, Leonard Woolf and Philip Noel-Baker. In fact, the great contemporary work that supported appeasement was Carr's *Twenty Years' Crisis*.[12] The same trope is used by Peter Wilson in a recent friendly criticism of my own work. While trying to apportion some of the blame for appeasement back on the critics of Chamberlain and E.H. Carr he argues that these critics were also responsible for creating the political climate that led to appeasement.[13] While I believe that Wilson errs by lumping in diverse writers into a single category, his argument (like my own earlier one) begs a really big question of whether there is any blame to apportion at all? So much of the discussions of inter-war international affairs and early IR involves passing around the hot potato of blame for appeasement and the rise of fascism. Yet, what if there is no blame at all? If no crime was committed then there cannot be any 'guilty men'.

The argument of this section is that we have been very much led up the garden path by the myth of appeasement and anti-appeasement. IR textbooks have a double layer of inaccuracy: they present a simplistic view of appeasement that blames the policy for the rise of Hitler, and then they pass the blame for the policy onto the wrong people. Arguments by more informed observers, such as myself and Wilson, are better able to present a sophisticated analysis for where the blame lies, but still assume that there is blame to be shared out. This said, my purpose here is not to provide a defence of the appeasers per se. On the contrary, my argument is that being an appeaser or an anti-appeaser did not make you necessarily right or wrong. In fact, I argue that there is more overlap between the two positions than we tend to give them credit for, and that the British policy that resulted from the political debates of the 1930s was a far more sophisticated response to the rise of Nazi Germany than we often give it credit for. There are mistakes and naïve arguments along the way, but these were rarely the sole property of one or another group. Indeed, one example of naivety is E.H. Carr's taking of Chamberlain at face value. The irony in the relationship between the thinking of Carr and the policy of Chamberlain is that the craftiness of the latter fed the wishful thinking of the former. This led to Carr falling into a trap that he had warned scholars about only a year earlier. Carr had correctly grasped part of Chamberlain's foreign policy, but had chosen to believe the rhetoric that hid the rest of it. Equally, hindsight has washed away some of the mistakes of both

Winston Churchill on the right, and of left-wing opinion formers such as the authors of *The Guilty Men* pamphlet that defined the common perception of appeasement both during and after the war.[14]

But didn't the policy of Allied governments lead us to the disasters of the early war? Surely there must be a failure somewhere in there. Yes, true, but whose failure? E.H. Carr in his masterful *Study of History* claimed that while we see distant historical events as inevitable due to structural causes, we often indulge in counter-factual and agency-driven 'what-if' scenarios for the recent past. IR scholars, as consumers rather than producers of history, tend to err on the side of seeing history as a structural given in which successful individual choices depend for their success on knowledge of these historical immutables. Also, because we look for explanations within our own areas of competence, we tend to stress the importance of global systemic forces over agency and luck. In this sense we have failed to learn the lessons taught us by Machiavelli: that it is in the management of the whims of the goddess fortune that the art of politics lies. Similarly, by our concentration on (and misreading of) the structures of power in 1938–40 IR scholars have missed how the course of the Second World War was as much a result of historical contingencies as it was about structural limits. As a result IR (and especially IR textbooks) drew the wrong lessons from the war. In short, it is time for IR to actually read the international historians who have written on this period. I will argue below that the blame for the initial (and, as it turned out, temporary) Axis successes of 1940–41 lies with very contingent and specific failings of the Allied war effort. It is these failings, and not the longer-term diplomatic policies that came before it, that are to blame for many of the very real changes in policies, power balances and ideological content that followed from 1945.

In the rest of this section I will explore three interlinked issues. The first focuses on the policy of appeasement as pursued by France and Britain in the late 1930s, pointing out the limits placed on Allied foreign policy-makers, and also the extent to which appeasement was not a stand-alone policy. The second will look at the anti-appeasers, and will stress the common ground with the advocates of appeasement. This section will particularly concentrate on the debate in Britain, and will argue that while there were clear differences between appeasers and anti-appeasers, these were often reducible to differences over means, rather than ends. That said, there were sections of British society and British opinion formers that were opposed to any confrontation with Germany, but these were increasingly marginalised after 1936. Also the problem posed by Nazi German revisionism was a recent phenomenon, and so extrapolations back to pre-1936 statements and policies are often unhelpful. Finally, I shall evaluate the extent to which (within the constraints it found itself) Allied diplomacy was a success or a failure leading into the Polish crisis of September 1939. I will balance this out with an analysis of the immediate causes of German success in 1940. Using the arguments of a number of international historians, I will stress the contingency and importance of the events of 1940 in shaping the course and outcome of the war.

Appeasement as a policy is not necessarily bad. The idea behind it is that a stronger party willingly enters into an agreement with a weaker that gives more concessions to the weaker party. The goal here is either to gain the support of the weaker for the stronger party, or to encourage the weaker party to identify more with the status quo. Thus, we can see the policy of the British 1906 Liberal government as appeasement. Concessions were made on union rights and Irish home rule in order to bring Labour and the Irish Party on board with government policy. Similarly, one of Neville Chamberlain's earlier diplomatic successes had been the 1938 agreement that appeased Ireland. The ending of the 'economic war' and the handing back of the Treaty ports created a working relationship with the strongly republican government of de Valera. Although it failed to bring Ireland into the war on the Allied side, it did guarantee that Ireland's neutrality was biased in favour of Allied interests.[15] It is, therefore, in many respects a tried and tested form of power politics. Yet, as we shall see below, appeasement strictly defined was only one part of the policy of the Allied governments between 1938 and 1939.

Before weighing up the merits and level of success of the appeasement policy associated with the British government and Neville Chamberlain I want to start by stating some of the weaknesses behind the policy. These need to be understood in order to form a rounded picture of both the policy and its main supporters. Appeasement in Britain was part of a foreign policy devised by men whose intellectual roots lay in the nineteenth century, even if that experience was influenced by the shock of total war between 1914 and 1918. Chamberlain and Halifax, the two key figures in the formation of British foreign policy in 1938–9, were products of a world populated by close-knit diplomatic circles made up of people with similar backgrounds and educations. Consequently, the behaviour of the dictators was alien to them. As a result, their responses were conservative and old-fashioned, although we can gauge from their personal correspondence that they were not slow in realising they were dealing with a new form of diplomacy. For example, even in the early stages of the Czechoslovak Crisis Chamberlain knew that the Germany he was dealing with was both untrustworthy and a bully.[16] The conservatism of Chamberlain's National government also coloured its attitude to foreign policy in general. The left was not slow to notice that British concessions to fascism were often in the interests of capitalism at home and abroad, and that this 'Tory policy of peace' only became tough when interests vital to British capital were threatened.[17] Certainly, in hindsight, British governments did not cover themselves with glory over the 1931 Manchurian Crisis, 1935–6 Abyssinian crisis, the Spanish Civil War from 1936–9, and the remilitarisation of the Rhineland in 1936. It is easy to contrast the belligerence of much of the left to fascism, and the comparative passivity of the National government. That said, we often forget that at the time it was not clear who the enemy was. Japan and Italy, not Germany, were the main disturbers of the peace before 1938, and (especially to men of a conservative disposition) the question of the role of the Soviet Union was not to be ignored. On top of this, Chamberlain's personality had its weaknesses. A successful businessman and local politician, he was often abrasive and far too sure of his own abilities. As Richard Overy puts it, he 'was an easy man to respect, a difficult man to like'.[18] In an era where it was uncommon for world leaders to travel, the elderly Chamberlain was a master at shuttle diplomacy, and his personal interventions often led to diplomatic breakthroughs, such as in the case of the Anglo-Irish agreement of 1938. Yet, there was hubris here. Chamberlain began to see himself as the man with a special touch in negotiations.[19] His air of superiority was particularly poorly received in the United States, and it is perhaps not surprising that the condemnation of Chamberlain (and the corresponding canonisation of his political rival and successor Churchill) is often more shrill in American popular narratives.[20]

These weaknesses aside, the form and nature of Chamberlain's foreign policy is not fully understood. Part of the fault for this lies with Chamberlain. Stock views of appeasement are often based on statements made by Chamberlain himself, even though there is a marked divergence between the policy Chamberlain followed, on the one hand, and the way that he sold the policy publicly on the other. Appeasement was basically a two-tier strategy. The first tier was the visible concessions and diplomatic niceties designed to reassure Germany that Britain was not its enemy. This often took the form of attempts to find out what Germany really wanted, and then see how far Germany could be accommodated without endangering British and French interests. The second was equally important. Chamberlain also presided over Britain's rearmament campaign that was designed to enhance the UK's diplomatic clout. This was coupled with frequent warnings to Germany that if a diplomatic line was crossed Britain (and with it France) would be prepared to go to war. As Chamberlain laid it out to the British House of Commons in 1938, the basis of his policy was 'By reason if possible – by force if not'.[21] The problem for Chamberlain was that until 1939 neither Britain nor France had the capability to intervene on the European continent in any strength, and therefore commitments to central European states before then would be meaningless. For Chamberlain good diplomacy was needed to make up for military deficiencies. While he certainly hoped that peace could be maintained, he was willing to threaten and countenance war if needs be. As the diplomatic wrangling with Germany continued between September 1938 and March 1939 Chamberlain became increasingly convinced that war was unavoidable.

Central to Chamberlain's appeasement policy was a return to the pre-1914 secret diplomacy that had in the 1920s been regarded in many circles, both on the left and the right, as a cause of the First World War. Chamberlain consciously chose secret great power diplomacy over the 'open' and multilateral diplomacy associated with the League of Nations. This had advantages, as Chamberlain was well aware. The decision-making at Geneva was hampered by the need to mobilise 'dozens of small nations' who had no direct 'responsibilities' for the crisis in hand. Thus, Chamberlain's return to the form of the 'old' diplomacy was seen by him as a necessary move in order to counter Germany with 'force and determination', even though in the same breath Chamberlain displayed his own dislike for the return of the old alliance system.[22] This advantage came with a cost, though. By largely ignoring Geneva and the League, Chamberlain took Britain and France down a lonely road without any clear backing from a wider coalition of states. Although, to be fair, Chamberlain and Halifax tried to rectify this disadvantage by bilateral deals designed to shore up the support or neutrality of other powers. Chamberlain's goal on taking office in 1936 was a final 'grand settlement' that would lay to rest most of the major problems in Europe, and avert another major war. He saw the settlement of outstanding problems between the great powers as a first stage in this. It was only after he realised the intransigence of the German position that he became pessimistic about achieving this goal, and lowered his sights accordingly.

Behind these diplomatic positions lay the question of French and British preparedness for war. Contrary to the myth of a disarmed Britain and France, both countries had actually been rearming since the middle of the 1930s. French rearmament had started in 1934, although a mix of problems meant that there were gross inefficiencies and a lack of planning in the early years.[23] Britain already had a programme for rearmament when Chamberlain came to power, and the new Prime Minister proved supportive of a further military build-up in order to boost the power of his diplomacy. Chamberlain strongly believed that without the force to back it up a threatening diplomatic stance was of no use at all.[24] British and French diplomacy remained cautious while rearmament was proceeding since both governments felt they did not have the power to threaten war. As late as the Munich Crisis of August–September 1938 the British military was warning the government that British military strength was not enough to make a threat of war viable.[25] There was a silver lining, however. British and French rearmament was due to reach full readiness for war in 1939, whereas the rearmament in Germany and Italy would peak in 1941 or 1942.[26] Thus, both Britain and France would have a military advantage within a year of Munich, and would be able to confidently call Germany's bluff. Until that time careful diplomacy was required if the Allies were to avoid threatening something that they could not follow through.

Linked to this preparedness for war issue was another that dogged Chamberlain and weakened his position. Since the end of the Great War the British Dominions had used their contributions to imperial defence to increase their own powers over foreign and defence policies. In the interests of Imperial burden-sharing Britain encouraged this, and at the 1919 Paris Peace Conference had pushed for separate signatures for India and the Dominions (except Newfoundland), and separate membership of the League for the Dominions (an option they all took up, again except for Newfoundland). After the 1931 Statute of Westminster this new independent policy for the Dominions was regularised and recognised. While Dominion policy varied, a common concern was the wish to avoid entanglement in another European war. As late as the Munich crisis it was fairly clear that the Dominions would not back a European war, and that if Britain went to war it could not expect the Dominions to follow. Like much of the British and French publics, the Dominion governments only gave their backing for war after Munich, and especially following the German occupation of rump Czechoslovakia in March 1939. The bottom line here is that any British war effort without the Dominions was likely to be compromised. The manpower and economic muscle of the Dominions were a necessary component of imperial defence. As it was, even in September 1939 Dominion support was not a given. There was opposition within the Canadian parliament, the South African parliament was deeply split and Ireland chose to remain neutral despite the deal over the treaty ports. This issue of Dominion support, so crucial to British abilities to fight a prolonged war, is often overlooked in popular discussions of appeasement.

Chamberlain came under particular fire during his premiership from both supporters of the Labour opposition and from anti-appeasers in his own party (especially Leo Amery, Anthony Eden and Winston Churchill). His policies were also ridiculed by the brilliant contemporary cartoonist David Low. There were specific criticisms of Chamberlain's policy that came from the anti-appeasers. One was that the return to a secretive old diplomacy amounted (in the words of the Labour Party's Advisory Committee on International Questions) to diplomatic disarmament because it lost Britain and France the support of the wider international community.[27] On the opposite side of the Party divide, Winston Churchill was urging the government in 1938 to oppose the Anschluss with Austria via a defence pact that was built upon the Covenant of the League of Nations.[28] By ignoring the institutions of the League, and the potential it could bring for support from other powers, the appeasers were (according to their opponents) undermining British security. Yet, while the question of whether it was a good tactical move to opt for great power diplomacy rather than a broader League front remains open, it is important to point out that the divide between the two sides was narrower than at first glance. The vast majority of anti-appeasers accepted that the dangers posed by Germany meant that some form of a return to alliance politics was called for in the last two years of peace. Given the threat to peace posed by Fascism several key opinion formers within the Labour Party – including Leonard Woolf, Herbert Morrison and Susan Lawrence – accepted that after 1936 the idea of League collective security could only be safeguarded by a closer alliance of pro-League powers in an old fashioned military alliance.[29] Under the influence of this growing group the Labour Party switched its policy to one of supporting a closer Anglo-French alliance. This was in line with Chamberlain and National government policy. Perhaps the one major difference between the anti-appeasers and appeasers on this issue was that for many anti-appeasers, such as H.N. Brailsford, this anti-fascist front should bring in other powers such as the Soviet Union and the United States.

The apparent exclusion of the USSR and the USA was another common criticism of the appeasers by the anti-appeasers. This seemed to be part of the 'diplomatic disarmament' that the critics of appeasement had levelled at the Chamberlain government. H.N. Brailsford was particularly strong on criticising Chamberlain for not including the Soviets, and there are indications that for much of the late 1930s the Soviets were interested in a closer relationship with the West. The Soviet exclusion from Munich, and the failure of Anglo-French talks with Stalin and the Soviet high command all seemed to point to a damaging exclusion from a pro-League anti-fascist front. While Brailsford was right that the addition of Soviet pressure on Germany would have been decisive, there still hangs over this the question of whether the Soviets would have been interested. Yes, it is true that Chamberlain made a point of excluding the Soviets from Munich,[30] but this did not necessarily cause a full rupture with the Soviets. The big sticking point for Soviet–Western accommodation was the extent to which the Western powers were able to contribute to any war, and specifically how it could take the pressure off the Soviets in the event of a full-scale war on the eastern front. Not unnaturally Stalin feared that any triple alliance between the USSR, France and Britain would see the USSR taking the brunt of the war as France and Britain fought to the last Russian. A combination of the failure of the Allied governments to commit to an alliance and the frank British admission that its contribution to any mutual defence would be only four divisions led to the Soviet decision to give up, in exasperation, any thought of an agreement with Britain and France.[31] Similarly, Chamberlain was reluctant to seek an understanding with the United States, despite Roosevelt's offers of meetings.[32] Yet, there was another side to this story of the freezing out of the Soviets and Americans. As well as being ideologically suspicious of the Soviets, both the British and French governments were unsure of how reliable Stalin would be. Indeed, Soviet officials often seemed more concerned about concessions from Poland. On the United States side, Chamberlain was concerned that there was little that Roosevelt could offer the Allies either militarily or diplomatically. America's dire military weakness and its powerful isolationist lobby made it a weak potential partner, and from Chamberlain's point of view the only effect of bringing the United States in to the negotiations with the fascist powers would have been to increase Hitler's sense of being surrounded. While the involvement of the Soviets in an anti-fascist pact remains an interesting counter-factual, there was little the United States could offer in the short term other than the credit and materiel that it provided to the Allies once war had broken out.

Perhaps the greatest contribution of the anti-appeasers was engaging in a task that, for political reasons, the National government was unable to contribute. Contrary to Wilson's claim, mentioned above, that the anti-appeasers of the left also contributed to appeasement by creating the conditions and public opinion that helped support appeasement, the group associated with the Labour Party Advisory Committee on International Questions (Norman Angell, Leonard Woolf, Philip Noel-Baker, Hugh Dalton, among others) actually agitated in the other direction. Faced with a Labour Party and wider country that was instinctively supportive of a peace at any price policy, the Advisory Committee engaged in a campaign in the 1930s to develop a policy of confrontation with the dictators. This spilled over into the Labour Party conference in 1935, when the question of support for League sanctions against Italy over Abyssinia saw a confrontation with the pacifist wing of the Party. This was followed up in Dalton's 1937 success in committing the Party to fight a war in self-defence, and the Party's decision to no longer oppose the defence estimates.[33] In sum, many of the anti-appeasers contributed actively to bringing the wider British public around to the need for confrontation with Germany. Despite the Party's past strong links with pacifism, Labour activists and leaders did this at the risk of being branded as the war party.[34] While they were able to use this as a party political tool, this activism actually helped the Chamberlain government's diplomacy through a sort of moral rearmament of the population. In this sense the confrontational Westminster model of government did its job.

Thus, there was clear common ground between appeasers and anti-appeasers. While the appeasers obviously had more direct links to government policy, anti-appeasers did more than just shout in the wilderness. Those anti-appeasers in the Labour Party did much to prepare the Party and its supporters for the acceptance of a policy that would lead to war. Similar work was carried out in Conservative ranks by Leo Amery, Winston Churchill and Anthony Eden, while the pro-League Conservative Robert Cecil acted as a link between the anti-appeasers in both groups.

Yet, Wilson is right about some groups. There were those who argued for peace at any price, although this group included both supporters and opponents of Chamberlain. The feminist and pacifist Helena Swanwick, for example, fully supported appeasement as a means of preventing war and curing the problem of fascism.[35] Interestingly there is much confusion about Chamberlain's own position due to the differences in his public and private pronouncements. Coming off the plane at Heston airport Chamberlain famously brandished the deal struck at Munich as 'peace for our time'. Later on the steps of 10 Downing Street he added the phrase 'peace with honour'. This was his public face. Driving between these two venues Chamberlain turned to Halifax and said 'All this will be over in three months'.[36] Chamberlain knew war was coming. Interestingly one of the victims of Chamberlain's two faced approach was E.H. Carr. Carr took the public Chamberlain at face value in *Twenty Years' Crisis*, seeing the goal of Chamberlain's diplomacy as a realistic power-aware approach that guaranteed peaceful change and a wider European settlement. Ironically in 1936, when he took up the chair of International Politics at Aberystwyth, Carr had warned that intellectual analysts of world affairs often engaged in wishful thinking when they looked at public pronouncements. In 1938 Carr became a victim of the very tendency he had noticed among supporters of League collective security.[37]

The immediate effects of Anglo-French diplomacy in the years 1938 and 1939 can be interpreted as a success, and indeed much recent international history is kinder to the diplomacy of appeasement than the vulgar and popular discourses found in venues such as IR textbooks. Looked at within the context of the constraints of the time the results can lead us to agree with Hitler's own self-assessment of his position in 1939. He had been diplomatically outmanoeuvred. Hitler's aim in 1938–9 had been French and British acquiescence to a German free-hand in central and eastern Europe. The goal of the British and French was to deny him that free hand, and buy time for their own rearmament. The reason that Hitler and his aides felt that they had been outmanoeuvred was because Britain and France had left the table at Munich with what they had wanted. Warned by their militaries that they were unable to fight a war to prevent German aggression, they had done the next best thing: through bluff they had forced the Germans to accept managed and diplomatic border changes.

Part of the problem with assessing Munich is that the popular discourse often ignores the constraints that the British and French governments faced. Both Britain and France needed time for rearmament, for the mental rearmament of their publics, and for the British Dominions to get on board. All three of these were achieved by early 1939, which is why British and French diplomacy could be that much tougher with Germany in the Polish crisis. The Allies, though, had not ignored other diplomatic avenues. Contact with Mussolini's government (which had its own deep concerns about military preparedness) had managed to guarantee Italian neutrality in the event of war. A deal on 27 May 1938 had made sure that the mineral-rich and strategically located Turkey stayed outside German influence, and remained until its own declaration of war against the Axis in 1945, a pro-Allied neutral. The much trumpeted guarantee to Poland, while it probably helped alienate the Soviet Union, sent a clear signal of Allied intentions in central Europe (a signal that the rather naïve Nazi leadership failed to read, unfortunately). If Germany went to war in 1939 it would find itself diplomatically isolated, and with no ally save its Slovakian puppet.

Because British and French rearmament reached war readiness in 1939, while the German programme still had 2–3 years to reach completion, the careful timing of the diplomacy of appeasement left British and French militaries on military par or better with the Germans in most areas of comparative military strength. With the larger manpower pool, access to raw materials and industrial production of the Allies, their military position could only strengthen, while Germany's (without some kind of miracle) would decline. For example, Germany's failure to plan for a long conflict meant that between 1939 and 1940 its strategic oil reserves had become seriously depleted. Its fuel reserves in May 1940 were a third less than it had been in September 1939.[38] Other minerals, such as rubber, were hard to find, and the iron ore supplies from northern Sweden were regularly disrupted during the winter when they had to be convoyed through Norwegian waters. In short, Germany had been caught on the back foot in September 1939.

Yet, if the policies of the British and French governments had left Germany at a disadvantage in September 1939, how then can we account for the success of the Axis in the early years of the war, and to the dramatic events of 1941–2 that came close to an Axis victory (at least in Europe and Russia)? As the historian Julian Jackson said of the events leading up to the fall of France 'when the outcome is known, the narrative tends to write itself too smoothly'.[39] The problem with much of the analysis of the Nazi blitzkrieg in 1939–42 is that we know how the story ends. As a result we tell the story as though the ending is an inevitability. For those living the events the outcome was much more uncertain. The position of Britain and France before May 1940 was actually a fairly secure one, while the German offensive of May 1940 was in many ways a desperate gamble.

In raw military terms the military balance between the Allies and Germany in 1940 gave no side a clear advantage. At sea the Allies clearly had an overwhelming superiority. British and French sea power swamped the surface fleet of the Kriegsmarine. Indeed, while the invasion of Norway in March 1940 was a success for Germany, it was a Pyrrhic victory that cost the Kriegsmarine more than half of its surface fleet.[40] With its submarines operating from its North Sea ports Germany was not even in a good place to carry out attacks on Allied shipping. On land the German Army was hampered by a lack of motorisation (the Germans relied heavily on horse-drawn transportation), which contrasted dramatically with the motorisation of British and French forces. France also outnumbered Germany in tanks, while the quality of French tanks was not necessarily inferior to the Germans (indeed, the latter had a shortage of heavy tanks). In artillery the Germans were clearly outgunned and outclassed, although the French were seriously short of anti-aircraft guns. The French had started to deploy superior anti-tank guns, although these were still in short supply in May 1940. The one advantage the Germans had here was the development of armoured divisions. Yet, even here the French were catching up. By May 1940 they had seven armoured divisions, with plans to develop more. In terms of army sizes, the French especially were not deficient. France had, in total, five million men under arms, against Germany's three million. While only about half of the French figure was available for defence of the north-east, the addition of the British 0.9 million BEF and the Belgian and Dutch forces gave the Allies a local advantage. Only in aircraft were the Germans superior. Earlier French aerial rearmament meant that many of its planes were now obsolete. Despite this, France and Britain were steadily building a modern fleet of planes, and France had arranged the purchase of American aircraft. The biggest German advantage was in bombers (1,680 German to 262 allied bombers), although in fighters the margin was much less (1,210 German versus 632 French, 416 British and 81 Belgian). Even the much maligned Maginot line played its part. The Maginot line is misunderstood as part of a toxic French defensive defeatism. Actually, the French plan was to use the Maginot line to allow offensive action in Belgian. The Maginot line would pin down German forces in the south, preventing an attack on France's industrial heartland, while allowing the rest of the motorised and armoured French army to swing into Belgium to meet a German offensive. British and French military planners were confident that they could repulse a German offensive early in the war, and then go onto the offensive once they had overwhelming military superiority. They projected the war ending in Allied victory in 1943.[41]

So why did the Allies not prevail? Basically, a desperate Germany took a gamble in May 1940, and due to bad luck, poor intelligence and weaknesses in the Allied general staff that gamble paid off. The success of the German offensive in May 1940, like so many military campaigns, was not a foregone conclusion. The French and British gambled that the Germans would take a different route through Belgium (and indeed this had been the German plan until 1940), and as a result their mobile reserve was in northern Belgium and unavailable to plug the gap caused by the sudden German attack on the Meuse and Sedan. As it was, stiff French resistance on the Meuse almost stopped the German advance. The German race to the sea, contrary to popular belief, was not accomplished by strategic brilliance, but by the leader of the armoured thrust, Guderian, losing contact with the general staff, and deciding to advance to the sea without infantry support. Even then the British and French situation was not dire. The German tanks were vulnerable to counter-attack and encirclement. Unfortunately a series of accidents ruined two Allied attempts to counter-attack. More seriously, and like the Anglo-American command (SHAEF) four-and-a-half years later during the 1944 Ardennes offensive, the Allied general staff and senior figures lost both their nerve and control of the battlefield. French resistance was dissipated in a lack of coordination. Basically, the fall of France in 1940 was the result of agency, not structure.

The fall of France changed the war dramatically. Italy decided to enter the war on what it thought was the winning side, the German armies were freed for action in the Balkans and then Russia. Britain abandoned its long-standing reliance on a French alliance and turned instead to the North Atlantic Anglo-American 'special relationship', which has been the cornerstone of British foreign policy ever since. On the other side of the world Japan began to plan for the conquest of the European and American possessions in the Far East and Pacific. Britain's decision to fight on was about the only bright light on the Allied horizon, and even that had not been guaranteed in May–June 1940.[42] The major event that defined the war, and also the Cold War western alliance that followed it, was not the 'failures' of appeasement diplomacy, but rather the contingencies and uncertainties of the battlefield in May 1940. The Allied diplomats had triumphed in 1938–9, but the Allied generals had failed miserably in 1940.

Turning to the IR textbooks: with perhaps the notable exceptions of Len Scott and Chris Brown they all have it horribly wrong. Heywood is wrong that appeasement encouraged Hitler. If anything he felt he had been the loser in 1938. The Allied diplomacy had given every indication that it would not allow Hitler a free hand in Central Europe. Rourke is wrong to state that Britain and France 'vacillated timorously'. Quite the contrary, they acted as determined and as strong as their resources allowed. Rather than giving in to Hitler's demands, they forced Hitler to compromise. Jackson and Sørensen are wrong that Britain and France let a great power get out of control. In fact, their diplomatic policy was the opposite: to manage and control German power so that it remained within limits. It is not clear, as Goldstein and Pevehouse claim, that Munich encouraged Hitler. At the same time there were no clever sceptical realists warning that appeasement was wrong. Roskin and Berry are probably wrong to argue that Britain and France would have enhanced their security by 'standing firm' in 1938. Indeed they stood as firm as their strategic position allowed. Len Scott is probably right about the lack of preparedness, but having said that he glosses over how actively engaged in rearmament the Allies were. Nye's claim that appeasement was the wrong policy against Hitler, and that Chamberlain was 'ignorant' of the realities of the situation is at least doubtful, and is certainly at odds with much current international historical research. Nye is probably right about Chamberlain's arrogance, though.

This brings us to Chris Brown's point. Is it right to judge a set of ideas based on historically contingent situations? This leads to a rather troubling conclusion for social science. Unlike many historians, IR scholars like to see the causes and nature of the world around them as the product of deep structures. This is as true for many critical approaches as it is for the many branches of realism. What a deep analysis of a historical case can show us is that contingency, irony and straight Machiavellian fortune often have a major role to play. The lesson of the narrative of the Second World War should not be, as IR textbooks tell us, a warning about failing to understand the importance of power. Rather, as recent studies by international historians show us, it does not matter how in tune with the realities of power you are the complexities of human political life can often give a high premium to plain dumb luck. Perhaps the structures of international politics did mean that eventually Germany would be defeated, but how that defeat would come about, and what shape the resulting settlement would take, are more reliant on complex questions of human agency than we fully understand. 'A strategic plan does not last beyond first contact with the enemy' claimed General von Moltke. In evaluating our own theories against 'reality' we need to realise the contingency and variability of that reality.

This still leaves us with the question of what then were the reasons that IR developed the way that it did? I shall return to this question in the next chapter. The goal of this chapter will be to chart the many different approaches to international affairs that existed in the years between 1936 and 1945 when global crisis and war were reshaping global politics. Having sketched the myriad of approaches that competed for attention as explanations of international affairs in this chapter, Chapter 8 will open by looking at how university-based IR came to favour some approaches over others in the formation of the academic field of IR after the war.

Perhaps one of the most interesting trends in the writings on international affairs in the decade between the mid-1930s and mid-1940s was that the immediate needs of foreign policy did not necessarily see a decline of longer-term epochal studies of the underlying influences on international relations. Indeed, attempts to understand the crisis in terms of wider historical and geographical factors seemed to increase, rather than recede. Two of these trends – the use of a longer-term history of civilisations, and the analysis of the relationship between statecraft and the geographical environment – actually seemed to gather steam during these years. The first of these will be explored in more detail in the next section, the second in the following two sections.

## International affairs as the rise and fall of civilisations

The early twentieth century saw a rise in the number of studies that tried to understand the fate of humanity through historical analogy with the history of past civilisations. To a certain extent this built on the pre-First World War works of writers such as Brooks Adams (see Chapter 5), who had tried to piece together patterns of the rise and decline of civilisations just as the full force of industrialised society appeared to change the nature of western society and its relationship with the rest of the world. A more immediate source of inspiration was the work of

Oswald Spengler, especially his *Decline of the West,* first published in German as *Der Untergang des Abendlandes* in two volumes between 1918 and 1922, and published in English translation in 1926–8.[43] His influence on Toynbee's later *A Study of History* cannot be ignored (despite Toynbee's public criticism of Spengler), and Toynbee was known to have a read an original German version before he started on his *magnum opus.*[44] Certainly, Spengler's view of civilisations as the proper units of history, as well as his view of the cyclical processes of rise and fall, find a home in Toynbee's approach, although Toynbee took issue with what he saw as Spengler's pessimism and determinism. Indeed, Spengler's use of an organic analogy for civilisations led E.H. Carr to place him in the same (realist and geopolitical) box as Rudolf Kjellén.[45] The study of classical texts in the educational institutions of the day also led to the use of historical analogies, especially from the classical world, in much of the writings on international affairs in the first half of the twentieth century. In Britain G. Lowes Dickinson, Alfred Zimmern and Gilbert Murray were all trained as classicists, and this classical training often informed their work through their use of classical texts to understand current global crises. Indeed, as Peter Wilson has pointed out, Murray's views on war were the result not of empirical studies in his own age, but rather through his studies of the role of war in classical Greek texts.[46]

Yet, there was a more empirical and scientific source for the history of civilisations that also influenced the work of writers such as Toynbee, and also helped to replace the simple progressivist view of history prevalent in the nineteenth century with one that at a minimum included a role for cycles of rise and decline.[47] This was the late nineteenth and early twentieth century revolution in archaeology as a source for historical knowledge. Heinrich Schliemann's ground-breaking work in Troy and Mycenae (not to mention his flamboyant self-promotion), Augustus Pitt Rivers' excavations in Britain in the late nineteenth century, Flinders Petrie's work in Egypt from the 1880s, Arthur Evans' discovery (and, some say, creation) of the Minoan civilisation on Crete at the turn of the century, and Mortimer and Tessa Wheeler's work in the 1920s and 1930s had all helped launch a revolution in archaeology that led to a fresh source of historical data that was separate from, and seen as more scientifically rigorous than, the ancient texts that had been the primary sources for past historians. One effect of this archaeological revolution, however, was to call into question the progressivist histories of the Victorians. Rather, what these archaeological digs appeared to reveal was that much of history involved the rise and fall of complex civilisations. In this sense Arthur Evans' work on Crete was particularly revealing. His discoveries seemed to suggest that a past island-based civilisation, previously unknown to historians, had created a sea-borne empire, before fading out of history with very little trace.[48] The lessons this suggested, especially to a British public that could not fail to grasp the similarities between Crete and Britain as sea powers, was that rather than history being a record of a slow progress to better societies, the archaeological evidence suggested that much of history was cyclical, with civilisations rising and falling with no real sense of a progress to something better. In fact, in archaeological circles there was a return of the pre-

Adam Smith notion that the success of a civilisation contained the seeds of destruction through the promotion of decadence. For Flinders Petrie, writing in 1911, it seemed that just as a society began to enjoy wealth and democracy so it began to experience decay and decline as a direct response of the ease and luxury its people now enjoyed.[49] These were natural cyclical rhythms for Petrie, and underscored how civilisation, rather than being a progressive development, was rather 'an intermittent phenomenon' obeying clear and precise rules of rise and decline.[50] In the more pessimistic era of the 1930s such views, based as they were on scientific studies of archaeological sites, inspired attempts to understand the current crisis by reference to the processes that seemed to influence the rise and decline of civilisations.

Arguably the most influential study in this genre was Arnold Toynbee's *A Study of History*, published between 1934 and 1961. Toynbee also wrote on current affairs in his role as the Director of Studies at the Royal Institute of International Affairs (RIIA) between 1929 and 1956, and was the editor of its annual *Survey of International Affairs* from 1920 to 1946. Classically trained, and the son-in-law of Gilbert Murray, he was also a major influence on the career and thought of one of the founders of the English School of IR, Martin Wight. Toynbee saw his *A Study of History* as both a distraction from his work for the RIIA (according to Wight, Toynbee's 'affectionate private name' for it was 'the nonsense book'[51]) and as a yoke mate 'in double harness' with his international affairs work.[52] Indeed Cornelia Navari, in her survey of Toynbee's work, considered the content and concerns of the *Surveys* from 1931 to 1937 as running parallel to those of the first six volumes of the *Study*.[53] The first three volumes of *A Study of History*, published in 1934, dealt with the origins and growth of civilisations, while volumes four to six dealing with the breakdown and disintegration of civilisations, appeared in 1939.[54] Toynbee regarded his work as both empirical and also comparative, although he was selective in the facts he used, and frequently used myth and mysticism in his accounts. It was empirical in as much as it was based on both texts and archaeological evidence, while it was comparative in the sense that it was premised on the idea that as products of the same human spirit all civilisations followed similar trajectories, and therefore could be compared to each other.[55] It was this inherent comparability that meant that culturally-related civilisations from different eras, especially for Toynbee the Greek and Western civilisations, could be compared in order to understand the future of a living civilisation. For Toynbee this was the 'Greek door to history', which could be used to answer the 'urgent questions of our own destiny'.[56]

In setting up this comparative study of civilisation Toynbee also rejected what he saw as the common mistake of historians of his time of seeing histories as fundamentally national. Nations were, for Toynbee, not self-sufficient entities, and therefore could never be regarded as the units of history. In writing national histories historians were portraying their tendency to 'illustrate rather than correct the ideas of the communities within which they live and work'.[57] In this sense *A Study of History* was a critical work that intended to challenge misconceptions that were based on a too shallow understanding of the deep historical processes involved in the shaping of human society. States and nationalism were also seen as a symptom of the problem. It had been, Toynbee argued, the disease of 'state-worship' that had eventually killed the Hellenic civilisation.[58] Thus, the national histories that dominated the historical analysis of Toynbee's time were simultaneously limited scholarship and also a symptom of a deeper disease that threatened Western civilisation in much the same way that the statism of the Peloponnesian war had threatened the Hellenic.

Like Petrie before him, Toynbee saw the processes involved in the rise and fall of civilisations as being internal and moral, and he firmly rejected the geopolitical view, explored by Ratzel and later by his American pupil Ellen Churchill Semple (see Chapter 5), that environmental factors explained the cyclical rise and fall of civilisations. That said, and despite his rejection of what he saw as Spengler's pessimistic determinism, there was a sense in which Toynbee's ideas of growth and decline were both determinist and also elitist. Like his father-in-law Gilbert Murray, Toynbee saw creativity of a civilisation as basically a top-down process. It was a creative minority that was the source of the responses to the challenges faced by a civilisation. Civilisations began to decline when this same minority ceased to be creative, and instead degenerated into a dominant minority (there are strong resemblances here to Petrie's notions of strife and challenge as necessary for the creativity and survival of a civilisation[59]). It was at this time that, in order to stave off the worst aspects of civilisational decline that the civilisation developed into a unitary state. Yet, rather than being the saviour of the civilisation, the unitary state was actually a symptom of decline. Dominated by an elite that was no longer creative, the unitary state helped create two proletariats: one inside the state made up of the lower classes, and one outside made up of neighbouring barbarians. Both of these, through various processes, worked to destroy the civilisation.[60]

Readers of Toynbee's *A Study of History* in the 1930s, living against the backdrop of a second descent into total war within living memory, could not fail but ask the question that Toynbee hinted at throughout his study: is western civilisation now entering a stage of decline? A question that Toynbee regarded as being part of the inter-war zeitgeist: 'It is worth noting' he wrote in 1939 'that our recognition of our civilisation's mortality is very recent'.[61] Here Toynbee's work on the history of civilisation melds with his work on international affairs. Also it is here that Toynbee's work can be grasped as less deterministic than on a first reading of *Study*. For although a civilisation in decline cannot return to growth once the creative minority has decayed into a dominant minority, there is a strong sense in his other writings that much can be done to prevent the spiral into decline. The immediate problem faced by western civilisation was the problem of war and militarism, a problem that had led to the decline of a number of civilisations, including the one that Toynbee most clearly used as the template for the lifespan of all his civilisations: the Hellenic. Like Gilbert Murray before him, Toynbee drew on the classical Greek tradition to argue for the 'suicidalness of militarism'.[62] It was here that the lessons of Thucydides' history of the

Peloponnesian war were, for Toynbee, still as fresh as they had been for Thucydides himself.[63] Militarism and war, which in turn would lead to an exhausted western civilisation finding a temporary peace in its declining years within a universal state, could be avoided by the creative development of a new global order that could promote peace, and thus save civilisation. In the 1930s Toynbee saw the best option for the preservation of western civilisation in a League of Nations order that managed to combine both collective security and a system of peaceful change.

Interestingly, and in an echo of Hegel's owl of Minerva only taking wing at dusk, Toynbee's detailed discussion of the importance of peaceful change and collective security came at a time when these were coming under their greatest threat during and directly after the Abyssinian crisis. Collective security and peaceful change were, for Toynbee, two necessary parts for a just international order that would avert the catastrophe of another war. Peaceful change represented a constitutional means for 'reconsidering and revising' the law, while collective security was the constitutional means for 'upholding and enforcing' the law.[64] Without a system of collective security peaceful change in a world of sovereign states would remain the exception (when compared to change brought by violence) and haphazard.[65] Similarly, without the promise of peaceful change collective security would remain merely the will of the status quo powers, and would be 'like a boiler without a safety valve': fated to boil up 'for a final shattering explosion'.[66]

At this point, despite his dislike for totalitarian regimes, Toynbee does endorse the idea of there being a difference between the 'have' societies of Britain, France and the United States, and the 'have-not' states of in Italy, Japan and Germany. This he shared with E.H. Carr. Yet, it is here that he took a different path to Carr. While Carr was to endorse the Munich Agreement of 1938 as a successful example of peaceful change when it gave the Czech Sudetenland to Germany, Toynbee opposed what he saw as narrowing the difference between 'have' and 'have-not' via 'violent change at the expense of the weak'.[67] Peaceful change, to be worthy of the name at all, had to be voluntary change too.[68] It also had to involve some sacrifice from the satisfied powers, especially from Britain (Munich saw the great powers sacrifice only the interests of a smaller power). Given these views, Toynbee approached the Munich agreement of 1938 with mixed emotions. He recognised that much of the redrawn boundaries were belated recognitions of the lack of impartiality in the drawing of the boundaries of central Europe in 1919. He also recognised that Munich had given Britain and France a breathing space, and that the western powers would be in a better position to deal with the German threat 'on its political and moral merits' once their defences were completed.[69] Up to those points the agreement was to be welcomed. The problem was that this peaceful change had been bought at the cost of a 'dominant Nazi Germany' and the 'mortal sickness of the League of Nations'.[70] The undermining of the League, as the 'heir to the whole of our heritage of international cooperation', left a void, and it left unfulfilled the need for the establishment of a world order based on some form of moral foundation.[71]

Here we see the crux of a problem that Toynbee never resolved. Like Carr he saw the sovereign state as a reality that, while it should and must be transcended in the future, was an immediate reality. This led Toynbee (again like Carr) to take the claims of the 'have-not' fascist powers seriously. While others, such as Norman Angell and Isaiah Bowman, rejected the have/have-not distinction (based on their view that it made little sense in an economically interdependent world), Toynbee tended to brush aside such economic arguments. Indeed, he seemed to discount the importance of economic factors in comparison to the psychological, political and cultural ones.[72] As a result, there was a tendency to play up power–political issues, even while he was arguing for their longer-term obsolescence or their short-term danger. Initially attracted to the League of Nations, he remained committed to collective security even after he ceased to see the League as a viable alternative to power politics in the wake of the Abyssinian crisis.[73] Despite some discussion of alternative world orders, and even of the functional alternative during the war years, Toynbee largely fell back on a more *ad hoc* society of states, often led by a British–American partnership. Immediately after the war Toynbee contrasted what he saw as the two most likely routes to an integrated world: either the 'one empire' that was familiar as his universal state in *A Study of History*, or a cooperative government based around the United Nations.[74] Toynbee clearly favoured the second.

In many ways this vision of a cooperative society of states should be familiar to many current scholars of IR theory. This is very similar to the idea of international society that is found in the English School. This link should not surprise us since Martin Wight, one of the key members of the English School, was mentored by Toynbee, and the two remained close in the decades after the war. Indeed, Wight also borrowed much of Toynbee's approach to history, including his comparative method. Also, Toynbee's defence of the viability of comparing civilisations carries more than a passing similarity with later post-war approaches to IR, such as Wight's Bull's or even Morgenthau's, who saw no intellectual problem with using insights from distant history to illuminate current issues. Both Toynbee and Wight were also concerned about the role of religious thought in international affairs, although Toynbee's religious beliefs remained less doctrinally fixed than Wight's.[75] Both had also become disillusioned with the League at about the same time. That said, there were also important differences that mark Toynbee off from the English School. Later volumes of *A Study of History* moved beyond a primary focus on civilisations to a concentration on the role of higher religions as agents in the progress of humanity. This view of religion was alien to Wight, who preferred to take a more pessimistic view of the role of religion in changing world order. Equally, as Toynbee's thought developed he became more aware of non-western traditions and the important role those traditions should and would play in world politics. As early as the 1930s he was agreeing with Leonard Woolf that native populations had a paramount claim to the colonial territories in which they lived, and that the mandate system should be extended to all colonial territories.[76] He was also more inclined to see the West as the aggressor, even accusing his own civilisation of 'turning the rest of the world upside down'.[77] Wight, on the other hand, was troubled by decolonisation and the breakdown of the western-dominated international society.[78] Thus, despite differences, there is a clear line of influence from Toynbee's inter-war and wartime work, and the development of ideas of international society in British post-war IR.

Toynbee's long-term view of history as essentially a moral and intellectual story existed alongside other long-term views that read history through the effects of environment and geographic space. While Toynbee had specifically rejected the idea that environment, along with race, influenced the course of civilisations, these other more geo-strategic and geo-political interpretations of international affairs remained popular in the late 1930s and early 1940s. Indeed, it was their very popularity that led to Toynbee's strong denunciation of them in his work. In the English-speaking world this geopolitical mindset was often developed as a conscious criticism of what was perceived as a similar (and altogether more sinister) form of geopolitics that was now dominating the thinking of the Nazi government in Germany. Given the important role that this perceived German geopolitics played in the development of its Anglo-American rival, the next section will explore this tradition in detail.

## German geopolitics: alternative international theory or straw man?

Once the United States entered the war a series of published works appeared that criticised the Axis through a sustained dissection of what was seen as the intellectual underpinnings of Nazi Germany's geopolitical strategy. Five criticisms of German geopolitics, often targeted specifically at Karl Haushofer and his Munich-based *Institut für Geopolitik*, were published in 1942 alone by the Geographers Isaiah Bowman, Derwent Whittlesey and Hans Weigert, the historian Andreas Dorpalen, and the polymath Robert Strausz-Hupé. Their interpretation of Haushofer and German geopolitics was to be reinforced by other works written in the immediate aftermath of the war, such as Edmund A. Walsh's analysis based on a first-hand account of meetings with Haushofer at the Nuremberg trials.[79] In the years that followed numerous works cited Haushofer and German geopolitics as the intellectual backbone of Nazi foreign policy.[80] While there were variants in this approach, the story followed similar lines, and can be summed up as follows: the ideas that informed the Nazi bid for world power were developed by a circle of geopolitics experts centred around the work of Karl Haushofer, a retired general and university professor. Haushofer was the head of the Institute for Geopolitics in Munich, and it was through this institute and his close association with Hess that Haushofer laid the groundwork for Germany's geo-strategic policies between 1933 and 1945. The basic ideas behind German geopolitics, according to these writers, were an amalgam of the work of Ratzel, Mackinder and Kjellén. States were like organisms that naturally competed for survival over the globe, and healthy societies needed to continue to expand to remain healthy. The result of this competition was that weaker societies must give way to the strong. The nature of this competition is dictated by spatial patterns, but racial characteristics also played their part, since this spatial competition was between national groups. It was from this that terms used by Ratzel, such as *Herrenvolk* and *Lebensraum* became central to Nazi ideology. The Germans, as a dominant race (*Herrenvolk*) needed space in which to expand (*Lebensraum*).[81]

This vision of the relationship between German geopolitics and Nazi strategy formed the foundation of an Anglo-American counter-movement that created a political geography that would underpin much of the post-1945 settlement (see the next section). In this sense, intellectually this notion of German geopolitics had a very real effect on the development of post-war American and British ideas. Having said this, though, the Anglo-American story of German geopolitics is also an over-simplistic myth that glosses over a much more complex story. Even the first task of defining what is meant by German geopolitics is troublesome, and more complex than the works cited above would suggest. There was no single centre or group of writers that can be readily identified as a clear school of geopolitics in Germany, and even the *Institut für Geopolitik* in Munich – the base upon which Haushofer was meant to have developed his school of geopolitics – never actually existed.[82] Indeed, when American forces reached Munich in 1945 their search for the *Institut für Geopolitik* yielded only a professor's office.[83] There certainly was a *Zeitschrift für Geopolitik* edited by Haushofer, and during the 1930s there was a working group that 'served primarily to feed news articles' to the press.[84] Overall, though, geopolitics in Germany was not wholly defined by Haushofer. Rather, what existed in Germany was a wide spectrum of geopolitical thought that can best be described as a vulgarised and popular political geography that (in the words of Albert von Hoffman) saw climate and topography as factors that predestined peoples to a 'particular destiny'.[85] Thus, rather than being the opposite of political geography, as writers like Bowman claimed, geopolitics in Germany (like the later geopolitics of wartime America) took ideas from political geography and applied them to the current concerns of international affairs.

Geopolitics in Germany goes back to before 1914, but it was only after the First World War that it became a popular way of interpreting international affairs. In this sense geopolitics was a product of the 1919 peace, and particularly of the grievances felt across much of the German political spectrum. In this sense the popularity and extension of geopolitics in Germany was a product of the Weimar years before the rise of the Nazis. Its forms of thought could be found both among conservative Social Democrats, who envisioned a Germany at the centre of a confederated Europe, and of democratic centrist views of an assertive, yet peaceful, German foreign policy.[86] While it is true that much of geopolitics was either sceptical or opposed to the League of Nations, it also had an uneasy relationship with the idea of an integrated pan-Europa. To a certain degree enthusiasts for a pan-European federation absorbed much geopolitical thought. The basis for the idea of a pan-European federation was 'that today national states are too small, politically and economically, for the purpose of playing and acquiring a big part in world politics'.[87] The new great powers would be continental in nature, and consequently only a federated Europe could compete with the other future continental powers. Yet, while ideas of a Pan-Europa shared the organic view of the state and its largely geo-strategic outlook with the rest of geopolitics, generally geopolitics in Germany supported a unilateral (and narrowly nationalist) foreign policy for Germany centred around revision of the Treaty of Versailles and the drawing of more 'natural' borders for Germany in the east.[88]

The work of Karl Haushofer represented a particularly right-wing and anti-democratic variety of geopolitics that took the work of Ratzel and Mackinder (see Chapter 5) and presented a vision of a global conflict over space in which Germany must expand, in alliance with Russia, to dominate the Eurasian landmass. That he certainly influenced the more geopolitical elements of Hitler's *Mein Kampf*, through his association with Rudolf Hess, is generally agreed. Hess, a member of the Nazi inner circle as well as Haushofer's wartime aide-de-camp and later research assistant, was Haushofer's major link with the Nazi leadership, as were (later) Haushofer's two sons. There is no denying that Haushofer tried to influence Nazi foreign policy, nor can his anti-democratic, militaristic and reactionary politics be ignored. What has been questioned, though, is his influence on Nazi grand strategy. Haushofer had blamed German defeat in the First World War on a lack of allies, and there is evidence that he and his son Albrecht were involved in the cooperation with Japan that led to the Anti-Comintern Pact with Japan. Similarly, his views on the need for an alliance with the Soviet Union against Britain fit with the 1939 Molotov–Ribbentrop pact between Germany and the USSR. Yet, after Hess' flight to Britain in 1941 Haushofer lost his influence with the Nazi leadership, and was briefly imprisoned in Dachau concentration camp because of his link to Hess.[89] Haushofer's reactionary world-view was premised on the importance of space, and was therefore at odds with the Nazi preoccupation with race. Perhaps the clearest distancing of the Nazis from Haushofer's ideas came with the invasion of Russia in 1941, which the contemporary American political geography Hans W. Weigert saw as 'undertaken in utter contempt' of Haushofer's views.[90] More recently, one author has gone further, and has argued that the rise of the Nazis actually led to a decline in the influence of geopolitics in Germany. Geopolitics 'flourished in the fertile pluralistic political settings of Weimar democracy', but 'ossified under the Nazis'.[91] In this sense, reactionary geopolitical ideas and concepts (the Nazi use of the terms *Herrenvolk* and *Lebensraum* stand out here) were freely used by the Nazis, but on the whole geopolitics played a secondary role to Nazi ideas of race and anti-Bolshevism.

This said, there can be little doubt that the idea of a dominant German geopolitics caught the imagination of many writers, and even filmmakers, in the Allied states, and particularly in the United States. Haushofer even played a central role in the Oscar nominated American film *Plan for Destruction* (1943), where he is presented as the mastermind behind an elaborate German plot to rule the world. There were two ways in which Haushofer influenced American thinking. On the one hand among political geographers, like Bowman and

Whittlesey, Haushofer's ideas were interpreted as the antithesis of proper international thinking. Here Haushofer became the foil for an alternative liberal global order. On the other, in the work of writers interested in geo-strategy, such as Nicholas Spykman, the ideas of geopolitics became something that could be adapted and used by a liberal United States. It is to these two reactions that we now turn.

## Anglo-American geopolitics and the planning of a New American-led world

When thinking about the role of political geography in planning the new *pax Americana* that would follow the Second World War the figure that comes to mind first is Isaiah Bowman. Bowman was, in the words of Neil Smith, 'Roosevelt's Geographer', and was part of the team around the President that did much of the planning that led to the agreements at Bretton Woods and San Francisco that gave the world the IMF, the World Bank and the United Nations. Bowman was certainly key in the development of this world, but space should also be given to another American political geographer writing at this time: Derwent Whittlesey. Whittlesey's work on the interplay between human society and the natural world, often written against the backdrop of the rise of totalitarianism, provided an intellectual justification for a global order at odds with autarky and increasingly economically interdependent. While Bowman certainly had the ear of the President, it was Whittlesey who developed a coherent theoretical geopolitics that justified the new American-led order that was being constructed.

States for Whittlesey were changeable institutions subject to human values, technological innovation and economic development as well as environmental factors. While the natural environment 'ceaselessly' modifies forces to shape the political world, cultures at the same time leave imprints of themselves on their environment.[92] For Whittlesey it was the spread of the European state over the rest of the world that was the most important geopolitical event of the last few centuries. This spread came about because of a technological transport revolution that altered the way that Europeans interacted with space.[93] For Whittlesey there were two implications to this:

1   The accomplishment of this global spread created an interdependent global economy that was a closed system.
2   The western European state was transferred to parts of the world that were significantly different in their physical environment to Western Europe.[94]

The transport revolution that led to global interdependence had two major implications according to Whittlesey. First, it had made larger territorial states both possible and also more efficient political entities. The European states, whose boundaries were a product of the stagecoach and canal era, increasingly found it hard to compete as great powers, and it is the larger states (especially the United States, the Soviet Union and the British Commonwealth) that now wield global power.[95] Against this trend, however, there was a counter-trend of nationalism that curtailed the creation of larger states, especially in Europe and latterly in the colonial world.[96] Second, and mirroring Bowman's earlier argument in *The New World* (see Chapter 6), Whittlesey saw that growing interdependence and the uneven spread of natural resources necessary for this new world had largely guaranteed that even the largest territorial state was incapable of self-sufficiency.[97] The spread of the western European idea of the state created a world of similar political units, with common European roots, but these new states interacted with the environmental conditions that they found, and even fostered the very intellectual revolutions that were bringing direct colonial rule to an end.[98] Thus, Whittlesey regarded the twentieth century world as marked by the conquest of the world by the Western European idea of the state, but that this European victory had eventually undermined Europe's power by favouring larger territorial states. The thirst for raw materials and the growth of interdependence of this new global order made even these large states such as the United States reliant on regions outside of their borders. In searching for the solution to this conundrum Whittlesey followed Bowman and Mackinder in seeing the answer to an interdependent largely western-led world in a global regime of interdependence regulated by international organisations and agreements.

Whittlesey's conception of the new order that was emerging was consciously constructed as an alternative to what he saw as the nationalist and autarkic world that dominated fascist thinking, especially the grand strategy that he associated with Karl Haushofer. Like Mackinder, Whittlesey traced the German mindset of the Second World War to deeper conditioning based on an education system dedicated to maps and the accumulation of geopolitical facts.[99] Failing to see that the problems of interdependence and raw material distribution could only be solved by a major change in the structure of world politics, the German geopoliticians (Whittlesey argued) accepted the state as a natural organism that needed to expand in order to survive. The result was the normalisation of war, and the establishment of an environment in which only a few states could struggle to reach self-sufficiency.[100] The impossibility of autarky led Whittlesey to agree with Bowman that currently the best answer to the problem of the lack of self-sufficiency was a global system of trade that allowed states to overcome their raw material problems and 'population pressures' through free exchange.[101] Behind the Nazi totalitarian geopolitical vision, Whittlesey saw a deeper problem. Totalitarianism for Whittlesey was a product of the major shifts in technology and economic power that had disturbed the structure of the state, and thrown it out of alignment with its physical environment. Whittlesey saw totalitarianism as an attempt by the state to reassert control in the face of technological flux. 'Human values' were discarded in the search for security.[102] The self-defeating nature of this approach was, according to Whittlesey, manifest in German geopolitics, and in order to confront the allure of totalitarianism full on it was necessary to work out an organisation of society in harmony with its finest traditions, an organisation not based on domination by any group ... The political history of the Occidental world since the early Middle Ages has moved toward the integration of larger and larger groups of people, as fast as improved transportation has increased contacts ... Thus further political integration appears to be inevitable.[103]

A reordering of the world was necessary to deal with the threat of totalitarianism. Here Whittlesey joined Bowman and Mackinder in calling for a new order that, while based on the 'realities' of the physical environment as expressed through recent major changes in technology and economic organisation, fundamentally changes the nature of global politics. Although Whittlesey did not go as far as Mackinder in reifying the organiser and idealist (see Chapter 5), there is still here a core idea that there are constraints on human action created by the realities of the natural world. For Whittlesey these constraints are very real, although for him it is the over-emphasis of these natural constraints that leads to the kind of dangerous environmental determinism found in the geopolitics of Haushofer. Where Whittlesey went further than Bowman and Mackinder was in his presentation of the natural environment as not just a conditioner of the social world, but also as something that is conditioned and changed by new ideas and social organisation. The physical world becomes mutable in a way that it was not even in Bowman. Thus, while Whittlesey's view of IR is still one dominated by the interplay of environmental and ideational forces, it becomes one in which it is ideas that have the power of not just interpreting the natural world, but actually changing substantially how the environment affects human society.

Bowman's own written contributions during the Second World War years were limited by his role in government. From 1942 he was a member of the Department of State Advisory Committee on Post-War Foreign Policy, and also acted as a special advisor to two wartime Secretaries of State. A member of Secretary Stettinius' 1944 London mission, he was also a member of the US delegation to Dumbarton Oaks, and an advisor at the 1945 San Francisco Conference.[104] His best known work from this period – 'Geography vs Geopolitics' – laid out both his criticisms of what he saw as the failings of fascist geopolitics, and also his own vision of what the basis of the American alternative should be.[105] Basically Bowman had accepted the notion, found in Haushofer, in Kjellén and in Ratzel, that human societies must expand. Where he parted company with them was in the notion that that expansion must be organised by states and against states in a zero-sum conflict. Here Bowman presented the future as being a conflict between a 'fatalism' that accepted the world as it was, and the 'human will' that was willing to (quoting F.S. Oliver) 'fling itself forward beyond its data' in order to create a new settlement after the war.[106] For Bowman this meant looking beyond the state and concentrating instead on free trade and the mobility of labour in order to allow expansions of trade and population that would not bring states into conflict.[107] Bowman helped to push this position in his roles at both the Dumbarton Oaks and the San Francisco conferences that would lay down the institutional framework for the new American-dominated global political economy of the second half of the twentieth century. While Haushofer's concept of *lebensraum* was of a German nation struggling to find its place in a hostile world, Bowman's conception of *lebensraum* would see societies expanding through free trade, economic development and migration. That is, each would engage in an economically-driven *lebensraum* without leading to wars between states. America's *lebensraum* would work through the new Bretton Woods system, and would constitute what Neil Smith would call the American Empire.[108]

To a certain degree this was a return, by Bowman, to Ratzel's intellectual definition of *lebensraum*, which could take a non-state, and even non-violent, aspect such as in the spread of the Chinese diaspora or the (perceived) development of the United States. This also perhaps explains why Harriet Wanklyn, in her 1961 study of Ratzel, singled out Bowman as the only twentieth century geographer who came close to having the same grasp of the field of political geography as Ratzel.[109] Bowman's preferred shape for the post-war settlement was, to a large degree, an attempt to return to the globalised world that had existed before 1914, but with the addition of a layer of international organisations to support the economic order and to regulate the political competition of states. In this sense it was not necessarily a radical step, and it stands in sharp contrast to the more left-wing visions discussed below, Bowman's vision did, to a large extent, become the global reality – first only in the US-dominated western sphere, and then after 1989 across the globe. We must see Bowman's approach to the problem of the international as one of the more successful theoretical visions of the mid-twentieth century. It was, though, not the only successful vision of the post-war age to emerge out of the United States at the time. While Bowman's political geography was primarily concerned with the political economy of the new world, another thinker who was also influenced by political geography, Nicholas Spykman, was developing a geopolitics that was firmly based on a political power politics model of the world.

Although Spykman was not a geographer, political geography played an important role in his development of what was primarily a power politics approach to world order. In this sense Spykman's approach stands on the cusp between political geography and what we would now call a classical realist interpretation of IR. Writing on international affairs from 1934 until his death at 49 in 1943, his final work appeared in 1944 edited by his research assistant at the Yale Institute of International Studies, Helen R. Nicholl. While his influence on wartime debates in the United States on the possible post-war order was strong, and he remained remembered at Yale for many years after the war, his early death meant that his name became less well-known to IR scholars in the decades after the war. While the classical realists that would dominate the subject of IR after 1950 would share Spykman's views on power, the balance of power and war, they would be less sympathetic to his use of political geography (not to mention his unabashed use of the word geopolitics to describe his ideas). Thus, Spykman's removal from the intellectual scene goes part of the way to explaining the declining influence of political geography within IR in the decades after the war.

Yet, at the same time, Spykman does also belong to the classical realist tradition that was to dominate American IR after his death.

There are two interlocking aspects to Spykman's international thought. The first was his notion of the role, nature and place of geographic factors in global politics. Here Spykman was careful to lay out the specific form that geographical influences took, and how they compared to other effects on foreign policy. While there are some similarities here with Bowman's political geography, there was also a glaring difference that puts more clear blue water between their views of international affairs than we might assume at first glance. Spykman's geopolitical outlook owed much to Halford Mackinder's 1904 analysis of the pivot area, although Spykman's interpretation put less emphasis on the Heartland/pivot area, and much more on Mackinder's Rimland. The second aspect was his view of power, and how this translated into his view of the balance of power and the role of international organisations in any post-war settlement. Here Spykman is much closer to the view of IR found in the work of Hans J. Morgenthau, particularly in his view of the inherent instability of the balance of power. That said, Spykman's tone when discussing war is significantly different from Morgenthau's, and it was perhaps Spykman's more blunt assessment of the role of war that accounts for both his greater popularity (compared to Morgenthau) during the war, but also the large number of negative reviews that the publication of his 1942 magnum opus *America's Strategy in World Politics* attracted.

Spykman viewed geography as only one of a number of factors that influenced foreign policy, yet having conceded this Spykman then laid out a reason why geographical factors were of central importance: 'the geographic characteristics of states are relatively unchanging and unchangeable, the geographic demands of those states will remain the same for centuries'. As a result, while conflict exists these geographic factors would continue to cause friction.[110] Thus, while Spykman is at pains to point out that geography is not the only factor, it is a factor that remains a constant even when other influences (such as the effects of communications technologies) enhance or reduce its power. By contrast, the non-geographic influences on foreign policy (the 'historical system of reference') tend to be ephemeral and more open to change. The result is that effects on foreign policy such as location have a geographical constant element ('through which we derive the facts of location'), and an historically contingent element ('by which we evaluate those facts').[111] Geographical influences, therefore, are something that cannot be wished away, as one might, for example, be able to do for ideological ones that are more open to human manipulation. 'For geography does not argue. It simply is.'[112]

So what was this geographical constant that Spykman saw in foreign affairs? Here he borrowed and adapted Mackinder's 1904 analysis, and in the process suggested a post-war grand strategy for the United States that bore a striking resemblance to the later policy of containment followed by the West during the Cold War. Like both Mahan and Mackinder before him, Spykman regarded the developments in communications technology as creating a truly global 'single field for the play of political forces'.[113] Where Mackinder had seen the danger of world empire coming from a state conquering the 'heartland' of Eurasia

(Eastern Europe, Russia and central Asia), Spykman was more concerned about the territories that Mackinder had referred to as the 'Rimland' (the area around the Heartland: Europe, the Middle East, south Asia, South-East Asia, China and North Asia). The strategic location and importance of the Rimland territories made these the crucial territories to control in order to prevent a conquest of Eurasia.[114] The area of the Rimland was strategically important for three reasons:

1   Because of the simple fact of its location (the Rimland territories were ideally placed so that they made control of all Eurasia easier[115]).
2   Because of the wealth in industry of the regions (they lay mostly in the globe's crucial 25° to 60° north latitudes where climate favoured first population and agricultural and then industrial power.[116]
3   Because they were the 'amphibious' zone where land power met sea power.[117] That these regions where the main battlegrounds of the Second World War lent immediate weight to Spykman's interpretation.

Spykman's work was, though, not simply a study of geo-strategic issues. Interwoven with the factors of location, climate and size were issues of power. For Spykman power was a potentially positive force that was responsible for the creation of civilisation. Usually a means towards an ethical end, in all societies power was manifest through cooperation, accommodation and conflict. International society was no different: examples of cooperation, accommodation and conflict could all be found. The problem was that the sovereign independence of states meant that international society was an 'anarchy' (i.e.: lacking any central authority), and so conflict and war were a natural part of interstate relations.[118] Since the two means of overcoming anarchy – conquest by one power or confederation of states – were both highly unlikely, then for Spykman it made sense that the study of international affairs should concentrate on the factors that run the international community of states: the balance of power.

The balance of power for Spykman was a product of the driving force behind the foreign policy of states in an anarchy: survival and the preservation of territorial integrity. Because of a lack of a central authority the search for power by independent states was carried out without any moderating moral values, and with each state concerned not with balance, but with their own striving to maintain a margin of superiority over their rivals. It was also a game played primarily by great powers, with the smaller powers acting more like stakes in the game than players. Like G. Lowes Dickinson, Spykman saw the international anarchy and the balance of power as a product of the collapse of medieval order, but he did not regard it as a system that naturally found its own equilibrium. On the contrary, the balance of power was always unstable because:

1   States sought a generous margin of power in their favour.
2   Power was difficult to calculate.
3   Forms of power were constantly changing, and never static.

As a result, war was a not infrequent part of the balance of power system, and human intervention was required to maintain a fragile political equilibrium.[119] In this view of the natural instability of the balance of power Spykman was in agreement with Hans J. Morgenthau (see Chapter 8). This human intervention could take many forms. One was the readiness to go to war. Another was the important role of international organisations. Interestingly, Spykman remained supportive of the League of Nations. The League for Spykman was a means by which the use of force between states could be redirected into less violent forms, and thus was not a replacement for the balance of power, but rather a more desirable form of it.[120] Indeed, up to his death he regarded the US failure to join the League as a mistake, and saw the return to a League-like system as important as 'a moral and legal basis for our indispensable participation in the power struggles of Europe and Asia'.[121] Thus, rather than seeing the balance of power as the opposite of a system of collective security, justice and democracy ('might' rather than 'right' in the words of Norman Angell), Spykman saw a successful balance of power in Europe and Asia between equal powers (and probably within a League-like organisation) as providing a stability that would make the spread of justice and democracy possible.[122] 'The first step from anarchy to order' Spykman argued in 1942, 'is not the disappearance of force, but its use by the community instead of individual members.'[123] In Spykman's view collective security emerges as a superior form of the balance of power, not its opposite.

Unlike Morgenthau, Spykman did not link his view of the struggle of power consciously to the idea of laws of history rooted in a common human nature, yet the underlying implication is there. For Spykman a combination of geographic constants (suitably modified by historical developments) with a common human struggle for power through history were the bases upon which the unchanging realities of world politics were based. Here we see a stark difference between Bowman and Spykman. Spykman sees constants that, while open to alteration by changes in political structure and technology, tend to determine human political behaviour throughout time. Bowman, on the other hand, reserves a much larger role for changes of spirit. Indeed, this was the whole point of Bowman's *The New World*, discussed in depth in the last chapter: the great changes in the world after 1919 were for Bowman fundamentally a result of changes in human spirit. Geographic factors were altered at a very fundamental level by these changes of spirit. For Spykman the human world was far less open to change, and had to be aware of the power of geographic and power political realities. That said, Spykman has been described as 'a steady user' of Bowman's *The New World*, and Bowman famously wrote a positive review of Spykman's 1942 *America's Strategy in World Politics*.[124] Bowman certainly thought that Spykman too readily confused geopolitics with geography, and he remained opposed to the blunt power politics found in Spykman's work, yet he was content to praise Spykman's realism up to a point.[125] Spykman's blunt realism also has to be considered in context, and without his chance to modify his position in the wake of the war, as many self-identifying realists did. The target of Spykman's work in the last decade of his life were the 'idealist' deniers of the role of power who at the time seemed to dominate American thinking in the debates between isolationists and interventionists (Spykman was strongly in favour of US intervention in world politics). Furniss believed that had Spykman lived through to the 1950s he would have equally been critical of the 'power-is-all' writers, since Spykman was well aware that power was not the only aspect effecting world politics.[126] It is even possible that Spykman would have followed a similar path as John Herz and Hans Morgenthau by endorsing David Mitrany's functional approach to world politics. Spykman's *America's Strategy in World Politics* contains a tantalisingly short discussion of global functional organisations in which he stated that 'International life … has problems that can be solved only in terms of a functional approach.' Although he does go on to say that he believed that a more regional approach remained the way to deal with political problems.[127]

Thus Spykman's ideas form a bridge between the political geographers like Bowman, Whittlesey and Mackinder and the founders of the post-war classical realist school that were to dominate IR in the United States universities from the late 1940s. Generally, though, the popularity of the political geographers in international thought reached its highest point in the early 1940s, buoyed up by its ability to simultaneously level criticism at a perceived Nazi ideology of world conquest, and to provide a blueprint for America's post-war strategy. In a dramatic reversal, though, its star would rapidly fall after 1945, making way for less geopolitical schools of thought. Unabashedly interventionist, it provided geostrategic reasons why the United States could not sink again into isolationism as it had done after 1919. It was equally unabashedly supportive of a global free-trade and capitalist order, and to a certain extent the work of Bowman in particular can be seen as laying the intellectual ground-work of the American-led international economic order that would come to dominate the globe once the Soviet alternative order had faltered. Yet, there were those, especially in Britain, for whom the political and strategic crises of the 1930s and 1940s were a product of capitalism. For them it was the problems caused by a declining and increasingly predatory capitalist system that was the most important problem faced by western civilisation, and a return to a global liberal economic order was out of the question.

## The crisis of capitalism

In 1935 an exchange of letters in the *New Statesman* brought a simmering debate about the relationship between capitalism and war to a head. These letters were soon published in an edited collection. The views expressed in the exchange revealed a split in the British left on whether capitalists as a class were potential allies in the attempt to move towards a world without war, or whether capitalism and capitalists were the cause of the instabilities that led to war. The debate would pitch the liberal socialists Norman Angell and Leonard Woolf against H.N. Brailsford and Harold Laski, and would influence debates on the left in the latter half of the decade. To a large extent the origins of the debate lay in an earlier split on the analysis of the nature of international society going back to before the First World War. This split has already been discussed in Chapter 5, and revolved around the pre-1914 work of Norman Angell, on the one hand, and J.A. Hobson, on the other. While Angell had regarded the spread of finance capital and economic interdependence as a major development that made modern war between great powers a potentially fatal threat to the prosperity of capitalism, Hobson regarded the particular nature of modern capitalism as a cause of current imperialist drives that destabilised the relationships between states. While Angell saw recent capitalist developments as compatible with global peace, Hobson saw them as a cause of imperialism and war. It has to be stressed that both writers were not talking about the nature of capitalism *per se*, but rather the specific form that the capitalist system was taking at the time. Angell also was not seeing capitalism as a panacea (indeed, he was aware of how brutal capitalist exploitation could be domestically), and Hobson was not necessarily anti-capitalist (his solution to the problem of capitalist exploitation abroad was social reforms at home that would redirect financial profits away from imperialism abroad and towards worker purchasing power in the metropole).[128] While Hobson's approach was both essentially liberal reformist and also concerned with the cause of imperialism as fundamentally a problem of domestic (and particularly British domestic) politics, the core of his approach was adopted in 1914 by H.N. Brailsford who, in his *The War of Steel and Gold* presented Hobson's theory of imperialism as one part of an international political economy approach that also attempted to show how the conditions of modern capitalist economics changed the nature of the balance of power between industrial great powers.[129]

It was these two approaches to the international role of capitalism that were to be played out in 1935. Although this split had been present throughout the 1920s too, it had largely taken a back seat while discussions on the left had revolved around the questions of the problems of the peace treaties and the proper structure of League of Nations collective security machinery (see Chapter 6). Yet, even then the problem of capitalism's compatibility with peace would resurface in the work of Brailsford. Even when praising the League's efforts in the 1920s Brailsford would still caution that 'I doubt the efficacy alike of arbitration and disarmament to solve the problem of war until we grapple with economic imperialism.'[130] In a more equivocal voice Hugh Dalton, a leading light in the Labour Party and a future cabinet minister, argued in 1928 that while Angell was right to argue that war did not benefit capitalism as a whole, it certainly did benefit some capitalists.[131] While Brailsford and Dalton might harbour these doubts about capitalism, it did not stop them supporting the same proposals for international institutional reform as Angell. The events that brought this latent split out into the open were the economic collapse that followed the Great Crash of 1929, and the seeming threat posed by capitalism to democracy after 1931. Certainly Brailsford was not alone in seeing the collapse of the British Labour government in 1931 and the rise of fascism in the early 1930s as products of capitalist *coup d'états* against potentially socialist governments that had come to power through democratic means. Suddenly the idea that peace could come through the building of international institutions, rather than through a dramatic change in the economic system, appeared naïve to many on the left.

The *New Statesman* exchange of 1935 saw Brailsford reiterate his interpretation of Hobson's analysis. While he did not dispute the logic of Angell's argument that war was a threat to the interdependent and international capitalist system, Brailsford argued that Angell's approach only existed in an ideal world. In the real world coercive sovereign states allow capitalists to keep an unequal share of the wealth, which causes under-consumption at home as workers with smaller pay packets are unable to purchase the goods produced by capitalist-owned domestic industries. This under-consumption means that capitalist profits cannot find worthwhile investment opportunities in the home market, and therefore require the state to engage in imperialism in order to create investment opportunities for finance capital abroad. Only the establishment of socialism domestically would remedy this situation.[132] Responding to Brailsford, Leonard Woolf argued that whereas Brailsford was right about the importance of economic structures, Angell was equally right that it was the delusion that it was possible to gain economically from war that had led to the Great War. Socialists, he argued, dismiss the non-economic and complex reasons for the outbreak of war at their peril.[133] Angell responded by arguing that it was the international anarchy that caused war between states, and that as a result an effective system of collective security was the solution to the problem of war. This was independent of any issue of under-consumption. Indeed, Angell was sceptical that there was a capitalist drive for imperial control, suggesting that investment abroad would just lead to more over-production, and that there did not seem to be a clear link between imperialism and investment since most British overseas investment was actually outside the Empire.[134] Brailsford was unapologetic, though, responding that capitalism was unstable, and that capitalist states by promoting only the interests of capitalists made for an unstable world.[135] Harold Laski backed Brailsford, and reiterated the point that Angell's view relied too much on reasoned argument, but that it was not reasoned argument that drove capitalists. Capitalists were not interested in the long-run implications for their actions, but rather in their own narrow interests.[136]

The basis of Brailsford and Laski's objections to Angell's (and to a certain extent, Woolf's) argument was that the root of politico-economic behaviour of capitalists was their short-term narrow interests. Brailsford's writing in the late 1930s was dominated by the view that the short-term interests followed by capitalist classes in the major western great powers were behind the policy of conciliation towards fascism. As long as core capitalist concerns about control over the wider extra-European empires were not threatened, he argued, then Britain (and by implication France and the United States too) was content to let fascists expand in Europe and Manchuria and Abyssinia.[137] While destructive to all civilisation in the long run, these interests were very real, and could not be easily dismissed as irrational and incorrect thought, as Brailsford felt Angell had done. Here, though, there had been a shift in Brailsford's view of how capitalism impacted on policy. In the 1935 exchanges Brailsford was firmly arguing that capitalism remained a cause of war between states, by 1938 he was making a different argument: that these short-term capitalist interests were actually leading to a reluctance by Britain, France and the United States to stand up to fascism at the possible cost of war. While the substance of Brailsford's analysis of the nature of capitalism had not changed, the appearance of fascism as a threat had changed how this capitalist short-termism manifested itself in foreign policy. Brailsford's pre-First World War analysis of international relations had hinged on the view that the conflicts between industrial capitalist states were fundamentally different, and were about conflicts over finance and market share, not land as in the older agrarian world. Fascism had changed the rules by resuscitating ideas of conquest of territory that had become alien to industrial capitalism.[138] While Brailsford remained sceptical of League of Nations collective security, seeing it as too reliant on Anglo-French military power and the threat of force,[139] he nevertheless was willing to support it when it confronted the older and more destructive logic of fascism. For Brailsford this collective security should be built around an Anglo-French alliance with the Soviet Union, which Brailsford saw as a natural ally against fascism.[140]

Ironically, Brailsford's return to, and re-endorsement of Hobson's approach to imperialism came at a time when Hobson himself had been re-evaluating his analysis of the causes of war. In a 1948 tribute to Hobson, Brailsford would argue that he and Hobson had put too much emphasis on the economic causes of war, and not enough on the psychological.[141] Interestingly enough Hobson had come to the same conclusion over a decade before. In a paper delivered to the South Place Ethical Society on 30 June 1935, Hobson argued that 'the war spirit cannot be explained in purely economic terms. Nations do not consciously range themselves behind their business men in a struggle for markets.'[142] Not only did Hobson criticise what he regarded as the 'Marxist' view of the causes of war, he also supported Angell's view of war as being caused by 'collective illusions and passions'.[143] While Brailsford seemed unaware of Hobson's views on the causes of war, he was not deaf to arguments that looked to nationalism and sovereignty as a major cause of international conflict. Towards the end of the Second World War Brailsford was singling out the sovereignty of the nation state as a major impediment to peace, arguing that it needed to be replaced by an ideal of the 'general good' of humanity.[144] That said, he clung to the idea that socialist states would be less likely to go to war against each other, and that a cooperative international order based on international planning could be built up through the establishment of social democratic planned societies at the national level first. This remained a major area of disagreement between Brailsford and his friend David Mitrany. The two had discussed the links between national and international planning between 1942–5, with Mitrany arguing that nationally planned socialist states would be as likely to fight each other over raw materials and market share as capitalist states, and thus the prevention of war would require the establishment of global institutions first. Brailsford was not totally won over by Mitrany's argument, but was troubled enough by the force of Mitrany's argument that he was willing to concede that socialism at the national level would not be enough to guarantee peace.[145]

Brailsford was not the only major British international expert to chart the way that capitalism distorted foreign policies and thus caused war. Harold Laski, who had previously taken a more liberal view of politics and international relations in the 1920s, had gradually moved to the left during the inter-war years. Another friend of Mitrany's, Laski – as we shall see in the next section below – was probably the first writer to apply the principles of functional government to the international, thus helping to create the functional approach to international relations. While this aspect of his work would inspire David Mitrany's research agenda from the 1930s onwards, Laski also remained closer to Brailsford in his analysis of the role of capitalism in international affairs.[146] Indeed, by 1933 he was arguing that the nature of capitalist society was such that it would never allow the international planning under the League of Nations that was required to create peace. As a result, a first step before an international order that could guarantee peace was the establishment of democratic socialism at home.[147] Laski firmly believed that the existence of the sovereign state was a major cause of war,[148] but his view of sovereignty was different from more liberal and conservative opponents of the international anarchy. While for writers like Gilbert Murray and Norman Angell sovereignty was an outdated concept that ought to be abandoned on the grounds of its irrationality, for Laski sovereignty was the rational creation of specific interests associated with the state. 'Sovereignty', he wrote in 1943, '… is the instrument through which the vested interests in any society wage … the war of steel and gold; and, under the cloak of government authority, they invoke the half-rational sentiment of nationalism to maintain their power abroad.'[149] Here Laski's argument shares much with what many would recognise as a classical realist position: that states are motivated primarily by their national interest, and that national interest is a product of the different groups within the specific national society.[150] Where Laski differs from the formulation of the national interest presented by (for example) Hans J. Morgenthau is that he saw this national interest in current western capitalist societies as predominantly the interests of a capitalist class that controlled state policy, and used sovereignty and nationalism as a means to further their economic goals through foreign policy.[151] It was the problems of capitalism, therefore, that led directly to the problems associated with sovereignty. As a result, it was the nature of capitalism that was of central importance when assessing the future success of any plan for international government that might attempt to move beyond the nation state.

Laski's view of capitalism was as a system that, after the First World War, no longer provided stability and security. Here the argument followed closely the earlier positions of Hobson and Brailsford. The basic problem was that capitalist vested interests desired greater profits, which they acquired by lowering wages and thus restricting demand. In a system capable of producing plenty, production was artificially restricted. The need to find outlets for profit under these conditions led to the use of sovereign state governments by capitalist vested interests in order to procure raw materials and markets abroad. The resulting international anarchy, along with economic hardship, produced insecurity for the great majority of people. For Laski insecurity was the enemy of democracy and freedom. Insecurity 'has bred in the hearts of men those fears and hates which are incompatible with freedom. For freedom can exist only where there is tolerance.'[152] This led Laski to conclude that only when the economy was growing was capitalism compatible with democracy. As soon as the economy ceased to grow, capitalist interests bread insecurity, which in turn led people to turn in fear away from democracy.[153] For Laski the reality of interdependence and the problem of capitalist vested interests led to the need for a two-track solution. International organisations dedicated to collective security needed to be established, but they would only succeed if:

1    They also dealt with the wider economic problems the world faced internationally.
2    Democratic socialist governments took over the reins of government and curbed the toxic effects of capitalist interests on foreign policy.[154]

At one level Laski's position appears at odds with more liberal socialist positions on the international (see the discussion in the last chapter), where reform of the international was seen as being possible without a major overhaul of capitalism, and also where it was the nature of the international anarchy, not necessarily the specific nature of individual capitalist states, that was central to stopping war. Many, such as Mitrany, were also sceptical of the idea that socialist states would be more peaceful than capitalist ones. Indeed, David Mitrany had even argued that planned socialist states were likely to be more war-prone since their wider economic functions would create more points of potential conflict with other states.[155] Yet, the links between Laski's thought and the broader trends within British liberal socialist thought were becoming more apparent during the 1940s in two ways. First, growing sceptism about the political effects of capitalism had grown among the left during the 1930s, leading some like Woolf to conclude that the Second World War was the direct result of 'Tory capitalism', and that 'the only way in which we can prevent history repeating itself is to rebuild the economic system and international society on Socialist principles'.[156] Equally as well, as we shall see in the next section, Laski's twin track approach of simultaneous international and domestic reform led him to develop the same ideas of functional international government that were found in the work of David Mitrany. Indeed, like Mitrany, Laski rejected federalist solutions to international order, and saw in functional organisations a way to bridge the gap between what he saw as necessary international and domestic reforms in an age where the economic interdependence of the globe had become a reality. That said, there is a difference of emphasis between Laski and Mitrany. While for Mitrany the focus was on the realities of interdependence and the failures of national solutions to the crisis, for Laski the central problem was the growing failure of a capitalist order to provide both prosperity and security. While there were major differences of opinion between Keynes and Laski, what they shared was the view that the old *laissez-faire* culture of the nineteenth century had failed. This theme of the failure of a whole ideology and its accompanying politico-economic order was also the major theme in the work of Karl Polanyi, whose war-time *magnum opus* took as its starting point the idea that the old liberal and free market society that had brought unprecedented prosperity in the nineteenth century was now in its death throes.

An often overlooked work dealing in part with the nature and crisis of the international system is Karl Polanyi's *The Great Transformation*. Still known in critical IPE – although even here usually mostly for the concept of the 'counter-movement' against the economic free market – Polanyi's work has been almost completely ignored by post-1945 IR theorists. This is despite the fact that the first two chapters explore the origins, structure and eventual demise of what he saw as the political and economic structures of the international system. At one level *The Great Transformation* is a work of international theory, albeit an approach that fuses both economics and politics, and international and domestic levels. It is not solely a work of international theory, however, for it is with the domestic conditions of nineteenth century liberal England that Polanyi's analysis concentrates. In addition to this, the development of the international part of his argument combines an analysis of political and economic conditions that, while appealing to earlier IR and later IPE scholars, puts Polanyi at odds with the thoroughly political arguments associated with the classical realist IR that emerged towards the end of the 1940s. Yet, despite this, the book remains an attempt to explain the dislocations that, from Polanyi's point of view, had destroyed an international order.[157]

Polanyi had been at pains to argue, throughout the process leading up to publication, that *The Great Transformation* was an exploration of 'the political and economic origins of the present world dilemma'.[158] In this sense it was not intended as a history of the liberal order, although so much of the writing concentrated on the origins of the crisis. Behind Polanyi's work lay the idea 'that man is rational … but that society tends to set him insoluble problems in the form of conflicting institutions …'. It is through institutions that human rationality needs to work. When institutions conflict, or break down, human rationality is unable to function adequately. The perceived irrationality of humanity in the 1930s 'merely reflect the institutional crisis in a transitional period'.[159] For Polanyi there were four reinforcing institutions that had created the long period of stability from the 1840s. These were the balance of power system, the gold standard, the self-regulating market and the liberal state.[160] For Polanyi, the first two out of the four institutions were international, and it was the unravelling of the balance of power after 1904, followed by the 'snapping of the golden thread' of the gold standard at the beginning of the 1930s that were the central crises that finally unravelled both the liberal state and the self-regulating market.

Polanyi's analysis of the balance of power centres on the role played by trade and finance in underpinning the stability of the balance. For Polanyi there was nothing natural about a political balance. While stable after the treaty of Utrecht, the balance had been maintained only by war.[161] On the contrary, it had proved to be a distinctly unstable system in the eighteenth century, while the attempt to recreate the eighteenth century balance after 1814, using hierarchy and religion, had proved short-lived. What made the balance of power work, and work for longer-term systemic peace, was the changing nature of finance and trade. Trade, which in a previous era had been 'military and warlike' linked to conquest, adventurers and privateers, now became reliant on an international finance that could only flourish with systemic peace.[162] *Haute finance* became the guarantor of the stability of the balance of power. While smaller wars, especially over colonial possessions, became commonplace, there was no 'great conflagration' to upset the balance. Although by the 1870s the era of free trade was over, and ceased to underwrite the stability of the system, international high finance reached its peak in the 1890s, and thus the system survived. Yet, even finance could not survive the polarisation of power that unravelled the system after 1904, creating two major alliance systems without a third power-balancing group.[163]

The collapse of the balance of power system that led to the First World War left the second international institution, the gold standard, in place. For Polanyi the immediate post-war period after 1919 represented an attempt to recreate a functioning balance of power and a stable financial system linked to the gold standard. The balance of power, he argued, was seriously compromised, but as long as the fiscal structures of the global economy remained in place the 1920s remained a stable, albeit conservative, decade. The economic collapse after 1929–31, which saw the abandonment of the gold standard, removed the last functioning international institution, and for Polanyi represented the end of the liberal civilisation that had emerged out of the 1840s. There were no longer any firm foundations on which human rationality could hang.[164]

Polanyi was certainly not the only person forecasting the end of the liberal *laissez faire* order, indeed a similar but less deep argument had been made by Norman Angell in his *Fruits of Victory* (1921), while J.M. Keynes had declared the death of *laissez faire* in 1926.[165] What made his analysis new was his notion of the inter-relationship between political and economic factors, and his notion that the political stability of the balance of power was dependent on factors rooted in the global economy. This relationship between politics and economics, where the realities of the global economy were responsible for the shaping of the struggle for power, was reversed in a work that appeared a year after Polanyi's *Great Transformation*. In his *National Power and the Structure of Foreign Trade* the economist Albert O. Hirschman (like Polanyi a European émigré) argued that international trade could be exploited for the purposes of enhancing or projecting national power. Taking the liberal idea that trade created interdependence, Hirschman went on to show how different degrees of dependence led to unequal gains in political dependence, and that as a result states were able to use trade as a part of their broader power-political struggles because trade brought different relative power gains for each of the trading partners. This he called the influence effect of foreign trade. In an echo of Brailsford's view of western capitalism, Hirschman argued that economic warfare 'can take the place of bombardments, economic pressure that of sabre rattling', and that even if war was eliminated from international affairs 'foreign trade would lead to relationships of dependence and influence between nations'.[166]

Hirschman's book was to influence both the dependency school of international development (he was to be regarded as its 'grandfather' for developing the idea that unequal trade led to permanent political dependence), and also the work of Stephen D. Krasner. Krasner's more power–political approach to international political economy owed much to Hirschman's study of trade (indeed Krasner had been taught by Hirschman), and there is more than a passing resemblance between Hirschman's take on the political uses of international trade and the wider classical realist tradition that will be explored in more detail below.[167] It also shows us the extent to which Polanyi's work represents a reversal of the classical realist view of the foundational nature of political power. Political power exists in the work of Polanyi (and also Brailsford and Laski), but it is dependent on deeper structures of economic organisation. Indeed, as Brailsford had argued, power here was viewed as a means, rather than an end. This marks a clear break between this political economy approach to the international and the classical realist tradition.

Within critical IPE, however, it is not Polanyi's view of the balance of power that is of interest, but rather his notion of the double- (or counter-) movement. The counter-movement for Polanyi is the steps taken by society to protect itself from the expansion of the market into areas that would threaten the stability of society.[168] References to the counter-movement in *The Great Transformation*, make it hard to pin down precisely what Polanyi meant by it (particularly, is it a means by which capitalism protects itself from its own excesses, or is it a threat to market stability, and the basis of institutional opposition to capitalism?). It is also a concept that Polanyi used mostly to describe relations between the market and the nature of society within the state, rather than outside of it. That said, the concept of the counter-movement is one that can be applied to international society as well. Indeed, Mitrany's conception of a functional approach to international politics, while it was certainly a response to the problems of the sovereign nation state in an anarchical society of states, can also be seen as a counter-movement to the globalisation of capitalism. Mitrany may have, like Angell, been suspicious of the blanket claim that capitalism caused war, but he was certainly keen to argue that it was the spread of economic interdependence, as well as the embedding of the counter-movement of planning as an alternative to capitalism, that made his functional alternative of vital importance to the search for a more peaceful and prosperous world. It is to this functional approach that we now turn.

## Planning for a new order. Functional alternatives to federalism and the nation state

David Mitrany is the scholar most associated with the development of the functional approach to international order, and indeed it was his work between the 1930s and the 1970s that did the most to develop a coherent functional international theory. That said, it was actually Harold Laski who was probably the first major expert to apply functional ideas to the problems of the international system.[169] Here Laski was taking an idea that had been earlier applied to domestic politics. In 1911 Mitrany's mentor L.T. Hobhouse had used the concept of function as a social purpose that a society needs fulfilled. He then used this to justify a centre-left interpretation of liberalism, in which individuals and groups in society carry out a range of different functions that allow society to operate.[170] After the war the idea of function was picked up by the British left, and became part of guild socialism, which advocated workers control of industry.[171] It can also be found in the work of the American management theorist Mary Parker Follett.[172] This also influenced H.G. Wells, who even sketched a guild socialist society (and went so far as to have one of his characters mention Laski) in his 1922 novel *Men Like Gods*. Laski then applied the idea to international governance. Basic to Laski's view of the international was that, in order to prevent future wars it was necessary to understand that the political, economic and social functions of global governance were intertwined, and that economics now played a central role in international affairs.[173] Thus, the question of the management of global affairs was now more complex than the old state-based diplomatic system was able to handle. Along with a fully functioning League of Nations system that included functional organisations like the International Labour Office (ILO), Laski advocated the development of a multitude of contacts across state boundaries 'outside the Foreign Offices of the State'. There was an urgent need for the development of an 'international administration' based not on the centralised power of the state, but on the many technical issues that now dominated international relations. Laski hoped that these functional links would allow problems to be solved before they became linked to wider political issues, and thus potential causes of war.[174]

As a student of Hobhouse and a friend of Laski's, it is probably little wonder that Mitrany was familiar with the idea of function and how it could be applied to international organisation. His turn towards functions based on needs as a basis of government also fit with his rejection of the idea that government could be based on reason. This idea he had taken from his other mentor at the London School of Economics, Graham Wallas. Wallas saw reason as a faculty that we brought in to justify our choices, and instead viewed politics as a product of social urges and entities.[175] Mitrany's view that modern society was based on fulfilling human needs, and that the future of global government lay in constructing functional organisations around human needs, was therefore a product of influences from Hobhouse, Wallas and Laski. Yet, Mitrany had also found corroboration for the idea of functional government from his earlier work on peasant agriculture and wartime government in south-eastern Europe.[176] His studies of peasant agriculture and war government had demonstrated to him how the economic means of production were not a separate apolitical world dominated by questions of efficiency, but were rather embedded in wider social and political concerns. The concentration in much economic theory on production efficiencies were, for Mitrany, misplaced. Rather his Balkan experience had shown him that the major problems in both peasant economics and war government were distribution and the related concern of whether human needs were being fulfilled.

What attracted Mitrany to the idea of international functional government was that it offered answers to the problems already discussed above of economic maldistribution in raw materials, population, trade and finance without interfering with the vexed problem of boundaries. It also offered a solution to the problems of conflict and war through the satisfaction of human needs, rather than through appeals to reason. It was, in this sense, a pragmatic solution to the problem of war that would by-pass the problems of national pride and even the vexed question of who had the right to own property. Mitrany's functional approach was also a third way in the debate between a *laissez-faire* free market system based on private property, and the idea of public ownership. For Mitrany the ideal remained the compromise that he saw working in peasant societies and in wartime government: where the property was privately owned, but production was carried out for a public good, not for private ones.

Mitrany's first articulation of a functional approach to the problem of the international came in 1933,[177] but it was not until a decade later, after the publication of his pamphlet *A Working Peace System* that his ideas reached a wider audience interested in the problems of post-war reconstruction. The ethos of the piece was a deep pessimism with both the form of the sovereign state system and with current constitutional and legalistic plans for solving the problem of war. This pessimism was not unique to Mitrany, and in fact was a hallmark of much of inter-war thinking in Britain,[178] but what was different about Mitrany was his scepticism about the possibilities of establishing a strong overarching 'political' security organisation along the lines of the old League of Nations. Thus Mitrany's functional approach should be seen as a response to both the doubts about the stability of a system of power politics and a pessimism about the League as a solution to the failings of power politics. According to Mitrany, the League failed because it was a far too rigid and formal structure that owed its shape to nineteenth century ideas of government, where security and policing were the primary concerns of government (the so-called 'nightwatchman state').[179]

The underlying argument of Mitrany's functional approach was that the first half of the twentieth century was witnessing major changes in both the form of the state and in expectations of what the state was expected to accomplish. These changes would also affect the form of international relations and Mitrany believed that any system of world politics based upon older principles of government would be insufficiently adaptable and thus doomed to failure. The central idea here was the change in the nature of the state from a primarily legalistic and constitutional 'nightwatchman' role, to a state based on services and the solving of practical problems of need and welfare regardless of their constitutional legality. He saw the nineteenth century concern with the constitutional constraint of authority as a necessary stage in human development that curbed arbitrary power and defined the relationship of the individual to the state. However, this nineteenth century political revolution was not able to address the serious social concerns that were being thrown up by recent industrial development.[180] The welfare state was replacing the nightwatchman state.[181] Where the earlier nineteenth century inspired constitutional government had stressed national difference as the basis for defining individual constitutional authorities (based on peoples), the new social politics involved solving issues of human need that often could only be effectively solved through international cooperation (indeed, Mitrany saw national planning and attempts to solve these social problems on an individual state level as a potential cause of further friction and war between states[182]). This gave a boost to international organisations designed to deal with special social and economic problems, and hence 'the lines of national and international evolution are not parallel, but converging'.[183] Thus, for Mitrany, new forms of government were developing that were centred on needs, rather than rational legal formulas, and that this needed to be reflected on the international stage as well.

It was for this reason that Mitrany rejected federalism as a solution to global problems. Federalism was a solution based on the old nineteenth century ideas of legal–constitutional government, failed to deal directly with problems of need, merely created larger states capable of fighting even more bloody wars, and was anyway naïve since the effort needed to integrate all levels of government simultaneously would be too long, involved, and likely to stir up national tensions. The form of the functional alternative, instead, is defined by the specific problems that it sets out to solve, and functional organisations are built up around specific social functions that are attempting to fulfil a single or narrow set of human needs. 'The problem of our generation', Mitrany wrote, 'is how to weld together the common interests of all without interfering with the particular ways of each.'[184] It was here that the constitutionalism of the federalist and League enthusiasts had come unstuck. The essential principle of the functional approach was to 'weld together' only those common interests that did not interfere with these particular ways. As a result, 'activities would be selected specifically and organised separately, each according to its nature, to the conditions under which it has to operate, and to the needs of the moment'.[185] Thus, functional organisations dealt with technical issues of need fulfilment, and their extent and scope were dictated by the requirements of the function in question. 'The functional *dimensions*', Mitrany argued, 'determine themselves. In a like manner the function determines its appropriate *organs*. It also reveals through practice the nature of the action required under the given conditions, and in that way the *powers* needed by the respective authority.'[186] In terms of principles of government, therefore, the functional approach would attempt to do internationally what the new service and welfare states were doing nationally: solve specific problems through the establishment of narrowly problem-focused international organisations that would evolve as the issue itself evolved.

Thus Mitrany's functional approach simultaneously attempted to deal with the problems thrown up by interdependence, and also tried to use this new global interdependence to create an interlocking set of global authorities that would make war less possible by satisfying global needs and robbing the state of its ability to mobilise all its economic, social and technical power for total war.[187] The scope and nature of international functional organisations would be defined by the scope and nature of the function itself. Thus air travel would be global, and would require an International Civil Aviation Organisation (ICAO) to regulate it, river basins could be regulated by an authority representing all the jurisdictions that shared the river, while train travel could be organised continentally, as is currently the case with RailNetEurope (RNE) at the moment. Mitrany already had a ready template for his idea of functional organisations in the Public International Unions discussed in Chapter 5, as well as the specialised agencies of the League of Nations. His ideas were also later to influence many of the functional organisations of both the United Nations system and what would later become the European Union. To a certain extent Mitrany's view of global governance via functional organisations has become a reality, and much of what passes for international relations in the technical, scientific, infrastructural, social, cultural and economic fields today are carried out by functional organisations.

It was immediately clear to Mitrany's contemporaries that *A Working Peace System* was an attack on the federalist solution to the problem of global governance and war. Advocates of federalism were critical of Mitrany's lack of a central political organisation.[188] Yet, despite these attacks Mitrany's ideas of international functionalism became widely accepted in British circles. Peter Wilson has even argued that the popularity of the functional approach in 1940s Britain was partially responsible for the decline in federalist thought in the UK after 1945.[189] There was, however, one group of theorists who were attracted to Mitrany's functional ideas for the reason that he rejected the 'utopianism' of federation, and accepted the problems and constraints posed by power relations and non-rational factors. These were the classical realists, who began to emerge during the 1930s and 1940s. E.H. Carr developed a functionalist solution to the problem of European order, although he failed to cite Mitrany.[190] John Herz, while he was concerned that a functionalist approach did not always take into consideration the importance of conflicts over power, thought that it could contribute to solving international problems.[191] Hans J. Morgenthau was far more enthusiastic than Herz, and his work has frequent references to functionalist solutions to global problems. Indeed, Morgenthau even wrote a preface for the 1966 American reissue of *A Working Peace System*.[192] This does not mean that all classical realists were supportive of Mitrany. Some, like the pro-federalist Georg Schwarzenberger, were hostile (although Mitrany reciprocated, once describing Schwarzenberger as 'a slimy little Germanic worm and I don't know who pays for or buys this kind of book'[193]). That said, while there might be disagreements between them on the role of power in political life, there were ties that bound both Mitrany's solution to the problem of global governance and many classical realist ideas, as we shall see in the next section.

## The power of power politics in an international society of states

In the early twentieth century there were three main ways of seeing power politics. At one extreme there were those like Mahan or Kjellén who saw the clash of powerful states as natural. On the other were those, such as the stricter pacifists like Arthur Ponsonby or Helena Swanwick, who denounced this system as irredeemably immoral. Between these poles were those who accepted that power politics was the natural resting place of international affairs in the absence of governmental structures and a proper system of international organisation. This group, which included such writers as Leonard Woolf, Nicholas Murray Butler, Norman Angell and G. Lowes Dickinson, among others, often believed that power politics (or the international anarchy, as it was frequently called) should be reformed and abolished, but accepted that it existed in any system that prioritised national interests and sovereignty over a system of international government based on international organisations. Throughout the 1930s and 1940s a group emerged that, in many respects, rested midway between this middle group and the extremes of Mahan and Kjellén. While less sure about the possibilities of international government, and therefore more inclined to see power politics as an immediate necessity that had to be faced and understood, they were still committed to reaching beyond the system of selfish sovereign nation states – whether this was via a functioning international society or some kind of reform that accepted the current realities of state power and interests. This group, which included a large number of émigrés from fascist Europe, was to form what would later be known as the classical realist and the English School traditions in post-1945 IR. Among their number was Nicholas Spykman, whose work has already been discussed above. While responsible for much of the theoretical groundwork of what we know as the contemporary realist tradition, they matched this concern for understanding power politics with normative arguments about the possible future direction of a world that would ameliorate, or even eliminate, power politics. In this sense, there was not as much distance between them and the works of people like Leonard Woolf as we might first assume. Yet, their concentration on the study of power politics still marks them out as significantly different in their approach.

What probably initially distinguished this group of early classical realists (and English School associates) from others writing at the time was their development of the idea of peaceful change, along with the concept of a difference between have and have-not states. Peaceful change had been the subject of the 1937 International Studies Conference (ISC) in Paris, and preparations for that conference resulted in the publication of two books, both with the title *Peaceful Change*, prepared and published on opposite sides of the Atlantic. One, published in Britain under the editorship of Charles Manning, was an edited collection bringing together the work of eight separate authors. The other, written by Frederick Sherwood Dunn of Yale University's Institute of International Studies, was a single-authored work that constituted the official report to the ISC of the American Coordinating Committee. Dunn began the work by distinguishing between two reasons for conflict between states. The first set were conflicts over what a state feels it is entitled to under the current status quo, while the others were conflicts that are aimed at changing the status quo. Dunn argued that the bulk of the work carried out to build a 'workable peace system' since 1919 had concentrated on conflicts of the first kind: those over rights under the current state of the world. The problem for Dunn was the second set: resolving peacefully conflicts that resulted from challenges to the current world order. These disputes that challenged the status quo necessarily involved a clash between two kinds of great power: the 'haves' that possessed adequate access to raw materials, access to relief from population pressures and control of colonial territories; and the 'have-nots', who lacked these conditions.[194] Peaceful change, therefore, aimed at dealing with the second set of conflicts, and consequently was a necessary addition to the collective security arrangements designed to deal with the first set.

In the end Dunn dismisses the argument that Germany, Japan and Italy are 'have-not' powers, pointing out that not only are there weaker states not seeking a change in the status quo, but that much of the problems outlined could be solved by a return to free trade. There is, though, a major issue of concern for Dunn: the problem of competition between states over relative power. The central issue is that, without some kind of international government that can manage global issues and foster some kind of sense of common purpose, states will be guided by self-interest and conflicts of power. With international machinery it would be possible to simultaneously give states the confidence not to pursue the accumulation of power for security, while reducing economic tensions through the promotion of global free trade.[195] In the absence of these the problems of peaceful change to the status quo would have to be dealt with through voluntary methods of diplomacy, conciliation, compromise and the marshalling of public opinion. Because these are voluntary though, states will always be able to opt out of these.[196] Unlike some post-1945 realists Dunn did not see the current problem of peaceful change as an older problem rooted in the laws of history, but rather as one that had its origins in 'the great technological advances of the nineteenth century' that had created the new economic networks that had burst the bounds of the sovereign state.[197] Thus the problems that dogged the power relations of states in the twentieth century were rooted in economic relations, and especially in the need to safeguard raw materials in both peace and war time. There is even a nod in Dunn's work to the arguments of the critics of capitalism. The need for international machinery to regulate and safeguard free trade was for Dunn a direct result of the work of national 'vested interests' that work against the establishment of free trade in the self-help state system.[198] In the final analysis it is the mix of a recently globalised economy (with the associated scramble for raw materials) and a state system dominated by the struggle over relative power that is the problem for Dunn. In the short-term he sees only voluntary arrangements as the likely tools for the promotion of peaceful change. Thus, in the foreseeable future the system remains unstable.

Not a dissimilar conclusion on peaceful change came from the British-based South African academic Charles Manning. Dunn had certainly been aware of Manning's work by at least 1939, since in that year he reviewed Manning's edited collection on *Peaceful Change*;[199] although it is more than likely that they were already acquainted via the 1937 International Studies Conference.

Active in the establishment of IR as a university discipline in Britain, Hidemi Suganami has even argued that Manning's influence on the direction that British IR took in the years after 1945 was 'decisive'.[200] Arguably he was an important influence on Hedley Bull, Martin Wight, Fred Northedge and Alan James. While his vision of a separate discipline of IR, distinct from both history and political science, proved unobtainable,[201] his concept of an international society living by certain international norms and rules even while its constituent parts remained sovereign and separate has remained a (albeit much modified) central part of the study of IR in Britain and beyond. A supporter of the League of Nations (Manning briefly worked for the League), he was critical of attempts by League supporters to set up a more legally binding system of collective security: the so-called 'closing of the gaps' in the Covenant discussed in the last chapter. That said, he supported the idea of the League as a club of states maintaining a weaker but more realistic system of collective security.[202] Looking back in 1975 Manning argued that his attempts to understand the nature of international affairs was in order to bring an 'understanding of things' to those he had met while working at the League (referred to by Manning as the 'children of light'). He hoped that his work would support those attempting to build a better and more peaceful world.[203] In this sense, Manning seemed happy with the League as already laid out in the Covenant in 1919. While Manning's vision of an IR separate from political science was alien to Dunn's view of an IR with political science at its core, yet there are also similarities with how they interpreted the world in the lead-up to the Second World War.

For Manning the initial problem with peaceful change was the failure to understand what it should be in a society of states. There was a widespread understanding that collective security needed some kind of peaceful change in order to replace force as the main means of affecting change between states. The problem was that peaceful change was framed as a legal problem: as a means of doing what is just. Rather, Manning argued, it needed to be seen as a response to 'pressure groups' and 'social forces', in other words as a product of interests. Rather than attempting (as would the legalistic approach) to solve a problem once and for all, peaceful change needed to be seen as a process that allowed breathing spaces for compromises between the parties involved. In this sense the notion of peaceful change would be very different from the notion of dispute settlement in domestic politics. Rather than the final and legal pronouncement of a legislature, international peaceful change would be the product of compromise within an international society of states (Manning here makes reference to the compromises found during the days of the concert of Europe).[204] Manning's return to the idea of the concert of Europe is a demonstration of the major differences between his own views and those of his contemporaries such as Woolf, Lowes Dickinson, Angell and Brailsford to be found on the centre and left of the political spectrum. For the left liberals discussed in the last chapter the 'international anarchy' of the concert of Europe was an unsustainable system that needed to be replaced by a new system of global governance based on principles found in domestic politics. For Manning the society of states (properly regulated in a loose structure such as the original League Covenant) was capable of stability. An international society of sovereign states fulfilling their obligations under international law was not just a possibility, but was an apt description of an international society of states that was radically different from domestic politics.[205] In this sense, Manning opposed the attempt to bring domestic norms into international affairs via legal changes to the structure of the League. In doing so he presented a model of a stable international society at variance with the 'international anarchy' ideas popular between the wars.[206] Most of this work, however, would not be fully developed in Manning's thought until after 1945.

Peaceful change also remained central to the international thought of the holder of the other professorial chair in British IR in the 1930s: E.H. Carr. Carr considered himself a friend to Manning,[207] and was the author of one of the best known IR texts from the 1930s. Indeed Carr in 1939 had hailed the September 1938 Munich Agreement as an example of successful peaceful change. Unlike Dunn, Carr was more willing to accept Germany's claim to be a have-not power, and in the 1930s he had endorsed the idea that Germany should be given a free-hand in eastern Europe as a way of lessening tensions between Germany and the 'Have' powers of Britain and France.[208] Unlike Manning, much has been written on Carr, and the wealth of secondary sources mean that his ideas have been both explored in detail and also been the subject of scholarly debates.[209] There were five main elements to Carr's thinking in the later 1930s and early 1940s. These were: the problem of public opinion; the split between 'have' and 'have-not' powers that also concerned Toynbee; the problem of the harmony of interests as applied to the relations between states; the nature of peaceful change under these conditions; and the prospects for the post-war (and post-national) world to come.

For Carr, writing in 1936, the crucial disconnect in much of the discussion in Britain on the problems of international order was rooted in a disconnect between the schemes of intellectuals and the position of 'the man in the street'. The rationalism of intellectuals leads them to assume that having a plan is the same as having a system. Quoting Charles Manning, Carr uses the example of a showman who has a plan for a display of elephants flying in formation. Having this plan will not, however, get the elephants to fly. In terms of international relations, these intellectuals assume that changes to the legal wording of the League's Covenant will lead to a new system of international intercourse. What they do not realise is that public opinion in Britain is less concerned about the legal structures of the League, and far more about the moral and emotional appeal of the League. The desire of British public opinion for peace means that they will oppose legal international machinery that will lead to wars in the name of collective security. Since politicians realise that they cannot propose international commitments that the public will not support, the realities of British foreign policy will never approximate the rational and legal schemes of the intellectuals. However much the showman perfects his plan, his elephants can never fly.[210] The problem was, as Carr would later state in *The Twenty Years' Crisis*, that while the nineteenth century liberals were probably right that public opinion would ultimately prevail, they were wrong to assume that it would be a force for rational decision making.[211] Two points from Carr's view of public opinion stand out here: that public opinion is moral and emotional, rather than rational; and that this moral and emotive response is more in touch with the realities of foreign policy than the rational and legalistic plans of the intellectuals.[212] Thus, from the 1930s onwards Carr took an increasingly different line from those (such as the liberal–socialists, or Robert Cecil) who saw the closing of the gaps in the Covenant as the solution to the problem of global order and international conflict.

If public opinion could be relied upon to oppose the use of force on emotive and moral grounds, this still left a problem for Carr. Post-1919 foreign affairs were dominated by the issue of the rights and wrongs of the peace treaties, and especially the Treaty of Versailles with Germany. The 1919 peace had been a product of democracy, and its opposition was correspondingly anti-democratic.[213] The problem was how to allow revisions of the treaties that would minimise the threats to democracy without at the same time encouraging wars for the revision of the treaties. There was, in short, a need for a means of peaceful change. Related to the question of peaceful change for Carr were the issues of the conflict between the 'have' and 'have-not' powers, and his criticism of the application of the nineteenth century liberal notion of the harmony of interests to international relations (on the harmony of interests see below). Underlying this was a deep-seated sense in Carr that Germany had been poorly treated by the Allied powers after 1918, and that one priority of British foreign policy in the late 1930s was the correcting of the wrongs imposed on Germany. As a result, Carr's concept of peaceful change came to be increasingly linked to one interpretation of the policy of appeasement. Although, as discussed above, Carr's notion of appeasement was crucially different from the approach taken by Chamberlain; and here, as I will discuss below, Carr became an unwitting victim of the tendency he had noted of intellectuals to apply a rational plan to an international sphere dominated by emotive and moral concerns.

Peaceful change for Carr meant, in the short run, reaching diplomatic compromises with Germany and other 'have-not' powers. In the first edition of *Twenty Years' Crisis* Carr wrote:

> If the power relations of Europe in 1938 made it inevitable that Czecho-Slovakia should lose part of its territory and eventually its independence, it was preferable … that this should come about as the result of discussions round a table in Munich.[214]

In effect Carr interpreted peaceful change as the unfolding of the same contest over power that had been the mark of the concert of Europe, but that war and the threat of war had been replaced by diplomacy. He was clearly less concerned than Toynbee that this would not mean sacrifices made by the 'have' great powers, but rather territorial concessions being forced on smaller powers. Carr's concern here was with both correcting the mistakes of Versailles, and ameliorating Germany's have-not status. It was here that Carr's attack on the harmony of interests came in. The utopian, Carr argued, assumes that ethics are prior to politics, and that we can come to a common set of interests via a rational understanding of what is right. The realist, on the other hand, sees politics as prior to ethics, and consequently that interests based on power clash.[215] In terms of the crisis of the 1930s this meant that not all states necessarily had the same interest in peace. 'Have' states clearly had a greater interest in peace and the status quo than did the 'have-not' powers. By recognising this it would be possible to organise negotiations that would ameliorate these differences, and hopefully save the peace by appeasing 'have-not' powers.[216] This, for Carr, represented a compromise between morality and power – between utopian and realist. Peaceful change is the recognition of the power relations at play, but it is also about the establishment of common procedures that will eventually build common feeling about what is reasonable, and from this a sense of 'give and take' emerges.[217]

And yet there is an irony here. Carr's argument is well crafted and devastating. His attack on the rationalist ethics of the Victorian age has struck chords with his readers ever since *The Twenty Years' Crisis* was first published in 1939. Yet, Carr had clearly misread the main political actors he was observing in 1938. We now know that Hitler was not willing to be appeased into accepting a new system of peaceful change, while Chamberlain, far from being the dupe of popular versions of the story, was well aware in 1938 that war would come (see the argument at the beginning of this chapter). Carr seems to have taken at face value Chamberlain's public declarations that Munich represented the basis of a new peace. The irony here is that Carr fell victim to the very trap that he accused internationalists of falling into in his 1936 'Public Opinion as a Safeguard of Peace' inaugural address discussed above. He had mistaken the public positions for policy. Criticisms have also been made of Carr's treatment of individual authors in *Twenty Years' Crisis*: His failure to use any of Norman Angell's work published after 1914 being one of many. Even Hans Morgenthau entered the lists against Carr, critical of Carr's conclusions about the Soviet Union, and Carr's apparent collapse of morality into power by endowing powerful forces with moral force.[218] That said, though, *Twenty Years' Crisis* is still a remarkable achievement in terms of IR theory, and justly deserves its status as a classic. His exploration of the balance between power and morality would become an important part of IR theorising in the very different world of the Cold War, despite Morgenthau's misgivings. If we also interpret it as a polemic that employs a complex rhetoric that steers a middle course between dichotomies, as Charles Jones labels and interprets it,[219] then the work can be judged on many different levels: policy relevance, its method, its literary style, as well as its underlying philosophy.

Yet, the split between utopians and realists does not exhaust Carr's contribution to international thought in this period. His wartime writings, which have not received as much attention as *Twenty Years' Crisis* are also important as contributions to the debates on the future of international affairs and the construction of the post-war settlement. Two of his books stand out here: *Conditions of Peace* and *Nationalism and After*. Both are premised on the death of the earlier moral and political order, and in that sense are in the same genre as

Polanyi's *Great Transformation*. Yet, while Polanyi largely looked back to understand the failed system, Carr (after what Haslam called 'a backward and nostalgic glance'[220]) looked forward to the coming peace. There was continuity with *Twenty Years' Crisis*. *Conditions of Peace* sought to lay out a system of justice within Europe that was also backed by power, while *Nationalism and After* wrestled with the attacks on the nation and nationalism from both a position of morality and a position of power. Carr's point of reference is what he saw as the failures of the 1919 peace process, and as a first condition for a more stable peace Carr criticises the 1919 model of peace as a single historical event, and instead interprets peace as a 'continuous process' over a prolonged period of time.[221] Carr foresaw the immediate relief effort in Europe as refocusing concerns on continent-wide issues, rather than national concerns, and as leading to a 'European planning authority' that would be able to solve economic planning problems that were out of the competence of individual nations in Europe.[222] Carr saw the fusing of political and economic power in the new nationally planned states as throwing up many problems, including the world wars, but multi-national and international planning offered a way out of this conundrum.[223] The European planning authority that Carr proposed in 1942 was by 1945 presented as an 'intermediate' and achievable organisation mid-way between the out-dated nation state and the far too utopian world government:

> ... the scope and constitution of different authorities must, on severely practical grounds, be determined according to the purposes which they are required to serve, on the principle of what has become to be called 'functional' instead of national organisation.[224]

This 'intermediate' organisation proposed for the peace of Europe bore a striking resemblance to David Mitrany's functional organisations discussed above, although Carr did not see fit to reference Mitrany here.

Without a doubt E.H. Carr is one of the most influential figures in IR from the late 1930s and early 1940s. His genius lay in his construction of an abstract theory based upon non-rational factors such as power and the moral sentiment of public opinion. From these factors he was able to construct a view of the international that shared much with the functional approach of David Mitrany. Carr was less successful when he applied his thinking to immediate policy issues. He certainly misread the nature of both Stalin and Hitler. In the case of the latter this led to a support for the appeasement policy of the Chamberlain government that misread Chamberlain's intent, took at face value Chamberlain's public pronouncements, and failed to grasp the underlying strategy being followed by the British government. In this sense Carr was a victim of the very tendency that he had criticised in the 'collectivist' supporters of the League, yet since he was not privy to internal government debates about foreign policy this lapse is excusable. As an intellectual he had constructed a view of what the international could be if peaceful change was taken seriously. Chamberlain and other appeasers had paid lip-service to this outlook, but actually had followed a policy that accepted the almost inevitable prospect of war. Rather than being a model for future change, as Carr had hoped, the Munich Agreement had only ever been a breathing space for Britain and France in their campaign to diplomatically isolate Germany in the war that they increasingly saw as inevitable. Even though he was also proved wrong on the post-national future for international affairs, his analysis has received praise for the excellence of his analysis of the nature of nationalism,[225] and his analysis of the imperative for a transnational organisation of Europe predicted the development of European integration in the decades to come.[226]

Carr is still a well-known figure in IR today. The same cannot be said for his British contemporary Georg Schwarzenberger. An expert on international law, his particular brand of pessimism meant that a selective reading of his work could lead a reader to conclude that Schwarzenberger was an advocate of power politics, as Mahan had been in the years before the First World War. In fact, Schwarzenberger's ideas on global order shared a number of assumptions and views of the international with Leonard Woolf. Like Woolf, Schwarzenberger saw power politics as the basic condition of a world dominated by states and nationalist loyalties to states. Like Woolf he also hoped for a way out of this that combined psychological and institutional changes. He also shared Woolf's view that functional organisations alone would not be enough to move the world beyond power politics, preferring the establishment of more direct and political organisations at the global level. That said, there are also differences with Woolf, especially in Schwarzenberger's greater concern with international law, and his stronger emphasis on the need for a change in the patterns of loyalty prior to the establishment of an alternative to power politics. Yet, Schwarzenberger's distance from Mahan is even greater. For Mahan armaments had a moral quality, and the pattern of power politics was a necessary structure for the survival of western civilisation. Schwarzenberger, by contrast, saw few redeeming qualities in power politics, although he saw even fewer immediate opportunities for the development of an alternative system. Interestingly, though, both Mahan and Schwarzenberger ultimately fell back on arguments drawn from Christianity. Here there are strong parallels with Hans J. Morgenthau and John Hertz. Perhaps these parallels are not all that surprising when we consider that all three were émigrés from Nazi Germany, and while Morgenthau was a German liberal, both Schwarzenberger and Hertz had been involved with the German social democratic party (SPD).

It was a concern for the role and limitations of international law that led to Schwarzenberger's interest in international order and power politics. For him the use made of law was dependent on 'the character of the human association' in which law and justice found 'their realisaton'.[227] To understand the nature of law Schwarzenberger used a modified version of the familiar sociological division found in Ferdinand Tönnies (among others) between two different kinds of human association, the first looser than the second: *gessellshaft* and *gemeinshaft*. For Schwarzenberger the distinction was between a society and a community. A community implies solidarity between its members, and the presence of a sense that the interests of the whole group is superior (or encompasses) the interests of the individual units. In a society, by contrast, the interests of the units take priority, and as a result the goal is 'the adjustment of divergent interests'.[228] 'The members of a community are united in spite of their individual existence, whereas the members of a society remain isolated in spite of their association.'[229]

While all law shares common characteristics, it was from this distinction between society and community that Schwarzenberger came up with three forms of law: the laws of power, coordination and reciprocity. The law of power existed in a society, and was marked by the members following their own individual interests, and as a result it was the individual power of each that was central to the nature of the association. Yet, in order to protect their own self-interests the members of a society construct a law to regulate their power relations and stabilise the relations of power, including protecting the society from the aberrant actions of some of its membership. Such a law of power was written for the great powers, and reflected their interests the most strongly. International law for Schwarzenberger fell mainly into the category of a law of power.[230] A full community was associated with the law of coordination. Like the law of power it was also intended to protect its members from aberrant behaviour, but by contrast it served the role of maintaining and developing the integration of the community, putting the shared values ahead of individual interests. As a result this form of law aims to develop the co-ordination of the efforts of all the members of the society for the common good. The laws of power and coordination represented the two extreme ideal poles of law. Between them lay the hybrid law of reciprocity, more common in the domestic politics of individual states, where elements of society and community co-exist. Under the law of reciprocity there is neither 'brutal domination' nor 'superhuman self-negation'. Rather law guarantees equal rights and reciprocal gains in an association in which power is balanced and there is a basic sense of shared interest.[231]

Thus the nature of law depended on the nature of the association in which it existed. In turn whether an association was a society, a community or a mix of both depended for Schwarzenberger mostly on the loyalties and psychological orientation of peoples. Thus, the reason why states formed a society rather than a community was that people's loyalties were primarily with the state (through nationalism), rather than to a wider political community (as had been the case in the European Middle Ages). It would take a psychological shift of loyalties to make out of the system of international organisations an effective international community.[232] This was a reversal of Mitrany's formula that the effective provision of services would create loyalty to the new level of government. Instead Schwarzenberger saw international organisations as empty of political force until there was a change of psychology away from nationalism. This position contained within it the essence of Bernard Bosenquet's idea that government could only extend as far as the general will extended. The difference between Bosenquet and Schwarzenberger was, however, that for Bosenquet the extension of government beyond the general will created oppressive government, while for Schwarzenberger it just translated into weakness. While Bosenquet took the lack of international will as the reason for not trying to establish international institutions, Schwarzenberger – living through a more unstable time – even argued that we should either develop a common loyalty at the international level, or take up Charles Manning's suggestion that statesmen should behave as though there is one.[233]

Nationalism was only one of two problems that Schwarzenberger saw at the root of the power politics of the society of states. The rise of the state had been facilitated by its alliances first with capitalism and then with nationalism.[234] The problems of capitalism and nationalism were linked to the twin cleavages that he saw as the major problems of the twentieth century: the cleavage between national loyalties and international order; and the cleavage between rapid economic interdependence and the much slower growth of our mental capacities[235] – the last point clearly mirroring Norman Angell's concerns in *The Great Illusion*. While Schwarzenberger was dismissive of so many plans for global order, and saw power at the root of international society, he was equally aware of the basic instability of power politics. Like Morgenthau, he saw the balance of power as the root ordering principle of power politics (he described it as 'universal'), but was equally aware that states aim for preponderance, rather than balance. The result is an inherent instability for the balance of power that often leads to war. As a result he argued that 'international anarchy' was an apt description of the international society.[236] Towards the end of *Power Politics* Schwarzenberger turns towards a common Christian ethics as the potential glue for an international (European-based?) community that would, in turn, have an international law with some teeth. Faith, he argued, in the long run was stronger than interests.[237]

Questions of faith and interest also intersected in the work of Reinhold Niebuhr on the other side of the Atlantic, although Niebuhr appears to have been more of an influence on Carr than on Schwarzenberger.[238] Niebuhr, along with Frederick Schuman, John Herz, Quincy Wright and Hans Morgenthau, was part of a growing group of writers in the United States that were interested in analysing the problems of international relations. This group would, with others, form what we now know as the early classical realist thinkers in American IR, and Niebuhr was generally recognised within this group as (in the words of George Kennan) 'the father of all of us'.[239] To Niebuhr the central problem of human societies was that, while individuals were capable of moral behaviour because they can sacrifice themselves, collectivities and societies of people were not. Rather, groups, including states, are amoral entities whose power can only be checked by another countervailing power.[240] The reason for this duality lay in the twin impulses in humans to be both moral and social. Our sociability, rooted in the desire to find security, led us to form groups that conflicted with our desire as individuals to be moral.[241] Thus a society of societies, such as the world of states, will be a fundamentally amoral one. States, and other societies, offer their members security, but after a time this security degrades to despotism, which in turn brings calls for revolts and calls for justice. There is, therefore an unstable equilibrium between security and justice: '… the same force which guarantees peace also makes for injustice'.[242]

In attacking what he saw as a rationalism rooted in the illusion that institutions were capable of improving individuals, Niebuhr effectively reversed Hobbes' view of human nature and society. For Hobbes the violent state of nature created by the existence of unsocial individuals could only be tamed by the creation of an authority that could impose a moral and legal order. Thus, the security of the leviathan allowed for the development of morality and the arts. Niebuhr reversed this relationship, seeing instead an innate spiritual morality in the individual that is superseded in communities formed out of the desire to security. Thus security and justice remain in an unresolved antimony throughout human political history. This dual nature of humanity plays itself out in Niebuhr's subsequent writings. It is our spiritual side that can also exacerbate the power struggles inherent in politics by causing us to reach beyond mere physical survival in order to strive for prestige and social approval.[243] It was here that Niebuhr developed his distinction between 'the children of light' and 'the children of darkness' – a duality that shares more than a passing resemblance to Mackinder's idealist and organiser ideal policy-maker types, and E.H. Carr's split between utopian and realist science. For Niebuhr the children of light recognise moral codes and are generally unselfish, and as a result they are naïve and often do not understand their best interests. The children of darkness, like Mackinder's organisers, understand self-interest and are manipulative. Like Mackinder and Carr, Niebuhr argues that the children of light need to be armed with the cleverness and understanding of the children of darkness without falling into the trap of a narrow malice.[244] The danger with developing a better understanding of the power-driven aspects of our natures was always a descent into a cynicism that was a hallmark of the children of darkness. After the war Niebuhr made this point in a dramatic comparison between British and German policy before the war. Yes British claims that its policy transcended self-interests were often hypocritical, while the German policy was blatantly cynical in its stated object of abandoning moral principle. Yet, the very appeal to moral principle gave British policy a strength which the German lacked.[245]

The problems of this duality were exacerbated by global economic interdependence, which increased the points of contact between people without necessarily increasing mutual trust and respect. Niebuhr was at pains to point out that interdependence alone could not guarantee the spread of a pacific world community, and that particularistic forces were stronger than naïve supporters of a univeralist future understood.[246] Even the hunt for security through the amassing of power increased the points of contact between both individuals and nations.[247] Here, though, Niebuhr saw hope in the practices and institutions of democracy. While it was the children of light who had established democracy, the system itself did justice to both the spiritual and social sides of the human character by supporting both the uniqueness and variety of life and the common necessities of humans as a whole. 'An ideal democratic order seeks unity within the conditions of freedom; and maintains freedom within the framework of order.'[248] His long-term prognosis for international order was less optimistic. While he saw a world community as the endpoint to which historical forces were driving us, it remained both possibility and impossibility at the same time because of the particularistic forces present in the world. In the final lines of *The Children of Light and the Children of Darkness*, Niebuhr leaves the accomplishment of this goal to the 'Divine Power' whose resources are 'greater than those of men'.[249]

While Niebuhr's Christian faith – and corresponding hope for a divine intervention to deal with the paradox of human political existence – was not necessarily shared with his fellow American and German–American classical realists, there was common agreement that much of the political problems faced by humanity were rooted in the often paradoxical relationship between interests and ethics. The one exception here is the figure of Waldemar Gurian, a devout Catholic and classical realist who, through his editorship of *The Review of Politics* pushed a classical realist position throughout the 1940s.[250] Whether religious or secular, the American classical realists also shared an unease about the scientific and quantitative methods that were beginning to take hold of the social sciences in the United States. Indeed, it was this disquiet that would be a catalyst for the formation of the committees and conferences that would form a distinctly classical realist IR in the United States after the Second World War. Yet, while Niebuhr was an inspiration to writers who would later identify themselves as realists during the 1930s and 1940s, and are now often referred to in the current IR literature as classical realists, that inspiration often led to different interpretations of both interest and power. In the case of Morgenthau, Herz and Schuman those interpretations had a distinctly secular quality. Morgenthau has been the subject of numerous appraisals and reappraisals in the last few decades, while Herz has recently been rediscovered and re-evaluated by IR scholars. Schuman is less well known in IR today, although his textbook on IR (first published in 1933) remained a standard textbook in the United States well into the 1950s.[251] A proper discussion of Morgenthau and Herz, however, does not belong in this chapter, since their major works on IR theory did not appear until after 1945. A short summary of the rise of classical realism in the United States and of the English School in Britain can be found in the next chapter.

## Conclusion

As the Second World War drew to a close the lessons in the lead up to the conflict did not point in any specific direction (despite the later textbook myth that it had somehow 'proved' a realist paradigm 'right'). Rather, there were several groups of scholars all drawing different lessons from the conflict. Arnold Toynbee, at the head of an influential British source of foreign policy research, was using his knowledge of history and archaeology to construct a longer-term view of the prospects for western civilisation. Political geographers, led by Isaiah Bowman, Derwent Whittlesey and Halford Mackinder, had constructed a world-view that was currently influencing both the Allied prosecution of the war and arguably dominating discussions about post-war planning in the United States. Figures on the left, especially H.N. Brailsford, Harold Laski and Karl Polanyi, were developing approaches to the international that placed the current crisis within a broader political economic failure of the contemporary global system of capitalism. David Mitrany had laid the seeds of what would later become the functional approach in world politics by suggesting that a new globalised social life required a radically different form of global governance based on functions. In addition to this, in both Britain and the United States scholars (some of whom were émigrés from Nazi Germany) had started to argue that the power political system that had often been pegged as the cause of the problems of the twentieth century, might be more durable, useable and capable of reform than previously thought. In addition to these strands, many influential writers from earlier decades were still dominating the debates on the nature of the international and the prospects for post-war reconstruction. Writers like Leonard Woolf, Norman Angell and Hugh Dalton were actively engaged in the cottage industry of speculating on the post-war order. There was no particular strand that was stronger than the others at the time, and there was certainly no sense that a realist power political approach had been vindicated. Indeed, in the United States the opposite appeared to be the case. In a 1944 article in *The Review of Politics* (a journal used by early classical realists edited by Waldemar Gurian) Hans Rommen saw the rising trend in the study of world affairs being what he called 'Utopianism'. Utopianism was defined as an approach that rejected sovereignty and power politics, and instead advocated regional federations and a system of international politics based on law. This was, for Rommen, an unsurprising response to the current military struggle, even if it was (in his view) based on error.[252] Looking back at 1945 from 1951, John Herz confirmed Rommen's view, arguing that the end of the war was 'an era of somewhat greater hopefulness' that saw 'planning for a brave new united world'. Herz saw his role back then as stressing the 'power facts' that were being overlooked. By contrast, by 1951 'the pendulum has swung to the other side'.[253]

Thus, there was no clear sign on how the study of world affairs would play out in the decades to come. Perhaps the smart money in the United States would have been on the political geographers. Mackinder had been rediscovered, Whittlesey was making a name for himself as a critic of German geopolitics, and Bowman was a senior advisor to the United States government. Non-geographers, such as the Yale professor Nicholas Spykman had discovered political geography, and was busy applying it to a power politics approach. What is more, their ideas that linked a geo-strategic literacy to the need to establish a liberal global order built on the power of the 'Big Three' Allied powers, seemed to catch the current realities of both global developments and the mood of the population and its political leadership. Yet, under the surface there were structural weaknesses in political geography. Isaiah Bowman, its major figure, worked against the establishment of a political geography community in the United States, and American Geography itself, under such key figures as Richard Hartshorne, was moving towards a less controversial definition of itself in which there was little place for political geography in the immediate future.[254] Other approaches were clearly up and coming. David Mitrany's functional approach, despite opposition from federalists, influenced the debate in the immediate post-war period in

Britain, and would later catch on in the United States after the 1966 publication of a collection of his essays (with an introduction from Hans Morgenthau) in the United States. Indeed, Peter Wilson has argued that Mitrany, along with Carr, was instrumental in undermining the older federalist tradition in Britain, steering much of the debate away from federal union towards the study of functional international organisations.[255] On the left the works of Laski and Polanyi particularly had caught the general anti-capitalist and pro-planning mood of the wartime generation, especially in Britain where the establishment of a welfare state had begun in earnest. The decline of an old-fashioned liberal capitalist order seemed as certain as the defeat of fascism.

Yet, despite this pluralism, a decade later it would be the classical realists in the United States and what would later be called the English School in the UK that would dominate the new university discipline of IR. The reasons for this change can be found in the peculiar conditions of late 1940s and early 1950s university life, not in the more diverse intellectual atmosphere of the 1930s and early 1940s. In this sense, while the inter-war period and wartime conditions left their imprint on future IR, it was the post-war decades that chose which of these approaches present before 1945 would eventually dominate in the seminar rooms and the lecture halls of the Anglophone universities.

## Notes

1  For an description of this event using eye witness accounts see Richard Overy, *The Road to War* (London: Vintage, 2009), 81–2.
2  Andrew Heywood, *Global Politics* (Houndmills: Palgrave Macmillan, 2011), 35.
3  John T. Rourke, *International Politics on the World Stage*, twelfth edition (New York: McGraw-Hill, 2008), 45.
4  Robert Jackson and Georg Sørensen, *Introduction to International Relations* (Oxford: Oxford University Press, 2007), 5.
5  Joshua S. Goldstein and Jon C. Pevehouse, *International Relations* (New York: Pearson, 2009), 28.
6  Bruce Russett and Harvey Starr, *World Politics. The Menu for Choice* (New York: Freeman, 2000), 25.
7  Michael G. Roskin and Nicholas O. Berry, *IR. The New World of International Relations* (London: Pearson, 2010), 203.
8  Len Scott, 'International History 1900–90', in J. Baylis, S. Smith and P. Owens (eds), *The Globalization of World Politics* (Oxford: Oxford University Press, 2011), 53.
9  Joseph S. Nye, *Understanding International Conflicts* (New York: Pearson, 2007), 110.
10  Nye, *Understanding*, 111.
11  Chris Brown with Kirsten Ainley, *Understanding International Relations* (Houndmills: Palgrave Macmillan, 2005), 28.
12  See Lucian M. Ashworth, *Creating International Studies: Angell, Mitrany and the Liberal Tradition* (Aldershot: Ashgate, 1999), ch. 5; Lucian M. Ashworth, 'Did the Realist–Idealist Great Debate Really Happen?', *International Relations*, 16(1), 2002, 33–51; and Lucian M. Ashworth, *International Relations and the Labour Party: Intellectuals and Policy Making from 1918–1945* (London: IB Tauris, 2007).
13  Peter Wilson, 'Where are we now in the Debate about the Great Debate?', in Brian C. Schmidt (ed.), *International Relations and the First Great Debate* (London: Routledge, 2012), 144.
14  'Cato', *Guilty Men* (London: Victor Gollancz, 1941).

15 On this story see Robert Fisk, *In Time of War: Ireland, Ulster and the Price of Neutrality 1939–1945* (London: Deutsch, 1983).

16 See, for example, the correspondence quoted in Robert Self, *Neville Chamberlain. A Biography* (Aldershot: Ashgate, 2009), 304.

17 See, for example, H.N. Brailsford, 'The Tory Policy of Peace', *Political Quarterly*, 1938, 9(3), 311–29; 'Vigilantes' [Konnie Zilliacus], *Inquest on Peace. An Analysis of the National Government's Foreign Policy* (London: Victor Gollancz, 1935).

18 Richard Overy with Andrew Wheatcroft, *The Road to War* (London: Vintage, 2009), 107.

19 Self, *Neville Chamberlain*, 299–300.

20 Indeed, the first of Sid Meier's *Civilization* series of video games rated you alongside Neville Chamberlain if you did particularly badly at the game.

21 Self, *Neville Chamberlain*, 297.

22 Self, *Neville Chamberlain*, 294.

23 See the discussion in Julian Jackson, *The Fall of France: The Nazi Invasion of 1940* (Oxford: Oxford University Press, 2001), 12–21.

24 Overy, *Road to War*, 109; Self, *Neville Chamberlain*, 297.

25 Overy, *Road to War*, 121.

26 Overy, *Road to War*, 121, 133, 184–5, 67–70, 233.

27 Labour Party Advisory Committee on International Questions (ACIQ), 'The Flight From Collective Security', memo no. 486a, March 1938. Labour Party Archives, Manchester.

28 Self, *Neville Chamberlain*, 295.

29 For a discussion of this switch see Lucian M. Ashworth, *International Relations and the Labour Party*, 143–5.

30 Overy, *Road to War*, 277.

31 Overy, *Road to War*, 283.

32 David Reynolds, *From World War to Cold War* (Oxford: Uxford University Press. 2006), 144–5.

33 Ashworth, *International Relations and the Labour Party*, 137–9.

34 See the wider study of Labour's developing foreign policy in Henry R. Winkler, *Labour Seeks a Foreign Policy* (Somerset, NJ: Transaction, 2004).

35 For a discussion of this see: Lucian M. Ashworth, 'Feminism, War and the Prospects for Peace. Helena Swanwick (1864–1939) and the Lost Feminists of Inter-War International Relations', *International Feminist Journal of Politics*, 2011, 13(1), 25–43.

36 Overy, *Road to War*, 123.

37 E.H. Carr, 'Public Opinion as a Safeguard of Peace', *International Affairs*, 1936, 15(6), 846–62.

38 Reynolds, *World War to Cold War*, 24.

39 Jackson, *The Fall of France*, 196.

40 See Anthony Cumming, 'The Navy and the Battle for Britain', *BBC History*, April 2010, 35–9.

41 On this balance see Jackson, *Fall of France*. For a summary of the position in 1940 see Laurence Rees, 'Hitler's Greatest Gamble', *BBC History*, May 2010, 22–9. See also Reynolds, *World War to Cold War*, ch. 2. There are also many recent military histories on the fall of France.

42 See the discussion in Reynolds, *World War to Cold War*.

43 Oswald Spengler, *The Decline of the West, vol. 1: Form and Actuality* (George Allen & Unwin: London, 1926) and *The Decline of the West, vol. 2: Perspectives of World-history* (London: George Allen & Unwin, 1928).

44 Richard Overy, *The Morbid Age. Britain and the Crisis of Civilization 1919–1939* (London: Penguin, 2010), 34.

45 E.H. Carr, *The Twenty Years' Crisis 1919–1939* (New York: Harper, 1964), 66.

46 Peter Wilson, 'Gilbert Murray and International Relations: Hellenism, Liberalism, and International Intellectual Cooperation as a Path to Peace', *Review of International Studies*, 2011, 37(2), 900.

47 For a discussion of the effects of archaeology on attitudes to decline, as well as its influence on Toynbee see Overy, *Morbid Age*, 33–4, 38.

48 An excellent account of Arthur Evans' discoveries in Crete, and their links to the prevailing philosophical trends of the time, can be found in Cathy Gere, *Knossos and the Prophets of Modernism* (Chicago: University of Chicago Press, 2009).

49 Flinders Petrie, *The Revolutions of Civilisation* (New York: Harper & Brothers, 1911), esp. 126. Also quoted in Overy, *Morbid Age*, 33.

50 Petrie, *Revolutions of Civilisation*, 5. For Petrie this rise and decline took on a racial tinge: a civilisation only lasted as long as the race at its heart remained creative. The collapse of a civilisation brought barbarian invasions that resulted in a racial mix, and consequent rejuvenation. While different from Nazi views of race, Petrie's interpretation was in line with the then popular ideas of eugenics (for a discussion of Eugenics see Overy, *Morbid Age*, ch. 3). Petrie's views on race, and his belief that racial characteristics produce better forms of government and civilisation, can be found in his *Janus in Modern Life* (London: Archibald Constable, 1907). While Toynbee certainly built on Petrie's ideas of civilisational decline, he also rejected race as an explanatory factor. Petrie is not specifically mentioned by Toynbee, but it is a good guess that his discussion of the irrelevance of race was meant as a direct criticism of Petrie and of eugenics (see Arnold J. Toynbee, *A Study of History*, vol. I (New York and London: Oxford University Press, 1947), 51–5).

51 Martin Wight, 'Arnold Toynbee: An Appreciation', *International Affairs*, 1976, 52(1), 12.

52 Overy, *Morbid Age*, 38.

53 Cornelia Navari, 'Arnold Toynbee (1889–1975): Prophecy and Civilization', *Review of International Studies*, 2000, 26(2), 294.

54 These six volumes are available in a handy and well-crafted one volume abridgement by D.C. Summerville: Arnold J. Toynbee, *A Study of History*, Volume I (New York and London: Oxford University Press, 1947).

55 Toynbee, *Study of History*, Volume I, 12–34.

56 Arnold J. Toynbee, 'The Greek Door to the Study of History', in J.A.K. Thomson and A.J. Toynbee (eds), *Essays in Honour of Gilbert Murray* (London: George Allen & Unwin, 1936), 308.

57 Toynbee, *Study of History*, Volume I, 1.

58 Toynbee, 'The Greek Door', 303, 308.

59 Petrie, *Revolutions of Civilisation*, 125–6.

60 Toynbee, *Study of History*, Volume I, Part IV.

61 Arnold J. Toynbee, 'The Downfalls of Civilizations', the text of his Hobhouse Lecture given in 1939, and republished in *Hobhouse Memorial Lectures 1930–1940* (London: Oxford University Press, 1948).

62 Toynbee, *Study of History*, Volume I, 336 ff.

63 Toynbee, 'The Greek Door', 303.

64 Arnold J. Toynbee, 'Peaceful Change or War? The Next Stage in the International Crisis', *International Affairs*, 1936, 15(1), 26–7.

65 Arnold J. Toynbee, 'The Lessons of History', in C.A.W. Manning (ed.), *Peaceful Change: An International Problem* (New York: Macmillan, 1937), 27–40.

66 Toynbee, 'Peaceful Change or War?', 27, 28.

67 Toynbee, 'Peaceful Change or War?', 28.

68 Toynbee, 'Lessons of History', 28.

69 Arnold J. Toynbee, 'A Turning Point in History', *Foreign Affairs*, 1939, 17(2), 317, 312.

70 Toynbee, 'A Turning Point in History', 318.

71 Toynbee, 'A Turning Point in History', 319.

72 This is discussed in Christopher Brewin, 'Arnold Toynbee, Chatham House, and Research in a Global Context', in David Long and Peter Wilson, *Thinkers of the Twenty Years' Crisis* (Oxford: Clarendon, 1995), 277–301.

73  See the discussion in Toynbee, 'A Turning Point in History', as well as Brewin, 'Arnold Toynbee', 282.
74  Arnold Toynbee, 'The International Outlook', *International Affairs*, 1947, 23(4), 463–76.
75  For the links between Toynbee and Wight, and a discussion of their similarities and differences, see Ian Hall, 'Challenge and Response: The Lasting Engagement of Arnold J. Toynbee and Martin Wight', *International Relations* 2003, 17(3), 389–404.
76  Toynbee, 'Peaceful Change or War?', 44 ff.
77  Toynbee, 'The Greek Door', 293.
78  See Ian Hall, 'The Revolt against the West: Decolonisation and its Repercussions in British International Thought, 1945–75', *International History Review*, 2011, 33(1), 43–64.
79  Isaiah Bowman, 'Geography vs. Geopolitics', *Geographical Review*, 1942, 32, 646–58; Derwent Whittlesey, *German Strategy of World Conquest.* (London: F.E. Robinson, 1942); Hans W. Weigert, *Generals and Geographers. The Twilight of Geopolitics* (New York: Oxford University Press, 1942); Andreas Dorpalen, *The World of General Haushofer. Geopolitics in Action* (New York: Holt, Rinehart and Winston, 1942); Robert Strausz-Hupé, *Geopolitics. The Struggle for Space and Power* (New York: G.P. Putnam, 1942); Edmund A. Walsh, *Total Power. A Footnote to History* (New York: Doubleday, 1948).
80  See, for example, Franz Neumann, *Behemoth: The Structure and Practice of National Socialism* (Oxford: Clarendon, 1942), 147, who called geopolitics 'nothing but the ideology of imperialist expansion'.
81  A condensed summary of the myth can be found in David Thomas Murphy, *The Heroic Earth. Geopolitical Thought in Weimar Germany, 1918–1933* (Kent, OH: Kent State University Press, 1997), vii.
82  See Gunthram Henrik Herb, *Under the Map of Germany. Nationalism and Propaganda 1918–1945* (London: Routledge, 1997), 3; also Murphy, *Heroic Earth*, vii.
83  Günter Wolkersdorfer, 'Karl Haushofer and geopolitics – the history of a German mythos', *Geopolitics*, 1999, 4(3), 152.
84  Murphy, *Heroic Earth*, vii.
85  Murphy, *Heroic Earth*, 17–19.
86  Murphy, *Heroic Earth*, 23.
87  Friedrich Naumann, quoted in David Mitrany, 'Pan-Europa – A Hope or a Danger?', *Political Quarterly*, 1930, 1(4), 460.
88  See the discussion in Murphy, *Heroic Earth*, ch. 9.
89  See Wolkersdorfer, 'Karl Haushofer and geopolitics', 148; and Gearóid Ó Tuathail, 'Introduction to Part One' in Gearóid Ó Tuathail, Simon Dalby and Paul Routledge, *The Geopolitics Reader*, second edn (London: Routledge, 2006) , esp. 26.
90  Weigert, *Generals and Geographers*, 258.
91  Murphy, *Heroic Earth*, viii.
92  Derwent Whittlesey, *The Earth and the State. A Study in Political Geography* (New York: Henry Holt, 1939), 556; Derwent Whittlesey, *Environmental Foundations of European History* (New York: Appleton-Century-Crofts, 1949), 5.
93  Whittlesey, *The Earth and the State*, 86 and 94; Whittlesey, *Environmental Foundations*, 118–19 and 133–4.
94  Whittlesey, *Environmental Foundations*,133–5.
95  Whittlesey, *The Earth and the State*, 12 and 23; Whittlesey, *German Strategy*, 192; Whittlesey, *Environmental Foundations*, 126–7.
96  Whittlesey, *The Earth and the State*, 23; Whittlesey, *Environmental Foundations*, 136–7.
97  Whittlesey, *The Earth and the State*, 31–2 and 52.
98  Whittlesey, *Environmental Foundations*, 118–19, 132–3 and 134–5.

99 Whittlesey, *German Strategy*, 30, 55.

100 Whittlesey, *German Strategy*, 69–73.

101 Whittlesey, *Environmental Foundations*, 139; Bowman, 'Geography vs. Geopolitics' 655; see also Isaiah Bowman, 'Introduction', in Isaiah Bowman (ed.) *Limits of Land Settlement. A Report on Present-Day Possibilities* (New York: Books for Libraries, 1937), 1–7.

102 Whittlesey, *The Earth and the State*, 55, 584.

103 Whittlesey, *German Strategy*, 192.

104 See Geoffrey J. Martin, *The Life and Thought of Isaiah Bowman* (Hamden, CT: Archon, 1980), 159, 169.

105 Bowman, 'Geography vs. Geopolitics', 646–58.

106 Isaiah Bowman, 'Peace and Power Politics', *Vital Speeches of the Day*, 1 April 1941, 7(12), 383.

107 Bowman, 'Geography vs. Geopolitics', 655.

108 Neil Smith, *American Empire. Roosevelt's Geographer and the Prelude to Globalization* (Berkeley, Los Angeles and London: University of California Press, 2003), especially 319.

109 Harriet Wanklyn, *Friedrich Ratzel: A Biographical Memoir and Bibliography* (London: Cambridge University Press, 1961). Also quoted in Smith, *American Empire*, 38–9.

110 Nicholas J. Spykman, 'Geography and Foreign Policy I', *American Political Science Review*, 1938, 32(1), 29.

111 Spykman, 'Geography and Foreign Policy I', 40.

112 Nicholas J. Spykman, 'Geography and Foreign Policy II', *American Political Science Review*, 1938, 32(2), 236.

113 Nicholas J. Spykman, *The Geography of the Peace*, edited by Helen R. Nicholl (New York: Harcourt and Brace, 1944), 35.

114 Spykman, *The Geography of the Peace*, 43–53.

115 Spykman, *The Geography of the Peace*, 43.

116 Spykman, 'Geography and Foreign Policy I', 41; Spykman, *The Geography of the Peace*, 28.

117 Spykman, *The Geography of the Peace*, 41.

118 Nicholas J. Spykman, *America's Strategy in World Politics. The United States and the Balance of Power* (New York: Harcourt and Brace, 1942), 11–16.

119 Spykman, *America's Strategy in World Politics*, 11–26.

120 Nicholas J. Spykman, 'States' Rights and the League', *Yale Review*, 1934, 24(2), 274–93; Spykman, *America's Strategy in World Politics*, 462. Nicholas J. Spykman and Abbie A. Rollins, 'Geographic Objectives in Foreign Policy I', *American Political Science Review*, 1939, 33(3), 391.

121 Spykman, *The Geography of the Peace*, 60.

122 Spykman's 1943 letter to *Life Magazine*, quoted in Edgar S. Furniss, 'The Contribution of Nicholas John Spykman to the Study of International Politics', *World Politics*, 1952, 4(3), 394–5.

123 Spykman, *America's Strategy in World Politics*, 463.

124 Martin, *The Life and Thought of Isaiah Bowman*, 105; Isaiah Bowman, 'Political Geography of Power [Review of Spykman's *America's Strategy in World Politics*]', *Geographical Review*, 1942, 32(2), 349–52.

125 Smith, *American Empire*, 288–9.

126 Furniss, 'The Contribution of Nicholas John Spykman', 384.

127 Spykman, *America's Strategy in World Politics*, 471.

128 See the discussions in Norman Angell, *The Great Illusion. A Study of the Relation of Military Power in Nations to their Economic and Social Advantage* (Toronto: McClelland and Goodchild, 1911); and J. A. Hobson, *Imperialism. A Study* (London: Nisbet, 1902).

129  H.N. Brailsford, *The War of Steel and Gold. A Study of the Armed Peace*, ninth edn (London: Bell, 1917).

130  H.N. Brailsford, 'Arbitrate or Disarm. A New View of Security', *New Leader*, 12 September 1924, 4.

131  Hugh Dalton, *Towards the Peace of Nations. A Study in International Politics* (London: Routledge & Kegan Paul, 1928), 15.

132  H.N. Brailsford, 'War and Capitalism', *The New Statesman and Nation*, 9 February 1935, 169–70. Reprinted in Henry Brinton (ed.), *Does Capitalism Cause War?* (London: H. & E.R. Brinton, 1935), 13–19.

133  Leonard Woolf, 'War and Capitalism', *The New Statesman and Nation*, 16 February 1935, 210. Reprinted in Brinton, *Does Capitalism Cause War?*, 21–3.

134  Norman Angell, 'Capitalism and War', *The New Statesman and Nation*, 23 February 1935, 241–3. Reprinted in Brinton, *Does Capitalism Cause War?*, 23–37.

135  H.N. Brailsford, 'Capitalism and War', *The New Statesman and Nation*, 2 March 1935, 278. Reprinted in Brinton, *Does Capitalism Cause War?*, 37–41.

136  Harold J. Laski, 'Capitalism and War', *The New Statesman and Nation*, 2 March 1935, 278. Reprinted in Brinton, *Does Capitalism Cause War?*, 41–2.

137  H.N. Brailsford, 'The Tory Policy of Peace', *The Political Quarterly*, 1938, 9(3), 325–33.

138  See the discussion in: H.N. Brailsford, *Towards a New League* (London: New Statesman and Nation, 1936).

139  H.N. Brailsford, *Why Capitalism Means War* (New York: Garland, 1972 [1938]), 53–7.

140  See the discussion in Brailsford, *Towards a New League*, especially Part IV.

141  H.N. Brailsford, *The Life Work of J.A. Hobson* (London: Oxford University Press, 1948), 26.

142  J.A. Hobson, 'Causes of War' unpublished and undated paper in the possession of David Long, 12–13. Now republished in John M. Hobson and Colin Tyler (ed.), *Selected Writings of John A. Hobson 1932–1938* (London: Routledge, 2011), 143–51.

143  Hobson, 'Causes of War', 15.

144  H.N. Brailsford, *Our Settlement with Germany* (Harmondsworth: Penguin, 1944), 14.

145  See the discussion in Lucian M. Ashworth, *International Relations and the Labour Party. Intellectuals and Policy Making 1918–1945* (London: IBTauris, 2007), 47.

146  Laski's intellectual shifts are explored in Peter Lamb, *Harold Laski: Problems of Democracy, the Sovereign State, and International Society* (New York: Palgrave Macmillan, 2004), ch. 6.

147  Harold J. Laski, 'Economic Foundations of Peace', in Leonard Woolf (ed.), *The Intelligent Man's Way to Prevent War* (London: Victor Gollancz, 1933), 543–7.

148  See, for example, Harold Laski, 'British Labour's Peace Aims', International Sub-Committee of the National Executive Committee (NEC), September 1939, p. 2. James Middleton Collection, Labour Party Archives, John Ryland's Library, Manchester, UK.

149  Harold J. Laski, *Reflections on the Revolution of our Time* (London: George Allen & Unwin, 1943), 217.

150  See, for example, Hans J. Morgenthau, 'Another Great Debate. The National Interest of the United States', *The American Political Science Review*, 1952, 46(4), 961–88.

151  Laski, 'British Labour's Peace Aims', 2–3; Laski, *Reflections on the Revolution of our Time*, 213.

152  Harold J. Laski, *Liberty in the Modern State* (Harmondsworth: Penguin, 1937), 17.

153  Laski, *Reflections on the Revolution of our Time*, 206.

154  Laski, *Reflections on the Revolution of our Time*, 249; Lamb, *Harold Laski*, 135 ff.

155  See David Mitrany, 'Interrelation of Politics and Economics in Modern War', *The Annals of the American Academy of Political and Social Science*, July 1937, 192,

84–5. See also the later work David Mitrany, 'International Consequences of National Planning', *Yale Review*, September 1947, 37(1), 24. This issue was also the subject of a series of letters between Mitrany and Brailsford in September 1945, which can be found in the Mitrany Papers, British Library of Political and Economic Sciences, LSE, London.

156  Leonard Woolf, *The International Post-War Settlement* (London: Fabian Society and Victor Gollancz, 1944), 3.

157  Karl Polanyi, *The Great Transformation. The Political and Economic Origins of our Time* (Boston: Beacon Press, 2001 [1944]), see, for example, the first line on page 3.

158  Letter from Karl Polanyi to Mr Cunningham, 25 March 1943, file: '47-13 Correspondence: Polanyi 1943', Karl Polanyi archives, Karl Polanyi Institute of Political Economy, Concordia University, Montreal (hereafter cited as Karl Polanyi Archives).

159  Letter from Karl Polanyi to Marshak, 29 January 1941, file: '47-11 Correspondence: Polanyi 1941', Karl Polanyi Archives.

160  Polanyi, *Great Transformation*, 3.

161  Polanyi, *Great Transformation*, 6–7.

162  Polanyi, *Great Transformation*, 16.

163  Polanyi, *Great Transformation*, 20.

164  Polanyi, *Great Transformation*, ch. 2.

165  Norman Angell, *The Fruits of Victory* (New York: Garland, 1970 [1921]); J. M. Keynes, *The End of Laissez Faire* (London: Hogarth Press, 1926).

166  Albert O. Hirschman, *National Power and the Structure of Foreign Trade* (Berkeley: University of California Press, 1945), 15.

167  Krasner's debt to Hirschman is mentioned in the interview of Krasner by Graham H. Stuart in 2003. The full text of the interview can be found at http://globetrotter. berkeley.edu/people3/Krasner/krasner-con1.html.

168  Polanyi, *Great Transformation*, 136.

169  His first use came in 1925. See Harold J. Laski, *A Grammar of Politics* (London: George Allen & Unwin, 1925), chapter 11.

170  L.T. Hobhouse, *Liberalism* (London: Williams and Norgate, 1911).

171  For a discussion of the use of function in the guild socialist works of R.H. Tawney and G.D.H. Cole see David Long, 'International Functionalism and the Politics of Forgetting', *International Journal*, Spring 1993, 48(2), 355–79. See specifically: R.H. Tawney, *The Acquisitive Society* (New York: Harcourt Brace, 1920); and G.D.H. Cole, *Guild Socialism* (New York: Stokes, 1920).

172  See especially Mary Parker Follett, *The New State* (London: Longmans, 1918).

173  Harold J. Laski, *A Grammar of Politics*, third edn (London: George Allen & Unwin, 1934), 587–8.

174  Laski, *Grammar of Politics*, 619.

175  Graham Wallas, *Human Nature and Politics* (Boston and New York: Houghton Mifflin, 1916 [1908]), pp. 21, 25, and ch. IV.

176  For Mitrany's work on peasant society and war government in south east Europe see: David Mitrany, *The Land and the Peasant in Rumania. The War and Agrarian Reform* (London: Humprey Milford and Oxford University Press, 1930); and David Mitrany, *The Effects of the War in South Eastern Europe* (New Haven: Yale University Press, 1936), chs 5–7.

177  David Mitrany, *The Progress of International Government* (London: Allen & Unwin, 1933).

178  For this pessimism see: Overy, *The Morbid Age*.

179  David Mitrany, *A Working Peace System* (Oxford: Oxford University Press, 1943), 8.

180  Mitrany, *Working Peace System*, 7.

181  Mitrany, *Progress of International Government*, 103; Mitrany, *Working Peace System*, 10.

182 See note 155 above.
183 Mitrany, *Working Peace System*, 9.
184 Mitrany, *Working Peace System*, 31.
185 Mitrany, *Working Peace System*, 33.
186 Mitrany, *Working Peace System*, 35. Emphasis in the original.
187 On this issue see David Mitrany, *The Road to Security* (London: National Peace Council, 1944).
188 See, for example, Lionel Curtis' response to Mitrany in David Mitrany, 'The Functional Approach to World Organization', *International Affairs*, 24 (1948), 362–3.
189 See Peter Wilson, 'The New Europe Debate in Wartime Britain', in Philomena Murray and Paul Rich (eds), *Visions of European Unity* (Boulder, CO: Westview, 1996), 57–8.
190 E.H. Carr, *Nationalism and After* (London, Macmillan, 1945), 47–74. Carr's use of Mitrany is mentioned in Ashworth, *Creating International Studies*, 113; and William Scheuerman, 'The (Classical) Realist Vision of Global Reform', *International Theory*, 2010, 2, 260. See also Wilson, 'New Europe Debate', 42–4.
191 John H. Herz, *International Politics in the Atomic Age* (New York: Columbia University Press, 1959), 327–9. See also: Scheuerman, '(Classical) Realist Vision', 264–6 and Casper Sylvest, 'Realism and International Law: the Challenge of John H. Herz', *International Theory*, 2010, 2(3), 436.
192 Hans J. Morgenthau, 'Introduction', in David Mitrany, *A Working Peace System* (Chicago: Quadrangle, 1966). See also Scheuerman, '(Classical) Realist Vision', 262–4.
193 David Mitrany's letter to A.P. Wadsworth of the *Manchester Guardian*, 15 September 1951, 338/1/122 Manchester Guardian Archive, John Rylands Library, Manchester University, UK.
194 Frederick Sherwood Dunn, *Peaceful Change. A Study of International Procedures* (New York: Council on Foreign Relations, 1937), 1–6.
195 Dunn, *Peaceful Change*, 10–13, 50.
196 Dunn, *Peaceful Change*, 84, 125.
197 Frederick Sherwood Dunn, *The Practice and Procedure of International Conferences* (New York: AMS Press, 1971 [1929]), 1.
198 Dunn, *Peaceful Change*, 48.
199 Frederick Sherwood Dunn, 'Review of C.A.W. Manning, *Peaceful Change: An International Problem*', *Political Science Quarterly*, 1939, 54(1), 128–9.
200 Hidemi Suganami, 'C.A.W. Manning and the Study of International Relations', *Review of International Studies*, 27(1), 104.
201 On this issue see David Long, 'C.A.W. Manning and the Discipline of International Relations', *The Round Table*, 2005, 94(1), 77–96.
202 See the discussion in Suganami, 'C.A.W. Manning', 95. Manning outlines his view of the League and collective security in C.A.W. Manning, 'The Proposed Amendments to the Covenant of the League of Nations', *The British Yearbook of International Law*, 1930, 11, 158–71.
203 C.A.W. Manning, *The Nature of International Society* (London: Macmillan, 1975), ix.
204 C.A.W. Manning, 'Some Suggested Conclusions', in C.A.W. Manning (ed.), *Peaceful Change. An International Problem* (New York: Macmillan, 1937), 169–90.
205 For Manning this was a western-dominated international order. Manning's support for western norms extended to his support for Apartheid South Africa, a position that alienated him from many students and colleagues in the years after the war.
206 Suganami, 'C.A.W. Manning', 101–2.
207 Carr calls Manning a friend in E.H. Carr, 'Public Opinion As a Safeguard of Peace', *International Affairs* 1936, 15(6), 853.

208  See Jonathan Haslam, *The Vices of Integrity. E.H. Carr, 1892–1982* (London: Verso, 1999), 59.

209  As well as the secondary texts mentioned below, Carr has also been the subject of an edited collection: Michael Cox (ed.) *E.H. Carr. A Critical Appraisal* (Houndmills: Palgrave, 2000). See also the comprehensive treatment of Carr in Sean Molloy, 'Dialectics and Transformation: Exploring the Theory of E.H. Carr', *International Journal of Politics, Culture and Society* 2003, 17(2), 279–306.

210  Carr, 'Public Opinion As a Safeguard of Peace', 853–9.

211  E.H. Carr, *The Twenty Years' Crisis. An Introduction to the Study of International Relations* (New York: Harper Torch, 1964 [originally published in 1939]), 31 ff.

212  Charles Jones is critical of Carr's analysis of public opinion, and argues that Carr's position was itself the result of wishful thinking. Other than the behaviour of elected representatives in Parliament, Carr had little or no evidence that his view of public opinion was right. Charles Jones, *E.H. Carr and International Relations. A Duty to Lie* (Cambridge: Cambridge University Press, 1998), 32–5.

213  Carr, 'Public Opinion As a Safeguard of Peace', 859 ff.

214  E.H. Carr, *The Twenty Years' Crisis. An Introduction to the Study of International Relations* (New York: Harper Torch, 1939), 278.

215  Carr, *Twenty Years' Crisis*, ch. 4.

216  Carr, *Twenty Years' Crisis*, 1964, 214.

217  Carr, *Twenty Years' Crisis*, ch. 13.

218  Hans Morgenthau, 'The Political Science of E.H. Carr', *World Politics*, 1948, 1(1), 127–134.

219  Jones, *E.H. Carr and International Relations*, 3 ff, 54–60.

220  Haslam, *The Vices of Integrity*, 97.

221  E.H. Carr, *Conditions of Peace* (London: Macmillan, 1942), 240.

222  Carr, *Conditions of Peace*, 247–56.

223  E.H. Carr, *Nationalism and After* (London: Macmillan, 1945), 27–8, 46–7.

224  Carr, *Nationalism and After*, 47–8.

225  See, for example, Ernst Gellner, 'Nationalism Reconsidered and E.H. Carr', *Review of International Studies*, 1992, 18(4), 285–93.

226  For Carr's (and Mitrany's) place in the debates on post-war Europe see: Peter Wilson, 'The New Europe Debate in Wartime Britain', in Philomena Murray and Paul Rich (eds), *Visions of European Unity* (Boulder, CO: Westview, 1996), 39–62.

227  Georg Schwarzenberger, 'The Three Types of Law', *Ethics*, January 1943, 53(2), 89.

228  Georg Schwarzenberger, *Power Politics. An Introduction to the Study of International Relations and Post-War Planning* (London: Jonathan Cape, 1941), 34–5.

229  Schwarzenberger, 'Three Types of Law', 90.

230  Schwarzenberger, 'Three Types of Law', 96–7.

231  Schwarzenberger, 'Three Types of Law', 90–3.

232  Schwarzenberger, *Power Politics*, 42–62. See also Georg Schwarzenberger, *The League of Nations and World Order* (London: Constable, 1936), 176 ff.

233  Schwarzenberger, *The League of Nations and World Order*, 181.

234  Schwarzenberger, *Power Politics*, 54–5

235  Schwarzenberger, *Power Politics*, 179

236  Schwarzenberger, *Power Politics,* 121–35.

237  Schwarzenberger, *Power Politics*, 433–4.

238  See the preface to the first edition of Carr's *Twenty Years' Crisis*.

239  Quoted in Kenneth W. Thompson, 'Beyond National Interest: A Critical Evaluation of Reinhold Niebuhr's Theory of International Politics', *The Review of Politics*, 1955, 17(2), 168.

240  Reinhold Niebuhr, *Moral Man and Immoral Society. A Study in Ethics and Politics* (New York: Charles Scribner, 1932), xii.

241  Niebuhr, *Moral Man and Immoral Society*, especially 25–7.

242  Niebuhr, *Moral Man and Immoral Society*, 6.
243  Reinhold Niebuhr, *The Children of Light and the Children of Darkness* (New York: Charles Scribner, 1944), 20.
244  Niebuhr, *The Children of Light and the Children of Darkness*, ch. 1.
245  Niebuhr in the summary report of the 1954 Rockefeller Conference on International Politics. Quoted in Robert C. Good, 'The National Interest and Political Realism: Niebuhr's "Debate" with Morgenthau and Kennan', *The Journal of Politics*, 1960, 22(4), 600.
246  Niebuhr, *The Children of Light and the Children of Darkness*, ch. 5.
247  Niebuhr also explores this idea in a much later monograph: *Christian Realism and Political Problems* (New York: Charles Scribner, 1953). He had also already discussed the problem of the hunt for security through power as impinging on the lives of others as early as 1945 in *Christianity and Society*, a journal he established and edited.
248  Niebuhr, *The Children of Light and the Children of Darkness*, 10.
249  Niebuhr, *The Children of Light and the Children of Darkness*, 190.
250  Gurian's work is best summarised in his 'On the Study of International Relations', *The Review of Politics*, 1946, 8(3), 275–82.
251  Frederick L. Schuman, *International Politics. An Introduction to the Western State System* (New York: McGraw-Hill, 1933). Perhaps the best summary of Schuman, who has not been well explored in recent analyses of classical realism, can be found in Scheuerman, 'The (Classical) Realist Vision of Global Reform', 251–3.
252  Hans Rommen, 'Realism and Utopianism in World Affairs', *The Review of Politics*, 1944, 6(2), 193–215. See especially page 196.
253  John H. Herz, *Political Realism and Political Idealism. A Study in Theories and Realities* (Chicago: University of Chicago Press, 1951), v.
254  See the discussion in Lucian M. Ashworth, 'Mapping a New World: Geography and the Interwar Study of International Relations', *International Studies Quarterly*, 2013, 57(1), 138–49. On Hartshorne and geography's change of direction see Gearóid Ó Tuathail, 'The Critical Reading/Writing of Geopolitics: Re-Reading/Writing Wittfogel, Bowman, and Lecoste', *Progress in Human Geography*, 1994, 18, 324–5.
255  Wilson, 'The New Europe Debate', 57–8.

# Part III

# Conclusion

International relations in living memory and lessons for the future

# 8 A new IR for a new world?

## The growth of an academic field since 1945

During the course of this book we have ranged over five centuries of history, and encountered many of the people who have forged our understanding of the international sphere. Some are well known in current narratives, while others have been sidelined or ignored, despite their contributions to the interpretations of other ages. We now stand on the threshold of living memory. Beyond this point those who still hold university positions in IR were either observers or participants in the history of international thought. To a certain degree this period's history (despite the fact that some of it is over half a century old) is still coalescing. Those who took part in it are still developing their ideas, and many are engaged in radical reassessments of the roles they played. This, and the fact that so much has been written on this period in IR, leads me to falter. The goal of this book, after all, has not been to make sense of IR as it is today, but to understand the currents that created the broader history of international thought. Like Moses this book is destined not to enter the Promised Land. But that said I would like to use this chapter to outline where IR has gone, before making some more general conclusions.

A word of warning is necessary here, however. To a large degree what we know as the field of IR does not necessarily exhaust the sum of international thought practised globally. IR, as discussed in Chapter 1, is effectively an Anglo-centric study of the global that itself emerged out of a broader western tradition. Telling its story is to exclude a wider non-western set of narratives that have also been dealing with the same crises of industrialisation, imperialism, war and the capriciousness of a world of states.[1] That these non-western theoretical narratives are found in different fora (including both academic and non-academic ones) does not stop them being legitimate parts of the story of international thought. The story I investigate in this book does not do these various non-western strands justice, mainly because of the serious work that still needs to be done in dissecting and understanding the western and narrower Anglophone traditions. My goal has been to explore a particular dominant western tradition that has over the last few hundred years coalesced into a predominantly western field. There was so much work to do here, and so many myths to expose and question that even this culturally narrow task is Herculean. Appreciations of the non-western traditions in current international thought are beginning to emerge. The missing piece in this story, though, still remains a comprehensive story of the historical origins of many non-western approaches. These have been hinted at in this study in a number of places, including:

1   The Islamic North African historical and philosophical traditions dating back to Arab scholars' dissections of Greek and Latin texts (Al-Farabi, Ibn Khaldun).
2   The involvement of non-western societies in the work of international organisations after the First World War.
3   Non-western reactions to imperialism and interdependence.

Yet, if westerners, especially Anglophones, are interested in studying the origins of the diverse non-western traditions it is helpful to understand the origins and nature of their own tradition. This has been the goal of this work.

I have two goals for this final chapter. The first is to lay out a short history of the development of IR since 1945. The goal here is to show the continuities and the breaks with the past. I do this in two sections. One will give a thumbnail sketch of the formation of the field between the end of the war and the 1960s. This roughly covers the period of the American and British committees that helped to define IR for the next few decades. The other looks at the developments since the 1960s, charting the introduction of behaviouralist methods, the development of international political economy, and the emergence of new theoretical perspectives that challenged what was seen as a realist orthodoxy in the field. Much of the analysis of this half-century has been dominated by a 'Great Debates' narrative. While, as I have made clear in Chapters 6 and 7, there was no first 'Great Debate', the evidence for further debates from the 1960s onwards is a little more fruitful. Although I argue that framing the history of the field in terms of debates is problematic, I am more sympathetic to using this Great Debate framework to understand the development of IR since the 1960s, as long as we realise that the notion of debate here is only a handy shorthand for a messier and more confused situation.

The second section of this chapter summarises the argument of this book, as well as suggesting how the history of international thought can help us understand the nature of IR today. I suggest that the concept of paradigm, which has become so entrenched in the categorisation of theories in IR following its wholesale adoption by scholars during the 1980s, should be abandoned. The concept of paradigm no longer serves any useful purpose, and has the effect of oversimplifying both the history of the field and its current form. I suggest instead that the increasingly popular concept of school – usually rooted to a specific university or set of universities, and which has found favour in IR over the last decade – is a more fruitful avenue. I use the recent work of Peter Galison in the history and philosophy of science to argue the case here. I also point out how detailed histories of international thought can have a critical theoretical edge when they challenge gatekeeping devices that use historical precedent to exclude certain approaches from the mainstream of the field. As we have seen from this journey so far, approaches as diverse as feminism, radical political economy, and political geography have all been part of the story of the development of international thought. A deeper historical analysis supports a broader definition of the field Finally, I take a more externalist line, arguing that the development of international thought has to be seen as a response to a series of revolutions that required a rethinking of the political universe. The first of these is the development of the modern state, an event still recognised as central through the myth of the Westphalian system debunked in Chapter 3. The second is the industrial revolution of the nineteenth century, which rarely gets a mention in IR textbooks, but is arguably the most important catalyst for the development of a recognisable field of IR (as I have argued in Chapters 4 and 5). IR is more a product of the hydrocarbon revolution that saw the development of a truly global and industrial civilisation dependent on first coal and then oil than it is of any other major development. If we also include the development of weapons of mass destruction, including nuclear weapons, during the course of the twentieth century as part of this process then the importance of the creation of an industrial hydrocarbon-dependent civilisation is thrown into even sharper focus.

## International relations 1945–60: an American social science in the shadow of the bomb

I started Chapter 6 by explaining why the idea of idealism and of a realist–idealist 'debate' was faulty, and also how it obscured and confused our understanding of the development of international thought after the First World War. There never was a recognisable 'idealist' paradigm. The situation with the post Second World War development of international thought and IR is different, but the general principle involved is the same. Ideas of a neat realist–idealist split have obscured our understanding of the post-war development of IR theory. There are, however, differences. While there is clearly no idealist school of thought in the 1920s and early 1930s, there is a self-conscious group of scholars calling themselves realists (or, at least, associated in clusters of scholars, some of which self-identify as realists). That said, we have to be careful about taking this self-identification at face value, and assuming that there is a sudden emergence of a realist paradigm – identical to current early twenty-first century thinkers who also call themselves realists – and that we are consequently looking at a sudden break in the historical record, followed by a long and tranquil period of theoretical stability. Rather, the argument of this section will stress both the continuities with the past, and also the discontinuities between the realists that emerged after the Second World War and the 'realism' that came to dominate academic IR especially in the United States from the 1960s. It is not for nothing that people who study the work of Hans J. Morgenthau, Frederick L. Schuman, Reinhold Niebuhr, Bernard Brodie or John Herz prefer to describe their subjects as 'classical realists'. Classical realism is in many important ways not only different from the neo-realism that emerged after the late 1970s, it was also very different from the quantitative, behaviouralist and system theory inspired 'realism' that emerged to challenge classical realism especially in the 1960s. In fact, the continuities between classical realism and many of the writers written off as 'idealist' are instructive. Both Morgenthau and Herz certainly felt an affinity with the work of David Mitrany, while Schuman's bitter denunciation of what he called the 'behaviouralists' was rooted in his view that work on IR that did not address the key normative issues that troubled international politics was largely useless and irrelevant.[2]

There are, though, two major trends that take place at this time which do mark a major discontinuity in the history of both international thought in general and the academic study of IR more specifically. The first trend relates to the eventual emergence of a separate academic study of international political economy (IPE) in the 1970s. Prior to 1945 much of the study of international affairs, often rather unconsciously, used a political economy approach to the study of the international. Whether it was Norman Angell's conception of a new interdependent global economy, Brailsford's views on the ways that capitalist imperialism caused wars, or Keynes' notion of the need for global economic institutions to safeguard peace, IR in the first half of the twentieth century *was* IPE. In short, the trend to limit IR to politics and security – manifest most clearly in Morgenthau's statement about the autonomy of the political sphere[3] – cut out the predominantly politico-economic interpretation of the international that had been a part of international thought since the mid-nineteenth century. This gap was later to be filled by the establishment of IPE, which was developed to fill an intellectual space that IR had dramatically abandoned. The second major trend was the marginalisation of feminism in IR. While feminism was hardly dominant in pre-1945 IR, it was at least a part of the emerging intellectual field, and occupied a place in the study of international affairs in the UK and the United States that gave it validity as an approach. This position was encouraged and promoted by the important link that existed between the League of Nations and gendered research. The important role of the Women's International League for Peace and Freedom in League work is a good example here. The disappearance of women from the academic field of IR after 1945 led to an almost four-decade period where feminism was shut out from IR scholarship. It was only with the dramatic return of feminism in the late-1980s that once again feminist scholarship found itself back where it had been half a century before. Perhaps the only difference was that now feminism was often regarded by non-feminist IR scholars as an 'add-on' that did not address the core issues in the field. Feminism once excluded, it seems, never regained the sense of belonging it had among writers on international affairs during the League years.

Thus, we have to see the emergence of classical realism in the United States, and of the English School as a complex development that involved both continuities and discontinuities. While many of those discontinuities are well known – such as the greater emphasis on power defined as interest – there were also two clear discontinuities that have largely gone unnoticed, despite the enormity of the effect these had on the development of a mostly security concerned masculinist field of IR in the second half of the twentieth century. That said, it would be wrong to write the classical realists off as conservative and reactionary. As I shall demonstrate below, many of the classical realists took a far more radical interpretation of the international than they have been given credit for.

While my study of this period of IR's history is arguing for a radical rethink of its place in the history of international thought, I am to a large degree on familiar ground for most IR scholars. The thinkers that I am dealing with are old friends (or foes) to most IR scholars, and the works I discuss are still studied by students today. I will first summarise the development of a classical realist tradition in the United States, and its relationship with the growth of the university field of IR within a broader political science context. After this I sketch out the parallel development of an IR in the UK in what would later be called the English School. It is now popular to regard this English school as a distinctly non-realist 'international society' approach. Certainly the 'English School' has a view of the international that is distinct from current (neo-)realist approaches. but then again so does the classical realism found in the United States in the 1950s. Both of these stories have been well documented in recent disciplinary histories.[4] The third will touch on the survival and growth of a third group within IR: the emerging functionalist and neo-functionalist interpretations of the international that (in whole or in part) drew their inspiration from the work of David Mitrany. Mitrany is one of the few non-realist scholars of the pre-Second World War stage in IR that survived to be major figures in the IR of the 1950s and 1960s. While there are many reasons why he survived, one of them is that his ideas of functional international government struck a chord with many of the classical realists in the United States (although he was less popular with the English School, with perhaps the possible exception of E.H. Carr during the Second World War, as we saw in the last chapter). This highlights an important part of the story sketched in this section. While I have divided up the discussion into three distinct 'schools', we have to be constantly aware that this division is a convenient fiction. The writers we will encounter often shared much with thinkers in the other sections, while thinkers lumped together (take, for example, Schuman and Niebuhr) often disagreed with each other on what they considered to be major issues.

In terms of the development of the classical realist tradition in the United States and the establishment of what would later be called the English School in the UK – there is an important link between the two in terms of the role of one particular funding agency. The Rockefeller Foundation provided the funding that supported both the American 1954 Conference on International Politics and the British Committee on the Theory of International Politics that first met in 1959. Kenneth W. Thompson was instrumental in organising the funding for both endeavours. While the British Committee would end up having a longer institutional history than its older American twin, the Rockefeller Foundation funding would go a long way in fostering and creating two related schools of IR on opposite sides of the Atlantic. Perhaps, though, it is important to point out that these groups of scholars form schools, rather than paradigms. A paradigm, at least as it has become interpreted in the IR literature of the last few decades, is usually marked out by common assumptions and shared theoretical positions. A school, on the other hand need only share a common intellectual language and intellectual proximity, whether through conferences, committees or the printed word. Language and proximity allow debate between the members of a school. The stories of the emergence of classical realism in the United States and of the English School in the UK are narratives about the founding and functioning of schools of thought. While these schools allowed for a certain level of dissent between their memberships, this is also a story of the creation of 'insiders' and 'outsiders', and thus questions of dialogues that are to be encouraged, and others that are to be marginalised. It is also the story of the establishment of IR as a university field, and thus something quite distinct from the much more open-ended intellectual environment of the inter-war period.

In June 2012 I attended a workshop in Edinburgh on classical realism organised by Sean Molloy (a former student and rising star in international political theory). At lunch a group of us started asking each other if anybody self-identified as a realist. Despite all of us having strong sympathies for the work of the classical realists, no one admitted to being a realist. Later one of our number asked the wider workshop whether any saw themselves as realists. No one admitted to being a realist. In part this could be explained by the fact that a scholar studying a past thinker does not have to be ideologically attuned to their subject to study them. That said, some people in that room were sympathetic to the political standpoints of their subject-matter, and yet they would not call themselves realists. The explanation lay mostly in another direction: that the term 'realist' as employed by IR scholars in the early twenty-first century means something that is quite distinct to what the classical realists saw as realism's defining characteristics. The workshop participants did not self-identify as realists (unlike their subject matter) not because they were not sympathetic to the classical realists, but because what the classical realists largely stood for is not well replicated in those who call themselves realist today. The next section may contain some clues to why this is. There were dramatic changes in IR after 1960 that moved the field away from the primary concerns of the classical realists.

Classical realism in the United States was a product of a series of events and meetings that occurred as a response to developments in political science. The net result of all this was the formation of a distinct field of IR theorising within the United States academy that would remain dominant until the later 1960s when new social scientific methods began to dominate IR theorising. This story has already been very eloquently told by Nicolas Guilhot in two recent publications.[5] Quincy Wright spoke for many in the United States in the decades either side of the Second World War who saw IR as a fundamentally interdisciplinary 'discipline', with Wright identifying at least eight disciplines that had contributed to the new field of IR.[6] Yet, by the late 1940s the reality in the United States was that IR was increasingly being viewed as part of political science. Guilhot's research, especially on the 1954 conference on international politics, shows how the classical realist tradition in the United States emerged not as a 'scientific' response to woolly-headed 'idealism', but rather as an attempt to insulate classical realist IR theory from the heavily behaviouralist political science. 'In this context, the theoretical approach to IR was first developed to insulate the field from the surrounding behavioural sciences. It was not meant to make it more scientific, but, quite the contrary, immune to science.'[7] In this sense, we need to take very seriously, as field-defining, such texts as Morgenthau's *Scientific Man vs Power Politics*. Central to Morgenthau's work was an attack on the competence of scientific reason and mathematics to understand political problems. 'Our Civilisation assumes', Morgenthau wrote, 'that the social world is susceptible to rational control conceived after the model of the natural sciences, while the experiences … of the age contradict this.'[8] Throughout the work Morgenthau argues that the 'rationalists' of the 'liberal ideology' using laws borrowed from the natural sciences have misunderstood the complex nature of humanity, the role of history and the place of power in our social existence. Instead Morgenthau replaced what he regarded as a pseudo-scientific rationalism with an understanding of politics based on an unresolved duality or antimony in humanity: an ongoing clash between our lust for power and the notion of a universal ethics. These opposites kept human action suspended between them 'as between the poles of an electrical field'.[9] This, in a nutshell, was the classical realist case: a philosophy of human society rooted in a tragic interplay between two opposites in human nature. This essence was not understandable through any natural science method, and produced a world that was not open to a science of society looking for the one best way to do things. This situation was all the more blatant in an international arena where no sovereign or powerful organisations existed that could dictate a peaceful order.[10]

Yet, as Guihot points out, the attempt to insulate IR theory from political science and its behaviouralism failed. In the next section I shall discuss the assault on IR theory from those trained in the social science methods that Morgenthau and his fellow attendees of the 1954 conference were trying to keep out of IR theory. Still, the membership of the 1954 conference was a roll-call of classical realist IR. They included not only Morgenthau, but Reinhold Niebuhr, William T.R. Fox, Arnold Wolfers, Dean Rusk, Paul Nitze, Kenneth W. Thompson, Dorothy Fosdick and Walter Lippman.[11] Guilhot also points out the vital role played by the Rockefeller Foundation in providing both financial and institutional support, and here the role of Morgenthau's student Kenneth W. Thompson needs to be acknowledged.[12] The Rockefeller Foundation also played an important role in the development of IR in Britain, through the funding of the 'British Committee on the Theory of International Politics'. Again Kenneth W. Thompson played a key role. The history of the British Committee has been ably told by Tim Dunne in his 1998 book,[13] and has been supplemented by a debate in the pages of *Cooperation and Conflict* between Dunne and his critics. These disagreements helped flesh out aspects of the story, and also to question the role of figures marginalised by the Committee (and, consequently, also marginalised in Dunne's account of the English School) such as Charles Manning (discussed in the last chapter). In addition to this literature, a new book by Ian Hall that looks at British IR scholars between 1945 and 1975 has added other layers to this story by casting the net wider than the English School and the British Committee.[14]

When I first studied IR as an undergraduate student in Keele in the early 1980s we made a distinction between American school and English school realists. We took it for granted that Martin Wight, Hedley Bull and Herbert Butterfield could be described as realists, but we recognised that there were substantial differences between their realism and that of, say Morgenthau or Waltz. That has now changed. The 'English School' is now presented as an alternative to realism. At one level there is truth to this. Much in the same way that classical realists in the United States are very different in their approach from twenty-first century neo-realists, so 'English School' scholars have little in common with current self-confessed realists in IR. Also, as David Long pointed out in his analysis of Charles Manning,[15] there was a substantial difference between the American classical realist view of the nature of the international and the English School's view. While classical realists like Morgenthau continued the tradition of seeing the international as an 'anarchy' that lacked something that domestic society had (a tradition popularised since the First World War by G. Lowes Dickinson, and found among British liberal socialists), the English School tended to see the international as a different kind of society that had value in itself. This difference, as I will discuss below, can help explain why David Mitrany's functional approach found more favour with American classical realists than it did with members of the English School. That said, there is substantial common ground with American classical realists and English school scholars. There is an emphasis on criticising overly rationalist solutions to global governance, and on outlining the limits that human nature places on what is possible at the international. As Herbert Butterfield wrote in 1951: advocates of the 'new diplomacy of the League and UN were "specialists in wishful thinking"', who failed to see that 'the kind of human predicament which we have been discussing is not merely so far without a solution, but the whole condition is a standing feature of mankind in world-history'.[16] So differences there are, but there is also an overlap.

Indeed Butterfield was an important link with the American Committee and the Rockefeller Foundation. He and Kenneth W. Thompson were friends, and it was during the course of their correspondence between 1954 and 1958 that the idea of the British Committee was discussed.[17] The Committee would later include such intellectual heavyweights as Martin Wight, Herbert Butterfield, Hedley Bull and Michael Howard, and had its first meeting in January 1959. While there were many themes that came out of the Committee's work, an important one, emphasised by Dunne, was the notion of 'international society': that there was a middle ground between an 'international anarchy' of power-hungry states, and more formal systems of cooperation that had been advocated by groups associated with experiments in international organisations. The emphasis here was on the means of cooperation between states without the necessity for formal government.[18] This cooperation was premised on there being a common diplomatic culture underpinning the norms that allowed the system of states to work. Yet, perhaps the biggest international issue facing Britain at the time of the foundation of the British Committee was also a challenge to this idea of common norms: decolonisation and the apparent 'revolt against the west' by the emerging 'Third World' of poorer states unaligned to either of the two superpowers. This challenge has been explored in detail by Ian Hall.[19] These new emerging forces challenged the idea that there were common and agreed rules that underpin a society of states. Wight's reaction to this was to see in it a confirmation of his view of the decline of international society, for Bull it became an aspect of his view of the split between order and justice in the international society (with the justice claims of the Third World as a counterpoint, and even threat, to international order). The exception was Adam Watson, who saw little essential change to the norms of international society.[20]

Yet, the membership of the British Committee was notable not only by who it included but also who it excluded. Tim Dunne's analysis of the archives suggests that many people were deliberately excluded, despite their high standing in British IR. Dunne mentions particularly E.H. Carr (ostensibly because of his high status that 'might deflect our discussions into channels opened up by his own work'), F.H. Hinsley (who saw Europe and the World 'as more of an anarchy and less of a society') and Charles Manning ('too idiosyncratic').[21] There were also some other notable exceptions. Georg Schwarzenberger had been critical of the more historical approach evident in the founder members of the British Committee, preferring a more legal and sociological approach that interpreted law and social norms as a product of a particular society (see my discussion of Schwarzenberger in the last chapter). This view, that put sociological structure ahead of norms, was not compatible with the international society views expressed by Wight and Bull. Indeed, Schwarzenberger's preferred answer to the problems of international society was a federal structure that would allow a stronger legal order. Another absence was a strong critic of federalism, David Mitrany. Mitrany's absence from the Committee, despite his links to the LSE, should not surprise us given his pessimism about the possibilities of a functioning international society composed of states. Yet, while Mitrany's functional ideas (explored in detail in the last chapter) found little common ground with 'English School' theorists, they did find an eager and interested audience in the United States.

David Mitrany was a not uncommon sight at American IR conferences and venues. Kenneth W. Thompson describes him as 'an unusual fellow … He had long flowing hair and looked like an Old Testament prophet. His impact was in many ways greater than that of full-time academic scholars.'[22] Ranging from cautious adaptation to enthusiastic adoption, Mitrany's functional approach found favour among many American classical realists due to the seeming pragmatic nature of his plan for dealing with the failures of the state system. John Herz, while concerned that a functionalist approach did not always take into consideration the universality of conflicts over power, believed that it could contribute to solving international problems, especially if it rested on broad public support.[23] Morgenthau was far more enthusiastic than Herz, and his work contains frequent references to functionalist solutions to global problems.[24] More importantly, it was Morgenthau's enthusiasm for Mitrany's *A Working Peace*

*System* that led to the republication of the pamphlet with other papers by Mitrany in 1966. The 1966 book-length version included an introduction by Morgenthau. In his introduction Morgenthau had presented the functional approach, through its ability to overcome a dangerous and obsolete nationalism, as the best hope for civilisation.[25] Thompson also lists Reinhold Niebuhr as an admirer,[26] a sentiment that seems to have been reciprocated if Mitrany's praise of Niebuhr's *Children of Light and Children of Darkness* is anything to go by.[27] Indeed, Niebuhr's criticism of federalist plans and his defence of the United Nations often bears a family resemblance to Mitrany's own position, even if both writers were coming to the problems from different angles and assumptions.[28] Later, Inis Claude's study of international organisation would include a chapter-length critical analysis of the functional approach that, while sceptical of certain assumptions of Mitrany's approach, acknowledged that it 'has the great merit of appealing both to humanitarian idealism and to national self-interest'.[29]

Here lay the appeal of Mitrany to the classical realists. The functional approach accepted the current power political nature of international affairs, and with it the forces of nationalism and ideology, as important constraints on reform of the global governance. Its idea of slowly replacing the system of states with organisations based around existing international functions offered a pragmatic alternative to the problem of bridging the practicalities of the system of power politics with the normative need to develop a better system of global order in the age of the atom bomb and of deep cultural and ideological rifts. American classical realists, who saw the anarchy of the international as a problem that needed fixing were, therefore, more open to Mitrany's ideas than were English School theorists of international society, who saw in the western-led world of states a functioning system that did not necessarily need replacing. Interestingly, although Mitrany's ideas had been adopted and adapted by the so-called neo-functionalists, who used his ideas to build up explanations for the successes and potential of European integration,[30] Mitrany was much happier with the way that his ideas were used by the classical realists. Mitrany was on balance content with the way that Morgenthau portrayed his ideas, but he was deeply critical with the way that neo-functionalists turned his ideas into a depoliticised and ultimately regional and federal project of integration.[31] Yet, it was the combination of Morgenthau's endorsement and Mitrany's high visibility in neo-functionalist writings that would lead to a renaissance of the functional approach in the 1960s and 1970s, and the attraction of a younger breed of scholars to the functionalist banner such as John Groom, Paul Taylor, Robert Boardman, James Patrick Sewell and Mark Imber.[32]

While the 1950s and early 1960s in American and British IR were largely dominated by the scholars of the two Rockefeller-funded committees, this dominance was to be short-lived. By the 1960s new challenges were rising, and within a few decades both groups, as well as the functional approach, would be marginalised by new emerging analyses of the international. While the label realist would still be taken up by a sizeable and apparently dominant group in the field (especially in the United States), the nature of what realism stood for would change significantly. At the same time many new approaches would emerge, and some of these new approaches would bring back methods and issue areas that had been prominent before the Second World War, but had been marginalised by the two committees.

## IR in living memory. New developments since the 1960s

Understandings of the recent history of IR have been strongly influenced by the idea of 'Great Debates' ever since Michael Banks suggested in 1985 that there had been three Great Debates that had forged the field.[33] While it has been shown above that the idea of a first realist–idealist 'Great Debate' was a myth based on faulty understandings of the inter-war and wartime period, Bank's view of the other two 'Great Debates' does deserve closer analysis. On top of Banks' three 'Great Debates, later analyses have also added the idea of further debates that have been seen as definers of the field since the 1980s. This series of four or five debates has now become something of a standard approach to the history of IR. Of the three or four debates recognised as occurring after 1960 these are usually interpreted as:

1   A 'second Great Debate' between traditional historical interpreters of IR and the behaviouralists who were using quantitative and systems theory methods to understand the international.
2   An 'Inter-Paradigm Debate' (Banks' main concern) between the three dominant approaches of realism, liberalism/pluralism and structuralism.
3   A 'Fourth Great Debate' (sometimes lumped in, or replacing, Banks' 'Inter-Paradigm Debate' as the 'Third Great Debate') over epistemological issues between positivist and post-positivist approaches.[34]
4   Chris Brown has suggested that there might be a 'Fifth Great Debate' over critical realism, although he was not particularly enthused about it.[35]

To a certain extent all these discussions of 'Great Debates' are attempts to reflect a reality that these writers were living through. In this sense they are useful devices for the historian of ideas. That said, it is also important never to take a text, even one written quite recently, at face value. First off, the idea of 'Debates' is itself misleading, and in many cases seems to be an attempt to anchor more recent scholarly divisions into a clear narrative that goes back to a perceived 'discipline-founding' first great debate. Steve Smith has even criticised the 'Debate' label on the grounds that more often than not scholars holding different views have merely ignored each other.[36] That said, even if we are critical of the framework that has been created by the 'Great Debate' paradigm, the fact that those who have constructed it lived through at least three, and maybe four, of the debates they describe means that they must have been interpreting a situation that they were also witnessing. The 'Debates' model may be open to criticism, but it does at least provide a starting point for examining the ebbs and flows of theoretical fashion in IR over the last half decade.

Turning to the idea of a 'Second Great Debate' between traditional/historical and scientific/behaviouralist approaches, there is at least a literature here that resembles a proper scholarly debate. Perhaps the most famous exchange took place in 1966 between Hedley Bull and Morton Kaplan.[37] Even here there were signs that the two sides were talking past each other. The classical realist approach discussed in the last section had emerged, as Guilhot points out, as in large part an attempt to isolate IR from the largely behaviouralist and social scientific branches of American political science at a time when IR in the United States was finding itself absorbed into political science departments in post-war universities. As Guilhot also pointed out, this attempt to create a qualitative IR dominated by philosophical and historical theorising ultimately failed, and quantitative behaviouralist approaches to IR were never completely kept out. Rather, by the 1960s new approaches that copied the quantitative and systemic approaches of both the physical and social sciences were becoming popular in the United States. For Bull these 'behavioural' approaches could also be classed as an outside intrusion: 'their thinking is certainly characterized by a lack of any sense of inquiry into international politics as a continuing tradition to which they are the latest recruits'.[38] Perhaps, though, it was less their parvenu status, and more the fact that the scientific approach did not say anything that could not be said using the classical tradition steeped in history and philosophy, and that the big questions of IR were moral questions that were not susceptible to abstract modelling. Frederick Schuman was equally as damning, claiming that the 'behaviouralists' were 'unconsciously motivated ... by a wish to avoid all confrontation with public policies', gain themselves good university careers with research grants 'on projects which pleasantly evade all normative issues in the name of a "science" without values and without judgements'.[39]

Kaplan's response to Bull was to pay back accusations of naivety with accusations of naivety. Those in the classical (or, as Kaplan called them, 'traditional') approach had a partial view of both the 'scientific' approach they were attacking and the traditional view they were defending. The scientific method, rather than just repeating what could be said in a traditional qualitative way without behaviourist jargon, was investigating systems of unconscious motivation that are open to a scientific systemic analysis. Indeed, these systems of unconscious motivation are more easily understood in a systemic scientific way using a precise language that can be mistaken for jargon.[40] Kaplan also cast doubt on Bull's claims that the classical or traditional approach had a monopoly on philosophy. Indeed, Kaplan was sceptical of the philosophical pretentions of Bull and the traditionalists, arguing that they did not understand the philosophy they quoted, and also were not aware of when philosophical approaches might be appropriate, and when they would be inappropriate. 'The traditionalists' Kaplan argued, 'mistake explicitly heuristic models for dogmatic assertions. They mistake assertions about deductions within the framework of a model for statements about the open world of history.'[41] Whatever the rights or the wrongs of the case, it was certainly the case that by the late sixties the quantitative methods of the behaviourists had taken hold in American IR, and that the approach of the classical realists were no longer dominant.

Outside of the United States the largely quantitative behaviourist approach to IR never gained a dominant position. The exception was peace research, where the figure of Johan Galtung – a mathematician and sociologist – stands as the best example.[42] British IR remained largely immune to these changes, as can be seen by the popularity of Charles Reynolds' 1973 study of theories and methods in IR, which scathingly attacked the scientific claims of behaviourists and quantitative methods.[43] Even in the United States the enormity of the change was masked by the continued use of the term 'realist' to describe both the early classical realists as well as some of the new approaches such as systems theory. Some, such as John Vasquez, even argued that the core assumptions of the behavioural approach remained realist, and so realism was unchallenged by the 'second debate'.[44] The eclipse of classical realism, whose domination of United States IR had begun in the late 1940s, seemed to be rendered complete by the 1980s as a new 'neo-realism' emerged with a stress on the systemic structures of the system of states over the philosophical inquiry into the nature of humanity and the laws of human history.[45] Realism became identified with a state-centric approach that looked for explanations in the structure of the system of states, instead of with the study of the tensions between humanity's ethical and power-maximising natures. If by 'realist' we mean the classical realism of Morgenthau, Herz, Niebuhr and Schuman based in qualitative methods taken from history and the law, then its dominance in the United States lasted little more than thirty years, and was challenged within a decade of its establishment. At the time of writing it is no exaggeration to say that, for example, the overwhelming majority of experts on the classical realism of (for example) Morgenthau live and work in Europe, Australia and Canada. The few Morgenthau scholars in the United States, such as the excellent Bill Scheuerman, are exceptions to the general rule. Bill, after all, is actually classed as a political theorist in his University Department.

In the flurry of publishing in IR that followed the establishment of the two IR committees on both sides of the Atlantic something got lost. The stress on international society, national interests, power politics and diplomatic practice sidelined an area of international thought that had been a central part of international theorising since the late nineteenth century: the nature of the international political economy. By the early 1970s the economic blindness of so much of the work being done in IR seemed increasingly indefensible. Exceptions remained. The functional approach of David Mitrany, which had a small but loyal following on both sides of the Atlantic, remained fundamentally an approach to global governance grounded in a politico-economic synthesis. Benjamin Cohen notes that in the decades before 1970 there was a cadre of mostly economists in the United States writing on the links between wealth and power.[46] Yet, on balance, the heavy hitters in both British and American IR were more concerned with war, power and diplomacy.

The impetus to change this came from many angles. The rise of dependency theory during the 1950s in international development studies (itself influenced by the work of Albert O Hirschman discussed in the last chapter) challenged the power–political model by introducing the global trading system as an arena of conflict, and the division between the rich north and the poor south as a more important division than a global bipolar balance of power between the West and the East. Decolonisation during the 1960s brought a whole new world to the diplomatic table, a situation that was formalised by the establishment of the 'Group of 77' developing states in 1964 at the United Nations Conference on Trade and Development (UNCTAD) that acted as a coalition for the advancement of economic development issues shared by the world's poorer states. The early 1970s also witnessed two shocks to the United States-led western economic system. In 1971 the United States went off the gold standard, leading to claims of declining US domination and the ushering in of a new mercantilist stage in the global economy with the loss of an international gold-based currency. This marked an end for the Bretton Woods Accord of 1944 that had stabilised the world economy by pegging currencies to a gold-convertible US dollar. Two years later in 1973 the oil embargo of many western countries by the Arab members of the Organization of Petroleum Exporting Countries (OPEC) led to shortages and price rises. The oil shock had many effects, one of which was to challenge the western view that the biggest foreign policy issue was relations with the Soviet Union. Here was a challenge from the so-called Third World that called into question the nature of both the international system and the issues that were of primary importance to IR. In Britain the troubles and eventual demise of the 'Sterling Zone' (the largest currency bloc in the world) between 1967 and 1979 also brought interest in the links between wealth and power into sharp focus. Indeed Susan Strange's interest in Sterling's decline in the late 1960s was one of the factors that led her to become one of the founders of post-1970 IPE.[47]

Like the formation of the realist-led orthodoxy after the Second World War, the formation of IPE occurred separately in both the United States and Britain. While the way it formed on both sides of the Atlantic was different, there were also crucial links and interconnections that meant that the two developments were never completely separate. Benjamin Cohen has given a blow-by-blow account, and readers interested in the formation of IPE are directed to his account. While Cohen is at pains to point out that the development of IPE took place over a longer period of time, 1970 comes across as an important year. In that year *The Political Economy of International Relations* book series was established by Basic Books, Charles Kindleberger published his *Power and Money: The Politics of International Economics and the Economics of International Politics*, and Susan Strange's call to arms 'International Economics and International Relations: A Case of mutual Neglect' was published in *International Affairs*. Cohen believes that Strange's article, in retrospect, deserves a special place in the history of IPE: 'Nowhere else had the issue been posed in such concise and focused terms.'[48] In Britain the study of IPE, in which Strange was particularly active, found its first institutional form in the estsablishment of the International Political Economy Group (IPEG), established under the auspices of the Royal Institute of International Affairs in 1971. IPEG is now a group within the British International Studies Association (BISA), although BISA was not formally established until 1975.[49]

A major push for the study of IPE came from the growing interdependence in the West and between the West and the underdeveloped world in the years following the Second World War. While it is true to say that the obituaries for the interdependent liberal free trade world order penned by Polanyi and others in the mid-1940s were writing against the back-drop of a steady nationalisation of economies, after the war, in the West and its dependencies at least, this trend began to reverse itself under US hegemony. In the United States influential texts, such as Robert Keohane and Joseph Nye's *Power and Interdependence* not only argued that growing complex interdependence was leading to greater transnational linkages, it was also changing the nature of power in politico-economic affairs. At the time their work was seen as a challenge to the dominant state centric 'realist' orthodoxy in IR, and therefore as well as an early IPE text, *Power and Interdependence* was also seen as part of a revival of a liberal approach to IR.[50] In Britain Susan Strange's approach comes across more as an attack on liberalism, and her discussions of the importance of power, made for a different approach. According to Strange power is the fundamental variable which defines the relations between authority and markets. Power takes two forms, relational and structural. Relational power corresponds to the realist definition of power, where it is 'the power of A to get B to do something they would not otherwise do'. Strange, however, saw the existence of a more profound power, which is inherent in the structure of the global society. Structural power is the power to write the rules: 'to shape and determine the structures of the global political economy'. The possessors of structural power are 'able to change the range of choices open to others, without apparently putting pressure directly on them . . . Such power is less "visible".'[51] Structural power, she argued is manifest in four structures: control over security, production, finance and knowledge. Yet, being opposed to realism, or trying to expand the definition of power, was not a necessary condition for writing on IPE. In the work of Robert Gilpin a largely realist state-centric approach is preserved and integrated into a broader IPE approach by adding the market to the state. Gilpin did not integrate politics and economics. Instead, he treated them as two separate spheres that nonetheless have a profound influence on each other. While the main political organisation is the state, the main economic one is the market. The rise of both the state and the market were accomplished, Gilpin claimed, because they were the two most efficient organisations in their spheres.[52]

By the mid-1980s it became fashionable to see IR as a field that contained not one, but three dominant disciplines. This oligopoly formed the basis of two 1985 surveys of the nature of IR theory: Kal Holsti's book *The Dividing Discipline*, and Michael Banks' influential chapter 'The Inter-paradigm Debate'.[53] These three were called by different names, but they boiled down to:

1  A classical or realist tradition.
2  A pluralist, or world/global society paradigm based on liberalism.
3  A structuralist, dependency or world capitalist systems approach.

In Banks we see the beginnings of a grid that would become familiar to all who had to use IR textbooks since the 1990s. Banks' grid summarised the three paradigms in the following way:

> On actors, realists see only states; pluralists see states in combination with a great variety of others; and structuralists see classes. On dynamics, realists see force as primary; pluralists see complex social movements; structuralists see economics. On dependent variables, realists see the task of IR as simply to explain what states do; pluralists see it more grandly as an effort to explain all major world events; and structuralists see its function as showing why the world contains such appalling contrasts between rich and poor.[54]

Although many IR scholars and students have probably never read this paragraph, this is arguably the most influential paragraph in the teaching of contemporary IR. Banks' definitions, although they borrow and interpret from a wide variety of sources, put in one place a clear and easily contrastable set of criteria that could be used to pigeonhole all IR theory into one of three categories. Its parsimony is the secret of its success. Although the grids used in textbooks in both Britain and the United States subtract and add details to fit the tone of the text, the basic idea has remained the same. Banks' division, for example, was one of two ordering principles that I used in my own IR comprehensive essay (October 1991) during the early stages of my PhD programme at a Canadian university. Where the textbooks lead, university courses follow. How many of us have sat through or designed courses in IR theory where we start with realism, move on to liberalism/pluralism, then round this off with a discussion of some radical paradigm, or collection of approaches under an umbrella term like constructivism? The more sophisticated might break the three up (classical realism and neo-realism; Gramscian IPE, Feminist IR and poststructuralist theories), but behind this all remains the origin point of Banks' neat grid.

Ironically, this notion of a tripartite inter-paradigm debate was actually already out of date when it was published, and was certainly superseded before the 1980s came to a close. Four years before, in June 1981, a professor at York University published an article in a journal run by students from Michael Banks' own Department. Robert Cox's article incorporated many insights from a glittering array of social theorists. Starting with the historian Fernand Braudel, Cox drew from the works of E.H. Carr, Giambattista Vico, Karl Polanyi and R.G. Collingwood. There was another social theorist who also found his way into Cox's theoretical world-view: Antonio Gramsci. Starting from the premise that IR had not properly dealt with the split between state and civil society, Cox quickly moved on from the world systems theory of Immanuel Wallerstein (often regarded as a major name in the structuralist paradigm), which he states can be criticised for a tendency to undervalue the state and to unwittingly help maintain an exploitative system by looking for equilibrium rather than contradictions. From this Cox made his famous distinction between problem solving theory (ahistorical, solves problems within prevailing institutions, ideas and power relationships) and critical theory (historically grounded, analyses of the prevailing limits, and transcending these limits). Cox takes Gramsci's notions of hegemony to distinguish between two different structures: one based on dominant dictatorial power (non-hegemonic), and another based on an unequal arrangement between classes (hegemonic). Here Cox reordered the radical tradition in IR, putting ideas (necessary to understand how hegemony works) alongside institutions and material capabilities as one of three forces that operate within the structure of international society. Cox then added to this his three interactive levels: social forces, forms of state and world orders.[55] This use of Gramsci to construct a view of the international order that took account of the role of ideas in creating a class-biased compromise between classes under capitalism became an important means for interpreting the rise of neo-liberalism, and the failure of anti-capitalist forces since the 1980s. Out of it came the neo-Gramscian approach to IPE.

While Banks placed Cox and Gramsci in his structuralist paradigm, Cox had clearly moved beyond the classes as actors and economic dynamics that Banks saw as a feature of structuralism. This was acknowledged by Mark Hoffman in 1987, where the critical theory approach used by Cox (and which Hoffman associates more directly with the Frankfurt School sociology of Max Horkheimer, Theodor Adorno, Herbert Marcuse and Erich Fromm) is seen as above and beyond the three paradigms of the inter-paradigm debate. Rather, this critical theory can be applied to all three paradigms with varying success, and represents the next stage of IR theory that will be post-realist and post-Marxist. Most importantly for Hoffman, critical theory offered a chance for IR theory to rejoin the mainstream of social theory.[56] Yet, Hoffman's piece had also fallen victim to the rapid changes in IR theory during the 1980s. In a response to Hoffman published a year later Nick Rengger (then a young researcher who had just finished his PhD the year before) argued that the 'Coxian critical theory' employed by Hoffman was far less critical than it claimed, since it shared with a more conservative rationalism the desire to find elements that were 'universal to world order'. Cox's critical theory was, therefore, based on the same search for foundations for truth as the approaches that Cox criticised. Rengger advanced an altogether more philosophical critical approach based on the idea 'that all our conceptions may simply be historically contingent, that there is, in other words, *nothing* that is "universal to world order" because there is "nothing that is universal at all"'.[57] To back up his argument Rengger quotes a work by another recent PhD – a young American called James Der Derian – who Rengger argues is a critical theorist whose work does not fit into the category of critical theory as outlined by both Cox and Hoffman. Rengger was alluding to a new approach within IR, associated with Michael Shapiro, James Der Derian, Rob Walker and many others, that was using various poststructuralist and broadly postmodern anti-foundationalist philosophies to chart a very different view of what the international meant.

When I wrote my comprehensives for my PhD in 1991 I was dimly aware of this new turn in IR. To my shame it was not until 1992 that I started reading their works. I felt that this was important, but I also felt out of my depth philosophically. With the support of the ever open-minded Tim Shaw, the PhD students in our Department invited James Der Derian up to give the keynote at a workshop on poststructuralism in IR during March 1994. At the end of the two-day workshop, in my closing address, I admitted that my exposure to poststructuralism had made me realise what a vulgar Hegelian I was. What I didn't tell them was that throughout 1992 I had struggled hard to understand an approach so different to what I was used to, at one point being awoken from a dream in which all I could see was text. Looking back I am glad I persevered, though my experience demonstrates both how different the poststructuralist approaches were to the IR that had gone before, and also why so many students of IR preferred uninformed hostility to trying to understand. That said, the basic idea that underscored all poststructuralist IR was deceptively simple: that there were no true-for-all-time foundations to thought. Instead, ways of seeing the world, whatever their claims to scientific objectivity, were products of their time and place. Much of the confusion about complexity resulted from the problem that a different approach to knowledge requires a different vocabulary to understand it, and it takes time to understand that vocabulary. Using insights from Michel Foucault, Jacques Derrida, Jean Baudrillard, and Jacques Lacan, poststructuralist IR scholars challenged the foundations on which IR's understanding of the international rested.

The works in poststructuralist IR were as varied in the subject matter, as they were united in their rejection of a foundation to international thought. What we mistook for foundations (especially the classical realist notion of a knowable human nature) were, they argued, the products of our traditions of thought, and owed more to being accepted as articles of faith than they did to rigorous scientific observations. Before 1990 at least three key books were published in this area: James Der Derian wrote on the traditions of diplomacy as a product of the mediation of estrangement between societies;[58] Rob Walker and Saul Mendlovitz brought together a number of scholars who interrogated the notion of state sovereignty;[59] and Der Derian and Michael Shapiro brought together scholars with a common interest in shaping poststructuralist analyses of the international.[60] Throughout these the need to interrogate commonly held definitions and assumptions came through. While the subjects analysed remained diverse, a common position was the questioning of the central role in IR of the division between international and domestic politics. Indeed, one of Richard Ashley's two suggestions for poststructuralist research was to live on the 'borderline' between the international and the domestic.[61] This, in different ways appeared as a theme in many poststructuralist works of the next decade, including Rob Walker's *Inside/Outside* and David Campbell's analysis of the construction of US foreign policy as a product of internal American discourses and worries.[62]

Alongside this adoption and adaption of poststructuralist thought there also emerged another anti-foundationalist approach that came to be called constructivism. The first major constructivist work in IR is arguably Nicholas Onuf's *World of our Making* from 1989 (the work in which the phrase was coined), although it is Alexander Wendt's 1992 article 'Anarchy is What States

Make of It' that is often quoted as the key text in this approach.[63] The basic idea behind constructivism comes from an idea common in the philosophy of science that it is scientists that create their knowledge, rather than knowledge being a product of the observation of a 'real world'. What distinguishes constructivism from poststructuralism is that constructivism still accepts the existence of an unproblematic reality outside of thought. Constructivism has become a popular theory in IR, and some textbooks have been known to lump poststructuralism and feminism in with constructivism as a 'third paradigm' alongside liberalism and realism.[64]

There was also another group of scholars that emerged in IR only a few years after the poststucturalists had begun to break into the field. The workshop on poststructuralism that we organised at Dalhousie included two speakers – Sandra Whitworth and Jane Parpart – whose work combined poststructuralism with feminism. Just a few years before three publishing events had heralded the arrival (or, should I say, return) of feminism in IR theory: the publication of Jean Bethke Elshtain's *Women and War* in 1987; a special issue of *Millennium* in 1988 entitled 'Women and International Relations'; and the 1989 publication of Cynthia Enloe's ground-breaking book *Bananas, Beaches and Bases: Making Feminist Sense of International Politics*.[65] The *Millennium* special issue had been preceded by a conference in London in 1988, while two further conferences on feminism and IR had been held in 1989 at the University of Southern California, and in 1990 in Wellesley College in Massachusetts. A collection of the papers from the Wellesley conference were later published as an edited collection.[66] During the early 1990s a number of works on feminism, women and IR were published, so that by 1995 feminist IR had acquired firm academic foundations.[67]

As with poststructuralism, the importance of the feminist incursion into IR in the 1980s and 1990s was not that it brought a feminist voice to analyses of already existing concepts in IR such as sovereignty, power and the state,[68] but that a feminist approach brought new insights by subjecting IR's assumptions to feminist criticism. This was the intent, for example, in J. Ann Tickner's feminist reformulation of Morgenthau's six principles of political realism, which underscored how notions of objectivity, power and the autonomy of the individual could be unpacked and criticised by feminists for their association with masculinity and masculine ways of interpreting social reality.[69] Masculinity here being a social construct endowed with power through its association with males. Indeed, it was the examination of masculinity and its effects on IR theorising – the 'Man Question' in IR – that required interrogation.[70] It was not enough to have women talking about IR concepts, rather the aim was to interrogate those very concepts using gendered lenses.[71] While at one level the successful intervention into IR by feminism and feminist approaches has marked a shift in the nature of IR, there is still disquiet among feminist scholars. While feminist approaches are now common in IR, the perception among feminist scholars is that they still remain marginal, and much of IR is still dominated by an 'add women and stir' mentality, perhaps most clearly demonstrated by how feminism is tagged on to the end of IR theory courses.[72]

Scholars in IR, it seems, are too quick to forget the important work played by feminists in the construction of international thought prior to 1945, as described in the last three chapters above.

It would be tempting to see all these changes as part of the end of the Cold War (of the confrontation between East and West that had such an important influence on the development of realist thought in the 1950s). The only problem with this is that much of these new developments actually preceded the fall of the Berlin Wall in 1989 and the collapse of the Soviet Union in 1991. In fact, many of the earlier critical works came from the period of the first Reagan Administration when the perception at the time was that the growing political cooperation between the US and USSR in the 1970s (Détente) had come to an end, and that the world had entered a 'second cold war'.[73] The failure of realist scholars to predict the end of the Cold War led to much soul-searching in IR circles,[74] and also to the adoption of four texts in many IR courses across the English-speaking world. Two supported the idea of a new peaceful liberal order, while two predicted new avenues of conflict. These were: George Bush snr's 'Toward a New World Order' speech published in 1990 that predicted a new period of cooperation between states; Francis Fukuyama's 1989 *The End of History* that predicted a new peaceful liberal capitalist world, the dissenting Samuel P. Huntington's 1993 *Clash of Civilizations?* that predicted that conflict over ideology would be replaced by clashes over culture; and the pessimistic 1994 *The Coming Anarchy* of Robert Kaplan that predicted a more violent post-Cold War world.[75] Yet, even here a decline in the popularity of a structural neo-realism (seeing states as the main international actors, and interpreting international behaviour as the product of the structure of the international system) may have begun in the early 1980s. Looking over the field in the United States over the last thirty years one study suggested that published articles using realism never reached above 15 per cent.[76] This study also noticed a steady rise of articles using quantitative methods, although this growth of quantitative IR seems to be restricted to the United States, and represents a major split between IR in the US and IR in the rest of the world. Outside of the United States approaches to IR tend to be qualitative, and also often dominated by work that rejects attempts to develop theories that emulate the physical sciences (usually called 'post-positivist' IR).[77] Even then, it is clear that qualitative and post-positivist approaches remain strong in the United States as well.

## Conclusions: diversity, the problem with paradigms, and the issues ahead

What this thumbnail sketch of the field of IR since 1945 reveals is the extent to which theoretical stability has eluded IR. It has been tempting for many textbooks to see a long period of realist stability stretching from the Second World War (a 'First Great Debate') all the way to the 1980s (an 'Interparadigm Debate'). This also has the benefit of sandwiching realism's domination between two world-changing external events: the last world war and the fall of the Soviet bloc. There are problems with this neat story at both ends of the narrative: classical realism really emerges in the early 1950s, and the many approaches that emerged in the discipline to form the 'dividing discipline' sketched by Kal Holsti actually emerged gradually (and mostly before the fall of the iron curtain and the Soviet Union). There is another problem with this story. It brushes aside the myth of the 'Second Great Debate', seeing it as a methodological conflict within realism. Yet, in many respects the 'Second Great Debate Myth', while up to a point an equally flawed and inaccurate story, is an explanation for a major turning point in IR theorising. One part of this was the rise of quantitative and positivist 'behaviouralist' IR in the 1960s that challenged the classical realist tradition of qualitative work based on historical and philosophical understands of human behaviour. The second part of this was the development after the 1970s of a 'neo-realist' approach (which had its roots in earlier studies in the 1950s and 1960s); which changed the definition of realism from an approach using power, interests and ethics to understand the laws of history that dominate human behaviour to an approach that stressed states as the main actors in IR and explained international behaviour in terms of an understanding of the nature of the structure of the international system of states.

The classical realism of Morgenthau and his contemporaries, therefore, had a short run at intellectual hegemony that may have only lasted less than two decades. Even the successor that took its name failed to gain a monopoly of the field after the 1980s, and there is a possibility that the common perception that (neo-) realism is dominant may owe more to the need by non-realist scholars to have a convenient foil for asserting their own ideas. Realists there are in IR, and some of them are even followers of the classical realists, but there are also liberals, feminists, poststructuralists, Marxists and constructivists. This is not a new 'descent into incoherence', but rather a feature of international thought and the field of IR throughout the short history of both. The dominance of particular approaches have tended to be limited both in time and also space. Even within the western IR 'core' of English-speaking societies different approaches to IR have tended to dominate at different times. There never was, in this sense, a realist golden age, although different approaches calling themselves realist have made major contributions to the field. There was no 'dividing discipline' mainly because it has always been divided.[78]

All of this leads me to a major weakness in much IR thinking on its past: the domination of the idea of catch-all paradigms. The idea of paradigms cuts to the core of the 'great debates' myth, and the idea that IR theory can be ordered by two great events: a debate between realist and idealist paradigms, and an inter-paradigm debate in a new pluralistic IR. The idea of using paradigms comes from Thomas Kuhn's influential masterpiece on the history of science *The Structure of Scientific Revolutions*,[79] although it may also be influenced by E.H. Carr's idea of the relationship between utopian and realist stages in the development of a science. In this story the emergence of realism is seen as following Kuhn's view of how scientific revolutions occur: that a dominant paradigm comes under threat from scientific anomalies that erode the dominance of a paradigm by requiring the development of increasingly complex and unwieldy explanations for the anomaly. When a paradigm is developed that can explain those anomalies more efficiently, and the problem of the anomalies has become so serious in the older paradigm as to lead to questions about its validity, the older paradigm is replaced by the new one in a scientific revolution. This was often the way that the realist–idealist debate was presented in IR: 'The response to the failure of Idealists to explain the dominant events of the 1930s', Steve Smith argued in 1987, 'was the emergence, in good Kuhnian fashion, of an alternative paradigm, Realism.'[80] Yet, there are two important ways in which, despite the evoking of Kuhn's name, the use of paradigms in IR are at odds with the way that Kuhn interpreted the concept. First, for Kuhn paradigms in science follow each other, each one dominating the practice of normal 'problem-solving' science at different times. In fact, discussions of paradigms in IR emerged most clearly in the 1980s when IR, it was claimed, was in a three-way debate between three paradigms. Paradigms, for Kuhn, do not 'debate', and certainly not in multiples greater than two. Second, paradigms in IR do not fulfil Kuhn's requirement of being incommensurate and incomparable ways of interpreting the world.[81] In fact, the definition of the main paradigms in IR seem not to be Kuhnian paradigms at all, but rather a hotchpotch of different characteristics that mix assumptions about the source of human action, ideas about the proper units of analysis, and issues that arise as the result of research such as the nature of global politics. These 'paradigms' are not even self-contained, and are often amenable to being amalgamated with each other to create new theoretical approaches, such as the combination of realist and liberal assumptions found in the 1970s work of Keohane and Nye mentioned above. In fact, the lists of paradigm attributes put together in textbooks are often misleading and useless. For example, the common claim that realists believe that human nature is bad, but liberals/idealists believe it is good would lead us to have to include Norman Angell and Immanuel Kant as realists (they both regarded human nature as naturally bad), and to throw Reinhold Niebuhr out of the realist camp (he saw individuals as capable of strong ethical and self-sacrificing behaviour). The argument that realists are state-centric would probably see Morgenthau barred from realism, particularly after his public endorsement of David Mitrany in 1966. Looking at IR in terms of paradigms is not only a poor use of Kuhn, it is also an exercise that commits so many errors in terms of ordering IR theories and theorists that it fails to properly understand the richness and diversity of international scholars.[82]

Recently Duncan Bell has argued for the application of the work of the historian of science Peter Galison to the history of IR theory.[83] Although Galison's method was developed to understand physics, he has been reinterpreted for use in exploring the social sciences by Joel Isaac.[84] Basic to Galison's work is the idea that communities of scholars form subcultures based on both contact and on a common language. These subcultures survive by recruiting new younger students, and communicate with other subcultures in 'trading zones', where academic 'pidgeon' languages and 'creoles' develop that allow them to trade ideas and findings. The crucial thing about Galison's subcultures is that, unlike Kuhnian paradigms, they are not self-sufficient (it is not for nothing they are called *sub*cultures), and in fact there is a lively intellectual cross-fertilisation between subcultures through intellectual trading zones. This model seems much more applicable to IR than does the 'paradigm' model used now, although some of the approaches in IR that often get called a 'paradigm' might be better classed as Galisonian subcultures. Thus, Gramscian IPE (a group of scholars talking the same language and communicating with each other) could be seen as an IR subculture. Similarly, it is also common in IR to refer to schools of thought that are often tied to one or more major universities. Thus, in strategic studies it is common to talk of the 'Copenhagen School' or the 'Welsh School'. Going further back, Kenneth W. Thompson's lucid 1996 account of the history of American IR divides the theory of the 1940s and 1950s into three schools, loosely based around Chicago, Harvard and Yale.[85]

This study also supports the move towards a subculture approach. There are just too many inter-linkages and multiple fissures for paradigms to be useful for the understanding of IR. Galison's subcultures have another advantage. The use of paradigms has centred around attempts to find common concepts and assumptions that are all-to-easily proved to be a poor way to distinguish thinkers. We tend to over-emphasise agreements within an identified paradigm, and under-play the commonalities between theorists in different paradigms (think the antipathy between Morgenthau and Carr, but the common ground between Mitrany and Morgenthau). Subcultures are not necessarily marked by common assumptions as they are by both proximity and common language. It also accepts that, through trading zones, even those in different subcultures can talk to each other. Since subcultures are lived communities we can much more easily account for their rise and fall through their relative effectiveness at attracting new members (whether that be for reasons internal or external to the discipline). If there is a space for Kuhn here then it is probably at a much bigger picture level. If there is an incommensurate and incomparable way of interpreting the world that we can call the dominant paradigm of IR it is the very notion that we can study the international as a separate part of human social existence. In this sense, the paradigm that dominates IR is the incommensurate and incomparable one that has been the subject of this book: the idea of the international itself. It is a paradigm that emerged out of the nineteenth century, took the form of a field in the twentieth century, and is the 'normal science' that we practise when we teach, research and mentor. Within this paradigm are many subcultures that interpret the field in many different ways. The scientific revolution, if and when it comes, will be a result of the growing anomalies building up as we find new and ingenious ways to account for the lack of autonomy of the international.

I have one final point to make here. In Chapters 4 and 5 I discussed how major changes to the shape of western society sparked an interest in the international, and eventually led to it becoming an intellectual field of study in its own right. IR, in this sense, is a product of industrialisation and the development of a hydrocarbon-based civilisation dependent first on coal, and then on oil. This new society created both a change in the nature of war and the development of a new imperialism, and it was the growth and interaction of these two that fed into the birth of IR as we know it. If IR was a product of these changes, then what do recent changes mean for the future of IR? Can IR give adequate answers to the problems posed by the end of oil and the advent of climate change? This brings in one approach to IR that I left out from my summary in the last section: 'green' IR.[86] The crises of climate change and of hydrocarbon depletion pose grave threats to the global society that IR was developed to study. To a certain extent this crisis has validated the study of the international. After all, these are crises that have a global reach, and the failures of states to manage the crises so far can be seen as a failure of international relations, and therefore well within the bailiwick of the field. If we add to this the crises associated with globalised capitalism – especially the growing inequalities between rich and poor, and the ongoing problems of global finance – then the relevance of the study of the international, by whatever name we call it, is unlikely to diminish in the near future.

## Notes

1  See A. Acharya, and B. Buzan, 'Why is There No Non-Western International Relations Theory? An Introduction', *International Relations of the Asia-Pacific*, 2007, 7, 287–312.
2  On the link between classical realism and David Mitrany see William Scheuerman, 'The (Classical) Realist Vision of Global Reform', *International Theory*, 2010, 2, 246–82. On Schuman's criticism of quantitative and behavioural IR see Frederick L. Schuman, *International Politics. Anarchy and Order in the World Society*, seventh edn (New York: McGraw-Hill, 1969), vii–viii.
3  Hans J. Mogenthau, *Politics Among Nations. The Struggle for Power and Peace*, fifth edn (New York: Alfred A. Knopf, 1973), 14.
4  On the American story see Nicolas Guilhot, 'The Realist Gambit: Postwar American Political Science and the Birth of IR Theory', *International Political Sociology*, 2008, 2, 281–304. On the British Committee see Tim Dunne, *Inventing International Society. A History of the English School* (Houndmills: Macmillan, 1998), especially chs 5 and 6.
5  Guilhot, 'The Realist Gambit'; and Nicolas Guilhot, *The Invention of International Relations Theory: Realism, the Rockefeller Foundation, and the 1954 Conference on Theory* (New York: Columbia University Press, 2011).
6  Quincy Wright, *The Study of International Relations* (New York: Appleton-Century-Crofts, 1955), 33.
7  Guilhot, 'The Realist Gambit', 295.
8  Hans J. Morgenthau, *Scientific Man vs Power Politics* (Chicago: University of Chicago Press, 1946), 2.
9  Morgenthau, *Scientific Man vs Power Politics*, 201.
10  Interest in Morgenthau has grown in recent years, and there are now several excellent discussions of his work that bring out the complexities of this thinking. These include: Christoph Frei, *Hans J. Morgenthau. An Intellectual Biography* (Baton Rouge: Louisiana State University Press, 2001); Sean Molloy, *The Hidden History of Realism: A Genealogy of Power Politics* (London and New York: Palgrave Macmillan, 2006); Sean Molloy, 'Truth, Power, Theory: Hans Morgenthau's Formulation of Realism', *Diplomacy and Statecraft*, 2004, 15(1), 1–34; Michael C. Williams (ed.) *Realism*

*Reconsidered. The Legacy of Hans J. Morgenthau in International Relations* (Oxford: Oxford University Press, 2007); William Sheuerman, *Hans J. Morgenthau: Realism and Beyond* (Cambridge: Polity Press, 2009).

11  Guilhot, 'The Realist Gambit', 295.

12  Guilhot, 'The Realist Gambit', 289–92, 293.

13  Dunne, *Inventing International Society*.

14  Ian Hall, *Dilemmas of Decline. British Intellectuals and World Politics, 1945–1975* (Berkeley: University of California Press, 2012).

15  David Long, 'C. A. W. Manning and the Discipline of International Relations', *The Round Table*, 2005, 94(1), 91.

16  Herbert Butterfield, *History and Human Relations* (London: Collins, 1951), 31.

17  Dunne, *Inventing International Society*, 90–1.

18  Dunne, *Inventing International Society*, especially ch. 5.

19  Ian Hall, 'The Revolt Against the West: Decolonisation and the Repercussions in British International Thought, 1945–1975', *International History Review*, 2011, 33 (1), 43–84; and Hall, *Dilemmas of Decline*, ch. 8.

20  See Hall's discussion above on the position adopted by these three members of the British Committee.

21  Dunne, *Inventing International Society*, 93.

22  Kenneth W. Thompson, *Schools of Thought in International Relations. Interpreters, Issues, and Morality* (Baton Rouge: Louisiana State University Press, 1996), 83–4.

23  John H. Herz, *International Politics in the Atomic Age* (New York: Columbia University Press, 1959), 327–9. See also: Scheuerman, '(Classical) Realist Vision', 264–6 and Casper Sylvest, 'Realism and International Law: the Challenge of John H. Herz', *International Theory*, 2010, 2(3), 436.

24  See also Scheuerman, '(Classical) Realist Vision', 262–4.

25  Hans J. Morgenthau, 'Introduction', in David Mitrany, *A Working Peace System* (Chicago: Quadrangle, 1966), 11.

26  Thompson, *Schools of Thought in International Relations*, 84.

27  See his review in *International Affairs*, 1945, 21(4), 524.

28  See Scheuerman, '(Classical) Realist Vision', 256–7.

29  Inis Claude, *Swords into Plowshares* (New York: Random House, 1956), 386.

30  See: Ernst B. Haas, *The Uniting of Europe: Political, Social and Economic Forces, 1950–57* (London: Stevens, 1958) and *Beyond the Nation State. Functionalism and International Organization* (Stanford: Stanford University Press, 1964); Leon N. Lindberg and Stuart A. Scheingold, *Europe's Would-Be Polity* (Englewood Cliffs, NJ: Prentice-Hall, 1970).

31  For Mitrany's objection to Haas' interpretation see 'Note to Ernst Haas', 14 February 1963, From the Mitrany Papers, British Library of Political and Economic Sciences, LSE, London.

32  See, for example, James Patrick Sewell, *Functionalism and World Politics. A Study Based on United Nations Programs Financing Economic Development* (Princeton: Princeton University Press, 1966); A.J.R. Groom and Paul Taylor, *Functionalism: Theory and Practice* (London: University of London Press, 1975). Mark F. Imber, 'Re-Reading Mitrany: A Pragmatic Assessment of Sovereignty', *Review of International Studies*, April 1984, 10(2), 103–23. Robert Boardman also acted as David Mitrany's research assistant in the 1970s, and in the early 1990s was my PhD supervisor on a project that looked at both Norman Angell and David Mitrany.

33  Michael Banks, 'The Inter-paradigm Debate', in Margot Light and A.J.R. Groom (eds), *International Relations: A Handbook of Current Theory* (London: Pinter, 1985), 7–26.

34  Yosef Lapid, 'The Third Debate: On the Prospects of International Theory in a Post-Positivist Era', *International Studies Quarterly*, 1989, 33, 235–54.

35  Chris Brown, 'Situating Critical Realism', *Millennium – Journal of International Studies*, 2007, 35(2), 409–16.

36  Steve Smith in C. Reus-Smit and D. Snidal (eds), *The Oxford Handbook of International Relations* (Oxford: Oxford University Press, 2008), 726.

37  Hedley Bull, 'International Theory: The Case for a Classical Approach', *World Politics*, 1966, 18(3), 361–77; and Morton Kaplan, 'The New Great Debate: Traditionalism vs Science in International Relations', *World Politics*, 1966, 19(1), 1–20.

38  Bull, 'International Theory: The Case for a Classical Approach', 375–6.

39  Schuman, *International Politics*, viii.

40  Kaplan, 'The New Great Debate', 3–6.

41  Kaplan, 'The New Great Debate', 20.

42  For his method at this time see Johan Galtung, *Theory and Methods of Social Research* (New York: Columbia, 1967).

43  See Charles Reynolds, *Theory and Explanation in International Politics* (London, Martin Robertson, 1973).

44  See John A. Vasquez, *The Power of Power Politics: A Critique* (New Brunswick, NJ: Rutgers University Press, 1983).

45  This approach was spurred on and championed by Kenneth Waltz. Although a qualitative IR scholar, his use of structure represented a departure from the political realism of Morgenthau, even though Morgenthau was quoted approvingly by Waltz as a structural theorist. See Kenneth Waltz, *Theory of International Politics* (Reading, MA: Addison-Wesley, 1979).

46  Benjamin Cohen, *International Political Economy. An Intellectual History* (Princeton: Princeton University Press, 2008), 20.

47  See Cohen, *International Political Economy*, 47. According to Cohen Strange started to study Sterling when she joined the Royal Institute of International Affairs in 1964. Her book on Sterling came out in 1971: Susan Strange, *Sterling and British Policy: A Political Study of an International Currency in Decline* (London: Oxford University Press, 1971).

48  Cohen, *International Political Economy*, 21.

49  Cohen traces its founding from an earlier 1974 meeting, while the idea was first formally agreed to in 1973. Interestingly, Susan Strange was also involved in the foundation of BISA.

50  Robert O. Keohane and Joseph S. Nye, *Power and Interdependence. World Politics in Transition* (Boston: Little Brown, 1977). For their place in a new liberal paradigm in IR see, for example, Banks, 'The Inter-paradigm Debate', 16–17 (although Banks singles out John Burton as the most important member).

51  Susan Strange, *States and Markets. An Introduction to International Political Economy* (London, Pinter, 1988), 24–5, 31.

52  Robert Gilpin, *The Political Economy of International Relations* (Princeton: Princeton University Press, 1987).

53  K.J. Holsti, *The Dividing Discipline. Hegemony and Diversity in International Theory* (Boston: Allen & Unwin, 1985); Banks, 'The Inter-paradigm Debate', 7–26.

54  Banks, 'The Inter-paradigm Debate', 12–13.

55  Robert W. Cox, 'Social Forces, States and World Orders: Beyond International Relations Theory', *Millennium: Journal of International Studies*, 1981, 10(2), 126–55.

56  Mark Hoffman, 'Critical Theory and the Inter-Paradigm Debate', *Millennium: Journal of International Studies*, 1987, 16(2), 231–49.

57  N.J. Rengger, 'Going Critical? A Response to Hoffman', *Millennium: Journal of International Studies*, 1988, 17(1), 81–9. The quote is from page 86. Emphasis in the original.

58  James Der Derian, *On Diplomacy* (Oxford: Blackwell, 1987).

59 R.B.J. Walker and Saul Mendlovitz (eds), *Contending Sovereignties: Redefining Political Community* (London: Lynne Rienner, 1990).

60 James Der Derian and Michael Shapiro (eds), *International/Intertextual Relations. Postmodern Readings of World Politics* (Lexington, MA: Lexington Books, 1989).

61 Richard K. Ashley, 'Living on Borderlines: Man, Poststructuralism, and War', in Der Derian and Shapiro, *International/Intertextual Relations*, 309.

62 R.B.J. Walker, *Inside/Outside: International Relations as Political Theory* (Cambridge: Cambridge University Press, 1993); David Campbell, *Writing Security: United States Foreign Policy and the Politics of Identity* (Manchester: Manchester University Press, 1998).

63 Nicholas Onuf, *World of Our Making: Rules and Rule in Social Theory and International Relations* (Columbia, SC: University of South Carolina Press, 1989); Alexander Wendt, 'Anarchy is What States Make of It: The Social Construction of Power Politics', *International Organization*, 1992, 46(2), 396–399.

64 See, for example, John T. Rourke, *International Politics on the World Stage*, twelfth edn (Boston: McGraw-Hill, 2008), 19.

65 Jean Bethke Elshtain, *Women and War* (Chicago: University of Chicago Press, 1987); Special Issue on Women and International Relations, *Millennium*, 1988, 17, 3; Cynthia Enloe, *Bananas, Beaches and Bases: Making Feminist Sense of International Politics* (Berkeley, CA: California University Press, 1989).

66 V. Spike Peterson (ed.), *Gendered States: Feminist (Re)Visions of International Relations Theory* (Boulder: Lynne Rienner, 1992).

67 J. Ann Tickner, *Gender in International Relations: Feminist Perspectives on Achieving Global Security* (New York: Columbia University Press, 1992); V. Spike Peterson and Anne Runyan, *Global Gender Issues* (Boulder, CO: Westview, 1993); Sandra Whitworth, *Feminism and International Relations: Towards a Political Economy of Gender in Interstate and Non-Governmental Institutions* (New York: Macmillan, 1994); Christine Sylvester, *Feminist Theory and International Relations in a Postmodern Era* (Cambridge: Cambridge University Press, 1994).

68 See the discussion of this in Annick T.R. Wibben, 'Feminist International Relations: Old Debates and New Directions', *Brown Journal of World Affairs*, 2004, 10(2), 97–114.

69 J. Ann Tickner, 'Hans Morgenthau's Principles of Political Realism: A Feminist Reformulation', *Millennium*, 1988, 17(3), 429–40.

70 See, for example, Marysia Zalewski and Jane Parpart (eds), *The 'Man' Question in International Relations* (Boulder, CO: Westview, 1998).

71 A point made very well in Marysia Zalewski, 'Well, What is the Feminist Perspective on Bosnia?', *International Affairs*, 1995, 71(2), 339–56.

72 See, for example, Jill Steans, 'Engaging from the Margins: Feminist Encounters with the "Mainstream" of International Relations', *British Journal of Politics and International Relations*, 2003, 5(3), 428–54.

73 See, for example, Fred Halliday, *The Making of the Second Cold War* (London: Verso, 1983).

74 See, for example, John Lewis Gaddis, 'International Relations Theory and the End of the Cold War', *International Security*, 1992–3, 17, 5–58.

75 George Bush, 'Toward a New World Order', *Dispatch*, 17 September 1990, 1(3), 91–4; Francis Fukuyama, 'The End of History?', *The National Interest*, 1989, 16, 3–18; and Samuel P. Huntington, 'The Clash of Civilizations?', *Foreign Affairs*, 1993, 72(3), 22–49; Robert D. Kaplan, 'The Coming Anarchy: How Scarcity, Crime, Overpopulation, Tribalism, and Disease are Rapidly Destroying the Social Fabric of our Planet', *Atlantic Monthly*, 1994, 273(2), 44–65.

76 Daniel Maliniak, Amy Oakes, Susan Peterson and Michael J. Tierney, 'International Relations in the US Academy', *International Studies Quarterly*, 2011, 55, 437–64.

77 See the contributions to Arlene B. Tickner and Ole Wæver (eds), *International Relations Scholarship Around the World* (London: Routledge, 2009).

78  Interestingly, my view expressed here contradicts the view of the 'three ages of IR' that I present in my own 'Interdisciplinarity and International Relations', *European Political Science*, 2008, 9, 16–25. I hope this represents a maturing of my thinking.

79  Thomas S. Kuhn, *The Structure of Scientific Revolutions* (Chicago: University of Chicago Press, 1962).

80  Steve Smith, 'Paradigm Dominance in International Relations: The Development of International Relations as a Social Science', *Millennium*, 1987, 16(2), 192.

81  See the discussion of this in Patrick Thaddeus Jackson and Daniel H. Nexon, 'Paradigmatic Faults in International Relations Theory', *International Studies Quarterly*, 2009, 53, 907–30.

82  This argument is made in my 'The Poverty of Paradigms: Subcultures, Trading Zones and the case of Liberal–Socialism in Interwar International Relations', *International Relations*, 2012, 26(1), 35–59.

83  Duncan Bell, 'Writing the World: Disciplinary History and Beyond', *International Affairs*, 2009, 85(1), 3–22.

84  See Bell, 'Writing the World', 3–22; Peter Galison, *Image and Logic: A Material Culture of Microphysics* (Chicago: University of Chicago Press, 1997); Joel Isaac, 'Tangled Loops: Theory, History, and the Human Sciences in Modern America', *Modern Intellectual History*, 2009, 6(2), 397–424.

85  Thompson, *Schools of Thought in International Relations.*

86  A recent example of this is Peter Newell and Matthew Patterson, *Climate Capitalism. Global Warming and the Transformation of the Global Economy* (Cambridge: Cambridge University Press, 2010).

# Bibliography

Acharya, A. and B. Buzan, 'Why is There no Non-Western International Relations Theory? An Introduction', *International Relations of the Asia-Pacific*, 2007, 7, 287–312.

Adams, Brooks. *The Law of Civilization and Decay* (New York: Vintage, 1943 [1896]).

Adams, Brooks, *The New Empire* (New York: Bergman, 1969 [1902]).

Alonso, Harriet Hyman. 'Nobel Peace Laureates, Jane Addams and Emily Greene Balch: Two Women of the Women's International League for Peace and Freedom', *Journal of Women's History*, 1995, 7(2), 6–26.

Anderson, Kevin B. *Marx at the Margins* (Chicago: University of Chicago Press, 2010).

Anderson, M. S. *War and Society in Europe of the Old Regime 1618–1789* (Stroud: Sutton, 1998).

Anderson, Perry. *The Lineages of the Absolutist State* (London: New Left Books, 1974).

Angell, Norman. *The Great Illusion. A Study of the Relation of Military Power in Nations to their Economic and Social Advantage* (Toronto: McClelland and Goodchild, 1911).

Angell, Norman. *Peace Theories and the Balkan War* (London: Horace Marshall, 1912).

Angell, Norman. *War and the Essential Realities* (London: Watts, 1913).

Angell, Norman. *The Foundations of International Polity* (London: William Heinemann, 1914).

Angell, Norman. 'Peace Terms', Labour Party Advisory Committee on International Questions memorandum no. 61, May 1919. People's History Museum Archives, Manchester.

Angell, Norman. *The Fruits of Victory* (New York: Garland, 1970 [1921]).

Angell, Norman. 'The International Anarchy', in Leonard Woolf (ed.), *The Intelligent Man's Way to Prevent War* (London: Victor Gollancz, 1933).

Anon, 'Revision of the Treaty of Versailles', Labour Party Advisory Committee on International Questions memorandum no. 254a, 1922. People's History Museum Archives, Manchester.

Anon, 'The Need for a League Foreign Policy', Labour Party Advisory Committee on International Questions memorandum no.287, 9 July 1923. People's History Museum Archives, Manchester.

Arnold-Foster, William. 'Commentary on the British Government's Observations to the League, on Arbitration and Security', Advisory Committee on International Questions memo no. 386, February 1928. People's History Museum Archives, Manchester.

Arnold-Forster William and Leonard Woolf. 'Proposed Recommendation to the Executive Regarding a Convention for Pacific Settlement', Advisory Committee on International Questions memo no. 355a, nd. People's History Museum Archives, Manchester.

Aron, Raymond. *Peace and War. A Theory of International Relations* (New York: Doubleday, 1966).

Ash, Rhiannon. *Tacitus* (London: Bristol Classical Press, 2006).

Ash, Ronald G. *The Thirty Years War. The Holy Roman Empire and Europe, 1618–1648* (Basingstoke: Macmillan, 1997).

Ashley, Richard K. 'Untying the Sovereign State: A Double Reading of the Anarchy Problematique', *Millennium: Journal of International Studies,* 1988, 17(2), 227–62.

Ashworth, Lucian M. *Creating International Studies. Angell, Mitrany and the Liberal Tradition* (Aldershot: Ashgate, 1999).

Ashworth, Lucian M. 'Bringing the Nation Back In?', in Lucian M. Ashworth and David Long (eds) *New Perspectives in International Functionalism* (Houndsmill: Macmillan, 1999), 69–71.

Ashworth, Lucian M. 'Did the Realist–Idealist Great Debate Really Happen?', *International Relations,* 2002, 16(1), 33–51.

Ashworth, Lucian M. 'Where are the Idealists in Interwar International Relations?', *Review of International Studies,* 2006, 32, 291–308.

Ashworth, Lucian M. *International Relations and the Labour Party:Intellectuals and Policy Making from 1918–1945* (London: IBTauris, 2007).

Ashworth, Lucian M. 'Interdisciplinarity and International Relations', *European Political Science,* 2008, 9, 16–25.

Ashworth, Lucian M. 'Rethinking a Socialist Foreign Policy: The British Labour Party and International Relations 1918 to 1931', *International Labor and Working Class History,* 2009, 75, 30–48.

Ashworth, Lucian M. 'Feminism, War and the Prospects for Peace. Helena Swanwick (1864–1939) and the Lost Feminists of Inter-War International Relations', *International Feminist Journal of Politics,* 2011, 13(1), 25–43.

Ashworth, Lucian M. 'The Poverty of Paradigms: Subcultures, Trading Zones and the case of Liberal-Socialism in Interwar International Relations', *International Relations,* 2012, 26(1), 35–59.

Ashworth, Lucian M. and Larry A. Swatuk, 'Masculinity and the Fear of Emasculation', in Marysia Zalewski and Jane Parpart (eds), *The Man Question in International Relations* (Boulder, CO: Westview, 1997).

Bacon, Francis. *The Essays 1601,* http://www.orst.edu/instruct/ph1302/texts/bacon/bacon_eaasays.html.

Baker, Ernest. *Political Thought in England 1848 to 1914* (London: Thornton Butterworth, 1928).

Balch, Emily Greene 'The Habit of Peace', *McCalls Magazine,* February 1919.

Balch, Emily Greene 'Women's Work for Peace', *The World Tomorrow,* November 1922, 336.

Banks, Michael. 'The Inter-paradigm Debate', in Margot Light and A. J. R. Groom (eds), *International Relations: A Handbook of Current Theory* (Boulder, CO: Lynne Rienner, 1985), 7–26.

Bartelson, Jens. *A Genealogy of Sovereignty* (Cambridge: Cambridge University Press, 1995).

Baylis, John and Steve Smith, *The Globalization of World Politics,* 3rd edition (Oxford: Oxford University Press, 2005).

Beaulieu, Paul Leroy. *Contemporary Wars (1853–1866). Statistical Researches Respecting the Loss of Men and Money Involved in Them* (London: Peace Society, 1869).

Bell, Duncan. 'Writing the World: Disciplinary History and Beyond', *International Affairs,* 2009 85(1), 3–22.

Bentham, Jeremy. *The Works of Jeremy Bentham* (New York: Russell and Russell, 1962).

Bentham, Jeremy. 'An International Code', in *Basic Texts in International Relations*, ed. Evan Luard (Basingstoke: Macmillan, 1992).

Bentham, Jeremy. *Colonies, Commerce and Constitutional Law* (Oxford: Oxford University Press, 1995).

Birn, D. S. *The League of Nations Union 1918–1945* (Oxford: Oxford University Press, 1981).

Bisceglia, Louis R. 'Norman Angell and the Pacifist Muddle', *Bulletin of the Institute of Historical Research*, 1972, 45, 104–19.

Black, Jeremy. 'Empire and Enlightenment in Gibbon's Treatment of International Relations', *The International History Review*, 1995, 17, 441–58.

Bloch, I. S. *Is War now Impossible?* (Aldershot: Gregg Revivals, 1991 [1899]).

Bodin, Jean. *The Six Bookes of a Commonweale* (Cambridge, MA: Harvard University Press, 1962).

Bosanquet, Bernard. 'The Function of the State in Promoting the Unity of Mankind', *Proceedings of the Aristotelian Society*, 1916–17, 17, 28–57.

Bosanquet, Bernard. *Social and International Ideals. Being a Study in Patriotism* (London: Macmillan, 1917).

Bosanquet, Bernard. *The Philosophical Theory of the State*, fourth edition (London: Macmillan, 1923).

Botero, Giovanni. *The Reason of State* (London: Routledge, 1956).

Botero, Giovanni. *A Treatise Concerning The Causes of the Magnificency and Greatness of Cities* (http://onlinebooks.library.upenn.edu/webbin/book/lookupid?key=olbp12563).

Boucher, David. *Political Theories of International Relations. From Thucydides to the Present* (Oxford: Oxford University Press, 1998).

Bourne, Randolph. *The State* (Tucson: Sharp, 1998).

Bowman, Isaiah. 'The Pioneer Fringe'. *Foreign Affairs*, 1927, 6, 49–66.

Bowman, Isaiah. *The New World. Problems in Political Geography*, fourth edition (Yonkers-on-Hudson: World Book Company, 1928).

Bowman, Isaiah. *International Relations* (Chicago: American Library Association, 1930).

Bowman, Isaiah (ed.), *Limits of Land Settlement. A Report on Present-Day Possibilities* (New York: Books for Libraries, 1937).

Bowman, Isaiah. 'Peace and Power Politics', *Vital Speeches of the Day*, 1 April 1941, 7(12), 383.

Bowman, Isaiah. 'Geography vs. Geopolitics', *Geographical Review*, 1942, 32, 646–58.

Brailsford, H. N. *The War of Steel and Gold. A Study of the Armed Peace*, ninth edition (London: Bell, 1917).

Brailsford, H. N. *A League of Nations* (London: Headley, 1917).

Brailsford, H. N. 'A Parliament of the League of Nations', Labour Party Advisory Committee on International Questions memorandum no. 44, January 1919. People's History Museum Archives, Manchester.

Brailsford, H. N. *After the Peace* (London: Leonard Parsons, 1920).

Brailsford, H. N. 'Arbitrate or Disarm. A New View of Security', *New Leader*, 12 September 1924, 3–4.

Brailsford, H. N. *Towards a New League* (London: New Statesman and Nation, 1936).

Brailsford, H. N. 'The Tory Policy of Peace', *The Political Quarterly*, 1938, 9(3), 325–33.

Brailsford, H. N. *Why Capitalism Means War* (New York: Garland, 1972 [1938]).

Brailsford, H. N. *Our Settlement with Germany* (Harmondsworth: Penguin, 1944).

Brailsford, H. N. *The Life Work of J. A. Hobson* (London: Oxford University Press, 1948).

Breight, Curtis C. *Surveillance, Militarism and Drama in the Elizabethan Era* (Houndmills: Macmilan, 1996).

Bright, John. *Selected Speechs of the Right Honourable John Bright MP on Public Questions* (London: J. M. Dent, 1907).

Brinton, Henry (ed.). *Does Capitalism Cause War?* (London: H & E.R. Brinton, 1935).

Brown, Chris, Terry Nardin and Nicholas Rengger. *International Relations in Political Thought. Texts from the Ancient Greeks to the First World War* (Cambridge: Cambridge University Press, 2002).

Brown, Chris. 'Situating Critical Realism', *Millennium – Journal of International Studies*, 2007, 35(2), 409–16.

Brown, Chris with Kirsten Ainley. *Understanding International Relations* (Houndmills: Palgrave Macmillan, 2005).

Brunhes, Jean. *Human Geography. An Attempt at a Positive Classification, Principles and Examples* (London: George G. Harrap, 1920).

Bull, Hedley. 'International Theory: The Case for a Classical Approach', *World Politics*, 1966, 18(3), 361–77.

Burns, Delisle, Bertrand Russell and G. D. H. Cole. 'The Nature of the State in View of its External Relations', *Proceedings of the Aristotelian Society*, 1915–16, 16, 290–325.

Burns, C. Delisle. 'Notes on the League', Labour Party Advisory Committee on International Questions memorandum no. 143, 8 June 1920. People's History Museum Archives, Manchester.

Burrow, John. *A History of Histories* (Harmondsworth: Penguin, 2009).

Bush, George. 'Toward a New World Order', *Dispatch*, 17 September 1990, 1(3), 91–4.

Butler, Nicholas Murray. *The International Mind. An Argument for the Judicial Settlement of International Disputes* (New York: Charles Scribner's Sons, 1912).

Butler, Nicholas Murray. *The Family of Nations. Its Need and its Problems. Essays and Addresses* (New York: Charles Scribner, 1938).

Butterfield, Herbert. *The Whig Interpretation of History* (New York: Norton 1981 [1931]).

Butterfield, Herbert. *History and Human Relations* (London: Collins, 1951).

Caedel, Martin. *Pacifism in Britain 1914–1945* (Oxford: Clarendon, 1980).

Caedel, Martin. *Living the Great Illusion. Sir Norman Angell 1872–1967* (Oxford: Oxford University Press, 2009).

Campbell, David. *Writing Security: United States Foreign Policy and the Politics of Identity* (Manchester: Manchester University Press, 1998).

Carr, E. H. 'Public Opinion as a Safeguard of Peace', *International Affairs*, 1936, 15(6), 846–62.

Carr, E. H. *The Twenty Years' Crisis 1919–1939: An Introduction to the Study of International Relations* (New York: Harper Torch, 1964 [1939]).

Carr, E. H. *Conditions of Peace* (London: Macmillan, 1942).

Carr, E. H. *Nationalism and After* (London: Macmillan, 1945).

Carr, E. H. 'Proudhon: The Robinson Crusoe of Socialism', in E. H. Carr, *Studies in Revolution* (London: Macmillan, 1950), 38–55.

Carvalho, Benjamin de, Halvard Leira and John Hobson, 'The Big Bangs of IR: The Myths That Your Teachers Still Tell You about 1648 and 1919', *Millennium*, 2011, 39(3), 735–58.

Cassirer, Ernst. *An Essay on Man. An Introduction to a Philosophy of Human Culture* (New Haven: Yale University Press, 1944).

'Cato', *Guilty Men* (London: Victor Gollancz, 1941).

Cavallar, Georg. *Kant and the Theory and Practice of International Right* (Cardiff: University of Wales Press 1999).

Cecil, Robert. *A Great Experiment* (London: Jonathan Cape, 1941).

Clark, Samuel. *State and Status. The Rise of the State and Aristocratic Power in Western Europe* (Montreal and Kingston: McGill-Queen's Press, 1995).

Claude, Inis. *Swords into Plowshares* (New York: Random House, 1956).

Cline, Catherine Ann. *Recruits to Labour. The British Party 1941–1931* (New York: Syracuse University Press, 1963).

Cobden, Richard. *Speeches on Questions of Public Policy by Richard Cobden MP* (London: Macmillan, 1903).

Cohen, Benjamin. *International Political Economy. An Intellectual History* (Princeton: Princeton University Press, 2008).

Colby, Charles Carlyle (ed.). *Geographic Aspects of International Relations* (Chicago: University of Chicago Press, 1938).

Cole, G.D.H. *Guild Socialism* (New York: Stokes, 1920).

Collini, Stefan. 'Hobhouse, Bosenquet and the State: Philosophical Idealism and Political Argument in England 1880–1918', *Past and Present*, 1976, 72, 86–111.

Comte, Auguste. *System of Positive Policy* (London: Longmans Green, 1877).

Cox, Michael (ed.). *E. H. Carr. A Critical Appraisal* (Houndmills: Palgrave, 2000).

Cox, Robert W. 'Social Forces, States and World Orders: Beyond International Relations Theory', *Millennium: Journal of International Studies*, 1981, 10(2), 126–55.

Cumming, Anthony. 'The Navy and the Battle for Britain', *BBC History*, April 2010, 35–9.

Curtis, Lionel. *Civitas Dei: The Commonwealth of God* (Macmillan: London, 1938).

Dallas, Gregor. *1918. War and Peace* (London: John Murray, 2000).

Dalton, Hugh. *Towards the Peace of Nations. A Study in International Politics* (London: Routledge & Kegan Paul, 1928).

Darwin, John. *After Tamerlaine. The Rise and Fall of Global Empires, 1400–2000* (Harmondsworth: Penguin, 2007).

Datta, Satya Brata. *Women and Men in Early Modern Venice: Reassessing History* (Aldershot: Ashgate, 2003).

Der Derian, James. *On Diplomacy* (Oxford: Blackwell, 1987).

Der Derian, James and Shapiro, Michael (eds). *International/Intertextual Relations. Postmodern Readings of World Politics* (Lexington, MA: Lexington Books, 1989).

Dickinson, G. Lowes. *The European Anarchy* (London: George Allen & Unwin, 1916).

Dickinson, Goldsworthy Lowes. *The International Anarchy 1904–1914* (London: Century, 1926).

Dickinson, G. Lowes. *The Autobiography of G. Lowes Dickinson*, edited by Denis Proctor and Noel Annan (London: Duckworth, 1973).

Dorpalen, Andreas. *The World of General Haushofer. Geopolitics in Action* (New York: Holt, Rinehart and Winston, 1942).

Drinkwater, Derek. *Sir Harold Nicolson and International Relations. The Practitioner as Theorist* (Oxford: Oxford University Press, 2005).

Dunn, Frederick Sherwood. *The Practice and Procedure of International Conferences* (New York: AMS Press, 1971 [1929]).

Dunn, Frederick Sherwood. *Peaceful Change: A Study of International Procedures* (New York: Council on Foreign Relations, 1937).

Dunn, Frederick Sherwood. 'Review of C. A. W. Manning, *Peaceful Change: An International Problem*', *Political Science Quarterly*, 1939, 54(1), 128–9.

Dunne, Tim. *Inventing International Society. A History of the English School* (Houndmills: Macmillan, 1998).

Earle, Edward Meade, 'Adam Smith, Alexander Hamilton, Friedrich List: The Economic Foundations of Military Power', in Edward Meade Earle (ed.), *Makers of Modern Strategy. Military Thought from Machiavelli to Hitler* (New York: Atheneun, 1967).

Elshtain, Jean Bethke. *Public Man Private Woman. Women in Social and Political Thought,* second edition (Princeton: Princeton University Press, 1981).

Elshtain, Jean Bethke. *Women and War* (Chicago: University of Chicago Press, 1987).

Enloe, Cynthia. *Bananas, Beaches and Bases: Making Feminist Sense of International Politics* (Berkeley, CA: California University Press, 1989).

Enloe, Cynthia. *The Morning After. Sexual Politics at the End of the Cold War* (Berkeley: University of California Press, 1993).

Estorick, Eric. *Stafford Cripps: Prophetic Rebel* (New York: John Day, 1941).

Farinelli, Franco. 'Friedrich Ratzel and the Nature of (Political) Geography', *Political Geography*, 2000, 19, 943–55.

Filmer, Robert. *Patriarchia: or the Natural Power of Kings* (London: Walter Davis, 1680).

Fisk, Robert. *In Time of War: Ireland, Ulster and the Price of Neutrality 1939–1945* (London: Deutsch, 1983).

Follett, Mary Parker. *The New State* (London: Longmans, 1918).

Fontanel, Jacques. Liliane Bensahel, Steven Coissard and Yann Echinard. 'French Utopian Economists of the Nineteenth Century', *Defence and Peace Economics*, 2008, 19(5), 339–50.

Foucault, Michel. *The Order of Things. An Archaeology of the Human Sciences* (London: Tavistock, 1970).

Foucault, Michel. *Politics, Philosophy, Culture. Interviews and Writings 1977–1984* (London: Routledge, 1988).

Foucault, Michel. *Madness and Civilization* (London: Routledge, 2001).

Freeden, Michael. *Ideologies and Political Theory. A Conceptual Approach* (Oxford: Oxford University Press, 1998).

Frei, Christoph. *Hans J. Morgenthau. An Intellectual Biography* (Baton Rouge: Louisiana State University Press, 2001).

Fukuyama, Francis. 'The End of History?', *The National Interest*, 1989, 16, 3–18.

Furniss, Edgar S. 'The Contribution of Nicholas John Spykman to the Study of International Politics', *World Politics*, 1952, 4(3), 382–401.

Gaddis, John Lewis. 'International Relations Theory and the End of the Cold War', *International Security,* 1992–3, 17, 5–58.

Galison, Peter. *Image and Logic: A Material Culture of Microphysics* (Chicago: University of Chicago Press, 1997).

Galtung, Johan. *Theory and Methods of Social Research* (New York: Columbia, 1967).

Gardiner, Stephen. 'A Discourse on the Coming of the English and Normans to Britain, Showing How Princes have Succeeded or Failed Depending Upon Whether They Ruled According to Reason or Appetite [1553–5]', in Peter Samuel Donaldson (ed.), *A Machiavellian Treatise By Stephen Gardiner* (Cambridge: Cambridge University Press, 1975).

Gellner, Ernst. 'Nationalism Reconsidered and E. H. Carr', *Review of International Studies*, 1992, 18(4), 285–93.

Gere, Cathy. *Knossos and the Prophets of Modernism* (Chicago: University of Chicago Press, 2009).

Gibbon, Edward. *An Essay on the Study of Literature* (London: Becket and de Hondt, 1764).

Gilpin, Robert. *The Political Economy of International Relations* (Princeton: Princeton University Press, 1987)

Gladstone, W. E. *The Turco-Servian War. Bulgarian Horrors and the Question of the East* (New York: Lovell Adam and Wesson, 1876).

Goldstein, Joshua S. and Jon C. Pevehouse. *International Relations* (New York: Pearson, 2009).

Gray, Colin S. 'In Defence of the Heartland: Sir Halford Mackinder and his Critics a Hundred Years on', *Comparative Strategy.* 2004, 23, 9–25.

Groom, A. J. R. and Paul Taylor, *Functionalism: Theory and Practice* (London: University of London Press, 1975).

Gross, Leo. 'The Peace of Westphalia 1648–1948', *American Journal of International Law*, 1948, 42(1), 20–41.

Grotius, Hugo. *De Jure Belli et Pacis Libri Tres* (Cambridge and London: John W. Parker, 1853).

Guicciardini, Francesco. *Maxims and Reflections of a Renaissance Statesman (Ricordi)* (Gloucester, MA: Peter Smith, 1970).

Guilhot, Nicolas. 'The Realist Gambit: Postwar American Political Science and the Birth of IR Theory', *International Political Sociology*, 2008, 2, 281–304.

Guilhot, Nicolas. *The Invention of International Relations Theory: Realism, the Rockefeller Foundation, and the 1954 Conference on Theory* (New York: Columbia University Press, 2011).

Haas, Ernst B. *The Uniting of Europe: Political, Social and Economic Forces, 1950–57* (London: Stevens, 1958).

Haas, Ernst B. *Beyond the Nation-State. Functionalism and International Organization* (Stanford: Stanford University Press, 1964).

Haas, Peter M. 'Epistemic Communities and International Policy Coordination'. *International Organization,* Winter 1992, 46(1), 1–35.

Hale, J. R. *War and Society in Renaissance Europe 1450–1620* (Stroud: Sutton, 1998).

Hale, Matthew. *The History of the Common Law of England* (Chicago: Chicago University Press, 1971).

Hall, Ian. 'Challenge and Response: The Lasting Engagement of Arnold J. Toynbee and Martin Wight', *International Relations* 2003, 17(3), 389–404.

Hall, Ian. *The International Thought of Martin Wight* (New York: Palgrave Macmillan, 2006).

Hall, Ian. 'The Revolt against the West: Decolonisation and its Repercussions in British International Thought, 1945–75', *International History Review*, 2011, 33(1), 43–64.

Hall, Ian. *Dilemmas of Decline. British Intellectuals and World Politics, 1945–1975* (Berkeley: University of California Press, 2012).

Halliday, Fred. *The Making of the Second Cold War* (London: Verso, 1983).

Hamilton Mary Agnes. *Remembering My Good Friends* (London: Jonathan Cape, 1944).

Hanson, Victor Davis. *The Western Way of War. Infantry Battle in Classical Greece* (Oxford: Oxford University Press, 1990).

Haslam, Beryl. *From Suffrage to Internationalism* (New York: Peter Lang, 1999).

Haslam, Jonathan. *The Vices of Integrity. E. H. Carr, 1892–1982* (London: Verso, 1999).

Hazard, Paul. *The European Mind 1680–1715* (Harmondsworth: Pelican, 1964).

Heather, Peter. *Empires and Barbarians. Migration, Development and the Birth of Europe* (London: Pan, 2010).

Henderson, Arthur. *The Peace Terms* (London: Labour Party, 1919).

Henderson, W. O. *Friedrich List: Economist and Visionary 1789–1846* (London: Frank Cass, 1983).

Herb, Gunthram Henrik. *Under the Map of Germany. Nationalism and Propaganda 1918–1945* (London: Routledge, 1997).

Herz, John. *Political Realism and Political Idealism. A Study in Theories and Realities* (Chicago: University of Chicago Press, 1951).

Herz, John H. *International Politics in the Atomic Age* (New York: Columbia University Press, 1959).

Hewlett, Charles F. 'John Dewey and Nicholas Murray Butler: Contrasting Conceptions of Peace Education in the Twenties', *Educational Theory,* December 1987, 37(4), 445–61.

Heywood, Andrew. *Global Politics* (Basingstoke: Palgrave Macmillan, 2011).

Hirschman, Albert O. *National Power and the Structure of Foreign Trade* (Berkeley: University of California Press, 1945).

Hirschman, Albert O. *The Passions and the Interests. Political Arguments for Capitalism Before its Triumph* (Princeton: Princeton University Press, 1977).

Hobbes, Thomas. *Leviathan* (Harmondsworth: Penguin, 1981).

Hobbes, Thomas. *De Cive. The English Version* (Oxford: Clarendon Press, 1983).

Hobhouse, L. T. *Liberalism* (London: Williams and Norgate, 1911).

Hobhouse, L. T. *The Metaphysical Theory of the State. A Criticism* (London: George Allen & Unwin, 1918).

Hobson, J. A. *The Evolution of Modern Capitalism* (London: Scott, 1894).

Hobson, J. A. *Imperialism. A Study* (London: Nisbet, 1902).

Hobson, J. A. *Richard Cobden. The International Man* (Toronto: Dent, 1918).

Hobson, J. A. 'Economic War after the War', Labour Party Advisory Committee on International Question memorandum no. 24, nd. People's History Museum Archives, Manchester.

Hobson, John M. *The Eurocentric Conception of World Politics. Western International Theory, 1760–2010* (Cambridge: Cambridge University Press, 2012).

Hobson, John M. and Colin Tyler (ed.), *Selected Writings of John A. Hobson 1932–1938* (London: Routledge, 2011).

Hoffman, Mark. 'Critical Theory and the Inter-Paradigm Debate', *Millennium: Journal of International Studies* 1987, 16(2), 231–49.

Hofstadter, Richard. *Social Darwinism in American Thought* (New York: George Braziller, 1955).

Holsti, K. J. *The Dividing Discipline. Hegemony and Diversity in International Theory* (Boston: Allen and Unwin, 1985).

Howard, Michael. *War and the Liberal Conscience* (New Brunswick, NJ: Rutgers Univerity Press, 1978).

Hume, David. 'Of the Rise and Progress of the Arts and Sciences (1742)' (http://www.utm.edu/research/hume/wri/essays/rise.htm).

Huntington, Ellsworth. *Climate & Civilization* (New Haven: Yale University Press, 1915).

Huntington, Samuel P. 'The Clash of Civilizations?', *Foreign Affairs,* 1993, 72(3), 22–49.

Imber, Mark F. 'Re-Reading Mitrany: A Pragmatic Assessment of Sovereignty', *Review of International Studies*, April 1984, 10(2), 103–23.

Isaac, Joel. 'Tangled Loops: Theory, History, and the Human Sciences in Modern America', *Modern Intellectual History*, 2009, 6(2), 2009, 397–424.

Jackson, Julian. *The Fall of France: The Nazi Invasion of 1940* (Oxford: Oxford University Press, 2001).

Jackson, Patrick Thaddeus and Daniel H. Nexon, 'Paradigmatic Faults in International Relations Theory', *International Studies Quarterly*, 2009, 53, 907–30.

Jackson, Robert and Georg Sørensen, *Introduction to International Relations* (Oxford: Oxford University Press, 2007).

James, William. 'The Moral Equivalent of War', in Harrison Ross Steeves and Frank Humphrey Ristine, *Representative Essays in Modern Thought* (New York: American Book Co, 1913), 519–33.

Johnson, Gaynor. *Lord Robert Cecil Viscount Cecil of Chelwood: Politician and Internationalist* (Aldershot: Ashgate, 2013).

Jones, Charles. *E.H. Carr and International Relations. A Duty to Lie* (Cambridge: Cambridge University Press, 1998).

Kant, Immanuel. *On History* (Indianapolis: Bobbs-Merrill, 1963).

Kant, Immanuel. *Perpetual Peace* (Indianapolis: Bobbs-Merrill, 1978).

Kant, Immanuel. *The Metaphysics of Morals* (Cambridge: Cambridge University Press, 1991).

Kaplan, Morton. 'The New Great Debate: Traditionalism vs. Science in International Relations', *World Politics*, 1966, 19(1), 1–20.

Kaplan, Robert D. 'The Coming Anarchy: How Scarcity, Crime, Overpopulation, Tribalism, and Disease are Rapidly Destroying the Social Fabric of our Planet', *Atlantic Monthly*, 1994, 273(2), 44–65.

Kendle, John E. *The Round Table Movement and Imperial Union* (Toronto: University of Toronto Press, 1975).

Keohane, Robert O and Joseph S. Nye. *Power and Interdependence. World Politics in Transition* (Boston: Little Brown, 1977).

Keynes, John Maynard. *The Economic Consequences of the Peace* (New York: Harcourt Brace and Howe, 1920 and London: Macmillan, 1920).

Keynes, John Maynard. *A Revision of the Treaty* (London: Macmillan, 1922).

Keynes, John Maynard. *The End of Laissez Faire* (London: Hogarth Press, 1926).

Keynes, John Maynard. 'The Change of Opinion (1921)', reprinted in his *Essays in Persuasion* (London: Macmillan, 1931).

Kilikowsky, Michael. *Rome's Gothic Wars* (Cambridge: Cambridge University Press, 2006).

Kjellén, Rudolf. *Der Staat als Lebensform* (Leipzig: Hirzel, 1917).

Knutsen, Torbjørn. 'A Lost Generation? IR Scholarship Before World War I', *International Politics*, 2008, 45(6), 650–74.

Krasner, Stephen D. 'Compromising Westphalia', *International Security*, 1995/6, 20(3), 115–51.

Kuhn, Thomas S. *The Structure of Scientific Revolutions* (Chicago: University of Chicago Press, 1962).

Labour Party. *Labour and the Nation*, first edition (London: Labour Party, 1928).

Labour Party. *Report of the Thirty-fifth Annual Conference* (London: Labour Party, 1935).

Labour Party Advisory Committee on International Questions (ACIQ), 'Short Statement on War Aims', Advisory Committee on International Questions memo no. 6, 25 June 1918, p1, Labour Party Archives, Manchester.

Labour Party Advisory Committee on International Questions (ACIQ). 'The Flight From Collective Security', memo no. 486a, March 1938. Labour Party Archives, Manchester.

Lamb, Peter. *Harold Laski: Problems of Democracy, the Sovereign State, and International Society* (New York: Palgrave Macmillan, 2004).

Lansbury, George. *My Life* (London: Constable, 1928).

Lansbury, George. 'To the Electors of Bow and Bromley,' electoral flyer for the 1935 General Election, 2–3. Paper no. 361, George Lansbury Papers, British Library of Political and Economic Science, London School of Economics and Political Science, London.

Lapid, Yosef. 'The Third Debate: On the Prospects of International Theory in a Post-Positivist Era' *International Studies Quarterly* 1989, 33, 235–54.

Laski, Harold J. *A Grammar of Politics* (London: George Allen & Unwin, 1925).

Laski, Harold J. 'Economic Foundations of Peace', in Leonard Woolf (ed.), *The Intelligent Man's Way to Prevent War* (London: Victor Gollancz, 1933).

Laski, Harold J. *A Grammar of Politics,* third edition (London: George Allen & Unwin, 1934).

Laski, Harold J. 'Capitalism and War', *The New Statesman and Nation*, 2 March 1935, 278. Reprinted in Brinton, *Does Capitalism Cause War?* 41–2.

Laski, Harold J. *Liberty in the Modern State* (Harmondsworth: Penguin, 1937).

Laski, Harold J. 'British Labour's Peace Aims', International Sub-Committee of the National Executive Committee (NEC), September 1939, p. 2. James Middleton Collection, Labour Party Archives, John Ryland's Library, Manchester, UK.

Laski, Harold J. *Reflections on the Revolution of our Time* (London: George Allen & Unwin, 1943).

Lea, Homer. *The Valour of Ignorance* (New York and London: Harper, 1909).

Lea, Homer. *The Day of the Saxon* (New York and London: Harper, 1912).

Leapman, Michael. *The World for a Shilling* (London: Headline, 2002).

Leibniz, Gottfried Wilhelm von. *Leibniz. Political Writings* (Cambridge: Cambridge University Press, 1988).

Leira, Halvard. 'Justus Lipsius, Political Humanism and the Disciplining of 17th Century Statecraft', *Review of International Studies*, 2008, 34, 669–92.

Lindberg Leon N. and Stuart A. Scheingold. *Europe's Would-Be Polity* (Englewood Cliffs, NJ: Prentice-Hall, 1970).

Lipsius, Justus. *Six Bookes of Politickes or Civil Doctrine* (London: Richard Field, 1594).

Lipsius, Justus. *Two Books of Constancie* (New Brunswick, NJ: Rutgers University Press, 1939).

List, Friedrich. *The National System of Political Economy* (New York: Augustus Kelly, 1966).

List, Friedrich. *The Natural System of Political Economy 1837* (London: Frank Cass, 1983).

Loades, D. M. *Politics and the Nation 1450–1660. Obedience, Resistance and Public Order* (Glasgow: Collins/Fontana, 1974).

Long, David. 'International Functionalism and the Politics of Forgetting', *International Journal*, Spring 1993, 48(2), 355–79.

Long, David. 'C. A. W. Manning and the Discipline of International Relations', *The Round Table*, 2005, 94(1), 77–96.

Long, David. 'Who Killed the International Studies Conference?', *Review of International Studies*, 2006, 32, 603–22.

Long, David and Brian Schmidt (eds). *Imperialism and Internationalism in the Discipline of International Relations* (Albany, NY: SUNY University Press, 2005).

Long, David and Peter Wilson, *Thinkers of the Twenty Years' Crisis* (Oxford: Clarendon, 1995).

Lothian, Marquess of (Philip Kerr). *Pacifism is Not Enough (Nor Patriotism Either)* (Oxford: Clarendon, 1935).

Lubac, H. de. *Un-Marxian Socialist: A Study of Proudhon* (London: Sheed and Ward, 1948).

MacDonald, James Ramsay. *Protocol or Pact? The Alternative to War* (London: Labour Party, nd [1925]).

Mackinder, Halford J. 'The Geographical Pivot of History', *The Geographical Journal,* 1904, 23, 421–37.

Mackinder, Halford J. 'Man-Power as a Measure of National and Imperial Strength', *National and English Review*, 1905, 45, 136–43.

Mackinder, Halford J. *Democratic Ideals and Reality. A Study in the Politics of Reconstruction* (London: Constable, 1919).

Mackinder, Halford J. *The Modern British State. An Introduction to the Study of Civics* second edition (London: George Philip, 1922).

Macmillan, Margaret. *Peacemakers* (London: John Murray, 2002).

Mahan, Alfred Thayer. *The Influence of Sea Power Upon History 1660–1783* (Boston: Little, Brown & Co., 1890).

Mahan, Alfred Thayer. *The Interest of America in Sea Power. Present and Future* (Boston: Little, Brown & Co, 1898).

Mahan, Alfred Thayer. *Some Neglected Aspects of War* (Boston: Little, Brown & Co., 1907).

Mahan, Alfred Thayer. *Armaments and Arbitration on the Place of Force in the International Relations of States* (New York: Harper, 1912).

Mahan, Alfred Thayer. *The Interests of America in International Conditions* (Boston: Little, Brown & Co., 1918).

Maliniak, Daniel, Amy Oakes, Susan Peterson and Michael J. Tierney, 'International Relations in the US Academy', *International Studies Quarterly,* 2011, 55, 437–64.

Manning, C. A. W. 'The Proposed Amendments to the Covenant of the League of Nations', *The British Yearbook of International Law*, 1930, 11, 158–71.

Manning, C. A. W. 'Some Suggested Conclusions', in C. A. W. Manning (ed.), *Peaceful Change. An International Problem* (New York: Macmillan, 1937).

Manning, C. A. W. *The Nature of International Society* (London: Macmillan, 1975).

Markwell, Donald. *John Maynard Keynes and International Relations. Economic Paths to War and Peace* (Oxford: Oxford University Press, 2006).

Martin, Geoffrey J. *The Life and Thought of Isaiah Bowman* (Hamden, CT: Archon, 1980).

Marx, Karl. 'Capital Punishment—Mr Cobden's Pamphlet—Regulations of the Bank of England', *New York Daily Tribune*, February 17–18 1853.

Marx, Karl. 'On the Question of Free Trade', in *Marx/Engels Collected Works*, Volume 6 (London: Lawrence and Wishart, 1976).

Marx, Karl. 'The Protectionists, the Free Traders and the Working Class [1848]', in *Marx Engels Collected Works*, Volume 6 (London: Lawrence and Wishart, 1976), 279.

Marx, Karl and Friedrich Engels. 'Manifesto of the Communist Party', in *Marx/Engels Selected Works*, Volume 1 (Moscow: Progress Press, 1969).

Marx, Karl and Friedrich Engels. *Marx/Engels Collective Works Volume 4* (Moscow: Progress Press, 1975)

Mauer, John H. 'Mahan on World Politics and Strategy: The Approach of the First World War, 1904–1914', in John B. Hattendorf (ed.), *The Influence of History on Mahan* (Newport, RI: Naval War College Press, 1991), 157–176.

McCrea, Adriana. *Constant Minds: Political Virtue and the Lipsian Paradigm in England 1584–1650* (Toronto: University of Toronto Press, 1997).

McNeill, William H. *The Pursuit of Power* (Oxford: Basil Blackwell, 1982).

Miles, Geoffrey. *Shakespeare and the Constant Romans* (Oxford: Clarendon, 1996).

Miller, Carol. *Lobbying the League: Women's International Organizations and the League of Nations* (Oxford: Oxford University Press, 1992).

Miller, D. H. *The Drafting of the Covenant*, volume I (New York: Putnam, 1928).

Milner, Helen. 'The Assumption of Anarchy in International Relations: A Critique', *Review of International Studies*, 1991, 17(1), 67–85.

Mitchell, Timothy. *Carbon Democracy. Political Power in the Age of Oil* (London: Verso, 2011).

Mitrany, David. 'Memorandum on Labour Policy Concerning Commissions to be Set up Under the Peace Treaty', Labour Party Advisory Committee on International Questions, memorandum no. 125, January 1920. People's History Museum Archives, Manchester.

Mitrany, David. *The Problem of International Sanctions* (London: Humphrey Milford and OUP, 1925).

Mitrany, David. *The Land and the Peasant in Rumania. The War and Agrarian Reform* (Yale: Yale University Press, 1930).

Mitrany, David. 'Pan-Europa – A Hope or a Danger?', *Political Quarterly*, 1930, 1(4), 457–78.

Mitrany, David. *The Progress of International Government* (London: Allen & Unwin, 1933).

Mitrany, David. *The Effects of the War in South Eastern Europe* (New Haven: Yale University Press, 1936).

Mitrany, David. 'Interrelation of Politics and Economics in Modern War', *The Annals of the American Academy of Political and Social Science*, July 1937, 192, 82–88.

Mitrany, David. *A Working Peace System* (Oxford: Oxford University Press, 1943).

Mitrany, David. *The Road to Security* (London: National Peace Council, 1944).

Mitrany, David. 'International Consequences of National Planning', *Yale Review*, September 1947, 37(1), 18–31.

Mitrany, David. *Marx Against the Peasant. A Study in Social Dogmatism* (London: Wiedenfeld and Nicolson, 1951).

Modelski, George. 'Agraria and Industria. Two Models of the International System', *World Politics*, 1961, 14(1), 118–43.

Molloy, Michael. 'Dialectics and Transformation: Exploring the Theory of E. H. Carr', *International Journal of Politics, Culture and Society*, 2003, 17(2), 279–306.

Molloy, Sean. 'The Realist Logic of International Security', *Cooperation and Conflict*, 2003, 38(2), 83–99.

Molloy, Sean. 'Truth, Power, Theory: Hans Morgenthau's Formulation of Realism', *Diplomacy and Statecraft*, 2004, 15(1), 1–34.

Molloy, Sean. *The Hidden History of Realism: A Genealogy of Power Politics* (London and New York: Palgrave Macmillan, 2006).

Montaigne, Michel de. *Essays* (Harmondsworth: Penguin, 1958).

Morefield, Jeane. *Covenants Without Swords. Idealist Liberalism and the Spirit of Empire* (Princeton: Princeton University Press, 2004).

Morgenthau, Hans J. *Scientific Man vs Power Politics* (Chicago: University of Chicago Press, 1946).

Morgenthau, Hans J. 'The Political Science of E.H. Carr', *World Politics*, 1948, 1(1), 127–34.

Morgenthau, Hans J. 'Another Great Debate. The National Interest of the United States', *The American Political Science Review*, 1952, 46(4), 961–88.

Morgenthau, Hans J. 'Introduction', in David Mitrany, *A Working Peace System* (Chicago: Quadrangle, 1966).

Morgenthau, Hans J. *Politics Among Nations. The Struggle for Power and Peace*, fifth edition (New York: Alfred A. Knopf, 1973).

Morgenthau, Hans J. *Politics Among Nations. The Struggle for Power and Peace*, sixth edition (New York: Alfred A. Knopf, 1985).

Morley, John. *The Life of Richard Cobden,* Volume I (London: Macmillan, 1908).

Murphy, Craig N. *International Organization and Industrial Change: Global Governance since 1850* (New York: Oxford University Press, 1994).

Murphy, David Thomas. *The Heroic Earth. Geopolitical Thought in Weimar Germany, 1918–1933* (Kent, OH: Kent State University Press, 1997).

Murray, Gilbert. 'National Ideals: Conscious and Unconscious', *International Journal of Ethics*, October, 1900, 11(1), 1–22.

Murray, Gilbert. *The Problem of Foreign Policy. A Consideration of Present Dangers and the Best Methods for Meeting Them* (Boston: Houghton and Mifflin, 1921).

Murray, Gilbert. 'Self-Determination of Nationalities*', Journal of the British Institute of International Affairs,* January 1922, 1(1), 6–13.

Murray, Gilbert. *The Ordeal of this Generation. The War, the League and the Future* (London: George Allen & Unwin, 1929).

Murray, Gilbert. 'Intellectual Cooperation', *Annals of the American Academy of Political and Social Science*, 1944, 235, 1–9.

Murray, Gilbert. *From the League to the U.N.* (Oxford: Oxford University Press, 1948).

Navari, Cornelia. 'Arnold Toynbee (1889–1975): Prophecy and Civilization', *Review of International Studies*, 2000, 26(2), 289–301.

Neumann, Franz. *Behemoth: The Structure and Practice of National Socialism* (Oxford: Clarendon, 1942).

Newell, Peter and Matthew Patterson. *Climate Capitalism. Global Warming and the Transformation of the Global Economy* (Cambridge: Cambridge University Press, 2010).

Nicholson, Peter P. 'Philosophical Idealism and International Politics: a Reply to Dr Savigear', *British Journal of International Studies,* 1976, 2(1), 76–83.

Nicolson, Harold. 'Modern Diplomacy and British Public Opinion', *International Affairs*, 1935, 14(5), 599–618.

Nicolson, Harold. 'The Foreign Service', *Political Quarterly*, 1936, 7, 208–22.

Nicolson, Harold. *Diplomacy: A Basic Guide to the Conduct of Contemporary Foreign Affairs* (New York: Harcourt Brace, 1939).

Nicolson, Harold. *Peacemaking 1919* (London: Methuen, 1964).

Niebuhr, Reinhold. *Moral Man and Immoral Society. A Study in Ethics and Politics* (New York: Charles Scribner, 1932).

Niebuhr, Reinhold. *The Children of Light and the Children of Darkness* (New York: Charles Scribner, 1944).

Niebuhr, Reinhold. *Christian Realism and Political Problems* (New York: Charles Scribner, 1953).

Noel-Baker, Philip. 'The Growth of International Society', *Economica*, 1924, 12, 262–277.

Noel-Baker, Philip. *Disarmament* (London: Hogarth, 1926).

Noel-Baker, Philip. *The League of Nations at Work* (London: Nisbet, 1927).

Nye, Joseph S. *Understanding International Conflicts* (New York: Pearson, 2007).

Onuf, Nicholas. *World of Our Making: Rules and Rule in Social Theory and International Relations* (Columbia, SC: University of South Carolina Press, 1989).

Osiander, Andreas. 'International Relations and the Westphalian Myth', *International Organization*, 2001, 55(2), 251–87.

Ó Tuathail, Gearóid. 'The Critical Reading/Writing of Geopolitics: Re-Reading/Writing Wittfogel, Bowman, and Lecoste', *Progress in Human Geography,* 1994, 18, 324–5.

Ó Tuathail, Gearóid. 'Introduction: Geo-Power', *Critical Geopolitics* (London: Routledge, 1996).

Ó Tuathail, Gearóid, Simon Dalby and Paul Routledge, *The Geopolitics Reader*, second edition (London: Routledge, 2006).

Overy, Richard (with Andrew Wheatcroft). *The Road to War* (London: Vintage, 2009).

Overy, Richard. *The Morbid Age. Britain and the Crisis of Civilization 1919–1939* (Harmondsworth: Penguin, 2010).

Parekh, Bhikhu and R.N. Berki, 'The History of Political Ideas: A Critique of Q. Skinner's Methodology', *Journal of the History of Ideas,* 1973, 34(2) 163–84.

Pecqueur, Constantin. *Economie sociale. Des Intérêts du Commerce, de l'Industrie et de l'Agriculture, et de la Civilisation en général, sous l'Influence des Applications de la Vapeur. Machines Fixes, Chemins de Fer, Bateaux à Vapeur* (Paris: Desessart, 1839).

Pecqueur, Constantin. *De la Paix, de son Principe et de sa Réalisation* (Paris: Capelle, 1842).

Pecqueur, Constantin. *Des Armées dan Leurs Rapports avec l'Industrie, la Morale et la Liberté* (Paris: Capelle, 1842).

Peterson, V. Spike (ed.). *Gendered States: Feminist (Re)Visions of International Relations Theory* (Boulder: Lynne Rienner, 1992).

Peterson, V. Spike and Anne Runyan. *Global Gender Issues* (Boulder, CO: Westview, 1993).

Petrie, Flinders. *The Revolutions of Civilisation* (New York: Harper & Brothers, 1911).

Pettman, Ralph. *International Politics. Balance of Power, Balance of Productivity, Balance of Ideologies* (Melbourne: Longman Cheshire, 1991).

Pietilä, Hilkka. *Engendering The Global Agenda* (New York and Geneva: UN NGLS, 2002).

Polanyi, Karl. *The Great Transformation. The Political and Economic Origins of our Time* (Boston: Beacon Press, 2001 [1944]).

Polanyi archives, UQAM, Montreal.

Ponsonby, Arthur. *Democracy and Diplomacy. A Plea for Popular Control of Foreign Policy* (London: Methuen, 1915).

Ponsonby, Arthur. *The Covenant of the League of Nations* (London: Union of Democratic Control, 1920).

Ponsonby, Arthur. *Now is the Time. An Appeal for Peace* (London: Leonard Parsons, 1925).

Porter, Bruce D. *War and the Rise of the State: The Military Foundations of Modern Politics* (New York: Free Press, 1994).

Prichard, Alex. 'Justice, Order and Anarchy: The International Political Theory of Pierre-Joseph Proudhon (1809–1865)', *Millennium: Journal of International Studies*, 2007, 35(3), 623–45.

Proudhon, Pierre-Joseph. *La Guerre et la Paix: Recherches sur le Principe et la Constitution Du Droit Des Gens*, two volumes (Paris: E. Dentu, 1861).

Proudhon, Pierre-Joseph. *The Principle of Federation and the Need to Reconstitute the Party of Revolution* (Toronto: University of Toronto Press, 1979).

Proudhon, Pierre-Joseph. *General Idea of the Revolution in the Nineteenth Century* (London: Pluto, 1989).

Pufendorf, Samuel. *On the Duty of Man and Citizen* (Cambridge: Cambridge University Press, 1991).

Quirk, Joel and Darshnan Vigneswaran. 'The Construction of an Edifice: The Story of a First Great Debate', *Review of International Studies*, 2005, 31, 89–107.

Raleigh, Walter. *A Discourse of the Originall and Fundamentall Cause of Naturall, Customary, Arbitrary, Voluntary and Necessary Warre* (London: Humphrey Moseley, 1650).

Raleigh, Walter. *Aphorisms of State, Grounded on Authority and Experience, and Illustrated with the Choicest Examples and Historical Observations* (London: Thomas Johnson, 1661).

Ratzel, Friedrich. *Politische Geographie* (Munich/Berlin: Oldenburg, 1897).

Ratzel, Friedrich. 'Flottenfrage und Weltlage', *Münchner Neuste Nachrichtung*, 1898, 51, 1–2.

Ratzel, Friedrich. *Anthropogeographie* (Stuttgart: J. Engelhorn, 1899).

Read, Donald. *Cobden and Bright. A Victorian Political Partnership* (London: Edward Arnold, 1967).

Rees, Laurence. 'Hitler's Greatest Gamble', *BBC History*, May 2010, 22–9.

Reeves, Julie. *Culture and International Relations: Narratives, Natives and Tourists* (New York: Routledge, 2004).

Reinsch, Paul S. *World Politics at the End of the Nineteenth Century As Influenced by the Oriental Situation* (New York and London: Macmillan, 1900).

Reinsch, Paul S. *Colonial Government an Introduction to the Study of Colonial Institutions* (New York and London: Macmillan, 1902).

Reinsch, Paul S. *Colonial Administration* (New York and London: Macmillan, 1905).

Reinsch, Paul S. *Public International Unions. A Study of International Administrative Law* (Boston and London: Ginn, 1911).

Rengger, N. J. 'Going Critical? A Response to Hoffman', *Millennium: Journal of International Studies* 1988, 17(1), 81–9.

Reynolds, Charles. *Theory and Explanation in International Politics* (London, Martin Robertson, 1973).

Reynolds, David. *From World War to Cold War* (Oxford: Oxford University Press, 2006).

Richelieu, Cardinal. *The Political Testament of Cardinal Richelieu*, edited and translated by Henry Bertram Hill (Madison: University of Wisconsin Press, 1961).

Riemens, Michael. 'International Academic Cooperation on International Relations in the Interwar Period: The International Studies Conference', *Review of International Studies*, 2011, 37, 911–28.

Rommen, Hans. 'Realism and Utopianism in World Affairs', *The Review of Politics*, 1944, 6(2), 193–215.

Roskin, Michael G. and Nicholas O. Berry, *IR. The New World of International Relations* (London: Pearson, 2010).

Rourke, John T. *International Politics on the World Stage*, twelfth edition (New York: McGraw-Hill, 2008).

Russett, Bruce and Harvey Starr. *World Politics. The Menu for Choice* (New York: Freeman, 2000).

'R. W.' *The Anatomy of Warre* (London: John Dalham, nd).

Rybczynski, Witold. *Home: A Short History of an Idea* (New York: Viking, 1986).

Savigear, P. 'Philosophical Idealism and International Politics: Bosenquet, Treitschke and War', *British Journal of International Studies*, 1975, 1(1), 48–59.

Scheuerman, William. *Hans J. Morgenthau: Realism and Beyond* (Cambridge: Polity Press, 2009).

Scheuerman, William. 'The (Classical) Realist Vision of Global Reform', *International Theory*, 2010, 2, 246–82.

Schmidt, Brian C. *The Political Discourse of Anarchy: A Disciplinary History of International Relations* (Albany, NY: State University of New York, 1998).

Schmidt, Brian. 'The American National Interest Great Debate', in Brian Schmidt (ed.), *International Relations and the First Great Debate* (London: Routledge, 2012), 94–117.

Schmidt, Sebastian. 'To Order the Minds of Scholars: the Discourse of the Peace of Westphalia in International Relations Literature', *International Studies Quarterly*, 2011, 55, 601–23.

Schuman, Frederick L. *International Politics. An Introduction to the Western State System* (New York: McGraw-Hill, 1933).

Schuman, Frederick L. *International Politics. Anarchy and Order in the World Society*, seventh edition (New York: McGraw-Hill, 1969).

Schwarzenberger, Georg. *The League of Nations and World Order* (London: Constable, 1936).

Schwarzenberger, Georg. *Power Politics. An Introduction to the Study of International Relations and Post-War Planning* (London: Jonathan Cape, 1941).

Schwarzenberger, Georg. 'The Three Types of Law', *Ethics*, January 1943, 53(2), 89–97.

Scott, Len. 'International History 1900–90', in J. Baylis, S. Smith and P. Owens (eds), *The Globalization of World Politics* (Oxford: Oxford University Press, 2011).

Self, Robert. *Neville Chamberlain. A Biography* (Aldershot: Ashgate, 2009).

Sellar W.C. and R. J. Yeatman. *1066 and All That. A Memorable History of England* (New York: Dutton, 1931).

Semple, Ellen Churchill. *Influences of Geographic Environment on the Basis of Ratzel's System of Anthropo-Geography* (London: Constable, 1911).

Sewell, James Patrick. *Functionalism and World Politics. A Study Based on United Nations Programs Financing Economic Development* (Princeton: Princeton University Press, 1966).

Sewell, Thomas. *Intellectuals and Society* (New York: Basic, 2009).

Sheehan, Michael. *Balance of Power: History and Theory* (London: Routledge, 1995).

Skinner, Quentin. 'Meaning and Understanding in the History of Ideas', *History and Theory*, 1969, 8(1), 53.

Skinner, Quentin. *Reason and Rhetoric in the Philosophy of Hobbes* (Cambridge: Cambridge University Press, 1996).

Smith, John Thomas. *Roman Villas: A Study in Social Structure* (London: Routledge, 1997).

Smith, Michael Joseph. *Realist Thought from Weber to Kissinger* (Baton Rouge and London: Louisiana State University Press, 1986).

Smith, Neil. 'Bowman's New World and the Council on Foreign Relations', *Geographical Review*, 1986, 76, 438–60.

Smith, Neil. *American Empire. Roosevelt's Geographer and the Prelude to Globalization* (Berkeley, Los Angeles and London: University of California Press, 2003).

Smith, Steve. 'Paradigm Dominance in International Relations: The Development of International Relations as a Social Science', *Millennium: Journal of International Studies*, Summer 1987, 16(2), 189–206.

Smith, Steve. 'Introduction', in T. Dunne, M. Kuki and S. Smith (eds), *International Relations Theories: Discipline and Diversity* (Oxford: Oxford University Press, 2007).

Smith, Steve in C. Reus-Smit. D. Snidal (eds), *The Oxford Handbook of International Relations* (Oxford: Oxford University Press, 2008).

Smuts, Jan. *The League of Nations: A Practical Suggestion* (London: Hodder and Stoughton, 1918).

Spencer, Herbert. *On Social Evolution* (Chicago: University of Chicago Press, 1972).

Spengler, Oswald. *The Decline of the West, vol. 1: Form and Actuality* (London: George Allen & Unwin, 1926).

Spengler, Oswald. *The Decline of the West, vol. 2: Perspectives of World-History* (London: George Allen & Unwin, 1928).

Spykman, Nicholas J. 'States' Rights and the League', *Yale Review*, 1934, 24(2), 274–93.

Spykman, Nicholas J. 'Geography and Foreign Policy I', *American Political Science Review*, 1938, 32(1), 28–50.

Spykman, Nicholas J. 'Geography and Foreign Policy II', *American Political Science Review*, 1938, 32(2), 213–36.

Spykman, Nicholas J. *America's Strategy in World Politics. The United States and the Balance of Power* (New York: Harcourt and Brace, 1942).

Spykman, Nicholas J. *The Geography of the Peace*, edited by Helen R. Nicholl (New York: Harcourt and Brace, 1944).

Spykman, Nicholas J. and Abbie A. Rollins, 'Geographic Objectives in Foreign Policy I', *American Political Science Review*, 1939, 33(3), 391–410.

Stannage, C. T. 'The East Fulham By-Election, 25 October 1933', *The Historical Journal*, March 1971, 14(1), 165–200.

Steans, Jill. 'Engaging from the Margins: Feminist Encounters with the "Mainstream" of International Relations', *British Journal of Politics and International Relations*, 2003, 5(3), 428–54.

Strange, Susan. *Sterling and British Policy: A Political Study of an International Currency in Decline* (London: Oxford University Press, 1971).

Strange, Susan. *States and Markets. An Introduction to International Political Economy* (London: Pinter, 1988).

Strange, Susan. 'The Westfailure System', *Review of International Studies*, 1999, 25(3), 345–54.

Strausz-Hupé, Robert. *Geopolitics. The Struggle for Space and Power* (New York: G. P. Putnam, 1942).

Stromberg, Roland N. 'The Idea of Collective Security', *Journal of the History of Ideas*, April 1956, 17(2), 250–63.

Sturmthal, Adolf. *The Tragedy of European Labour. 1918–1939* (London: Victor Gollancz, 1944).

Suganami, Hidemi. 'C. A. W. Manning and the Study of International Relations', *Review of International Studies*, 27(1), 91–107.

Swanwick, H. M. *The Future of the Women's Movement* (London: Bell, 1913).

Swanwick, H. M. *Women and War* (London: Union of Democratic Control, 1915).

Swanwick, H. M. 'Towards a Permanent Peace VI: The Case for Women's Participation in National and International Affairs'. *Labour Leader*. 29 April 1915, 5.

Swanwick, H. M. *The Peace Treaties Explained. No. 1 The Covenant of the League of Nations* (London: Women's International League, 1920).

Swanwick, H. M. *New Wars for Old* (London: Women's International League, 1934).

Swanwick, H. M. *I Have Been Young* (London: Victor Gollancz, 1935).

Swanwick, H. M. *Collective Insecurity* (London: Jonathan Cape, 1937).

Swanwick, H. M. *The Roots of Peace* (London: Jonathan Cape, 1938).

Swanwick, H. M. and W. Arnold-Forster, *Sanctions of the League of Nations Covenant* (London: London Council For Prevention of War, 1928).

Sylvest, Casper. 'Continuity and Change in British Liberal Internationalism, *c.*1900–1930', *Review of International Studies*, 2005, 31, 263–83.

Sylvest, Casper. *British Liberal Internationalism, 1880–1930* (Manchester: Manchester University Press, 2009).

Sylvest, Casper. 'Realism and International Law: the Challenge of John H. Herz', *International Theory*, 2010, 2(3), 410–45.

Sylvester, Christine. *Feminist Theory and International Relations in a Postmodern Era* (Cambridge: Cambridge University Press, 1994).

Tawney, R. H. *The Acquisitive Society* (New York: Harcourt Brace, 1920).

Teschke, Benno. *The Myth of 1648* (London: Verso, 2003).

Thompson, Kenneth W. 'Beyond National Interest: A Critical Evaluation of Reinhold Niebuhr's Theory of International Politics', *The Review of Politics*, 1955, 17(2), 167–88.

Thompson, Kenneth W. *Schools of Thought in International Relations. Interpreters, Issues, and Morality* (Baton Rouge: Louisiana State University Press, 1996).

Tickner, Arlene B. and Ole Wæver (eds), *International Relations Scholarship Around the World* (London: Routledge, 2009).

Tickner, J. Ann. 'Hans Morgenthau's Principles of Political Realism: A Feminist Reformulation', *Millennium*, 1988, 17(3), 429–40.

Tickner, J. Ann. *Gender in International Relations: Feminist Perspectives on Achieving Global Security* (New York: Columbia University Press, 1992),

Tillyard, E. M. W. *The Elizabethan World Picture. A Study in the Idea of Order in the Age of Shakespeare, Donne and Milton* (New York: Vintage, nd).

Toulmin, Stephen. *Human Understanding Volume 1* (Oxford: Clarendon, 1972).

Toulmin, Stephen. *Cosmopolis: The Hidden Agenda of Modernity* (Chicago: University of Chicago Press, 1995).

Toynbee, Arnold J. 'Peaceful Change or War? The Next Stage in the International Crisis', *International Affairs* 1936, 15(1), 26–56.

Toynbee, Arnold J. 'The Greek Door to the Study of History', in J. A. K. Thomson and A. J. Toynbee (eds), *Essays in Honour of Gilbert Murray* (London: George Allen & Unwin, 1936).

Toynbee, Arnold J. 'The Lessons of History', in C. A. W. Manning (ed.), *Peaceful Change: An International Problem* (New York: Macmillan, 1937), 27–40.

Toynbee, Arnold J. 'A Turning Point in History', *Foreign Affairs,* 1939, 17(2), 305–20.

Toynbee, Arnold J. *A Study of History*, in two volumes, edited by D. C Summerville (New York and London: Oxford University Press, 1947).

Toynbee, Arnold. 'The International Outlook', *International Affairs*, 1947, 23(4), 463–76.

Toynbee, Arnold J. 'The Downfalls of Civilizations', the text of his Hobhouse Lecture given in 1939, and republished in *Hobhouse Memorial Lectures 1930–1940* (London: Oxford University Press, 1948).

Tuck, Richard. *Philosophy and Government 1572–1651* (Cambridge: Cambridge University Press, 1993).

Turner, Frederick Jackson. *The Frontier in American History* (Tucson: University of Arizona Press, 1994).

Vasquez, John A. *The Power of Power Politics: A Critique* (New Brunswick, NJ: Rutgers University Press, 1983).

Vellacott, J. *Pacifists, Patriots and the Vote* (Houndsmill: Palgrave Macmillan, 2007).

Vico, Giambattista. *The New Science of Giambattista Vico* (Ithaca: Cornell University Press, 1968).

'Vigilantes' [Konnie Zilliacus], *Inquest on Peace. An Analysis of the National Government's Foreign Policy* (London: Victor Gollancz, 1935).

Walker, R. B. J. *Inside/Outside: International Relations as Political Theory* (Cambridge: Cambridge University Press, 1993).

Walker, R. B. J. and Saul Mendlovitz (eds). *Contending Sovereignties: Redefining Political Community* (London: Lynne Rienner, 1990).

Wallas, Graham. *Human Nature and Politics* (Boston and New York: Houghton Mifflin, 1916 [1908]).

Walsh, Edmund A. *Total Power. A Footnote to History* (New York: Doubleday, 1948).

Waltz, Kenneth. *Theory of International Politics* (Reading, MA: Addison-Wesley, 1979).

Wanklyn, Harriet. *Friedrich Ratzel: A Biographical Memoir and Bibliography* (London: Cambridge University Press, 1961).

Ward-Perkins, Bryan. *The Fall of Rome and the End of Civilization* (Oxford: Oxford University Press, 2006).

Watson, Adam. *Diplomacy: the Dialogue Between States* (London: Eyre Methuen, 1982).

Weigert, Hans W. *Generals and Geographers. The Twilight of Geopolitics* (New York: Oxford University Press, 1942).

Wells, H. G. *Outline of History* (Toronto: Doubleday, 1925).

Wendt, Alexander. 'Anarchy is What States Make of it: The Social Construction of Power Politics', *International Organization,* 1992, 46(2), 391–425.

White, Lynn. *Medieval Technology and Social Change* (Oxford: Oxford University Press, 1962).

Whittlesey, Derwent. *The Earth and the State. A Study in Political Geography* (New York: Henry Holt, 1939).

Whittlesey, Derwent. *German Strategy of World Conquest* (London: F. E. Robinson, 1942).

Whittlesey, Derwent. *Environmental Foundations of European History* (New York: Appleton-Century-Crofts, 1949).

Whitworth, Sandra. *Feminism and International Relations: Towards a Political Economy of Gender in Interstate and Non-Governmental Institutions* (New York: Macmillan, 1994).

Wibben, Annick T. R. 'Feminist International Relations: Old Debates and New Directions', *Brown Journal of World Affairs*, 2004, 10(2), 97–114.

Wight, Martin. 'Arnold Toynbee: An Appreciation', *International Affairs*, 1976, 52(1), 11–13.

Williams, Andrew. *Failed Imagination? The Anglo-American New World Order from Wilson to Bush* second edition (Manchester: Manchester University Press, 2007).

Williams, Andrew. 'Norman Angell and His French Contemporaries, 1905–1914', *Diplomacy and Statecraft*, 2010, 21(4), 574–92.

Williams, Michael C. 'Rousseau, Realism and Realpolitik', *Millennium*, 1989, 18, 185–203.

Williams, Michael C. (ed.) *Realism Reconsidered. The Legacy of Hans J. Morgenthau in International Relations* (Oxford: Oxford University Press, 2007).

Williams, William Appleman. 'The Frontier Thesis and American Foreign Policy', *The Pacific Historical Review*, 1955, 24, 379–95.

Wilson, Peter. 'The New Europe Debate in Wartime Britain', in Philomena Murray and Paul Rich (eds), *Visions of European Unity* (Boulder, CO: Westview, 1996), 39–62.

Wilson, Peter. 'Gilbert Murray and International Relations: Hellenism, Liberalism, and International Intellectual Cooperation as a Path to Peace', *Review of International Studies* 2011, 37(2), 881–909.

Wilson, Peter. 'Where are we now in the Debate about the Great Debate?', in Brian C. Schmidt (ed.), *International Relations and the First Great Debate* (London: Routledge, 2012).

Winkler, Henry R. *Paths Not Taken. British Labour and International Policy in the 1920s* (Chapel Hill: University of North Carolina Press, 1994).

Winkler, Henry R. *Labour Seeks a Foreign Policy* (Somerset NJ: Transaction, 2004).

Wohlforth, William C. et al. 'Testing Balance-of-Power Theory in World History', *European Journal of International Relations*, 2007, 13(2), 155–85.

Wolkersdorfer, Günter. 'Karl Haushofer and Geopolitics — The History of a German Mythos', *Geopolitics*, 1999, 4(3), 145–60.

Woolf, Leonard. *International Government* (London: George Allen & Unwin, 1916).

Woolf, Leonard. *Mandates and Empire* (London: League of Nations Union, 1920).

Woolf, Leonard. 'The League of Nations and Disarmament', Labour Party Advisory Committee on International Questions, memorandum no. 251, 1922. People's History Museum Archives, Manchester.

Woolf, Leonard. *The International Post-War Settlement* (London: Fabian Society and Victor Gollancz, 1944).

Wooton, David (ed.). *Divine Right and Democracy. An Anthology of Political Writing in Stuart England* (Harmondsworth: Penguin, 1986).

Wright, Quincy. *A Study of War*, volume II (Chicago: Chicago University Press, 1942).

Wright, Quincy. *The Study of International Relations* (New York: Appleton-Century-Crofts, 1955).

Wyatt-Walter, Andrew. 'Adam Smith and the Liberal Tradition in International Relations', *Review of International Studies*, 1996, 22(1), 5–28.

Zalewski, Marysia. 'Well, What is the Feminist Perspective on Bosnia?', *International Affairs*, 1995, 71(2), 339–56.

Zalewski, Marysia and Jane Parpart (eds) *The 'Man' Question in International Relations* (Boulder, CO: Westview, 1998).

# Index

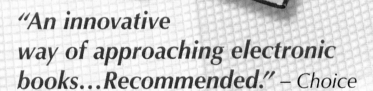